Pitchess Privileges and the CPRA

Police Officer Personnel and Investigative Records Privileges and their Intersection with the California Public Records Act

AF810937

by

Tony M. Sain, Esq.

With Foreword & Special Contributions By

Abigail R. McLaughlin, Esq.

www.lewisbrisbois.com

***Pitchess* Privileges and the CPRA:**
Police Officer Personnel and Investigative Records Privileges and their Intersection with the California Public Records Act

Copyright © 2014 (Original Edition), 2015, 2018, 2021, 2022, 2023, 2024, 2025 (Revised Editions) by Tony M. Sain, Esq.

With Foreword & Special Contributions By Abigail Ryan McLaughlin, Esq.

All Rights Reserved.

Published in the United States by the law firm of
Lewis Brisbois Bisgaard & Smith, LLP
633 West Fifth Street, Suite 4000
Los Angeles, California 90017

Telephone: (213) 250-1800
www.lewisbrisbois.com

ISBN 978-1495314216 (2014 Version)
ISBN 978-0-578-33864-4 (2022+ Versions)

9th Edition

DEDICATION

To the brave men and women in blue who work so tirelessly to keep us safe and protect our rights under the law.

We are proud of you and honored to serve with you.

1. OVERVIEW: Introduction to the Primer on the *Pitchess* Privilege.

California law provides a statutory protection to peace officer personnel file information that causes officer personnel record information to be presumed confidential. Thus, under the peace officer personnel file information privileges, officer personnel record information may not be discovered or disclosed, unless an exception to the statutory privileges applies or by order of the court. Normally, under California's *Pitchess* procedure, which applies in both state criminal and civil court cases, any information that meets the statutory definition of peace officer "personnel file" information is protected from discovery or disclosure to persons/parties outside the scope of the privilege — regardless of where such information is stored; even if it's stored in the officer's memory/mind.[1]

Under the *Pitchess* procedure then, where a party seeks to obtain/discover or publish/disclose officer personnel file records/information, that party must make a motion for a court order showing good cause for the records/information to be discovered/produced to the moving party, or published/disclosed to some other party: such as to a jury at trial.[2]

The *Pitchess* procedure has several detailed technical requirements — including specificity, good cause, materiality/manifest necessity, and reasonable belief mandatory thresholds and other procedural mandates — all of which must be met before the moving party can obtain *in camera* review by the court

---

1 *See, e.g.*, Cal. Penal Code §§ 832.5, 832.7, 832.8; Cal. Evid. Code §§ 1040-1047; *Commission on Peace Officer Standards & Training [POST] v. Superior Ct.* (2007) 42 Cal.4th 278, 293; *Hackett v. Superior Ct.* (1993) 13 Cal.App.4th 96, 99-101; *Haggerty v. Superior Ct.* (2004) 117 Cal.App.4th 1079, 1085-1087; *City of San Diego v. Superior Ct.* (1981) 136 Cal.App.3d 236, 239.

2 *See People v. Mooc* (2001) 26 Cal.4th 1216, 1226-1229; *Zanone v. City of Whittier* (2008) 162 Cal.App.4th 174, 187-189.

of the personnel file records/information sought: and only after the court conducts such *in camera* review may any personnel file records/information be produced/discovered to the moving party and/or published/disclosed to a non-party, such as the trial jury.[3] Furthermore, even *after* the court issues a *Pitchess* production/discovery and/or publication/disclosure order, the *Pitchess* procedure imposes several restrictions on what can be discovered/disclosed and on what must remain protected by court order.[4]

In light of the complexities of the *Pitchess* procedural requirements, as a new wave of attorneys moves into the practice of litigating civil rights, employment, and other civil actions involving peace officers and their law enforcement agencies, that new wave is often breaking upon the rocky shoal of the privilege protections that preserve certain peace officer personnel file records, and related information, from being disclosed in discovery or placed into evidence at trial — needlessly frustrating their discovery attempts and resulting in countless hours of lost time and resources for both the party attorneys seeking discovery or disclosure of protected matters and the party attorneys seeking to preserve their clients' privileges. Indeed, many lawyers who are experienced in the customary rules and procedures in civil case discovery struggle needlessly, and in a manner that is time-consuming and unduly costly to all parties, regarding discovery related to peace officer personnel file information. However, one can trace a substantial amount of this frustration and improvident expenditure of time to a lack of understanding of the scope of the protections governing peace officer personnel file information — and the related disclosure procedures — in both state and federal cases.

Thus, in an effort to reduce the undue consumption of the time and resources of the parties, their counsel, and the courts that can otherwise result from often futile or improper discovery or disclosure attempts, this primer attempts to present an overview on and explanation of the operation of the peace officer personnel file record privileges — which are generally referenced

3 *See, e.g., Alford v. Superior Ct.* (2003) 29 Cal.4th 1033, 1036-1046; *City of Santa Cruz v. Municipal Ct.* (1989) 49 Cal.3d 74, 94; *Warrick v. Superior Ct.* (2005) 35 Cal.4th 1011, 1021-22; *Haggerty, supra*, 117 Cal.App.4th at pp. 1085-1087; *City of Hemet v. Superior Ct.* (1995) 37 Cal. App.4th 1411, 1424-1425; *Zanone, supra*, 162 Cal.App.4th at p. 187 n. 14; *People v. Gwillim* (1990) 223 Cal.App.3d 1254, 1269-1270.

4 *See* Cal. Evid. Code §§ 1045(b)-(d), 1047; *Warrick, supra*, 35 Cal.4th at pp. 1027-1028; *cf. Mooc, supra*, 26 Cal.4th at p. 1229; *Alt v. Superior Ct.* (1999) 74 Cal.App.4th 950, 957; *City of San Jose v. Superior Ct.* (1993) 5 Cal.4th 47, 55-57; *Chambers v. Superior Ct.* (2007) 42 Cal.4th 673, 679-680.

FOREWORD

The relationship between the public and the government has always been a delicate balance between transparency and privacy, access and confidentiality. In California, the laws governing this balance are shaped by principles rooted in both democratic ideals and legal precedents. Among these laws, the California Public Records Act ("CPRA") and the *Pitchess* privilege stand out as two crucial instruments that help define the boundaries between public oversight and personal or governmental privacy, especially in the realm of law enforcement.

While the CPRA was designed to empower the public by granting access to government records, with the intent of fostering transparency and accountability in all areas of public administration, when it comes to law enforcement, the application of this principle becomes more nuanced: balancing the public's right to know against the need to protect the privacy, integrity, and operational effectiveness of law enforcement agencies – as they strive to serve the public and protect them from all manner of dangers and crimes. Moreover, law enforcement is uniquely affected by certain privileges that are designed to balance the privacy rights of officers and the integrity of investigations against the public interest in transparency and good governance. Navigating these intricacies can be atypically challenging: both for members of the public seeking records, as well as for the government agencies tasked with complying with public records requests.

This book delves deep into the nuances of both the *Pitchess* privilege in peace officer personnel file information and its complex intersection with the CPRA's public access laws: offering clarity on how these laws interact, overlap, and – at times – conflict. This reference manual thus explores the intricacies of legal procedures, recent case law, and practical consideration for navigating the often-complex terrain of determining what police-related records can be obtained by public records requests and/or in civil discovery.

Whether you are a legal professional, a government employee, or a law enforcement officer, this book offers an indispensable guide to understanding the ins-and-outs of the CPRA and *Pitchess* privilege in an ever-evolving legal landscape. While both the statutes and case law governing the CPRA and *Pitchess* privilege may seem complicated, this book provides a clear path to success in navigating the procedural process and best representing the interests of law enforcement in doing so. If anyone is considering working in this realm, this book should be at the top of your reading list: and remain on your top shelf, as a practical guide to support your representation of the interests of those who risk their lives protecting our communities.

As an attorney whose entire practice centers on the defense of law enforcement officers, this book has been an invaluable resource that I have consulted countless times in order to ensure that I am providing proper guidance to both entity clients and individual law enforcement officers about their rights and disclosure obligations when it comes to the CPRA, and whether certain documents are subject to *Pitchess* privilege.

Abigail J. R. McLaughlin, Esq.
Attorney, Partner, and Appellate Advocate

Contents

as the "*Pitchess*" privileges — in state and federal cases, and to answer some of what appear to be the most frequently asked questions about such protections.

In addition to the introductory overview on the scope and discovery mechanisms at issue in civil cases involving peace officers, this primer also addresses some emerging trends in discovery related to peace officer personnel record information — including developing trends where the peace officer is in an adversarial position to the public entity that is the custodian of the officers' personnel file information — as well as the impact and overlap of the California-law peace officer record privileges upon federal privileges and discovery in federal cases.

A. Overview Of The Recent Exceptions To The *Pitchess* Protections: A Revolution In The Scope Of The Peace Officer Personnel File Record-Information Privilege-Confidentiality.

On September 30, 2018, the California Governor signed into law two bills (SB 1241 and AB 748) ostensibly designed to advance the public's "strong compelling interest in law enforcement transparency because it is essential to having a just and democratic society."[5] The new laws amended Cal. Gov. Code § 6254 (AB 748; now recodified as Cal. Gov. Code § 7920.000 *et seq.* as of January 1, 2023)[6] and Cal. Penal Code §§ 832.7 and 832.8 (SB 1241) to transform otherwise *Pitchess*-protected officer personnel file records/information — including associated criminal and administrative investigations records — about officer-involved shootings ("OIS") against persons and uses of force ("UOF") against persons where death or great bodily injury results, as well as audio and video recordings of such critical incidents and records of sustained officer sexual assaults/policing dishonesty, into public records accessible under a California Public Records Act ("CPRA") request — with some limitations. (The revisions to the Penal Code were slated to go into effect on January 1, 2019; the revisions to the Government Code were slated to go into effect on July 1, 2019.)

In essence, the revolutionary statutory changes would remove from the *Pitchess* protective procedures records of investigation and recordings of "serious" police uses-of-force (OIS against persons, or UOF against persons where

---

5 Senate Bill no. 1241, § 4; *accord* Assembly Bill no. 748.

6 *See also* Cal. Gov. Code § 7923.630 (recodification not intended to alter substance of former Section 6254).

death or serious bodily injury results — which the new laws also reference as "critical incidents"), sustained investigative records of sexual assault by officers against non-officers/non-employees, and/or sustained investigative records of job-related officer dishonesty. Moreover, by subjecting such records to CPRA production requirements, any interested person need not even obtain a subpoena or serve a civil or criminal discovery request to obtain such now-public records.

The implications of these bombshell statutes on the subtleties of *Pitchess* privilege law will be addressed throughout this revision, where applicable to existing *Pitchess* privileges/procedures.

2. SCOPE: What Is the Extent of the Protected Matter Under the Peace Officer Personnel File Record Privileges?

The cornerstone to understanding how the *Pitchess* privileges operate rests upon knowing that "personnel file" information has a fixed definition under the law. The definition of what constitutes a peace officer's "personnel file" is specified under California law as "any file maintained under that individual's name by his or her employing agency and containing records related to any of the following": (a) personal data, including marital status, family members, educational and employment history, home addresses or similar information; (b) medical history; (c) election of employee benefits; (d) employee advancement, appraisal, or discipline; (e) complaints, or investigations of complaints, concerning an event or transaction in which he or she participated, or which he or she perceived and pertaining to the manner in which he or she performed his or her duties; or (f) any other information the disclosure of which would constitute an unwarranted invasion of personal privacy.[1]

---

1 *See* Cal. Penal Code § 832.8; *Commission on Peace Officer Standards & Training [POST] v. Superior Ct.* (2007) 42 Cal.4th 278, 293 (holding that physical inclusion of a document in a peace officer's personnel file is insufficient to trigger the *Pitchess* privilege; rather, only those documents specifically identified in Cal. Penal Code § 832.8 as personnel records are entitled to *Pitchess* procedural protections); *see also* Cal. Penal Code § 832.5(b) (**mandating that complaints and "any reports or findings related to these complaints" against a peace officer must be retained in a peace officer's personnel file, or a separate file designated by that department's policy, "for a period of at least five years"**); *Zanone v. City of Whittier* (2008) 162 Cal.App.4th 174, 187-189 (holding that to trigger the *Pitchess* privilege, the "complaint or investigation of a complaint must both concern an event that involved the officer as a participant or witness *and* pertain to the officer's performance of his or her duties," and exempting from the *Pitchess* procedure a statement from a memorandum written by a witness officer about another officer's racial discrimination where that statement by that witness officer impeached his defense-favorable testimony in an employment discrimination case).

Under California law, "[p]eace officer or custodial officer personnel records and records maintained by any state or local agency pursuant to Section 832.5, or information obtained from these records, are confidential and shall not be disclosed in any criminal or civil proceeding except by discovery pursuant to [Cal. Evid. Code §§ 1043 and 1046]."[2] Thus, for example, "internal [affairs type] investigations are considered confidential and part of an officer's personnel records.[3]

Significantly, the *Pitchess* privileges apply to such personnel file information even if the information at issue is contained — or otherwise obtainable from sources — *outside* of the peace officer's physical or digital personnel file, including information otherwise obtainable in publicly available records, or by queries to the officer: in other words, **as long as the information at issue falls within the statutory definition of a personnel record, it is irrelevant to the evaluation of the *Pitchess* privilege issues that such information may be duplicated and available outside of the actual personnel file of that officer.**[4]

This is due to the fact that the legislative history of the *Pitchess* statutes shows that the California Legislature intended such personnel file information to be kept confidential regardless of <u>where</u> it was stored.[5] Thus, "the statutes which protect personnel records *and information from such records* also protect

---

2 *See* Cal. Penal Code § 832.7(a); *but see* Cal. Penal Code § 832.7(a)-(f) (**exempting** from the statutory confidentiality requirement: investigations by a grand jury, city attorney, or district attorney; statements made by a party making a complaint to a law enforcement agency and released to that complaining party at the time the complaint is filed; *discretionary* dissemination by the employer department or agency of data regarding the number, type, and disposition of complaints where the individuals involved are not identified; and *discretionary* dissemination by the employer department or agency of factual information concerning a disciplinary investigation if a peace officer makes a knowingly false statement concerning a disciplinary investigation or its outcome to the news or entertainment-communications media).

3 *Haggerty v. Superior Ct.* (2004) 117 Cal.App.4th 1079, 1085.

4 *Hackett v. Superior Ct.* (1993) 13 Cal.App.4th 96, 99-101 (evaluating the legislative history of the *Pitchess* statutory procedure and holding that testimony about an officer's personal contact information, birth date, and driver's license was not subject to discovery/disclosure without a good cause showing through the *Pitchess* procedure, even if that personnel file information was otherwise obtainable from public records).

5 *Hackett, supra*, 13 Cal.App.4th at pp. 99-101.

NOTE: The inverse of this precept is that non-confidential information is likely CPRA-disclosable regardless of who possesses it. *See, e.g.*, *First Amendment Coalition v. Superior Ct.* (2023) 98 Cal.App.5th 593, 611 (holding that CPRA disclosable records must be produced regardless of which agency, state or local, possesses them: this is because "it [is] 'unlikely [that] the Legislature intend[ed] to render documents confidential based on their location, rather than their content.'").

the identical information about personnel history which is within the officers' personal recollections" because "[t]here would be no purpose to protecting such information in the personnel records if it could be obtained by the simple expedient of asking the officers for their disciplinary history orally."[6]

The converse also appears to be true. To elaborate, where such records/recording are *not* statutorily-defined officer personnel file records, the mere placement of such records/recordings into an officer's personnel file likely does *not* transform such records into protected officer personnel file records.

Incident Videos Are *Not* Personnel File Records. For example, where an arrest video was *not* created during the administrative investigation against the subject officer, but was created before such investigation (and not for the purpose related to the advancement, appraisal, or discipline of an officer), even though such recording was used during the administrative investigation, and copies saved to the officer's personnel file, such video was *not* a protected officer personnel file record subject to the *Pitchess* system.[7]

Where Outside Investigations Are *Not* Part Of The Officer Disciplinary System, Their Records Are Not *Pitchess* Protected Officer Personnel Files. Similarly, when a public agency retains an outsider to conduct an independent investigation of alleged law enforcement officer misconduct, but that investigation cannot result in discipline against the officer, that investigation record is *not* an officer personnel file record subject to *Pitchess* protections: and may thus be CPRA-disclosable.[8]

Thus, for example, where a county hired an outside counsel to conduct an investigation into allegations of harassment misconduct by an elected Sheriff, and that investigator prepared a related report, because the County had no power to discipline or terminate the Sheriff, that investigation report was *not* a *Pitchess*-protected officer personnel file record, and it was thus

---

6 *City of San Diego v. Superior Ct.* (1981) 136 Cal.App.3d 236, 239 (reversing a trial court that had granted a motion to compel to force officers to testify at deposition about subject matters contained in personnel file records for which that trial court had denied discovery-disclosure after a *Pitchess* motion and *in camera* review).

7 *City of Eureka v. Superior Ct.* (2016) 1 Cal.App.5th 755, 763-764.

8 *See Essick v. County of Sonoma* (2022) 81 Cal.App.5th 941, 945-946, 951-954; *accord Pasadena Police Officers Assn v. Superior Ct.* (2015) 240 Cal.App.4th 268, 274-275, 288.

CPRA-disclosable.[9] Similarly, where – after a series of officer-involved shootings ("OIS") – a city hired an outside consultant to conduct an independent review of its police department's policies, because that review did *not* affect the "advancement, appraisal or discipline of the officers involved in the shooting," the related report was *not* an officer personnel file record: and it thus lacked *Pitchess* protection and was CPRA-disclosable.[10]

The *Pitchess* System Is The (Near) Exclusive Mechanism For Obtaining Such Records. As a result, absent an applicable exception (as will be discussed later in this primer), a party to any civil or criminal case may *not* obtain discovery or disclosure of any peace officer's personnel file records — or obtain testimony about information contained in such records — unless that party first complies with the so-called "*Pitchess* procedures" of the Evidence Code.[11] In other words, in California state court cases, unless the CPRA otherwise makes such a disclosable public record, the *Pitchess* procedure is the **exclusive** method for obtaining both peace officer personnel records and the information contained in them.

A. Mandatory 5 Year Retention Of Complaints/Investigations Of Officer Misconduct; Unless Sustained, Then 15 Year Retention Required.

Even under the 2019 revisions, police agencies are still required to maintain/preserve records of complaints/investigations of officer misconduct for at least **5 years.**[12] While the law makes such records part of the officer's personnel file, agencies are generally permitted (but not required) to segregate such records from the "general personnel file" of the officer into a separate personnel file just consisting of such complaints/investigations.[13]

9 *See Essick, supra*, 81 Cal.App.5th at pp. 945-946, 951-954.

10 *See Pasadena Police Officers Assn, supra*, 240 Cal.App.4th at pp. 274-275, 288.

11 *See, e.g.*, Cal. Evid. Code §§ 1040, 1043, 1045; *City of Santa Cruz v. Municipal Ct.* (1989) 49 Cal.3d 74, 81-82; *Haggerty, supra*, 117 Cal.App.4th at p. 1085 (holding that the *Pitchess* statutory procedure applies to discovery in both civil and criminal cases); *Davis v. City of Sacramento* (1994) 24 Cal.App.4th 393, 401 n. 2 (barring testimony on *Pitchess*-privileged matters); *cf. Pitchess v. Superior Ct.* (1974) 11 Cal. 3d 531 (the case that controlled such discovery and disclosure before the statutory procedures were enacted); *City & County of San Francisco v. Superior Ct.* (1981) 125 Cal.App.3d 879, 882 (evaluating peace officer records privileges under the right to privacy).

12 Cal. Penal Code § 832.5(b).

13 Cal. Penal Code § 832.5(b). PRACTICE NOTE: Absent a litigation hold or comparable notice in a specific case, there is no benefit to the police agency to retain records of officer misconduct complaints/investigations for more than 5 years from the incident date(s).

However, as of January 1, 2022, statutory revisions have further mandated two significant changes for officer personnel file record retention.

First, **where the department or agency has sustained a finding of misconduct** by the peace officer or custodial officer, the 2022 revisions now mandate that the agency retain the records of the complaint, related reports/investigations, and findings for at least **15 years** — triple the prior officer personnel record retention requirement.[14]

Second, the 2022 statutory revisions now *mandate* that records pertaining to complaints, reports/investigations, and findings of officer misconduct that resulted in a frivolous, unfounded, or exonerated finding must be kept separate from the officer's general personnel file — even though, as separate officer personnel file records, they still otherwise enjoy the *Pitchess* privilege.[15]

Read in conjunction, the revised portions of the statute effectively mandate that records pertaining to complaints, reports/investigations, and findings of officer misconduct that resulted in a frivolous, unfounded, or exonerated finding must be retained under the 5 year requirement, not the 15 year requirement.[16]

B. The 2019 Exception: Critical Incident Recordings & Some Investigation/Complaint Records Are Now Public Records.

Under the 2019 statutory revisions, while all complaints against peace/custodial officers and administrative investigations against them (*e.g.*, IA-type investigations) remain "personnel file" records-information that, in most cases, are presumed confidential and protected under the *Pitchess* privilege procedure, the California Legislature has carved out a large exemption to the presumption of confidentiality. In essence, California law now makes some officer personnel file records/information a matter of public record (exempt from the confidentiality presumption, and presumed to be public records) — discoverable upon submission of a California Public Records Act ("CPRA") request to a public/police agency.

---

14 Cal. Penal Code § 832.5(b) (amend. 2022).

15 Cal. Penal Code § 832.5(c) (amend. 2022).

16 *Compare* Penal Code § 832.5(b) (amend. 2022) *with* Penal Code § 832.5(c) (amend. 2022).

With some potential temporary withholding or limited redaction available under a variety of specified circumstances, upon compliance with certain technical requirements (all of which will be explored later in this book), the 2019 revisions to the Government Code and to the Penal Code make the following police records into public records, even when they otherwise satisfy the definition of officer personnel file records: (1) audio/video recordings of "critical incidents" — which the laws also define as "serious" uses of force; (2) complaints/investigation records/information regarding critical incidents; (3) complaints/investigation records/information regarding <u>sustained</u> allegations of officer sexual assault against non-officers/persons who are not employees of the subject officer's agency; and (4) complaints/investigation records/information regarding <u>sustained</u> allegations of officer policing-related dishonesty.[17]

The new laws use the terms "critical incident[s]" and "serious" uses of force interchangeably to mean incidents where: (1) there was an **officer-involved shooting ("OIS")** of/at a person, regardless of injury; or (2) there was an **officer use-of-force ("UOF")**, *of any kind*, on a person, where the UOF resulted in (a) **death**, or (b) "**great bodily injury**". Notably, the term "critical incident" does <u>not</u> extend to officer sexual assault or officer dishonesty.[18]

While the nuances and details of the 2019+ *Pitchess* exception will be explained in a later chapter of this book, their significance here is that, for these specified categories of officer personnel file records/information, **they are no longer presumed confidential**. Rather, even where they constitute officer personnel file information, **these categories of records/information are presumed to be matters of public record.** In other words, for these specified categories of police records, they are effectively **exempt** from the *Pitchess* privilege and procedural requirements.

---

17 Cal. Gov. Code §§ 7923.60-7923.625 (formerly Cal. Gov. Code § 6254(f)); Cal. Penal Code §§ 832.7-832.8 (amend. 2019).

18 *See id.* PRACTICE NOTE: The law is very specific about the critical incident being defined as against a <u>person</u>. Thus, an OIS against an animal, or an OIS where a person was not hit, or a UOF against a non-person arguably all do <u>not</u> fall within the critical incident definition: and thus such non-person OIS/UOF events appear to retain their *Pitchess* confidentiality.

TION PROCEDURE: What Procedure st a Party Follow to Obtain *Pitchess* vileged Matter in a California te Case?

rview of the *Pitchess* Procedure.

ke other California discovery procedures, such as those found in nia Code of Civil Procedure, "the Evidence Code procedure begins sumption of confidentiality": except for the newly exempted records.[1] "seeker of the information under section 1043 must show that the on sought is relevant to the subject matter of the lawsuit — not simply shes to obtain it."[2]

s is because in enacting the *Pitchess* procedures, such as those codified ce Code sections 1043 and 1045, the Legislature intended to place mitations and procedural safeguards on the disclosure of peace officer l files.[3] Thus, the *Pitchess* statutory procedure recognizes that a peace as a strong privacy interest in his or her personnel records and that

City of Hemet v. Superior Ct. (1995) 37 Cal.App.4th 1411, 1424-1425; *cf.* Cal. Evid. 3; Cal. Penal Code § 832.7; *Alford v. Superior Ct.* (2003) 29 Cal.4th 1033, 1036-1046 (sum-*itchess* procedures); *People v. Superior Ct.* (*Johnson*) (2015) 2015 Cal. LEXIS 4647, *14-24, summarizing *Pitchess* procedures and rationale); *People v. Mooc* (2001) 26 Cal.4th 1216; l. Penal Code §§ 832.7-832.8 (amend. 2019) *and* Cal. Gov. Code §§ 7923.600-7923.625 Cal. Gov. Code § 6254(f)) (police records/recordings of critical incidents and records of ual assault on non-officers or officer policing dishonesty are matters of public record).

City of Hemet, supra, 37 Cal.App.4th at pp. 1424-1425 (reversing order for disclosure l affairs investigation records due to lack of good cause).

City of Santa Cruz v. Municipal Ct. (1989) 49 Cal. 3d 74, 94.

3. JURISDICTION: Doe Privilege and Procedu State *Civil* Cases or On *Criminal* Cases?

Pitchess privilege issues most often ari covery and criminal trials, presumably becau peace officers are criminal cases.[1] However, C *explicitly* holds that the *Pitchess* privileges anc as well: in other words, "[t]hese statutes **appl discovery**."[2]

Thus, a civil practitioner may often find from California state criminal cases when addr in her civil litigation. However, a civil litigator *Pitchess* procedures, even in her civil case.

1 *See, e.g.*, *Pitchess v. Superior Ct.* (1974) 11 Cal. 3d deputy sheriffs); *People v. Mooc* (2001) 26 Cal.4th 1216 (a crimin on a peace officer).

2 *See Haggerty v. Superior Ct.* (2004) 117 Cal.App.4th for obtaining these confidential personnel records **in civil** and crim Code §§] 1043 through 1047 and [Cal. Penal Code §§] 832.5, 832 *see also* Cal. Penal Code § 832.7 ("Except as provided in subdivis peace officers and custodial officers and records maintained by a to [Penal Code] Section 832.5, or information obtained from th shall not be disclosed in any criminal or civil proceeding except b 1043 and 1046 of the Evidence Code.") (emphasis added); *cf. Mooc*

4. MO Mu Pri Sta

A. Ov

Unli the Califo from a pre Thus, the informati that he w

Thi in Evide specific l personn officer "

1 Code § 10 marizing 33-40 (als *but see* C (formerly officer se

2 of intern

3

such records should not be disclosed unnecessarily"—even if the evidence contained in the officer's personnel file could be pertinent to the lawsuit.[4]

Indeed, part of the rationale underlying the *Pitchess* procedure of Evidence Code § 1043 *et al.* is that it creates "detailed and careful procedures [in order] to assure that the sensitive information contained in records relating to allegations of police misconduct will be disclosed *only* upon a showing of **manifest necessity**."[5] Thus, in the balance of the "legitimate concerns of peace officers to shield from disclosure confidential information not essential to an effective" presentation of a party's case, the intent of the *Pitchess* procedure is to protect officer personnel files from discovery or disclosure unless crucial information "essential" to the moving-party's case is not "otherwise obtainable from other nonprivileged sources."[6]

Accordingly, in order "[t]o balance these competing interests [between a party's interest in discovery-disclosure and a peace officer's interest in non-disclosure of the officer's personnel file information], the Legislature 'require[d] the intervention of a neutral trial judge, who examines the personnel records *in camera*...and orders disclosed to the [moving party] only those records that are found both relevant and otherwise in compliance with statutory limitations.'"[7] "In this manner, the Legislature has attempted to protect [a party's] right to a fair trial and the officer's interest in privacy to the fullest extent possible."[8]

However, before a court may even conduct an *in camera* review of peace officer personnel files, and certainly before such records may be disclosed or

---

4 *Haggerty v. Superior Ct.* (2004) 117 Cal.App.4th 1079, 1085 ("discovery of police officer files [is permitted] on a proper showing of materiality, relevance, and necessity...[however, the] *Pitchess* statutory scheme recognizes that evidence contained in a law enforcement officer's personnel file may be relevant in a lawsuit, but that the officer 'has a strong privacy interest in his or her personnel records and that such records should not be disclosed unnecessarily.'").

5 *City of Hemet, supra*, 37 Cal.App.4th at pp. 1424-1425 (emphasis added); *but see* Cal. Penal Code §§ 832.7-832.8 (amend. 2019) *and* Cal. Gov. Code §§ 7923.600-7923.625 (formerly Cal. Gov. Code § 6254(f)) (police records/recordings of critical incidents and records of officer sexual assault on non-officers or officer policing dishonesty are matters of public record).

6 *City of Santa Cruz, supra*, 49 Cal. 3d at p. 94.

7 *Haggerty, supra*, 117 Cal.App.4th at p. 1085 (citing *Mooc, supra*, 26 Cal.4th at p. 1227).

8 *Haggerty, supra*, 117 Cal.App.4th at pp. 1085-1086 (holding that trial courts are granted wide discretion regarding motions to discover-disclose law enforcement officer personnel records, and that a reviewing court should reverse the trial court's determinations only on a showing that the court abused its discretion).

produced to the moving party, a moving party's motion to compel production or disclosure of peace officer personnel file records (a "*Pitchess* motion") must meet *all* of the following requirements.

First, the moving party's *Pitchess* motion must **specifically describe** the type of records sought, and the identity of the officer(s) whose records are sought, so as "to ensure that the [moving party's] request is not so broad as to garner all information which has been obtained by the [other party]...but is [instead] limited to instances of officer misconduct related to the misconduct asserted by [the moving party]."[9]

Second, the *Pitchess* motion must be supported by a **sworn declaration-affidavit showing good cause** for the disclosure.[10]

Third, the moving party's showing of good cause must demonstrate the "'**materiality** of the subject matter of the pending litigation...'"; in other words, there must be a "logical link" between the items to be disclosed and the party's claims.[11]

Finally, the *Pitchess* motion's declaration must show that the moving party has a "**reasonable belief** that the agency has the type of information sought."[12]

---

9 *See Warrick v. Superior Ct.* (2005) 35 Cal.4th 1011, 1021-22; *Uybungcov v. Superior Ct.* (2008) 163 Cal.App.4th 1043, 1048-1049.

PRACTICE NOTE: In most practitioners' parlance, the terms "disclose" and "produce" are often treated as fungible — even though to "disclose" is to reveal the *existence* of something, while to "produce" is to actually hand over that something. However, in the context of a *Pitchess* motion, it may be wiser for us all to be more precise in the use of these terms because the function of a *Pitchess* motion varies depending on how the *Pitchess*-privileged matter is to be used in the case. Technically, when a moving party seeks to obtain "discovery" or "production" of *Pitchess*-privileged matter, they are seeking to obtain access to that information for themselves. When a moving party seeks to "disclose" *Pitchess*-privileged matter, they are seeking the court's approval to *publish Pitchess*-privileged matter to the jury at trial (i.e., to have the otherwise-privileged evidence deemed admissible) or to other persons or entities besides the involved officer and the custodial government agency. As the standards for discovery *before* trial are similar to, and yet distinct from, the standards for disclosure *at* trial, the best practice is for the moving party to clarify for which use — pre-trial discovery or disclosure at trial — the moving party is seeking court authorization. *See generally Zanone, supra*, 162 Cal.App.4th at p. 187 n. 14.

10 *See Haggerty, supra*, 117 Cal.App.4th at pp. 1085-1086.

11 *See Warrick, supra*, 35 Cal.4th at pp. 1016, 1021-1022, 1024-1025 (emphasis added).

PRACTICE NOTE: The evaluation of "materiality" largely overlaps the issue of "manifest necessity": it is thus simplest to think of the materiality requirement as a requirement to show the manifest necessity for the peace officer personnel file information at issue.

12 *See Warrick, supra*, 35 Cal.4th at p. 1016; *Haggerty, supra*, 117 Cal.App.4th at p. 1086.

- Did the Protective Order Limit Use of the Officer Personnel File Only to the Action at Issue?

- Did the Protective Order Mandate End-of-Action Return or Verified Destruction of the Officer Personnel File Records-Information Discovered-Produced to the Movant?

Please see below and the chapters thereafter for a full explanation of the mechanics, rules, authorities, and rationales underlying each of the above *Pitchess* motion checklist items.

2. *APPEALS: Standard of Review for Appeals of Pitchess Rulings.*

Along related lines, it should be noted that a Court's decision on a *Pitchess* motion is *normally* subject to **appellate review** on an **<u>abuse of discretion</u>** standard, and requires a showing of prejudicial error where the appellant alleges the *Pitchess* procedures were violated by the court.[15]

However, where the facts are undisputed, and the correctness of the trial court's ruling turns on a question of law, then the appellate court will review the trial court's *Pitchess* ruling ***<u>de novo</u>***.[16]

B. <u>SERVICE: Notice and Service Requirements of the *Pitchess* Procedure and Related Standing Issues.</u>

To address the more technical considerations of the *Pitchess* procedure, a *Pitchess* motion must be filed with the "appropriate court or administrative body upon written notice to the governmental agency which has custody and control of the records" at issue.[17] Furthermore, a *Pitchess* motion must be noticed in conformity with the requirements of Code of Civil Procedure section 1005(b), and it must include the time and place of the hearing within

---

15 *See People v. Gaines* (2009) 46 Cal.4th 172, 176, 178, 180-181; *Haggerty, supra*, 117 Cal.App.4th at pp. 1085-1086.

16 *See Banuelos v. Superior Ct.* (2024) 2024 Cal.App.LEXIS 705, *8 ("Generally, a trial court's ruling on a *Pitchess* motion is reviewed for abuse of discretion. [citation] But where, as here, the facts are undisputed and the correctness of the court's *Pitchess* ruling turns on a question of law, our review is de novo."; citing *Brown v. Valverde* (2010) 183 Cal.App.4th 1531, 1546).

17 *See* Cal. Evid. Code §§ 1043(a).

the motion.[18] It is then the duty of the custodial governmental agency upon whom the *Pitchess* motion is served to "immediately notify the individual whose records are sought."[19]

However, because the *Pitchess* procedure incorporates the service requirements of Code of Civil Procedure section 1005(b), which in turn incorporates section 1013, and because these sections require service of moving and opposing papers on "each party" to an action, in civil cases, where the records sought are from the personnel file of an officer who is a party to the action, in addition to serving the governmental agency that is reasonably believed to be the custodian of the records sought, the safest practice is for the moving party to also serve its *Pitchess* motion on the individual party-officer at issue.[20]

Additionally, "full compliance with the notice provisions" of Evidence Code section 1043 is a prerequisite to the *Pitchess* motion being heard by the court — unless the moving party shows "good cause for noncompliance, or upon a waiver of the hearing by the government agency identified as having the records."[21]

The waiver option of the governmental agency is significant because it and other authority shows that "the privilege against disclosure of official police records is held both by the individual officer involved *and* by the police department."[22] The rationale underlying this dual standing in the confidentiality of peace officer records is that the *Pitchess* protective procedure reduces the incentive for governmental agencies to unnecessarily or hastily destroy

---

18 *See* Cal. Evid. Code § 1043(a).

19 *See* Cal. Evid. Code § 1043(a).

20 *See See* Cal. Evid. Code § 1043(a); Cal. Code Civ. Proc. §§ 1005(b), 1013.

PRACTICE NOTE: In a *criminal* action, unless the peace officer in question is a defendant, the officer for whom personnel file records are sought will *not* be a party to the action.

21 *See* Cal. Evid. Code § 1043(a) (emphasis added).

22 *See Davis v. City of Sacramento* (1994) 24 Cal.App.4th 393, 401 (holding that waiver of *Pitchess* privileges by a peace officer is *not* sufficient to require disclosure of personnel file information where the peace officer's employer has not waived the *Pitchess* privileges) (emphasis added); *cf.* Cal. Evid. Code §§ 1040 (a "public entity has a privilege to refuse to disclose official information," such as confidential information acquired by a public employee in the course of his or her duties, where the disclosure is forbidden by state or federal law or is against the public interest in the confidentiality of the information), 1043(c); *San Francisco Police Officers' Ass'n v. Superior Ct.* (1988) 202 Cal.App.3d 183, 189.

their records.[23] Accordingly, on a practical level, this means that both the law enforcement agency or government agency *and* the individual officer whose personnel records are sought have standing to oppose the moving party's *Pitchess* motion.[24] However, it must be noted that *only* the governmental agency, *not* the individual officer, has the power to waive the right to a *Pitchess* motion hearing.[25]

There are significant implications arising from the fact that **the custodial public entity and the peace officer are joint holders of the *Pitchess* privilege**, particularly in light of the fact that the public entity receives superior privilege/access rights to an officer's personnel file. However, these implications will be explored in a subsequent chapter.

---

23 *See San Francisco Police Officers' Ass'n v. Superior Ct.* (1988) 202 Cal.App.3d 183, 189-190 (holding that the legislative history of the *Pitchess* statutes shows that the purpose of the *Pitchess* privilege "is to give the peace officer and...employing agency the right to refuse to disclose any information concerning the officer or complaints or investigations...in both criminal and civil proceedings" so as to avoid the incentive for destruction of records).

24 *See Davis, supra*, 24 Cal.App.4th at p. 401 n. 1 (observing that giving the governmental agency the privilege against disclosure was intended to avoid the incentive for destruction of records); *San Francisco Police Officers' Ass'n, supra*, 202 Cal.App.3d at pp. 191-192.

25 *Michael v. Gates* (1995) 38 Cal.App.4th 737, 744.

5. MOTION THRESHOLD: What Showing Must a Party Make to Get an *In Camera* Hearing for Potential Discovery or Disclosure of *Pitchess* Privileged Matter in a State Case?

As noted above, in order for a moving party to obtain the *in camera* hearing that is generally prerequisite to discovery-disclosure of *Pitchess*-privileged matters, the moving party's *Pitchess* motion must: (1) **specifically describe** the type of records sought, and the identity of the officer(s) whose records are sought; (2) be supported by a sworn declaration/affidavit showing **good cause** for the discovery or disclosure; (3) show the **materiality** of the records-information sought to the moving party's claims/defenses in the action; and (4) show a **reasonable belief** that the government agency from whom the records are sought has such records in its custody or control.[1]

A. The Specificity Requirement of the *Pitchess* Procedure (Scope).

In order to obtain disclosure of records from a peace officer's personnel file, the moving party must include in its *Pitchess* motion a specific "description of the type of records or information sought," as well as the specific "peace or custodial officer whose records are sought," and the moving party must identify "the governmental agency which has custody and control of the records" sought.[2] This specificity requirement of the *Pitchess* procedure is intended to

---

1 *Ass'n for L.A. Deputy Sheriffs (ALADS) v. Superior Ct.* (2019) 8 Cal. 5th 28, 40-43 (summarizing the *Pitchess* motion process and standards, including citation to many of the cases cited herein below); *see also People v. Nuno* (2024) 105 Cal.App.5th 1030, 1052-1056 (summarizing the general rules for analysis of *Pitchess* motions).

2 *See* Cal. Evid. Code § 1043(b)(1)-(2).

force the moving party to "show that the information sought is relevant to the subject matter of the lawsuit — not simply that he wishes to obtain it."[3] Thus, the specificity requirement for a *Pitchess* motion is designed to "preclude the possibility of a.... [moving party's] simply casting about for any helpful information."[4] In other words, the "specificity requirement excludes requests for officer information that are irrelevant to the pending" issues of the case.[5]

For example, in an excessive force and false arrest civil case where plaintiffs sought production of the *entire* personnel files of the defendant officers through a *Pitchess* motion, after performing an *in camera* review, the trial court granted the motion and ordered the production of the *entirety* of the defendant officers' personnel files.[6] However, the appellate court reversed the trial court's order because the moving party had failed to satisfy the specificity (and related materiality) requirement(s) of the *Pitchess* procedure: in other words, the appellate court ruled that the moving party was *not* entitled to production of the *entire* personnel file — which included complaints about conduct unrelated to the allegations at issue in plaintiffs' action, performance evaluations, and other such matter — because the plaintiffs' *Pitchess* motion was not specific and narrow enough in the subject matters for which it sought discovery-disclosure.[7] At most, in light of plaintiffs' claims in that action, the reviewing court held that the moving party would have been entitled to the names and addresses of other persons who had complained against the defendant officers for excessive force or false arrest — and even then the moving party would *not* have been entitled to discovery of the entire investigative files for such complaints, absent a proper showing of good cause for such.[8]

Notably, there is a growing body of authority indicating that the <u>scope</u> of a *Pitchess* motion is <u>not</u> limited to officers who participated in or witnessed the alleged misconduct at issue in the litigation: as long as good cause is established, a *Pitchess* motion may be brought seeking discovery or disclosure of any peace

---

3 *City of Hemet v. Superior Ct.* (1995) 37 Cal.App.4th 1411, 1424-1425.

4 *See People v. Mooc* (2001) 26 Cal.4th 1216, 1226.

5 *See Warrick v. Superior Ct.* (2005) 35 Cal.4th 1011, 1021-1022.

6 *City of Azusa v. Superior Ct.* (1989) 191 Cal. App. 3d 693, 695-697.

7 *City of Azusa, supra*, 191 Cal. App. 3d at pp. 695-697; *cf. Warrick, supra*, 35 Cal.4th at pp. 1021-1022.

8 *City of Azusa, supra*, 191 Cal.App.3d at pp. 696-697.

officer.[9] However, it should also be noted that, where the misconduct at issue involves an arrest, Evidence Code § 1047 bars disclosure of the personnel file records/information of uninvolved officers.[10]

B. The Good Cause Requirement of the *Pitchess* Procedure

The moving party's burden for showing good cause for discovery-disclosure of *Pitchess*-privileged matter is a "'relatively low threshold'" that can be met by a sworn attorney declaration or affidavit, made on information and belief; however, such declaration must still demonstrate good cause for the discovery or disclosure by showing: (1) a "plausible [factual] scenario of officer misconduct...that might or could have occurred...that is both internally consistent [in light of the pertinent documents] and supports" the claims of the moving party; (2) that the requested "discovery sought may lead to relevant evidence or may itself be admissible direct or impeachment evidence" under some theory of admissibility at trial; and (3) how the requested *Pitchess* disclosures sought would support the moving party's claims.[11]

The moving party can satisfy its burden of showing a plausible factual scenario for officer misconduct in a number of ways — including referencing affidavits, police reports, witness statements, and other relevant documents — and alleging, on information and belief, a theory of officer misconduct that is both internally consistent and supports the moving party's claims: corroboration of that alleged officer misconduct is not required, so long as it is something that plausibly could have occurred under the circumstances.[12]

---

9 *Riske v. Superior Ct.* (2016) 6 Cal.App.5th 647, 661-662 (Cal. Evid. Code § 1047 "only applies if the discovery request relates to an incident *involving* an arrest or its equivalent. When, as here, the discovery request is unrelated to an arrest, Evidence Code section 1047's limitation does not apply.... If the [moving party] can show the confidential personnel records of officers who were not involved in the injury are nonetheless material to the litigation, he or she has demonstrated the good cause necessary to obtain *in camera* review.")(emphasis in original).

10 *See* Cal. Evid. Code § 1047(a); *Riske, supra*, 6 Cal.App.5th at pp. 661-662.

11 *See Warrick, supra*, 35 Cal.4th at pp. 1024-27.

12 *Warrick, supra*, 35 Cal.4th at pp. pp. 1019, 1024-1026; *Brant v. Superior Ct.* (2003) 108 Cal.App.4th 100, 105 (reversing trial court's denial of a *Pitchess* motion where criminal defendant properly alleged false reporting by the officers); *but see* Cal. Evid. Code § 1046 (requiring attachment to the *Pitchess* motion of related incident police report(s) where excessive force allegations are being made).

However, as part of showing the materiality of the information sought to the moving party's claims (a key aspect of the good cause showing), the moving party must also show that the information sought is either itself admissible into evidence at trial or could reasonably lead to the discovery of evidence that is admissible at trial.[13] Thus, even under the "relatively relaxed" standards for showing good cause for discovery-disclosure of peace officer personnel files, "the requisite allegations must 'establish some cause for discovery other [than] a mere desire for the benefit of all information which has been obtained.'"[14] Accordingly, **where information in an officer's personnel file is irrelevant to the claims at issue in the action, there cannot be good cause to discover or disclose that information**, and it is thus *not* discoverable.[15]

Furthermore, in deciding whether there is good cause for the trial court to review personnel file records *in camera* for potential discovery or disclosure, "only documentation of past officer misconduct which is similar to the misconduct alleged by the [moving party] in the pending litigation is relevant and therefore subject to discovery."[16] Thus, even though "evidence of habit or custom [is generally] admissible to show that a person acted in conformity with that habit or custom on a given occasion," where the personnel file information that the moving party seeks regards *dissimilar* alleged misconduct, or is irrelevant to the claims at issue in the action, that personnel file information is *not* discoverable.[17]

---

13 *See Warrick, supra*, 35 Cal.4th at p. 1026; *Haggerty v. Superior Ct.* (2004) 117 Cal.App.4th 1079, 1083-1084, 1086 (holding that where a plaintiff alleging excessive force in custody sought *Pitchess* production of the internal affairs report into the incident at issue in his excessive force claims, because it was "self-evident" that facts from that report could be admissible evidence, or could reasonably lead to the discovery of admissible evidence, plaintiff had satisfied the materiality element of the good cause showing in his *Pitchess* motion).

14 *See City & County of San Francisco v. Superior Ct.* (1994) 21 Cal.App.4th 1031, 1035 (reversing order for production of an incident-related internal affairs investigation report, for lack of good cause, in an excessive force civil damages case).

15 *See Warrick, supra*, 35 Cal.4th at p. 1022 (emphasis added); *accord People v. Hustead* (1999) 74 Cal.App.4th 410, 416-418.

16 *California Hwy. Patrol v. Superior Ct.* (2000) 84 Cal.App.4th 1010, 1021.

17 *California Hwy. Patrol, supra*, 84 Cal.App.4th at pp. 1021-1022; *cf.* Cal. Evid. Code §§ 1101(a), 1105; *Holdgrafer v. Unocal Corp.* (2008) 160 Cal.App.4th 907, 928-929 (excluding "habit" evidence of conduct that was too dissimilar from the misconduct at issue in the action on the grounds that "evidence of a [party's] prior bad acts or bad character is generally inadmissible to prove propensity or disposition to engage in conduct on a specified occasion"); *but cf.* Cal. Evid. Code § 1101(b).

For example, where a moving party's supporting declaration to a *Pitchess* motion had failed to allege that a specific officer had falsified any reports, and failed to set forth a specific factual scenario supporting an allegation of such dishonest misconduct *by that officer*, the court held that the movant lacked good cause for discovery-disclosure of that officer's personnel file — even though the moving party made an "unsupported allegation" that all officers are dishonest and likely to lie at trial about fellow officers' use of excessive force.[18]

Similarly, where the prosecution had dropped a resisting arrest charge, but the moving party still sought review-disclosure of the arresting officer's personnel files regarding excessive force complaints, the court held that because excessive force was no longer relevant to the case, the trial court correctly declined even to review the officer's personnel files on those issues.[19]

By way of contrast, where that same moving party alleged that several statements in the arresting officer's police report on the incident were misrepresentations, and where the moving party attached the report to its *Pitchess* motion as well as made a specific factual showing as to how the statements were materially false, the reviewing court held that whether the arresting officer had a history of making misrepresentations in his reports was a relevant issue, and thus that the trial court should have reviewed the personnel files *in camera* on that misrepresentation issue so as to determine if such reports were discoverable and whether such reports should have been produced to the moving party.[20]

In sum, in order to make a proper showing of good cause for disclosure-discovery of specific information from a peace officer's personnel file records, a moving party must not only state a plausible factual scenario of officer misconduct (via its declaration/affidavit), but the moving party must show how that information — if it exists — could reasonably be admissible at trial, or lead to the discovery of admissible evidence, and the moving party must show how that information is material to the claims at issue in the action.[21]

18 *See California Hwy. Patrol, supra*, 84 Cal.App.4th at pp. 1023-1025 (reversing order for disclosure).

19 *See Hustead, supra*, 74 Cal.App.4th at pp. 416-418.

20 *See Hustead, supra*, 74 Cal.App.4th at pp. 416-418.

21 *See generally* Cal. Evid. Code § 1045(b)(3).

1. *Use of Privileged Information to Establish Good Cause.*

According to recent controlling authority, a moving party need no longer choose between preserving privileged information from disclosure and meeting the threshold for establishing good cause for *Pitchess* discovery or disclosures. Thus, where the moving party's affidavit-declaration would result in disclosure of **privileged information**, the moving party is entitled to file the *Pitchess* motion or affidavit-declaration **under seal**.

In such circumstances, the moving party's motion must clearly assert the privileges claimed, and the court must review the motion's alleged privileged information (*i.e.*, the affidavit-declaration containing the purportedly privileged information) *in camera*. Moreover, the opposing party must be permitted to propound questions to be asked by the court during the *in camera* hearing that go to whether the privilege claimed by the moving party applies to the information for which a court sealing order is sought.[22]

Notably, this *in camera* procedure for reviewing a *Pitchess* motion *under seal* is designed to prevent the opposing party from receiving the allegedly privileged matter upon which good cause for disclosure-discovery rests; however, even if the *Pitchess* motion itself were reviewed *in camera*, the court would still be required to conduct a *separate in camera* review of the records possessed by the custodial government agency, unless the moving party was the custodial government agency.[23]

C. The Materiality Requirement of the Good Cause Showing Under the *Pitchess* Procedure.

As intimated above, in order to show good cause for *Pitchess* disclosure, and so as to move the process toward an *in camera* review by the court, a moving party must show that the personnel file information sought is material to the claims at issue in the action: in other words, the moving party must show that there is a "logical link" between the items to be disclosed and that party's claims/defenses.[24] This is because, under the presumed confidentiality of the

22 *See Garcia v. Superior Ct.* (2007) 42 Cal.4th 63, 73.

23 *Garcia, supra*, 42 Cal.4th at p. 73; *cf.* Cal. Evid. Code §§ 915(b), 1045; *Mooc, supra*, 26 Cal.4th at pp. 1226-1229; *Haggerty, supra*, 117 Cal.App.4th at p. 1086.

24 *See Warrick, supra*, 35 Cal.4th at pp. 1024-1025.

Pitchess privileges, the *Pitchess* statutes prohibit the discovery or disclosure of personnel file information that is irrelevant to the claims at issue.[25] Thus, as noted above, where the moving party is only making allegations of X specific misconduct by an officer, personnel file information about Y conduct is *not* material to the moving party's claims — and the courts will thus find that there is no good cause for disclosure-discovery of such matter in that case.[26]

For example, in an excessive force civil case regarding a man who was being detained in a cell, where plaintiff alleged that county deputies began beating him for failing to comply with a command to move a calendar away from a light, and where plaintiff learned that the department had conducted an internal affairs type investigation into the incident, the reviewing court partly affirmed the trial court's order that the internal affairs report on the incident must be produced-disclosed by the relevant law enforcement agency to plaintiff — on the grounds that the materiality of an internal investigative report regarding the incident at issue in plaintiff's claims was essentially "self-evident."[27]

Similarly, in a criminal case regarding a charge of resisting arrest, where the defendant claimed that the arrest was unlawful in part due to the use of excessive force by the arresting officer, and where the defendant's *Pitchess* motion sought production of prior complaints of excessive force against the arresting officers on the theory that such complaints might constitute or lead to the discovery of admissible habit evidence on the issue of making unlawful arrests by use of excessive force, the California Supreme Court reversed the Court of Appeal and affirmed the trial courts' orders for discovery-disclosure of such complaints — on the grounds that such personnel records were sufficiently material to the defendant's claims (defenses) as to warrant production under the *Pitchess* procedure.[28]

---

25 *Warrick, supra*, 35 Cal.4th at pp. 1024-1025; *City & County of San Francisco, supra*, 21 Cal.App.4th at p. 1035; *California Hwy. Patrol, supra*, 84 Cal.App.4th at p. 1021.

26 *California Hwy. Patrol, supra*, 84 Cal.App.4th at pp. 1023-1025; *Hustead, supra*, 74 Cal.App.4th at pp. 416-418.

27 *Haggerty, supra*, 117 Cal.App.4th at pp. 1083-1084, 1086 (but also holding that the report to be produced must redact the investigating officers' conclusions, which are *not* discoverable).

28 *City of Santa Cruz v. Municipal Ct.* (1989) 49 Cal. 3d 74, 79-80, 85-86.

D. The Related Requirement of "Manifest Necessity" for Discovery or Disclosure and Its Impact on the Process Where the Information Sought Is Available From Non-Privileged Sources.

As noted above, unlike other California discovery procedures, under the *Pitchess* procedure of the Evidence Code, the court *must* presume that the peace officer's personnel file records are confidential and *not* discoverable, unless the moving party makes the proper showing to overcome that presumption.[29] In other words, unless an exception applies, California law requires that such personnel records be kept confidential absent "a showing of **manifest necessity**."[30]

Thus, in the balance of the "legitimate concerns of peace officers to shield from [discovery-]disclosure confidential information not essential to an effective" presentation of a party's case, the intent of the *Pitchess* procedure is to shield personnel files from discovery or disclosure unless crucial information that is "essential" to the moving-party's case is *not* "otherwise obtainable from other nonprivileged sources."[31] In other words, as a result of the policies underlying the *Pitchess* privileges, **where the confidential personnel records sought are unlikely to affect the outcome of a proceeding, or are *unnecessary* to the presentation of the moving-party's case (such as where comparable information can be obtained elsewhere), such personnel files are *not* discoverable.**[32]

As an example of the operation of the requirement of manifest necessity, in a recent criminal case, prior to a preliminary hearing, the defendant's *Pitchess* motion sought the arresting officer's personnel records on prior complaints or discipline for excessive force, false arrest, fabrication or dishonesty — on the grounds that such records would support his defense of lack of probable cause for his arrest: however, the trial court denied the *Pitchess* motion for lack of

---

29 *See City of Hemet, supra*, 37 Cal.App.4th at pp. 1424-1425; *but see* Cal. Penal Code §§ 832.7-832.8 (amend. 2019) *and* Cal. Gov. Code §§ 7923.600-7923.625 (formerly Cal. Gov. Code § 6254(f) (amend. 2019) (making critical incident records/recordings, and sustained officer sexual assault/dishonesty records presumed public records).

30 *See City of Hemet, supra*, 37 Cal.App.4th at pp. 1424-1425 (emphasis added).

31 *See City of Santa Cruz, supra*, 49 Cal.3d at p. 94; *accord California Hwy. Patrol, supra*, 84 Cal.App.4th at p. 1024.

32 *See City of Santa Cruz, supra*, 49 Cal.3d at p. 94; *accord California Hwy. Patrol, supra*, 84 Cal.App.4th at p. 1024; *City of Azusa v. Superior Ct. (Madrigal)* (1987) 191 Cal.App.3d 693, 696 (holding that the Evidence Code requires that the reviewing court consider whether the requested materials-information can be obtained from other, non-confidential sources).

good cause.[33] On review, the California Supreme Court affirmed the denial on two grounds: first, the Court concluded that prior to filing his *Pitchess* motion, the defendant knew the identity of "various relatives and neighbors of petitioner [who] were present at his arrest and witnessed some, if not all, of the officers' conduct."[34] Accordingly, because the defendant had other sources — namely, eyewitness testimony — to present his case for lack of probable cause and otherwise to contest the officer's version of events, the disclosure of the arresting officer's personnel file records was *unnecessary*.[35] Second, the Court concluded that because the threshold for holding a person to answer for a crime at a preliminary hearing was so low, it was unlikely that the personnel file information would have changed the outcome of the preliminary hearing: accordingly, the trial court did not err by denying that *Pitchess* motion without prejudice.[36]

By way of contrast, in another criminal case, the defendant asserted that he was not at all present where the crime charged had occurred.[37] The prosecution then offered a former police officer who claimed that defendant made admissions supporting the defendant's guilt.[38] During an investigator's interview, the former officer said that he had been separated from his department due to a disability.[39] However, the defendant then filed a *Pitchess* motion supported by the statements of another police department's officers alleging that the former officer had resigned to avoid pending discipline on an issue of moral turpitude.[40] On review, the appellate court held that because the credibility of that former officer was central to that case, and because the defendant supported his *Pitchess* motion with the impeaching statements of the other department's officers, the defendant had shown good cause for the former officer's personnel file to be reviewed *in camera* by the trial court under the *Pitchess* discovery-disclosure procedure.[41]

---

33 *See Galindo v. Superior Ct.* (2010) 50 Cal.4th 1, 9-10.

34 *See Galindo, supra*, 50 Cal.4th at pp. 9-10.

35 *See Galindo, supra*, 50 Cal.4th at pp. 9-10.

36 *See Galindo, supra*, 50 Cal.4th at pp. 9-10.

37 *See Abatti v. Superior Ct.* (2003) 112 Cal.App.4th 39, 58-60.

38 *See Abatti, supra*, 112 Cal.App.4th at pp. 58-60.

39 *See Abatti, supra*, 112 Cal.App.4th at pp. 58-60.

40 *See Abatti, supra*, 112 Cal.App.4th at pp. 58-60.

41 *See Abatti, supra*, 112 Cal.App.4th at pp. 58-60 (reversing the *Pitchess* motion denial).

As a practical matter, it is perhaps simplest to consider the materiality requirement and the manifest necessity requirement to be overlapping or linked: to show materiality for the good cause showing, one must show manifest necessity, and vice versa.

1. *Summary Implications of the Recent Pitchess Exemption For Critical Incidents and Sustained Findings of Officer Sexual Assault or Officer Dishonesty: No Good Cause Required.*

As explained briefly above and in more detail in a subsequent chapter, effective 2019, California law removed the presumption of *Pitchess* confidentiality for four categories of police records/information, even when such are otherwise-confidential officer personnel file records/information: (1) audio/video recordings of "critical incidents" — which the laws also define as "serious" uses of force (OIS against persons, and UOF against persons where death or great bodily injury results); (2) complaints/investigation records/information regarding critical incidents; (3) complaints/investigation records/information regarding sustained allegations of officer sexual assault against non-officers/non-employees; *and* (4) complaints/investigation records/information regarding sustained allegations of officer policing-related dishonesty.[42] Effective 2022, the California Legislature added four more categories (for a total of eight categories) of officer misconduct to this list of CPRA-disclosable police officer records, including: (5) sustained allegations of excessive force; (6) sustained allegations of failure to intervene to stop clear excessive force; (7) sustained allegations of discrimination; and (8) sustained allegations of unlawful arrest or unlawful search.[43]

This means that, as to these specified categories of records/information, if the party seeking discovery or disclosure did so by means of a *Pitchess* motion (as opposed to a CPRA request), **there would be no requirement to show good cause or manifest necessity**: as such records are presumed to be public records under the 2019 and 2022 statutory revisions.

---

42 *See* Cal. Gov. Code §§ 7923.600-7923.625 (formerly Cal. Gov. Code § 6254(f) (amend. 2019); Cal. Penal Code §§ 832.7-832.8 (amend. 2019 & 2022).

43 *See* Cal. Penal Code § 832.7 (amend. 2022).

E. <u>The *Pitchess* Procedure Requirement of a Reasonable Belief That the Government Agency From Whom Discovery-Disclosure Is Sought Possesses the Personnel File Information at Issue.</u>

Additionally, in order to make an adequate showing for *Pitchess* disclosure, and so as to advance the issue toward an *in camera* review, the final threshold a moving party must cross is to show that, with regard to "the governmental agency which has custody and control of the records" sought, the moving party has a "reasonable belief that the governmental agency identified [in the *Pitchess* motion] has the records or information from the records."[44]

However, the moving party is *not* required to have personal knowledge that the government agency in question has such records: rather, the moving party may allege *on information and belief* its reasonable belief regarding the government agency's custody or control of such records.[45] As long as the moving party bases its sworn declaration asserting that a specific government agency has such records upon a "rational inference from known or reasonably assumed facts," the moving party can satisfy the reasonable belief requirement of the *Pitchess* procedure.

Nevertheless, we may presume that where — during the *in camera* review or otherwise — a government agency shows that it has no records in its possession, custody, or control that are at all responsive to the items sought for disclosure-discovery in the *Pitchess* motion, the government agency is *not* required to disclose or discover the records it lacks.[46]

F. <u>The *Pitchess* Threshold Requirements Must Be Met.</u>

In light of the foregoing, in order to show good cause for discovery or disclosure, and so as to proceed to an *in camera* review of the records sought by the court, a moving party must emphasize the *necessity* for the discovery or disclosure in the particular case at issue so as to overcome the statutory presumption against discovery-disclosure.

---

44 *See* Cal. Evid. Code § 1043(b)(1), (3).

45 *City of Santa Cruz*, *supra*, 49 Cal. 3d at pp. 90-91.

46 *See generally* Cal. Evid. Code §§ 1043(a), 1045(d); 1047.

Only if a moving party has satisfied its threshold burden for showing good cause for discovery or disclosure of the records identified in its *Pitchess* motion (in other words, only if the moving party has met the specificity, good cause, materiality/manifest necessity, and reasonable belief elements), shall the court then proceed to the *in camera* review phase of the *Pitchess* procedure. The details of the *in camera* review procedure are detailed in the next chapter.

6. HEARING PROCEDURE: Once a Party Wins an *In Camera* Hearing for Potential Discovery-Disclosure of *Pitchess* Privileged Matter, What Procedures Must Be Followed During the *In Camera* Proceeding in a State Case?

In event that a moving party "establishes good cause [for discovery-disclosure of *Pitchess*-privileged matter], the court *must* review the records [at issue] *in camera* to determine what, if any, information should be disclosed."[1] Notably, once good cause is established, the court's *in camera* review of the specified personnel file records is *mandatory*: that proceeding cannot be skipped, even if the court so chooses.[2]

A. The Custodian's Role, Attendance at the Review, the Custodian's Oath, and the Record of the *In Camera* Proceeding.

Thus, once the court determines that the moving party has met its threshold burdens for *in camera* review, "'the custodian of records [of the government agency identified by the moving party in its motion] should bring to the court all documents potentially relevant to the [*Pitchess*] motion.'"[3] On a practical level, many courts will order the *in camera* review to occur at some date *after*

1 *See Chambers v. Superior Ct.* (2007) 42 Cal.4th 673, 679 (emphasis added); *see also* Cal. Evid. Code § 1045.

2 *See People v. McDaniel* (2021) 12 Cal.5th 97, 134.

3 *See Haggerty v. Superior Ct.* (2004) 117 Cal.App.4th 1079, 1086; *accord Warrick v. Superior Ct.* (2005) 35 Cal.4th 1011, 1019; *People v. Mooc* (2001) 26 Cal.4th 1216, 1229; *see generally* Cal. Evid. Code §§ 1040, 1043, 1045, 1046, 1047.

the *Pitchess* motion hearing date — particularly if the government agency's custodian of records is not present at the *Pitchess* motion hearing or did not bring the identified personnel file records to the motion hearing.

Although "[d]ocuments clearly irrelevant to a [moving party's] *Pitchess* request need not be presented to the trial court for *in camera* review...if the custodian has any doubt whether a particular document is relevant, he or she should present it to the trial court" because "[s]uch practice is consistent with the premise of Evidence Code sections 1043 and 1045 that the locus of decisionmaking is to be the trial court, not the [opposing party] or the custodian of records."[4]

At the *in camera* review proceeding, the "trial court 'shall [then] examine the information [at issue] in chambers...out of the presence and hearing of *all* persons except the person authorized [to possess the records, i.e., the custodian of records,] and such other persons [that the custodian of records] is willing to have present.'"[5]

In other words, during the court's *in camera* review of the identified personnel file records for which the court has found good cause for potential discovery-disclosure, ***only* the following persons may be present in chambers** for the *in camera* review: (1) the **custodian of the records** at issue; (2) the **holder of the *Pitchess* privilege** — *i.e.*, the custodial governmental agency and/or the officer whose *Pitchess*-privileged records are being reviewed (in most cases), *unless* (arguably) the officer is the moving party (see below); and (3) **any person the privilege holder(s) want(s) to have present**, such as an

---

4 *See Mooc, supra*, 26 Cal.4th at p. 1229; *see generally* Cal. Evid. Code §§ 1040, 1043, 1045, 1046, 1047.

PRACTICE NOTE: Although the custodian of records is *not required* to do so, it is often customary for the custodian to bring the *entire* personnel file record for the officer identified in the motion to the *in camera* review. *See Mooc, supra*, 26 Cal.4th at p. 1229 n. 4. However, the law only requires — and many judges only expect — the custodian to bring those personnel file records that are potentially relevant to the specific materials requested by the moving party's *Pitchess* motion. *See Mooc, supra*, 26 Cal.4th at p. 1229-1230; *People v. Superior Ct. (Johnson)* (2015) 2015 Cal. LEXIS 4647, *40-41 ("The custodian of the records can assist the trial court by focusing the court's attention on what is relevant.")

5 *See Haggerty, supra*, 117 Cal.App.4th at p. 1086 (emphasis added); *see also* Cal. Evid. Code § 915(b) (only the person authorized to claim the privilege, or the person from whom the disclosure of privileged matter is sought (or both) under Cal. Evid. Code § 1040 *et seq.*, "and any other persons as the person authorized to claim the privilege is willing to have present" may be in chambers when a court is ruling on a claim of privilege).

attorney for the government agency or an attorney for the identified office whose records are to be reviewed (unless the officer is the moving party).[6]

Neither the moving party, nor its attorney, nor any other persons outside of the court's staff are permitted or entitled to be present during the court's *in camera* review of the identified personnel records, and such review is to be conducted outside of their hearing.[7]

Notably, the authorities are less than definitive about whether *all* privi-lege holders are entitled to be present during the *in camera* review when the *Pitchess* motion moving party is also the officer whose records are at issue. Bu the law does provide some guidance on the matter.

1. *Limitations On Officer's Right To Inspect Officer's Own Personnel File.*

On the one hand, during the time that the officer is employed by the cus-todial government agency, under the Government Code, an officer is entitled to reasonable inspection of his or her personnel file upon request (without resort to a *Pitchess* motion) for the purpose of discovering whether "any materials

---

6 *See* Cal. Evid. Code §§ 915(b), 1045(b); *Mooc, supra*, 26 Cal.4th at pp. 1226-1229; *Haggerty, supra*, 117 Cal.App.4th at p. 1086.

7 *See* Cal. Evid. Code §§ 915(b), 1045; *Mooc, supra*, 26 Cal.4th at pp. 1226-1229; *Haggerty, supra*, 117 Cal.App.4th at p. 1086.

PRACTICE NOTE: Since the custodian of records for the government agency, and the officer asserting the *Pitchess* privilege in his records, are both entitled to have any other person present in chambers whom they are "willing" to have present, the best practice is for the custodian and/or the officer to specifically identify, on the record, before proceeding into the judge's chambers, that the custodian/officer wants its/his/her attorney present during the *in camera* review. This will permit the custodian/officer to consult with counsel during the *in camera* review process, which could facilitate a more effective defense of the *Pitchess* privilege. In the event that the moving party or its counsel also "requests" to be present in chambers during the *in camera* review, and/or argues that counsel for the opposing party agency or officer should not be present if the moving party counsel cannot be present, the custodian and/or officer (or their attorneys) should remind the court that: (a) *only* persons the custodian/officer is "willing" to have present in chambers may be present during the review of privileged materials; (b) the custodian/officer is *not* willing to have the moving party or its counsel present during the *in camera* review; and (c) the entire purpose and function of the *in camera* review is for the court to decide which privileged materials should be disclosed **outside the presence of the party seeking disclosure**, or that moving party's counsel — thus, **it is wholly improper for the moving party or its counsel to be present while privileged materials and information are being reviewed by the court, especially when such materials have not been previously disclosed to such party/counsel.**

have been 'mistakenly or unlawfully placed in the file'" and so as to permit the officer to seek removal of improper matter or to submit a response.[8]

On the other hand, even under the Government Code, an officer is only entitled to inspect the records in his personnel file which constitute/contain adverse comments: the underlying supporting or investigative materials upon which such comments are based are *not* subject to the officer's Government Code inspection right, particularly where they are stored separately from the officer's personnel file, such as in an internal affairs file.[9]

When read in conjunction with the underlying purposes of the *Pitchess* procedure, where the officer is the moving party to a *Pitchess* motion regarding his or her own records, it is likely that officer may be entitled to attend the *in camera* review, but as a practical matter, **the court should take care during the *in camera* review to avoid disclosure to the moving-party officer of those personnel file materials to which the officer does not already have a statutory inspection right.**

Once in chambers, the court reporter shall **place the custodian of records under oath**: this is because "administering the oath to the custodian of records who testif[ies] at *Pitchess* [*in camera* review] hearings is necessary to

---

8 *See* Cal. Gov. Code §§ 3305, 3306, 3306.5; *Barber v. Department of Corr. & Rehab.* (2012) 203 Cal.App.4th 638, 651-655 (§ 3306.5 only applies prior to the officer's termination); *McMahon v. City of Los Angeles* (2009) 172 Cal.App.4th 1324, 1335-1337 (holding that Gov. Code § 3306.5 did not permit the officer to inspect internal affairs file materials that were not used in making adverse comments in the officer's personnel file and were stored separately from the personnel file); *Brutsch v. City of Los Angeles* (1992) 3 Cal.App.4th 354, 360 (holding that the inspection regime of Gov. Code § 3305 applies to information that might affect the officer's status of employment, such as information that could be used to discipline the officer, and did not include a right to inspect unfavorable comments made in connection with a promotional exam); *Sacramento Police Officers Assn. v. Venegas* (2002) 101 Cal.App.4th 916, 924-930 (holding that while Gov. Code § 3306.5 gives an officer the right to inspect internal investigation records kept separately from the officer's personnel file where such investigation records were used to impose discipline against him or constitute comparable adverse comments that could result in discipline, an officer does not have the right to inspect the entirety of the Department's investigative record where it is not stored within the officer's personnel file or does not constitute adverse comments affecting the status of the officer's employment); *cf. Aguilar v. Johnson* (1988) 202 Cal.App.3d 241, 249 (evaluating comparable limits under the Government Code).

9 *See id.*; *McMahon*, *supra*, 172 Cal.App.4th at pp. 1335-1337; *cf.* Cal. Penal Code § 832.5(b)-(c) (regarding storage of complaints and related investigations in separate files from the officer's personnel file).

establish the accuracy and veracity of the custodian's representations regarding the completeness of the record submitted for the court's review."[10]

The trial court should then make a record of what documents it examined before ruling on the *Pitchess* motion. Such a record will permit future appellate review. If the documents produced by the custodian are not voluminous, the court can photocopy them and place them in a confidential file. Alternatively, the court can prepare a list of the documents it considered, or simply state for the record what documents it examined.... Of course, to protect the officer's privacy, the examination of documents and questioning of the custodian should be done *in camera* in accordance with the requirements of Evidence Code section 915[,] and **the transcript of the *in camera* hearing and all copies of the documents should be sealed.**[11] Notably, the moving party is <u>not</u> entitled to know the number of documents reviewed, the substantive content of the undisclosed materials, or even the general nature of the protected material: as such information remains confidential if the court did not rule that it should be discovered or disclosed.[12]

During the *in camera* review, "[t]he custodian should be prepared to state in chambers and for the record what other documents (or category of documents) not presented to the court were included in the complete personnel record, and why those [records] were deemed irrelevant or otherwise nonresponsive to the [moving party's] *Pitchess* motion."[13] However, the court is *not* required to have the custodian specifically identify each of the records from the personnel file that the custodian did *not* deem to be responsive to the moving party's *Pitchess* motion: in other words, the court is *not* required to make a record of specific personnel file records that were *not* brought to the *in camera* review proceeding.[14]

---

10 *See People v. White* (2011) 191 Cal.App.4th 1333, 1340; *see also Mooc, supra*, 26 Cal.4th at pp. 1226-1229 (observing that the purpose of conducting the *in camera* review on the record is to "document the custodian's statements, as well as any questions the trial court may wish to ask the custodian regarding the completeness of the record").

11 *See Mooc, supra*, 26 Cal.4th at p. 1229 (observing that "[w]ithout some record of the documents examined by the trial court, a party's ability to obtain appellate review of the trial court's decision, whether to disclose or not to disclose, would be nonexistent"); *Brown v. Valverde* (2010) 183 Cal.App.4th 1531, 1541.

12 *See Herrera v. Superior Ct.* (1985) 172 Cal.App.3d 1159, 1163-1164.

13 *See Mooc, supra*, 26 Cal.4th at p. 1229.

14 *See Mooc, supra*, 26 Cal.4th at p. 1229; *People v. Fuiava* (2012) 53 Cal.4th 622, 646-647.

Notably, **the court is *required* to conduct the *in camera* review and to do so *on the record*,** and where the court fails to do so, on a showing of prejudice related to such *Pitchess* motion and the court's violations of the *Pitchess* procedures, a party may obtain appellate relief: however, the relief available is largely limited to remand to the trial court with an order to conduct such *in camera* review on the record if the court had not previously done so.[15]

B. Mandatory Exclusions from Discovery-Disclosure During the *In Camera* Review Proceeding.

Additionally, in conducting its *in camera* review of the officer personnel file records at issue, and as part of its determination of which records are subject to discovery or disclosure under the *Pitchess* procedure, the **court is *required* to exclude** from any discovery-disclosure: (1) "the conclusions of any officer investigating a complaint" of officer misconduct; and (2) "[f]acts sought to be disclosed that are so remote as to make disclosure of little or no practical benefit."[16]

Significantly, California case law has held that, as to routine destruction of officer personnel files *after* the five (5) year retention required by the Penal

---

15 *See People v. Gaines* (2009) 46 Cal.4th 172, 176, 178, 180-181; *Haggerty, supra*, 117 Cal.App.4th at pp. 1085-1086.

16 *See* Cal. Evid. Code § 1045(b)(1)-(2); *Warrick, supra*, 35 Cal.4th at p. 1019; *Haggerty, supra*, 117 Cal.App.4th at pp. 1087-1088; *cf. Galindo, supra*, 50 Cal.4th at pp. 9-10 (aff'g exclusion from discovery-disclosure personnel file information that was not necessary to the moving party's case, and thus so remote as to be of little or no practical benefit to the moving party's case).

PRACTICE NOTE: Until 2022, the Evidence Code had a third subsection to Section 1045(b) that mandated that judges exclude from *Pitchess* production "[i]nformation consisting of complaints concerning conduct occurring more than five years before the event or transaction that is the subject of the litigation in aid of which the discovery or disclosure is sought." However, SB 16 deleted that subsection and renumbered former subsection (2) as new subsection (1), and former subsection (3) as new subsection (2). The removal of the five-year limit to *Pitchess* discovery-disclosure means that there are only two temporal limits to officer personnel file record production under the Pitchess or CPRA systems: (1) strict agency adherence to its document retention policy, namely, retaining no more records than the law requires; and (2) the too "remote" in time argument available under newly-renumbered subsection 1045(b)(2). Notwithstanding the foregoing, ***under the Penal Code,* it is clear that an agency is *only* required to retain personnel records of officer misconduct complaints and investigations for a period of <u>five</u> years — *unless* the investigations result in a sustained finding, at which point the <u>fifteen</u> year retention requirement is activated.** Cal. Penal Code § 832.5(b)-(c) (amend. 2022). Thus, in their document retention policies and training, it may be advisable for agencies to reference the explicit Penal Code retention limit, rather than the implicit Evidence Code limit. Additionally, although other statutes may affect government agency record retention requirements, that issue that is beyond the scope of this guidebook. *But see id.*

Code (or fifteen years, in the case of sustained findings of officer misconduct) has expired, such routine destruction by police agencies is constitutional and lawful.[17]

With regard to the "conclusions of any officer investigating a complaint" of officer misconduct that *must* be excluded from any *Pitchess* discovery-disclosure, this term "denotes the thought processes of, and factual inferences and deductions drawn by, an officer investigating a complaint, concerning such matters as the credibility of witnesses or the significance, strength, or lack of evidence"; however, this exclusion does *not automatically* extend to "the investigating body's ruling on the complaint or the nature of any discipline imposed."[18]

Furthermore, although, on its face, the language of Evidence Code section 1045 appears to limit the mandatory exclusion of investigating-officer conclusions only to *Pitchess* motions brought in "criminal proceeding[s]," because the *Pitchess* statutes require the non-disclosure of "facts that 'are so remote as to make disclosure of little or no practical benefit,'" absent persuasive articulation by the moving party showing how the conclusions of an officer investigating alleged misconduct would be of "meaningful benefit in the litigation… [Evidence Code section 1045(b)] mandates exclusion of the [investigating] officer's untested preliminary conclusions" in civil cases as well.[19] For example,

---

17 *City of Los Angeles v. Superior Ct.* (2002) 29 Cal.4th 1, 10-12 (holding that a criminal defendant's Due Process constitutional rights were not violated where, after the five-year mark had passed, consistent with a routine records destruction plan, a police agency destroyed old officer personnel file records, and suggesting that a different outcome might be required where the destruction was conducted with a spoliating intent as to a specific case); Cal. Evid. Code § 1045(b)(2) (court shall exclude personnel file records about conduct that is too remote from the incident at issue in the action); Cal. Penal Code § 832.5(b)-(c) (amend. 2022) (mandating that officer personnel file records be preserved for 5 years; unless there's a sustained finding of officer misconduct, then mandating personnel record retention for 15 years).

18 *See City of San Jose v. Superior Ct.* (1993) 5 Cal.4th 47, 55 (discipline imposed *may* be disclosed after a *Pitchess* motion is granted, but not the underlying reasoning); *see also* Cal. Evid. Code § 1045(b).

19 *See Haggerty, supra*, 117 Cal.App.4th at pp. 1088-1089 (affirming *Pitchess* production of an internal affairs report, but only after redaction of the investigating officers' conclusions); *Arcelona v. Municipal Ct.* (1980) 113 Cal.App.3d 523, 531 (excluding from disclosure officer performance evaluations as being too remote and immaterial to the issues of the case); *City of Azusa v. Superior Ct.* (1989) 191 Cal. App. 3d 693, 696 (excluding performance evaluations, officer medical records, criminal records, and evaluations of credibility as being too remote and immaterial to the issues of the case); *cf. Warrick, supra*, 35 Cal.4th at p. 1019 (citing *Haggerty*); *Coito v. Superior Ct.* (2010) 182 Cal.App.4th 758, 775-776 (defining mental impressions and opinions in the context of the attorney work product protection).

evidence pertaining to post-litigation or post-prosecution acts may be excluded as irrelevant character evidence.[20] The rationale of this exclusionary mandate re investigating officer conclusions is that it "imposes a further safeguard to protect officer privacy where the relevance of the information sought is minimal and the officer's privacy concerns are substantial."[21]

Additionally, the court **must** exclude from disclosure the records of peace officers, including supervisors, who were "not present during the arrest or had no contact with the party seeking disclosure from the time of the arrest until the time of booking, or who were not present at the time the conduct is alleged to have occurred within a jail facility...."[22] In other words, in arrest-related or seizure-related cases (such as where a suspect is killed before an arrest), the *Pitchess* statutes "prohibit discovery of [peace officer] personnel records for officers not involved in the incident giving rise to particular litigation"; but where the misconduct at issue is unrelated to an arrest, this blanket restriction may not apply.[23]

Moreover, "in determining relevance where the issue in litigation concerns the policies or pattern of conduct of the employing agency, the court shall consider whether the information sought [from the peace officer's personnel file] may be obtained from other records maintained by the employing agency in the regular course of agency business which would not necessitate the disclosure of individual [confidential] personnel records."[24]

Furthermore, generally, upon such *in camera* review, the court may "disclose only bare-bones information about prior complaints, so that the seeking party can conduct his own investigation."[25] Accordingly, the court may disclose "only the **outcome** of the investigation, rather than verbatim reports or records of investigations" into complaints of officer misconduct—so as to avoid inhibiting either the subject's or the investigator's candor during such officer

---

20 *See, e.g., People v. Breaux* (1991) 1 Cal.4th 292, 312.

21 *See Warrick, supra*, 35 Cal.4th at p. 1019.

22 *See* Cal. Evid. Code § 1047.

23 *See Alt v. Superior Ct.* (1999) 74 Cal.App.4th 950, 957 (citing *Davis v. City of Sacramento* (1994) 24 Cal.App.4th 393, 400); Cal. Evid. Code § 1047; *but see Riske v. Superior Ct.* (2016) 6 Cal. App.5th 647, 661-662.

24 *See* Cal. Evid. Code § 1045(c); *Haggerty, supra*, 117 Cal.App.4th at pp. 1087-1088.

25 *See City of Hemet v. Superior Ct.* (1995) 37 Cal.App.4th 1411, 1425.

misconduct investigations.[26] In other words, discovery or disclosure of records of alleged officer misconduct investigations thus "ordinarily involves revelation only of the name, address, and phone number of any prior complainants and witnesses and the dates of the incidents in question."[27]

However, "the practice of disclosing only the name of the complainant and contact information must yield to the requirement of providing sufficient information to prepare for a fair trial": thus, where the names and contact information "prove to be inadequate information to prepare [the moving party's] case," on a showing of good cause, the moving party can obtain further discovery, including witness statements contained in the officer's personnel file (particularly of complainants who are unavailable or whose memories have faded).[28]

1. *Implications of the Recent Revisions to Pitchess Confidentiality Upon the Mandatory Exclusions.*

With the 2019 revolution in the scope of *Pitchess* confidentiality, with a follow-up expansion in 2022, the aforementioned restrictions on production of investigations of officer misconduct arguably no longer apply, or are at least moot, when it comes to the eight categories of records that are now CPRA discoverable and presumed to be public records: (1) criminal and administrative records and incident recordings of officer-involved shootings of/at persons

---

26 *See City of San Jose*, *supra*, 5 Cal.4th at pp. 55-57 (holding that the "thought processes of, and factual inferences and deductions drawn by, an officer investigating a complaint, concerning such matters as the credibility of witnesses or the significance, strength, or lack of evidence" are generally not discoverable, but that any discipline imposed can be discoverable); *accord Haggerty*, *supra*, 117 Cal.App.4th at pp. 1088-1089 (holding that in a civil excessive force action, Cal. Evid. Code § 1045(b) often bars the discovery of such investigating officer conclusions as well); *cf. Alt*, *supra*, 74 Cal.App.4th at p. 955.

27 *See Chambers*, *supra*, 42 Cal.4th at pp. 679-680.

28 *See Alvarez v. Superior Ct.* (2004) 117 Cal.App.4th 1107, 1112; *accord Haggerty*, *supra* 117 Cal.App.4th at pp. 1086-1090 (permitting disclosure of an entire internal affairs report as long as the investigating officer's conclusions were redacted).

PRACTICE NOTE: It is likely a safer practice for a moving party to include such items as witness statements in its specific identification of materials it seeks to be produced-disclosed by its *Pitchess* motion: the more narrowly tailored and specific the list of sought-after materials, the more likely it is that the court will deem that the moving party has complied with the specificity and materiality requirements of the good cause showing. Additionally, in its statement of good cause the *Pitchess* motion moving party can increase its prospects for disclosure-discovery by customizing its argument for good cause and materiality to be tailor-fit to each specific type of records for which the moving party seeks disclosure or production.

("OIS"), regardless of injury; (2) criminal and administrative records and incident recordings of other officer uses of force on persons ("UOF") where death or "great bodily injury" results; (3) criminal and administrative records of *sustained* investigations of officer sexual assault against non-officers/non-employees; (4) criminal and administrative records of *sustained* investigations of officer dishonesty in policing; (5) criminal and administrative records of *sustained* investigations of officer excessive force; (6) criminal and administrative records of *sustained* investigations of officer failure to intervene to stop excessive force; (7) criminal and administrative records of *sustained* investigations of officer discrimination; and (8) criminal and administrative records of *sustained* investigations of officer unlawful search or unlawful arrest.[29]

Thus, when it comes to the four categories of officer personnel file records that are now public records, either such records would be exempt from the mandatory exclusions of the *in camera* review process — and thus producible *in their entirety* (save statutorily-authorized redactions and/or temporary withholding), or — as to these categories of records only — the *Pitchess* motion would likely need to be denied for lack of good cause: because such records could be obtained by alternative, non-privileged means, namely a CPRA request.

29 Cal. Penal Code §§ 832.7-832.8 (amend. 2019 & 2022); Cal. Gov. Code §§ 7923.600-7923.625 (formerly Cal. Gov. Code § 6254(f) (amend. 2019).

7. DISCOVERY-PRODUCTION LIMITS: What Limitations Control the Discovery-Production of Pitchess Privileged Matter After the In Camera Hearing in a State Case?

In sum then, during the court's *in camera* review, the court will review on the record those documents from the identified officer's personnel file for which the court has found (sight unseen) good cause for potential discovery-disclosure; at that *in camera* review, the court will then review and identify those specific records for production-disclosure for which it found there was good cause for such discovery-disclosure, but excluding those records which fall within the mandatory exclusions of the *Pitchess* procedure; the court will then order specific conforming records to be produced, or authorized for disclosure at trial, subject to certain protective order limitations as required or authorized under the *Pitchess* statutes. In other words, the process and function of the court's *in camera* review proceeding is thus for the court to ensure that the *only* personnel records that are produced or disclosed are those records that, by its review, the court finds to be: (1) responsive to the moving party's *Pitchess* motion requests; (2) within the scope of the types of records for which the court found good cause for discovery-disclosure; and (3) and which are not otherwise excluded by the presumptions or requirements of the *Pitchess* statutes.[1]

During the *in camera* review, "[t]he custodian should be prepared to state in chambers and for the record what other documents (or category of documents) not presented to the court were included in the complete personnel

---

1 *See, e.g., Haggerty v. Superior Ct.* (2004) 117 Cal.App.4th 1079, 1086-1090.

record, and why those [records] were deemed irrelevant or otherwise non-responsive to the [moving party's] *Pitchess* motion."[2] However, the court is *not* required to have the custodian specifically identify each of the records from the personnel file that the custodian did *not* deem to be responsive to the moving party's *Pitchess* motion: in other words, the court is *not* required to make a record of specific personnel file records that were *not* brought to the *in camera* review proceeding.[3]

Notably, the court is *required* to conduct the *in camera* review and to do so *on the record*, and where the court fails to do so, on a showing of prejudice related to such *Pitchess* motion and the court's violations of the *Pitchess* procedures, a party may obtain appellate relief: however, the relief available is largely limited to remand to the trial court with an order to conduct such *in camera* review on the record if the court had not previously done so.[4]

1. ***The Pitchess Order for Discovery-Disclosure.***

After the completion of its *in camera* review, the court should then order which specific documents are to be produced or disclosed to the moving party (and the court *must* order the transcript of the *in camera* review proceeding to be sealed).[5] On a practical level, some courts will then order the custodian of records to produce or disclose specifically identified records, while other courts will have copies made by the court staff of the conforming *Pitchess* materials the court is ordering to be produced or disclosed to the moving party.

2. ***The Mandatory Protective Order.***

In any event, with regard to any documents or information that the court decides is/are to be disclosed-produced to the moving party, the court is **required** to issue a protective "order [mandating that] the records disclosed or discovered may not be used for any purpose other than a court proceeding pursuant to applicable law."[6]

---

2 *See People v. Mooc* (2001) 26 Cal.4th 1216, 1229.

3 *See Mooc, supra*, 26 Cal.4th at p. 1229; *People v. Fuiava* (2012) 53 Cal.4th 622, 646-647.

4 *See People v. Gaines* (2009) 46 Cal.4th 172, 176, 178, 180-181; *Haggerty, supra*, 117 Cal.App.4th at pp. 1085-1086.

5 *See Mooc, supra*, 26 Cal.4th at pp. 1229-1230.

6 *See* Cal. Evid. Code § 1045(e); *Warrick, supra*, 35 Cal.4th at pp. 1027-1028.

3. *The* ***Discretionary*** *Protective Order.*

However, on a showing of good cause "by the governmental agency which has custody or control of the records...or by the officer whose records are sought," the court is **permitted** to issue "any order which justice requires to protect the officer or agency from unnecessary annoyance, embarrassment or oppression."[7]

---

7 *See* Cal. Evid. Code § 1045(d); *Warrick v. Superior Ct.* (2005) 35 Cal.4th 1011, 1027-1028; *cf. Mooc, supra*, 26 Cal.4th at p. 1229 (holding that the court should also order the transcript of the *in camera* review proceeding and any associated documents to be sealed).

PRACTICE NOTE: The party seeking a specific protective order (as opposed to the statutory minimum) should include the argument for that order as an alternative argument in any opposition to the *Pitchess* motion, and should include a copy of the proposed protective order with any opposition to the *Pitchess* motion — which can be framed as an alternative motion for a protective order. This is due to the fact that where a party waits until the *Pitchess* motion hearing or the *in camera* review proceeding to move for a protective order that goes beyond the minimum order required by § 1045(e), many courts are likely deem such an attempt as untimely and/or a waiver of any right to a more extensive or customized discretionary protective order under § 1045(d). Additionally, a party opposing *Pitchess* disclosure-production should consider preparing a proposed protective order that limits use of the disclosed-produced *Pitchess* materials *only to that action*, and that requires such *Pitchess* materials to be returned to the government agency or verifiably destroyed by the moving party within a specified time after the action has been dismissed, resolved, or otherwise terminated — so as to prevent the moving party, or its counsel, from recycling *Pitchess*-privileged materials in other civil or criminal cases.

8. DISCLOSURE-PUBLICATION LIMITS: What Are the Limits to *Disclosing Pitchess* Privileged Matter in a State *Trial*?

The *Pitchess* statute uses two terms to describe the end results that a *Pitchess* motion may seek: "discovery **or** disclosure."[1] While, at first blush, these terms would seem to be synonymous and fungible: and while these terms are routinely used interchangeably by many courts — on closer inspection of the case law, as well as the function of and purposes behind the *Pitchess* statutory procedure, it is perhaps more precise to construe these two terms as meaning *different* things. Specifically, it is probably best to construe "discovery" of *Pitchess*-privileged matter to mean *pre-trial disclosure and production* of the matter by the custodial government agency to the moving party — in other words, "discovery" under the *Pitchess* statutes is best construed to mean obtaining information" that the seeker does not already possess (or over which is not already in the seeker's custody); and it is probably best to construe "disclosure" of *Pitchess*-privileged matter to mean *publication at trial* of such matter by the moving party to the jury and/or by the governmental agency to a person/entity outside the scope of the privilege.[2]

1 *See, e.g.*, Cal. Evid. Code § 1043(a), (b)(1) (emphasis added); *but see* Cal. Gov. Code §§ 7922.525-7922.545, 7923.600-7923.625 (formerly Cal. Gov. Code §§ 6253, 6254(f)) (using the term "disclosure" in a manner more consistent with the word "production"; which is more of an outside-of-court type of process, like discovery).

2 *See, e.g.*, *Michael v. Gates* (1995) 38 Cal.App.4th 737, 743-744 (observing that "discovery" under the *Pitchess* statutes involves production to an adverse party by the custodian of records and holding that "disclosure" of *Pitchess*-privileged matter at trial also requires compliance with the *Pitchess* statutes); *accord People v. Superior Ct. (Gremminger)* (1997) 58 Cal.App.4th 397, 404-407 (interpreting *Michael* to stand for the proposition that review of personnel records by the governmental agency's attorney does not constitute "discovery or disclosure" that would be subject to the *Pitchess* procedures); *Zanone v. City of Whittier* (2008) 162 Cal.App.4th 174, 187 n. 14; *see also People v. Superior Ct. (Johnson)* (2015) 61 Cal.4th 696, *713-716, 719-720.

In any event, with regard to disclosure-publication of *Pitchess*-privileged material *at trial*, it appears that "the *Pitchess* procedures affect not only discovery of personnel [record] information but also its admissibility" at trial.[3] Thus, even where a party to an action is not required to comply with the *Pitchess* procedure in order to obtain *discovery* of *Pitchess*-privileged matter — such as would the case where the custodial agency's attorney was reviewing an officer's personnel record in preparation of the agency's case at trial — absent waiver by both the agency and the officer (the holders of the *Pitchess* privilege in a peace officer's personnel records), in order to *disclose* that personnel record to the jury *at trial* — *i.e.*, to offer that record or *Pitchess*-privileged information into evidence at trial (or to otherwise publish it beyond the scope of the *Pitchess* procedural exceptions)—a party to an action must comply with the *Pitchess* procedures, **even if the party seeking disclosure at trial is the custodial agency.**[4]

In other words, prevailing case law holds that where a party to an action seeks to offer *Pitchess*-privileged records or information into evidence *at the time of trial*, unless all of the holders of the *Pitchess* privilege in a personnel record waive that privilege against disclosure, **before the party can offer the *Pitchess*-privileged matter into evidence (disclosure), the offering party must first obtain a court order authorizing such disclosure to the jury by complying with the *Pitchess* procedure** — including by filing a noticed motion, satisfying the good cause requirement, and proceeding through an *in camera* review by the court.[5]

---

3 *See Zanone, supra*, 162 Cal.App.4th at p. 187 n. 14.

4 *Michael, supra*, 38 Cal.App.4th at pp. 743-745; *accord Zanone, supra*, 162 Cal.App.4th at p. 187 n. 14; *People v. Gwillim* (1990) 223 Cal.App.3d 1254, 1269-1270 (holding that a prosecutor may review an officer's personnel file, such as an immunized statement made regarding on-duty conduct, without resort to the *Pitchess* procedures because of the investigative exception of the *Pitchess* statutes, but also reasoning that *use* of such personnel file records during the prosecution, such as at trial, may *not* be permitted by Cal. Penal Code § 832.7 — and thus implying that a *Pitchess* motion may be required where the prosecution seeks to use protected material at trial, even if a court order was not necessary to discover/obtain such material from the governmental agency).

5 *See* Cal. Penal Code § 832.7(a); *Michael, supra*, 38 Cal.App.4th at pp. 743-745; *accord Zanone, supra*, 162 Cal.App.4th at p. 187 n. 14; *Gwillim, supra*, 223 Cal.App.3d at pp. 1269-1270.

PRACTICE NOTE: The *Pitchess* statutes do "not apply to investigations **or proceedings** concerning the conduct of peace officers or custodial officers, or an agency or department that employs those officers, conducted by a grand jury, a district attorney's office, or the Attorney General's office." *See* Cal. Penal Code § 832.7(a). Thus, under a strict construction of the statutes, a criminal prosecutor need *not* comply with the discovery *or* the disclosure requirements of the *Pitchess* procedure where the investigation or proceeding concerns the conduct of peace officers or their agency. *Cf.* Cal. Evid. Code § 1043; *but see* 66 Ops. Cal. Atty. Gen. 128, 128-130 (1983) (concluding that a district attorney is *not* required to obtain a court order before accessing or reviewing a peace officer's personnel records under § 832.7, as long as he or she is "duly investigating 'the conduct of police

However, it must be emphasized that the clarity of this point of law is still developing.[6]

A. Do the *Pitchess* Procedures Apply To State Administrative Proceedings?

In California, outside of federal cases and outside of state courtrooms, there are many examples of administrative proceedings that are like trial: where an officer's professional future is decided. Some examples of these quasi-judicial administrative proceedings include: (a) hearings/proceedings before an administrative law judge ("ALJ"); (b) hearings/proceedings before a State or County or City personnel board, or comparable public employee disciplinary or related board (such as the State Personnel Board, or the Department of Fair Housing and Employment, or the Workers' Compensation Appeals Board); (c) hearings/proceedings before an arbitrator, pursuant to an employment agreement or memorandum of understanding ("MOU") — such as a *Skelly* or post-*Skelly* disciplinary appeal; and/or (d) comparable proceedings before a quasi-judicial person or board with limited adjudicatory powers.[7]

In such administrative proceedings, an administrative hearing officer is empowered to issue rulings and orders on motions for *Pitchess* discovery or

---

officers or a policy agency,'" **but** also concluding that the district attorney "would not be authorized under section 832.7 to release that information to the public. . . ."). However, in proceedings that do *not* concern the conduct of police officers or their agency, the prosecutor is *not exempted* from the *Pitchess* procedure under § 832.7. Moreover, notwithstanding the strict statutory construction, it is the best practice of the criminal prosecutor to obtain a *Pitchess* order from the court before offering *Pitchess*-privileged matter into evidence at trial (disclosure) — even if the trial concerns the conduct of a police officer or police agency — so as to avoid potential disputes. *See also* Cal. Evid. Code § 1042; *Fagan v. Superior Ct.* (2003) 111 Cal.App.4th 607, 618. Additionally, **the moving party should consider seeking discovery *and* disclosure in its *Pitchess* motion, and preparing a proposed order that properly distinguishes the two**, so as to avoid the need for duplicative motion work and undue consumption of judicial resources. Otherwise, an opposing party may be able to argue that a court order for *discovery* of *Pitchess*-privileged matter to the moving party did not automatically authorize *disclosure* of that matter to the jury at trial and/or to the public.

6 *See Zanone, supra*, 162 Cal.App.4th at p. 187 n. 14; *cf. Johnson, supra*, 61 Cal.4th at p. *713-716 (adopting *Michael, supra*, 38 Cal.App.4th 737 and *Gremminger, supra*, 58 Cal.App.4th 397 for the proposition that that the custodial government entity need not obtain a *Pitchess* order before reviewing officer personnel file information already in its possession, and implicitly, those lower courts' reasoning that even a custodial government agency must obtain a *Pitchess* order before disclosing such materials to persons outside the *Pitchess* privilege in such personnel files).

7 *See, e.g.*, Cal. Gov. Code §§ 3304, 3304.5 (re officer administrative appeals).

disclosures.[8] However, because administrative disciplinary proceedings are private, not public, officer personnel records produced at "administrative disciplinary proceedings are not subject to public disclosure" but instead retain their *Pitchess* confidentiality protections.[9]

This means that the *Pitchess* procedural protections do apply to administrative proceedings, such as those regarding allegations or investigations of officer misconduct and/or discipline; but it also means that the administrative hearing officer (the person acting in a judicial-like capacity, such as the ALJ or arbitrator) has the power to hear/decide *Pitchess* motions brought before such officer. This rule also means that such hearing officer is bound to follow the *Pitchess* procedure just as any court judge would be bound, including all of the restrictions such procedure imposes.[10]

---

8 *Riverside County Sheriff's Assn. v. Stiglitz* (2014) 60 Cal.4th 624, 640-648; *but see Brown v. Valverde* (2010) 183 Cal.App.4th 1531, 1549-1550, 1558 (holding that *Pitchess* discovery is not available in administrative proceedings and administrative hearing officers have no legal authority to rule on *Pitchess* motions or make *Pitchess* orders).

9 *See Stiglitz, supra*, 60 Cal.4th at p. 640.

PRACTICE NOTE: Interestingly, as a practical matter, since administrative hearing officers are empowered to review *Pitchess* motions, including conducting an *in camera* review, and because public entities can waive a right to a hearing on a *Pitchess* motion and proceed directly to *in camera* review, the public entity should be able to authorize the hearing officer at a private administrative disciplinary hearing to have the hearing itself construed as an *in camera* review, for *Pitchess* purposes. Thus, if the custodial government agency wished to permit the officer personnel file records to be disclosed at the administrative hearing, it could waive the motion hearing and permit the administrative hearing to be construed as the *in camera* review to which the appealing officer and others were deemed parties the custodian of records is "willing" to permit to attend the *in camera* review. Thus, from a practical standpoint, as long as the custodial government agency so authorizes, there should be no need the administrative officer to order disclosure at the administrative proceeding of *Pitchess*-protected materials subject to the moving party's *Pitchess* motion for discovery. This, in turn, means that the custodial government agency appears to be empowered to permit the disclosure of *Pitchess*-protected materials at an administrative proceeding that is subject to a *Pitchess* motion for discovery; and that the custodial government agency is likewise empowered to waive the bar to *Pitchess* discovery to the appealing officer, if it so chooses.

10 *See id.*

PRACTICE NOTE: Where records/recordings are exempted from *Pitchess* confidentiality provisions, an officer in an administrative hearing would not be required to follow the *Pitchess* procedure to obtain discovery or disclosure of exempt/public records. *See generally* Cal. Penal Code §§ 832.7-832.8 (amend. 2019); Cal. Gov. Code §§ 7923.600-7923.625 (formerly Cal. Gov. Code § 6254(f) (amend. 2019).

1. ***Practical Implications In Administrative Proceedings.***

To elaborate, as a practical matter, the issue of *Pitchess* privileges in administrative proceedings is most likely to arise in officer-agency disputes over discipline. While, as a matter of law, the officer challenging the police agency's disciplinary finding is only entitled to that part of his own personnel file that constitutes "adverse" comments/findings[11], many agencies — either as a custom or as part of their MOU — will permit an officer to have much (if not all) of his personnel file upon request.

In such instances, the police agency should at least consider requiring the officer to execute a non-disclosure agreement to avoid publication of the personnel file record outside of counsel and those witnesses deemed essential to the officer's rebuttal/appeal of the discipline. But in any event, absent some kind of written agreement or reservation, for the agency that discovers-produces more of the personnel file to the officer than the officer is entitled to have, that agency is likely to be considered to have waived its own *Pitchess* privileges in the personnel file records/information — so as to arguably remove the *Pitchess* limitations on the recipient officer's disclosure-publication of those records.

However, where the agency declines to produce those parts of the officer's personnel file that do not constitute adverse comments, in the administrative proceeding context of an officer-agency dispute, in order to obtain discovery-production or the right for disclosure-publication at the proceeding, the officer would be required to proceed with the *Pitchess* procedure, making his motion to the hearing officer (or by writ to a superior court); and the hearing officer would then be bound to comply with all of the *Pitchess* procedural requirements. This means that, in such cases, the agency must be cautious as to whether it is opposing only discovery-production of the personnel file records/information to the officer or whether it is opposing disclosure-publication of such at the administrative hearing. Notably, in cases where the hearing officer is also the factfinder (such as where an ALJ or arbitrator is the sole potentate deciding the dispute), because the hearing officer will be conducting *in camera* review of disputed records, there will be disclosure-publication in such cases *before* there is discovery-production.

---

11 *See, e.g.*, Cal. Gov. Code §§ 3303, 3305, 3306, 3306.5.

Given the complexities of the implications of *Pitchess* procedures on administrative proceedings, and given the police agency's superior right of file/information ownership and waiver, in officer-agency disputes, it may be simpler for the agency to voluntarily produce the subject officer's personnel file records/information upon his/her request, even if the records discovered-produced do not necessarily reflect adverse comments, in exchange for the officer's written agreement to forego publication-disclosure outside of the administrative hearing or to persons who are not the counsel/representative of the officer at such proceeding or who are not such officer's principal incident witnesses.

However, the police agency should also be sure to embrace the *Pitchess* procedural protections, even in administrative proceedings, in those cases where there is sensitive information that the agency believes is inappropriate to discover-produce to the officer, or where there is legitimate concern that the officer will use such information outside of the administrative proceeding: such as in a news media release or in a related criminal or civil case.

9. STATUTORY EXEMPTIONS to the Otherwise Mandatory *Pitchess* Procedure.

The *Pitchess* statutes also include some exemptions from the confidentiality and discovery-disclosure requirements of the *Pitchess* procedure of which practitioners should likely be aware, specifically: (a) the exception for criminal prosecutors' investigations; (b) the exception for release of a complaint statement to the complainant; (c) the exception for discretionary release of anonymous data by a government agency; (d) the exception for discretionary release of rebuttal facts by a government agency when an officer lies to the media about a disciplinary investigation; and (e) the 2019 exception for critical incident recordings, critical incident investigative/disciplinary records, and sustained officer sexual assault and officer dishonesty-in-policing investigative/disciplinary records.

A. The Criminal Prosecutor's & POST Investigation Exception.

First, the statutes expressly hold that, regarding the requirement that peace officer personnel file records be kept confidential, and only discovered or disclosed pursuant to California Evidence Code sections 1043 and 1046, such *Pitchess* privilege protections "shall not apply to investigations or proceedings concerning the conduct of peace officers or custodial officers, or an agency or department that employs those officers, conducted by a grand jury, a district attorney's office, or the Attorney General's office" or investigations by the California Commission on Peace Officer Standards and Training ("POST").[1]

In other words, "the exception contained in [Penal Code] section 832.7 affords the district attorney the ability to review confidential peace officer personnel files when investigating police misconduct without notice to the individuals involved"; however, "it [also] requires the district attorney to maintain

1 Cal. Penal Code § 832.7(a) (amend. 2022).

the nonpublic nature of the files absent judicial review of the relevance of the information to a criminal or civil action."[2] Thus, "[w]here the exception afforded the district attorney by section 832.7, subdivision (a) is inapplicable, [the prosecutor or POST investigator] must proceed according to the provisions Evidence Code section 1043."[3]

For example, where a prosecutor is reviewing records from a peace officer's personnel file, such as an immunized officer statement made regarding on-duty conduct, the investigative exception to the *Pitchess* procedure permits such review *without* resort to a *Pitchess* motion (but *may* require resort to a *Pitchess* motion to disclose/use such information at trial). But where the prosecution is *not* against the officer whose personnel records are sought, and where the criminal prosecution is unrelated to the defendant-officer's *conduct as a peace officer*, the investigative exception does *not* apply—and, in such an event, even the prosecutor must go through the *Pitchess* motion procedure before the prosecutor can review/discover or disclose the protected peace officer records.[4]

B. The Exception for Release of a Complainant's Statement to the Complainant.

Second, when a person lodges a complaint with a government agency about a peace officer, even though that complaint will be placed into that officer's personnel file, at the time the complainant lodges the complaint, the government agency is *required* to release a copy of the statements made by

---

2 *Fagan v. Superior Ct.* (2003) 111 Cal.App.4th 607, 618; *cf. City of Los Angeles v. Superior Ct.* (2002) 29 Cal.4th 1, 18 (Brown, J., concurring) (noting that it is unsettled as to whether the *Pitchess* exception for prosecutorial investigation permits a prosecutor to examine a witness officer's personnel file for the purpose of identifying material to be disclosed pursuant to the prosecutor's duty to disclose potentially exculpatory material under *Brady v. Maryland* (1963) 373 U.S. 83, 87); *but see People v. Superior Ct. (Johnson)* (2015) 61 Cal.4th 696, 710-716 (holding that because a "police officer does not become the target of an investigation merely by being a witness in a criminal case," the criminal prosecutor investigation exception does not apply unless the officer is the subject of the criminal investigation/prosecution).

3 *Fagan, supra*, 111 Cal.App.4th at p. 618; *accord People v. Superior Ct. (Gremminger)* (1997) 58 Cal.App.4th 397, 404 (also holding that the statutory exception for prosecutorial investigations does not apply where the criminal defendant is not employed as a peace officer at the time of the alleged criminal act and/or the subject of the criminal charge does not involve the defendant's conduct as a peace officer).

4 *See Johnson, supra*, 61 Cal.4th at pp. 713-715 (holding that because a "police officer does not become the target of an investigation merely by being a witness in a criminal case," the criminal prosecutor investigation exception does not apply unless the officer is the subject of the criminal investigation/prosecution); *Gremminger, supra*, 58 Cal.App.4th at pp. 404-407; *People v. Gwillim* (1990) 223 Cal.App.3d 1254, 1269-1270.

that complainant to the complainant who requests them.[5] In other words, a complainant is *not* required to submit a *Pitchess* motion in order to obtain a copy of the statement he has made at the time of his complaint.

C. The Exception for Discretionary Release of Anonymous Data by a Government Agency.

Third, a government agency is *permitted*, but *not* required, to disclose "data regarding the number, type, or disposition of complaints (sustained, not sustained, exonerated, or unfounded) made against its officers if that information is in a form which does not identify the individuals involved."[6] In other words, departments are permitted to release anonymous statistics without going through the *Pitchess* process.

D. The Exception for Discretionary Release of Rebuttal Facts by a Government Agency When an Officer Lies About a Disciplinary Investigation to the Media/Public.

Fourth, where a peace officer who is the subject of a disciplinary investigation (or his representative) "publicly makes a statement he or she knows to be false concerning the investigation or the imposition of disciplinary action," a government agency is *permitted*, but *not* required, to disclose "facts contained in the officer's personnel file concerning the disciplinary investigation or imposition of disciplinary action that specifically refute the false statements made public by the peace or custodial officer or his or her agent or representative"—but only if the false statement was "published by an established medium of communication, such as television, radio, or a newspaper."[7]

E. The CPRA Exception for Specified Officer Misconduct.

Fifth, the California Legislature has created a new exception from *Pitchess* confidentiality, effective in January and July 2019: a pair of amended California

---

5 *See* Cal. Penal Code § 832.7(c) (amend. 2019); *San Diego v. City of San Diego Civ. Serv. Comm'n* (2002) 104 Cal.App.4th 275, 284-285; *cf. Haynie v. Superior Ct.* (2001) 26 Cal.4th 1061, 1067 (refusing to decide an alternative argument on the issue of disclosure of a complainant's statements).

6 *See* Cal. Penal Code § 832.7(d) (amend. 2022); *San Diego*, *supra*, 104 Cal.App.4th at pp. 284-285.

7 *See* Cal. Penal Code § 832.7(e) (amend. 2019); *San Diego*, *supra*, 104 Cal.App.4th at pp. 284-285.

statutes that represent a revolutionary shift in the *Pitchess* privilege — by effectively exempting an important segment of officer personnel file records/information from the *Pitchess* confidentiality presumption and transforming such officer personnel file records/information into presumed-public records. The Legislature has also expanded and slightly revised the 2019 exceptions with additional legislation effective January 1, 2022.

By revisions to California Penal Code §§ 832.7 and 832.8, as well as by rollbacks to the exemptions from the disclosure requirements of the California Public Records Act ("CPRA"; Cal. Gov. Code § 7920.000 *et seq.* (formerly Cal. Gov. Code § 6250 *et seq.*) that were available under former California Government Code § 6254(f), the California Legislature has **removed *Pitchess*-privilege presumptions of confidentiality**, and the related procedural protections, for that portion of peace/custodial officer personnel file records that constitute **officer-involved shootings and "serious" use-of-force investigations, and associated incident recordings, as well as sustained investigations of officer sexual assault on non-officers, officer dishonesty in policing, officer excessive force, officer failure to intervene to prevent excessive force, officer unlawful arrest or unlawful search, and officer discrimination against protected classes.**

These revisions and their effect are explained in detail in this chapter below.

1. *Overview of the Recent Revisions to Officer Personnel File Records-Information Confidentiality (2019 and 2022 Changes).*

In essence, where peace officer personnel file records and information (as well as most police investigatory records) were once completely exempt from CPRA disclosure, <u>the 2019 and 2022 amendments effectively create a limited *exception* to this CPRA exemption</u>: and, by so doing, the expanding CPRA exception operates as a de facto statutory exception to the *Pitchess* privilege system that makes eight specified categories of officer personnel file records related to specified misconduct into de jure public records — with some restrictions that will be explained herein below.[8]

Although, under the 2019 amendments, there are several mechanisms for temporary withholding, or redaction, of such records in response to a CPRA

8 *Compare* Cal. Gov. Code §§ 7927.705, 7930.180 (formerly Cal. Gov. Code §§ 6254(k), 6276.34) *with* Cal. Penal Code § 832.7(b).

request, the new laws essentially make the following types of records/recordings discoverable without the need to obtain a *Pitchess* order from a court — whether the records are from a criminal or an administrative investigation.

Thus, under the new laws, investigation/complaint records of the following types of events are now discoverable in response to a CPRA request:

(1) [OIS] **officer-involved shootings ("OIS")** of/at persons ("discharge of a firearm at a person"), regardless of injury, including incident audio/video recordings thereof;

(2) [UOF-D/GBI] **officer uses of force** ("UOF") on persons, **where death or great bodily injury ("D/GBI") resulted,**[9] including incident audio/video recordings thereof;

(3) [Excessive Force] **officer uses of unreasonable or excessive force,** but only where the agency's investigation resulted in a *sustained* finding;

(4) [Failure to Intervene to Prevent Excessive Force] **where officers fail to intervene against another officer using force that is clearly unreasonable or excessive,** but only where the agency's investigation resulted in a *sustained* finding;

(5) [Sexual Assault — Specified] **officer sexual assault on non-officers/non-employees,** with a customized definition of what constitutes officer sexual assault, but only where the agency's investigation resulted in a *sustained* finding;

(6) [Policing Dishonesty] **officer dishonesty in law enforcement duties,** but only where the agency's investigation resulted in a *sustained* finding;

(7) [Discrimination] **officer discriminatory conduct or writings against members of a protected class,** but only where the agency's investigation resulted in a *sustained* finding; and

---

9 In the context of incident video/audio recordings, the new laws refer to OIS and death/great bodily injury uses of force as "critical incidents" or "serious" uses of force. *See, e.g.*, Cal. Penal Code §§ 832.7 cmt (2018); *cf.* Cal. Gov. Code § 7923.625 (formerly Cal. Gov. Code § 6254(f)(4)). NOTE: Even after the 2022 revisions, the definition of "great bodily injury" remains ambiguous, as explained more fully below.

(8) **[Unlawful Arrest & Unlawful Search]** officers' unlawful arrests or unlawful searches, but only where the agency's investigation resulted in a *sustained* finding.[10]

The new laws also provide specific grounds for withholding or redacting otherwise-discoverable officer records/information and critical incident recordings, with detailed procedures, that can be generally *summarized* as follows.

For non-exempt (CPRA-discoverable) officer personnel file records, where the police agency makes a *written* showing that the non-disclosure interest clearly outweighs the public interest in disclosure, such records **may *only* be withheld**: (1) **while the incident criminal investigation is pending** (against the officer or against another person), but then only up to 60 days, with an available extension up to 18 months; (2) **where any incident-related criminal charges are filed** (against the officer or against another person), and until there is a verdict or non-withdrawable guilty/no-contest plea; (3) **while an administrative investigation against the officer is pending**, but then only up to 30 days after the associated criminal case closes, with an available extension up to 180 days.[11] If *produced*, such non-exempt personnel file records **may *only* be redacted**: (a) for **officer personal information** (*e.g.*, home address, phone number, family member identities); (b) for **complainant and witness names/identifying information** (to "preserve the[ir] anonymity")[12]; (c) for **medical, financial, or federally-protected/ comparable information**; (d) to **preserve the physical safety of an officer or others from a specific, articulable, particularized danger**; and (e) where

10 *See First Amendment Coalition*, *supra*, 98 Cal.App.5th at p. 612 ("Senate Bill 16 amended section 832.7(b) to increase transparency. The legislation enlarged the scope of the required disclosure to include records relating to additional types of sustained findings and records of officers who resign before an investigation concludes." This expanded the excepted records disclosable under the CPRA to now include records for sustained findings of: (1) "unreasonable or excessive force" [*e.g.*, Cal. Penal Code §§ 832.7(b)(1)(A)(iii), (iv)]; (2) "prejudice or discrimination against protected classes" [*id.*]; (3) "unlawful arrest or search" [*e.g.*, Cal. Penal Code §§ 832.7(b)(1)(D) (s), 832.7(b)(1)(E)]; and (4) where officers resign in lieu of receiving sustained findings on the foregoing [*e.g.*, Cal. Penal Code § 832.7(b)(3)].)

11 *See* Cal. Penal Code § 832.7(b)(8)(C) (amend. 2022).

12 Notably, the *addresses* of incident witnesses and "involved persons" are CPRA-discoverable to crime victims and insurers [*see* Cal. Gov. Code § 7923.605 (formerly Cal. Gov. Code § 6254(f))], and arrestee information and crime reports (which often include witness addresses) are CPRA-discoverable to all persons — except arrestees and criminal defendants. *See* Cal. Penal Code § 7923.610 (formerly Cal. Gov. Code § 6254(f)(1)); Cal. Penal Code § 841.5.

the **particularized public interest in non-disclosure clearly outweighs the public disclosure interest**.

For non-exempt (CPRA-discoverable) "critical incident" video/audio recordings, where the police agency makes a *written* showing that the non-disclosure interests in preserving an investigation from interference clearly outweigh the public interest in disclosure, and with the provision of an *estimated date of disclosure* in most cases, such **recordings may *only* be withheld** in two cases. (1) **While the incident criminal investigation is pending** (against the officer or against another person) ***or* the incident administrative investigation is pending** — but then only up to 45 days, with an available extension of up to 1 year; or over 1 year, on a showing by *clear and convincing evidence* that the non-disclosure interest clearly outweighs the public interest in disclosure — with a reporting requirement due every 30 days after the initial 45-day period. (2) **On recording-subject privacy protection grounds**, with no time limit, such as where redaction cannot adequately protect the privacy interest — but such recording may *not* be withheld from the subject whose privacy was raised as the basis of withholding, or from the subject's parents/heirs/representatives, as applicable, unless disclosure to the subject would substantially impair the investigation.[13] If *produced*, such non-exempt critical incident recordings may *only* be **redacted** — *e.g.*, by blurring/obscuring technology — to protect the privacy interest raised by the police agency.[14] However, the redaction cannot impair one's ability to "comprehend" the incident events on the recording, and other edits are prohibited.[15]

Additionally, as explained more fully below, the 2019 and 2022 amendments overlap and conflict when it comes to critical incident recordings and police records, including conflicts in the timelines and standards for withholding and redaction. The best policy is thus to treat non-administrative critical incident recordings (audio and video) as "recordings" subject to Government Code § 7923.625 (formerly section 6254(f)(4), AB 748) and all other recordings that fall within one of the aforementioned categories as "records" subject to Penal Code §§ 832.7 and 832.8 (SB 1421).

---

13 *See* Cal. Gov. Code § 7923.625(a)-(b) (formerly Cal. Gov. Code § 6254(f)(4)(A)-(B).

14 Cal. Gov. Code § 7923.625(b)(1)-(3) (formerly Cal. Gov. Code § 6254(f)(4)(B)(i)-(iii)); *see also* Cal. Gov. Code § 7922.570 (formerly Gov. Code § 6253.9) (requiring materials stored in electronic format to be produced as such).

15 *See* Cal. Gov. Code § 7923.625(b)(1)-(3) (formerly Cal. Gov. Code § 6254(f)(4)(B)(i)-(iii)).

2. *Pitchess Procedures and Other Privileges Unaffected by the Revisions.*

The new laws are also notable for what they do *not* change. First, personnel file records and incident recordings that do *not* directly relate to the specified categories of officer misconduct retain their full *Pitchess* privilege protections, where otherwise applicable.[16] Indeed, the California Supreme Court has held that SB 1421 "does not 'affect the discovery or disclosure of information contained in a peace or custodial officer's personnel file pursuant to Section 1043 of the Evidence Code [citing Cal. Penal Code § 832.7(g)]. Nor does it 'supersede or affect the criminal discovery process outlined in...[Evidence Code] section 1054..., or the admissibility of [such] records pursuant to...*Pitchess*...."[17]

Second, records/information protected by ***other*** **privileges remain(s) exempt** from the CPRA disclosure requirement. This is because both SB 1421 and AB 748 reflect revisions *only* to Cal. Gov. Code §§ 7923.600-7923.625 (formerly Cal. Gov Code § 6254(f)) — the subsection exempting some, but not all, police records from CPRA discoverability. However, **Cal. Gov. Code § 7927.705** (formerly Cal. Gov. Code § 6254(k)) (exempting Evidence Code privileged matters from the CPRA) **remains unchanged by the new laws.** Thus, records/information subject to such statutory privileges — such as the

---

16 However, the new laws also leave untouched the recent Supreme Court holding that the names of officers involved in police shootings cannot be withheld from a CPRA request. *See* Cal. Penal Code § 832.7(i) (amend. 2019) (adopting *Long Beach Police Officers Assn. v. City of Long Beach*, 59 Cal.4th 59 (2014)).

17 *See Ass'n for L.A. Deputy Sheriffs (ALADS) v. Superior Ct.* (2019) 8 Cal. 5th 28, 36-37, 50 n. 5, 56 (holding that a law enforcement agency does not violate Cal. Penal Code § 832.7 by disclosing to a prosecutor (such as by a *Brady* list or otherwise) the fact an officer of that agency who is a witness in a pending criminal prosecution may have information in the officer's personnel file that tends to exonerate the criminal defendant); *see also id.* at pp. 46-47 ("Senate Bill 1421 does not 'affect the discovery or disclosure of information contained in a peace or custodial officer's personnel file pursuant to Section 1043 of the Evidence Code [citing Cal. Penal Code § 832.7(g)]. Nor does it 'supersede or affect the criminal discovery process outlined in...[Penal Code] Section 1054 [or Evidence Code section 1043] [et seq.]..., or the admissibility of records pursuant to [Cal. Penal Code § 832.7(a), which codifies the court decision in *Pitchess v. Superior Court* (1974) 11 Cal.3d 531...."); *see also id.* ("[E]ven if Senate Bill 1421 does not increase the amount of information that a defendant [or moving party] can *compel* an agency to disclose, the bill, by making certain records nonconfidential, reduces the amount of information that agencies are *forbidden* from disclosing voluntarily.... [O]ur conclusion that records described in section 832.7(b) are 'not confidential' does not mean that they are invariably open for public inspection over the agency's objection.") (emphasis in original); *see also id.* at p. 50 n. 5 (holding that the 2019 amendments emphasize that *Pitchess* protections are intended to shield confidentiality of peace officer personnel file information from the *public*, *not* from government agencies).

attorney-client privilege,[18] the settlement communications privilege,[19] the spousal privilege,[20] the physician-patient privilege,[21] and the official government information privilege[22] — remain free of the new CPRA-discovery exception.[23] Similarly, the exemptions from CPRA disclosure obligations remain for: (a) **drafts**, notes, and intra-agency memos that are not ordinarily retained in the course of business[24]; (b) **records pertaining to pending litigation** in which the public agency is a party[25]; and (c) records whose **disclosure is prohibited by federal law**, among other unchanged provisions.[26]

Third, the new laws do <u>not</u> alter the normal process for criminal case discovery, including the exemption from *Brady*-style disclosures of records that the prosecutor does not possess.[27] (However, the complex intersection of

---

18 Cal. Evid. Code § 954; *but see* Cal. Penal Code § 832.7(b)(12) (amend. 2022; adopting and clarifying prior case law by mandating that facts relayed by a public entity to its attorneys, or "factual information discovered in any investigation conducted by, or on behalf of, the public entity's attorney" are exempt from the attorney-client privilege).

NOTE: However, "Senate Bill 16 also clarified that, for purposes of section 832.7(b), the lawyer-client privilege does not prohibit the disclosure of factual information provided by the public entity to its attorney or factual information discovered in an investigation, even when the investigation is conducted by the attorney." *See First Amendment Coalition, supra*, 98 Cal.App.5th at p. 612.

19 Cal. Evid. Code § 1119.

20 Cal. Evid. Code § 970.

21 Cal. Evid. Code §§ 990, 1010.

22 Cal. Evid. Code § 1040.

23 Indeed, by specifically adopting the holding of *Pitchess v. Superior Ct.* (1974) 11 Cal.3d 531, the new version of Cal. Penal Code § 832.7 — at subsection (h) — also implicitly underscores that the official information privilege remains available, when applicable.

24 Cal. Gov. Code § 7927.500 (formerly Cal. Gov. Code § 6254(a)).

25 Cal. Gov. Code § 7927.200(a) (formerly Cal. Gov. Code § 6254(b)).

26 Cal. Gov. Code §§ 7927.700, 7927.705 (formerly Cal. Gov. Code § 6254(c), (k)); *see also Becerra v. Superior Ct.* (2020) 44 Cal.App.5th 897, 914-918, 920-921, 923-929 (holding that the "[n]otwithstanding…any other law" language of Section 832.7(b)(1) "cannot reasonably be read to do away with the entire CPRA" and that, as a result, the CPRA categorical exemptions remain in effect, except as to records that specifically fall into the SB 1421 (and presumably SB 16) categories of disclosable police personnel file records).

27 *Compare* Cal. Penal Code § 832.7(h) *with* Cal. Penal Code § 1054.1; *see also People v. Superior Ct. (Johnson)* (2015) 61 Cal.4th 696, 713-723 (holding, among other things, that even where the criminal prosecuting attorney is employed by the same public entity that is the custodian of records of officer personnel files, because the prosecuting attorney represents the People of the State of California in a criminal case, and *not* the custodial public entity, the criminal prosecutor — the State — cannot be said to have possession of the officer's personnel file records: and, thus, in a case where the officer is not the subject of the criminal prosecution/investigation, such personnel file records can only be obtained by the prosecutor by a *Pitchess* motion — making them equally

the *Brady* disclosure duty and the *Pitchess* privilege merits further exploratio See the *Brady* disclosure chapter for additional details.)

Fourth, the new laws do not alter the process for obtaining discover disclosure of *Pitchess*-protected materials under Cal. Evid. Code § 1043 by *Pitchess* motion.[28]

Fifth, lest agencies be tempted to return to the old ways, the new laws d not change the agency's requirement to preserve records of officer miscondu complaints/investigations for 5 years; and, in fact, the 2022 revisions expan that retention requirement to 15 years where there are sustained findings o officer misconduct of any kind.[29] Nor do the new laws alter the obligation t produce the complainant's statement to the complainant, the agency's option t publish anonymous policing statistical data, or to publish findings in rebutt to a subject officer's publicity mischaracterizations.[30]

Furthermore, the new laws do not alter the CPRA provision that permit compliance to be satisfied (in most cases) by posting the non-exempt/CPR discoverable records/recordings on the agency's website.[31]

3. *Retroactive Effect of SB 1421.*

Contrary to the contentions of some, SB 1421 and its sibling statute apply *retroactively*: this means that their CPRA disclosure provisions apply t *all* police records, regardless of when such records were created – even if suc were created *before* the 2019 enactment of SB 1421.[32]

---

available to the prosecution as to the defense, and thereby excluding them from a prosecutor *Brady* disclosure duty); *ALADS*, *supra*, 8 Cal. 5th at pp. 46-47; *see generally* Cal. Penal Code § 1054. (regarding prosecutorial criminal-case disclosure requirements echoing *Brady v. Maryland* (1963 373 U.S. 83).

28 *See* Cal. Penal Code § 832.7(f); Cal. Gov. Code § 7923.625(f) (formerly Cal. Go Code § 6254(f)(4)(E)); Cal. Evid. Code § 1043.

29 *See* Cal. Penal Code § 832.5(b) (amend. 2022).

30 *See* Cal. Penal Code § 832.7(c)-(e).

31 *See* Cal. Gov. Code § 7922.545 (formerly Cal. Gov. Code § 6253(f)); *see also* Cal. Pena Code § 13650 (mandating Internet publication of CPRA-discoverable police policies, procedure and training manuals/materials).

32 *See Ventura County Sheriffs' Assn. v. County of Ventura* (2021) 61 Cal.App.5th 58 589-590, 594; *accord Walnut Creek Police Officers' Assn. v. City of Walnut Creek* (2019) 33 Cal.App.5t 940, 942.

4. *The Debate Over Whether Training Logs, Training Records, Training Manuals, and Training Certificates Are Disclosable Under the CPRA.*

Taking effect in 2019, as enacted in Penal Code section 13650, California law makes law enforcement "training materials that would otherwise be available to the public" under the CPRA into records that must be posted on the agency's website.[33] However, on its face, **the statute does *not* hold that such officer "training materials" are automatically disclosable public records**: rather it states that *if* officer training records are non-exempt public records, in addition to being disclosed to a CPRA requester, they must also be posted on the agency's website, without awaiting such a request.[34]

However, this 2019 law raises new questions without clear answers: as it *suggests*, but does *not* mandate, that officer "training materials" — such as curriculum reading material in any medium (documents, videos, presentations, etc.), manuals, handouts, training logs, or training certificates — are supposed to be disclosable public records under the CPRA.

The notion that officer training records are non-exempt public records does have at least *some* support under other sections of the Government Code. Chief among these is the fact that, within Government Code sections 7928.410, 7926.220 (formerly included in section 6254), while there *is* an express exemption from disclosure for training records for public employees who have *no* collective bargaining rights under California law: and since law enforcement officers have such collective bargaining rights, on a cursory review, this express exemption would seem *not* to apply to peace officers' training records.[35] In other words, because the express CPRA exemption for public employee training records seems *not* to extend to officer training records, at first blush, such records would appear to be CPRA-disclosable.

However, significantly, the contrary position is supported by the Penal Code: which expressly defines protected officer "personnel file" records to

---

33 Cal. Penal Code § 13650.

34 Cal. Penal Code § 13650.

35 *See* Cal. Gov. Code §§ 7928.410, 7926.220 (formerly Cal. Gov. Code § 6254(p)(2)-(q)); Cal. Gov. Code § 3508.

include all records "relating" to an officer's "educational…history…."[36] Thus, by operation of Government Code section 7927.705 (formerly section 6254(k)) [the statutory privilege and protection incorporation provision], officer training logs-manuals-records remain exempt from CPRA disclosure as *Pitchess*-privileged officer personnel file records.[37]

In balancing the vagaries of these competing authorities, **the most supportable position is likely to be that officer training records — including training curriculum materials/handouts, training videos/demonstrations, training logs, training certificates, and so forth — are *Pitchess*-protected officer personnel file records**; and, thus, unless there are portions that can be segregated to reveal non-exempt information, such records are likely exempt from CPRA disclosure — and thus discoverable *only* by operation of the *Pitchess* motion system, and *not* through the CPRA process.[38]

Notwithstanding the foregoing, particularly in light of Penal Code section 13650, the issue of whether officer training records are CPRA-disclosable is one for which monitoring of legal developments in the case law is sagely recommended.

5. *Practical Implications on the Burdens of Production and Related Considerations of the CPRA Exception.*

For litigators used to the lower-threshold of discoverability available in federal courts, the revolution to the scope of the *Pitchess* protection may seem like much ado about nothing: as even the newly-modified California *Pitchess*

---

36 *See* Cal. Penal Code §§ 832.7(a), 832.8(a)(1); *Commission on Peace Officer Standards & Training [POST] v. Superior Ct.* (2007) 42 Cal.4th 278, 285-286, 293-295, 300-303 (holding that, absent case-specific security concerns, such as uncover officer status, identities and employer names of peace officers in POST's possession was not exempt from the CPRA because such was not within the enumerated categories of information specified in Cal. Penal Code § 832.8).

37 *See id.*; *see also Northern Cal. Police Practices Project v. Craig* (1979) 90 Cal.App.3d 116, 118-119, 123-124 (holding that CHP training manuals re law enforcement procedures, weapons tactical training, and related safety and security protocols were generally exempt from CPRA disclosure, but where the materials contained non-exempt information, such materials should be produced if the exempt material could be segregated from the non-exempt material); *City of Fresno v. Superior Ct.* (1988) 205 Cal.App.3d 1459, 1465-1466 (on review of a *Pitchess* motion, presuming that policy manuals, training materials, training handouts and "other documents which have been used in the training of the police officers listed" in the motion were *Pitchess*-protected officer personnel file records); *see also, e.g.*, Cal. Evid. Code §§ 1043, 1045.

38 *See id.*

procedures still provide broader protections from discovery-production/disclosure-publication than would be available in a federal case.

However, for police agencies, this revolution represents nothing less than the opening of the floodgates. By removing "critical incident" investigations and recordings from *Pitchess* confidentiality, and making such records/recordings discoverable with nothing more than a CPRA request (as well as those for sustained findings of the other categories of specified officer misconduct), police agencies are seeing criminal defendants, civil litigants, and the news media take full advantage of the new bypass around the *Pitchess* procedural protections to obtain as much of these records as they want: bombarding and often burying public agencies in sometimes vast public records requests.

Without the good cause requirement and judicial review that, under the *Pitchess* procedure, protected agencies from unwarranted fishing expeditions, and without the same kind of judicial intervention that a motion to quash a subpoena or a motion for protective order from written discovery could have afforded, police agencies are finding themselves either on the defensive end of trying to oppose a suit to enforce a CPRA request or in the throes of making complex determinations about voluminous production of these now-public records/recordings.

As a result, to better cope with this post-revolutionary world, police agencies should at least consider some steps to mitigate the burden issues raised.

First, agencies should consider re-training their patrol officers and their criminal/administrative investigators to be more mindful of their presentation: to act on recordings as they would want to be seen/heard on the news, and to write their investigative reports/findings with a sharper eye on how such will be viewed, once published.

Second, given the volume of production the new laws have inspired, and given the highly-technical and limited nature of the remaining exemptions and conditional options available for withholding or redacting such police records/recordings, police agencies should consider hiring additional unsworn personnel whose sole or primary function would be to process such CPRA requests, and to manage associated evaluations of the application of the exemptions and determinations on production, under department-approved procedures, and preferably in consultation with experienced legal counsel. Either alternatively or in conjunction with increasing staff, police agencies should also explore retaining vendors who specialize in digital records management, and who may be better equipped to assist with processing the production or redaction of incident audio and video recordings.

Third, in cases where the "critical incident" or other excepted officer misconduct incident raises no extraordinary liability risk, threat to the investigation, or public/officer safety risk, police agencies should consider developing a routine procedure for posting such records/recordings on their website: preferably with a senior supervisory-level review before final posting. However, importantly, police agencies should also develop procedures, and retain experienced counsel to assist them, for how to proceed to withhold or redact CPRA-discoverable records/recordings when the "critical incident" *does* involve issues raising an unusual liability exposure, an unusual danger to the successful completion of the investigation, or a specific/articulable threat to an involved officer or other person: so that the withholding or redaction can be conducted in full compliance with the highly-technical requirements of the new laws and in a manner more likely to withstand legal challenge.

6. *Overview: Key Details of the CPRA Revisions to Officer Personnel File Confidentiality Procedures: Public Records, Withholding, and Redaction Rules.*

There are several important subtleties to the amended statutes that are likely to affect how police agencies respond to requests for the now-public-record portions of peace/custodial officer personnel file records/information. These subtleties are explained below.

7. *Key Detail: Which Peace/Custodial Officer Personnel File Records-Information Are Now Public?*

Under the 2019 and 2022 statutory revisions, while the definition of "personnel file" records generally still applies to such officer records/information, the *confidentiality provisions no longer apply* to investigation/complaint records regarding:

(1) [OIS] **officer-involved shootings ("OIS")** of/at persons ("discharge of a firearm at a person"), regardless of injury, including incident audio/video recordings thereof[39];

---

39 Cal. Penal Code §§ 832.7(b)(1)(A)(i) (amend. 2022).

(2) [**UOF-D/GBI**] **officer uses of force** ("UOF") on persons, **where death or great bodily injury ("D/GBI") resulted,**[40] including incident audio/video recordings thereof[41];

(3) [**Excessive Force**] **officer uses of unreasonable or excessive force,** but only where the agency's investigation resulted in a *sustained* finding[42];

(4) [**Failure to Intervene to Prevent Excessive Force**] **where officers fail to intervene against another officer using force that is clearly unreasonable or excessive,** but only where the agency's investigation resulted in a *sustained* finding[43];

(5) [**Sexual Assault — Specified**] **officer sexual assault on non-officers/non-employees,** with a customized definition of what constitutes officer sexual assault,[44] but only where the agency's investigation resulted in a *sustained* finding;

---

40 In the context of incident video/audio recordings, the new laws refer to OIS and death/great bodily injury uses of force as "critical incidents" or "serious" uses of force. *See, e.g.*, Cal. Penal Code §§ 832.7 cmt (2018); *cf.* Cal. Gov. Code § 7923.625 (formerly Cal. Gov. Code § 6254(f)(4)). NOTE: Even after the 2022 revisions, however, the definition of "great bodily injury" remains ambiguous, as explained more fully below.

41 Cal. Penal Code §§ 832.7(b)(1)(A)(ii) (amend. 2022).

42 Cal. Penal Code §§ 832.7(b)(1)(A)(iii) (amend. 2022).

43 Cal. Penal Code §§ 832.7(b)(1)(A)(iv) (amend. 2022).

44 Cal. Penal Code §§ 832.7(b)(1)(B)(i)-(iii) (amend. 2022). NOTE: The statute specifically *excludes* the employees/officers of the subject officer's agency from the scope of sexual assault investigations that may be CPRA-discoverable, where sustained; however, it specifically *includes* cadets, explorers, or other youth program members within the scope of CPRA-discoverable sexual assaults by the agency's officers, where sustained. *See* Cal. Penal Code § 832.7(b)(1)(B)(iii). Thus, for example, where a subject officer had a sustained finding of a sexual assault against an employee of that officer's employing agency, the associated investigation records would fall *outside* the scope of the new CPRA *Pitchess* exception: and would remain confidential and discoverable only by the traditional *Pitchess* process. Additionally, "sexual assault" for purposes of CPRA disclosure is defined as: the "commission or attempted initiation of a sexual act with a member of the public by means of force, threat, coercion, extortion, offer of leniency or other official favor, or under the color of authority. For purposes of this definition, the propositioning for[,] or commission of[,] any sexual act while on duty is considered a sexual assault." *See* Cal. Penal Code § 832.7(b)(1)(B)(ii). This arguably means that a sustained finding that an officer had *consensual* on-duty sex with a member of the public would be CPRA-disclosable. *See id.*

(6) **[Policing Dishonesty] officer dishonesty in law enforcement duties,**[45] but only where the agency's investigation resulted in a *sustained* finding;

(7) **[Discrimination] officer discriminatory conduct or writings against members of a protected class,** but only where the agency's investigation resulted in a *sustained* finding[46]; and

(8) **[Unlawful Arrest & Unlawful Search]** officers' unlawful arrests or unlawful searches, but only where the agency's investigation resulted in a *sustained* finding.[47]

Significantly, the revised statutes expressly confirm that, non-exempt, CPRA-discoverable officer personnel file records must be produced regardless of medium or sub-type including: (a) all investigative reports; (b) all photographic, video, and audio evidence; (c) all transcripts or recordings of interviews; (d) all autopsy reports; (e) all materials submitted to the prosecutor who is deciding whether to criminally charge an involved officer regarding an incident; (f) all materials submitted to the agency or entity/body that is deciding whether an involved officer's incident actions were consistent with the law and/or department policy — where the purpose of such agency's review is to decide whether to impose discipline or take corrective action against the officer; (g) all documents setting forth the recommendations-findings associated with such administrative review; and (h) all copies of disciplinary records associated with the incident, including but not limited to letters of intent to impose discipline, modifications of discipline after an officer's appeal (*e.g.*, post-*Skelly*), and/or letters re final imposition of discipline or corrective action.[48] However, the 2019 and 2022 statutes explicitly exempt unfounded, frivolous, and exonerated complaints from the scope of CPRA-discoverable personnel file records/information, as explained below.

---

45 *See* Cal. Penal Code §§ 832.7(b)(1)(C) (amend. 2022), 832.8 (amend. Jan. 2019); Cal. Gov. Code §§ 7923.600-7923.625 (formerly Cal. Gov. Code § 6254 (amend. July 2019). PRACTICE NOTE: The statute is clear that the new exemption applies only to acts of dishonesty by the officer in his/her official law enforcement function: such as false reporting, perjury as a police officer witness, and such. *See id.*

46 Cal. Penal Code §§ 832.7(b)(1)(D) (amend. 2022).

47 Cal. Penal Code §§ 832.7(b)(1)(E) (amend. 2022).

48 Cal. Penal Code § 832.7(b)(3) (amend. 2022).

a. Temporary Extension Of Withholding Time For Ongoing Investigations re Pre-2022 Incidents.

Interestingly, for all incidents that occurred prior to January 1, 2022, where the ongoing criminal or ongoing administrative caveat would otherwise apply to temporarily stay the disclosability of records (but not necessarily recordings) for specified officer misconduct, in the 2022 revisions that expanded the categories of CPRA-disclosable officer misconduct from four (OIS, UOF-D/GBI, sexual assault, dishonesty) to eight (adding excessive force, failure to intervene, discrimination, and unlawful arrests/searches), the Legislature enacted a blanket extension of the time for withholding such ongoing investigations until January 1, 2023.[49]

In other words, where the ongoing investigation was for (1) an incident that occurred before January 1, 2022; *and* (2) regarding officer misconduct pertaining to (a) excessive force, (b) failure to intervene to protect against excessive force, (c) officer discrimination against a protected class, or (d) officer dishonesty in law enforcement; in that event, rather than navigate the complex under-60-day, over-60-day, and over-180-day temporary withholding provisions of Penal Code section 832.7(b)(8), the 2022 revisions to the ongoing investigation caveat simply allow the agency to withhold that ongoing investigation from CPRA disclosure until January 1, 2023: and, thereafter, presumably, if applicable, the time limits of subsection (b)(8) would then apply, in the unlikely event that the investigation was still ongoing at that time.[50]

b. The Exemption for Unfounded, Frivolous, And Exonerated Complaints/Investigations: A Caveat to the New Exception.

However, as to investigation/complaint records, where the investigation resulted in an unfounded finding, or where the complaint was deemed frivolous (pursuant to Cal. Code Civ. Proc. § 128.5), or (presumably) where the agency's investigation exonerated the officer, even as to OIS and UOF investigations, such unfounded investigation records are <u>not</u> CPRA-discoverable. But, it is important to note, that **the exemption for unfounded/frivolous complaints/investigation applies only to *records*** (SB 1421): **it does <u>not</u>**

---

49 Cal. Penal Code §§ 832.7(b)(2) (amend. 2022).

50 *See id.*

apply to critical incident *recordings* (AB 748) that are CPRA-discoverable under these laws.[51]

Put another way, for example, where the OIS or UOF investigation resulted in an unfounded finding, the complaint/investigative records would remain *Pitchess* confidential, but the associated incident audio/video recordings would not. Rather, such recordings would be presumed public records under the CPRA, even if they otherwise qualified as officer personnel file records/information.

8. *Key Detail: Important Definitions Associated With These Categories of CPRA-Disclosable Police Records.*

The 2019 and 2022 laws also contain or reference some key terms that directly bear on the scope of what is CPRA-discoverable versus what is or remains *Pitchess*-confidential or CPRA-exempt.

<u>**Critical Incidents & "Serious" Uses Of Force**</u>. The 2019 laws use the terms "critical incident" and "serious use of force" interchangeably to refer to: (1) **officer-involved shootings** ("OIS") ("discharge[s] of a firearm") of/at persons, regardless of injury; <u>and</u> (2) officer **uses of force (by any means)** ("UOF") at persons **where death or great bodily injury results.**[52] It logically follows that the following officer uses of force are <u>not</u> critical incidents/serious uses of force triggering the new *Pitchess* exception: (1) OIS that were <u>not</u> fired at and did not strike/injure any person; (2) other UOF that were <u>not</u> directed at and did not strike/injure any person; and/or (3) UOF (other than OIS) that struck/injured a person, but where death or great bodily injury did <u>not</u> result.

<u>**Officer Dishonesty**</u>. The 2022 revision to the new laws specifically defines CPRA-discoverable (*Pitchess*-excepted) officer dishonesty as "dishonesty by a peace officer or custodial officer directly relating to the reporting, investigation, or prosecution of a crime, [--] or directly relating to the reporting of, or investigation of misconduct by, another peace officer or custodial officer, [--]

51 *Compare* Cal. Penal Code § 832.7(b)(9) (amend. 2022) *with* Cal. Gov. Code § 7923.625 (formerly Cal. Gov. Code § 6254(f)(4) (amend. 2019).

52 *See* Cal. Penal Code § 832.7(b)(1)(A)(i)-(ii) (amend. 2019); Cal. Gov. Code §§ 7923.600-7923.625 (formerly Gov. Code § 6254(f) (amend. 2019). NOTE: As explained more fully below, the definition of "great bodily injury" is ambiguous and disputed; as is the meaning of "resulted in" — as to whether such means "caused by" or "followed by" (each with vastly different implications).

including, but not limited to, false statements[;] filing false reports[;] destruction, falsifying, or concealing of evidence[;] or perjury."[53] The implications of this definition are that officer dishonesty regarding matters *other than* his or her law enforcement duties are *not* CPRA-disclosable: even when a related investigation results in a sustained finding.

Sexual Assault. The new laws specifically define CPRA-discoverable (*Pitchess*-excepted) officer "sexual assault" for *Pitchess* and CPRA purposes as the "commission or attempted initiation of a sexual act with a member of the public by means of force, threat, coercion, extortion, offer of leniency or other official favor, or under the color of authority. For purposes of this definition, the propositioning for[,] or commission of[,] any sexual act while on duty is considered a sexual assault."[54]

Sexual Assault — Member of the Public. But, significantly, the "**member of the public**" definition *excludes* officer/employee victims of the subject officer's agency from the public records exception to *Pitchess* confidentiality. This is because "member of the public" is defined as "any person not employed by the officer's employing agency and includes any participant in a cadet,

53 Cal. Penal Code § 832.7(b)(1)(C) (amend. 2022).

54 Cal. Penal Code § 832.7(b)(1)(B)(i)-(iii) (amend. 2022). NOTE: This arguably means that a sustained finding of on-duty consensual sex would be considered CPRA-disclosable "sexual assault" — an odd byproduct of the inartful drafting of these statutes.

PRACTICE NOTE: While, at first blush, the last sentence defining "sexual assault" seems broad enough to include on-duty consensual sex, such construction is inconsistent with CPRA and other case law. Generally speaking, to be a public record, the record must concern a government actor's performance of his or her duties: purely personal tasks, even if performed with government resources or on-duty, do not necessarily qualify. For example, where a public agency possesses a government actor's personal grocery shopping list, that list would *not* be viewed as a public record. *See San Gabriel Tribune v. Superior Ct.* (1983) 143 Cal.App.3d 762, 774 (home/personal shopping list, friend's letter to public officer unrelated to government activities, and comparable personal records are *not* public records, even when in the possession of a public entity); *see also* Cal. Penal Code § 11165.1 ("sexual assault" does *not* include voluntary conduct between adults). As a result, the "propositioning" language of Penal Code § 832.7 is more reasonably construed as referencing an *attempt* to physically force, or to use official authority to coerce, sex from a member of the public. This is because the alternative would be absurd: under the alternative, if an officer was on-duty, but during her duty shift she went home on a break and had sex with her willing adult husband in order to meet a strict fertility schedule, that officer would be committing a "sexual assault" for CPRA purposes — making her efforts to conceive publicly disclosable. *See generally Michael v. Gates* (1995) 38 Cal.App.4th 737, 745 (statutes should be construed to avoid absurd results); *accord Becerra v. Superior Ct.* (2020) 44 Cal.App.5th 897, 917. Given the California Constitution's strict deference for privacy, such a construction seems unlikely to be correct. *See* Cal. Const., art. I, § 1. However, the issue has not been clearly resolved by case law.

explorer, or other youth program affiliated with the agency."[55] Notably, this definition does *not* include employees/officers of that same agency. Thus, for CPRA/*Pitchess* purposes, a sexual assault is only CPRA-discoverable if it is committed against someone who is *not* an officer/employee of that officer's agency. But, even then, to be discoverable, the officer sexual assault must have resulted in a sustained investigative finding.[56] Otherwise, if these conditions do not apply, to be discoverable, the seeking party must proceed through the *Pitchess* procedures. The definitions of a "sustained" investigative finding and an "unfounded" one remain unchanged by the new laws, as explained below.

Protected Classes & Discrimination. The 2022 statutory revisions that extend CPRA-disclosure to public records of officer misconduct pertaining to discrimination specifically include records pertaining to a sustained investigation finding that an "officer engaged in conduct, including, but not limited to, verbal statements, writings, online posts, recordings, and gestures, involving prejudice or discrimination against a person on the basis of race, religious creed, color, national origin, ancestry, physical disability, mental disability, medical condition, genetic information, marital status, sex, gender, gender identity, gender expression, age, sexual orientation, or military and veteran status."[57]

Sustained. The definition remains essentially the same: namely, an investigative finding is "sustained" where, after an opportunity to have an administrative appeal pursuant to Cal. Gov. Code §§ 3304 and 3304.5 (Peace Officers' Bill of Rights Act), the police agency's administrative process makes a final determination that the subject officer violated the law or a department policy.[58] However, a slight revision to the 2022 version of the statute extends the definition to include a sustained finding by "any oversight agency": presumably including POST.[59]

55 Cal. Penal Code § 832.7(b)(1)(B)(iii) (amend. 2019).

56 Cal. Penal Code § 832.7(b)(1)(B)(i) (amend. 2019).

57 Cal. Penal Code § 832.7(b)(1)(D) (amend. 2022).

58 *See* Cal. Penal Code §§ 832.7(b)(1); 832.8(b) (amend. 2019, defining "sustained"); *Collondrez v. City of Rio Vista* (2021) 61 Cal.App.5th 1039, 1055 (applying statutory construction to hold that, because the alternative would be to defeat the purpose of the 2019 revisions to the CPRA and Penal Code, a finding is "sustained" once the agency makes its final determination and the officer has an *opportunity* to appeal; the statute does *not* require the appeal to be completed before the finding is sustained for purposes of determining CPRA disclosure).

59 Cal. Penal Code §§ 832.7(b)(1)(B)-(E) (amend. 2022).

Thus, under the CPRA, as detailed in Cal. Penal Code § 832.8, a "sustained nding" of disclosable officer misconduct results when the administrative ivestigation into such reaches a "final determination" for which there is no ther administrative appeal available under Cal. Gov. Code §§ 3304 or 3304.5.[60]

Unfounded. The definition remains largely the same: namely, an investigative finding is "unfounded" where the "investigation clearly establishes ıat the allegation is not true."[61] [As explained above, investigation/complaint ecords are not CPRA-discoverable if the investigation revealed they are nfounded or were frivolous (as defined by Cal. Code Civ. Proc. § 128.5).[62]]

Clear and Convincing Evidence. Under California law, clear and convincing evidence is evidence that persuades that it is highly probable that the act at issue is true.[63]

Great Bodily Injury. Under California law, "**great bodily injury**" is somewhat vaguely defined; and the 2019 and 2022 statutory amendments do *not* include a custom definition regarding the CPRA exception to the *Pitchess* privilege.[64] The scope of the term is thus the subject of debate.

9. *The Debate Over Defining Great Bodily Injury (GBI) for the CPRA Exception & Statutory Construction Issues.*

Significantly, there are at least two potential definitions of "great bodily injury" (or "GBI") in California law: and which definition applies *dramatically* affects the scope of potentially CPRA-disclosable materials under the statutory amendments.

---

60 *See Collondrez, supra*, 61 Cal.App.5th at pp. 1051-1055.

61 Cal. Penal Code § 832.8(c) (amend. 2019).

62 Cal. Penal Code § 832.7(b)(9) (amend. 2022); *accord* Cal. Penal Code § 832.5(d) (amend. 2022). By contrast, "**Exonerated**" means that the agency's investigation clearly established that the peace/custodial officer actions that were the subject of the complaint were not violations of law or department policy. *See* Cal. Penal Code § 832.5(d).

63 *See In re Angelia P.* (1981) 28 Cal.3d 908, 919; Cal. Evid. Code §§ 115, 500; Judicial Council of Cal. Civ. Jury Instruction ("CACI") no. 201.

64 *See* Cal. Penal Code § 832.7(b)(1)(A)(ii) (amend. 2019 & 2022); Cal. Gov. Code §§ 7923.600-7923.625 (formerly Cal. Gov. Code § 6254(f)).

<u>Penal Code GBI & Its Flaws: The Broad Definition.</u> The **broad definition** of GBI rests largely on the <u>Penal Code</u>: but, due to case law defining the Penal Code version of GBI to include physical pain, and given the legislative history indicating that, in the CPRA context, police use of force was *not* intended to be so broadly disclosable, this definition of GBI is problematic.

Specifically, Penal Code section 12022.7(f) defines GBI as "a significant or substantial physical injury"[65]: as opposed to "moderate harm" or "trivial or insignificant injury."[66] On its face, this definition thus seems innocuous.

Under the <u>broad definition</u>, one could argue that, for practical purposes, if one also applies the Penal Code definition of serious bodily injury, great/serious bodily injury (GBI) is *at least* the "impairment of physical condition, including but not limited to, the following: loss of consciousness; concussion; bone fracture; protracted loss or impairment of function of any bodily member or organ; a wound requiring extensive suturing; and serious disfigurement."[67]

Indeed, a limited construction of Penal Code GBI is tempting when one considers the controlling case law that holds that, under California law, there is no material distinction between the term "great bodily injury" and "serious bodily injury": and "serious bodily injury" (or "SBI"), even when it comes to police use of force.[68]

However, case law associated with the Penal Code definition of GBI is much more expansive: and it **stretches GBI to include a broad array of injuries resulting in abrasions/scrapes, contusions/bruises, burns, punctures, lacerations, and even just physical pain.**[69]

---

65 *See* Cal. Penal Code § 12022.7(f).

66 *See also People v. Escobar* (1992) 3 Cal.4th 740, 746; Cal. Penal Code § 12022.7(f) ("As used in this section, 'great bodily injury' means a significant or substantial physical injury.")

67 Cal. Penal Code § 243(f)(4); *see also* Cal. Penal Code §§ 198.5, 12022.7(f).

68 *See People v. Knoller* (2007) 41 Cal.4th 139, 143 n.2; *accord People v. Burroughs* (1984) 35 Cal.3d 824, 831; *People v. Arnett* (2006) 139 Cal.App.4th 1609, 1613 ("great bodily injury" and "serious bodily injury" "have substantially the same meaning").

69 *See People v. Washington* (2021) 210 Cal.App.4th 1042, 1047-1048 ("some physical pain or damage, such as lacerations, bruises, or abrasions" constitutes great bodily injury under Cal. Pen. Code, § 12022.7(f)); *People v. Jung* (1999) 71 Cal.App.4th 1036, 1042 (same); *People v. Wallace* (1993) 14 Cal.App.4th 651, 665-666 (cuts and burns from being flex-tied, burning sensation from an insecticide-like substance were great bodily injury); *People v. Bustos* (1994) 23 Cal.App.4th 1747, 1755 (multiple abrasions, lacerations, and contusions were great bodily injury); *People v. Corona*

Proponents of the broad definition of GBI for CPRA purposes contend that, under California law, the statutory definition of SBI is narrower than the statutory definition of GBI: and that, since, in drafting the 2019 amendments, the California Legislature chose the term GBI, *not* SBI, the Legislature must have intended the broader definition of GBI, rather than SBI, to apply to the CPRA exception.[70]

While the broad definition of GBI for CPRA seems at odds with California law defining GBI as greater than a regular injury – and a regular "injury" is defined as "any physical injury which requires professional medical treatment" (which should often *omit* things like physical pain, bruises, scrapes, and so forth)[71] – the ambiguity of the 2019 amendments renders the broad definition of GBI to be at least colorable, if not persuasive.

However, the practical implications of the broad definition must be considered. If the broadest Penal Code definition of GBI [Section 12022.7(f)] were held to apply to the CPRA exception to the *Pitchess* privilege, the CPRA exception would essentially devour the privilege. This is because, in such an event, *virtually any and all police uses of force would fall into the CPRA-discoverable category of officer uses of force resulting in death or GBI.* In other words, the broad GBI definition would effectively void the *Pitchess* privilege in uses of force that resulted in minor scrapes, bruises, abrasions, burns, lacerations, or even physical pain.

Given the overly broad scope of such a hole in the *Pitchess* privilege, and given that the 2019 amendments appear to take great pains to preserve the *Pitchess* privilege at its core, there is little support for the contention that the broadest Penal Code definition [GBI – Section 12022.7(f)] – or even the narrower Penal Code definition [SBI – Section 243(f)(4)] that case law equates with GBI – apply to the CPRA exception to *Pitchess* privilege here.

(1989) 213 Cal.App.3d 589 (a swollen jaw, bruises to head and neck and sore ribs were "great bodily injury"); *People v. Sanchez* (1982) 131 Cal.App.3d 718 (multiple abrasions and lacerations to victim's back and bruising of eye and cheek were "great bodily injury") *disapproved on other grounds in People v. Escobar* (1992) 3 Cal.4th 740, 751, fn. 5; *People v. Jaramillo* (1979) 98 Cal.App.3d 830, 836–837 (multiple contusions, swelling and discoloration of the body, and extensive bruises were "great bodily injury").

70 *See, e.g., Research Article* by Tenaya Rodewald, Esq., Sheppard, Mullin, Richter & Hampton, 2020 for an astute analysis of the issue; *compare* Cal. Pen. Code, § 12022.7(f) (defining GBI) *with* Cal. Pen. Code § 243(f)(4) (defining SBI).

71 Cal. Penal Code § 243(f)(5).

This is particularly the case when one considers that, as shown below, relative to police uses of force, GBI is used interchangeably with SBI to refer to a kind of force likely to result in injuries far more severe than mere abrasions, contusions, lacerations, punctures, minor burns, or physical pain. Specifically, in the context of police use of force, GBI is typically paired with death as the type of result that, in order to be avoided, deadly force may be used.

Significantly then, applying the broad Penal Code definition of GBI to the police use of force and CPRA context would also have the bizarre side effect of lowering the threshold for when officers could use deadly force. This is because, under both California and federal law, law enforcement officers are authorized to use deadly force when, from the perspective of a reasonable officer under the totality of the circumstances known to the force-wielding officer at the time, it is objectively reasonable for the force-wielding officer to reasonably believe that he or she faces an immediate threat of death or great bodily injury (GBI).[72]

Although, in the police use of force context, GBI has *not* been defined down by the case law to the Penal Code level of embracing mere physical pain, if the broad Penal Code GBI definition applied to police use of force and CPRA disclosures thereof, officers would be authorized to shoot for nothing more than a reasonable belief that they were about to face a painful bruise.[73]

---

72 *See, e.g., Palm v. Las Vegas Metro. Police Dept.*, 1998 U.S. App. LEXIS 7939, *5-6 (9th Cir. 1998) ("A police officer has a right to use...deadly force[] as is necessary under the circumstances to protect himself and other from what he reasonably believes to be a threat of great bodily injury or harm."); *id.* at pp. 7-8 (holding deadly force to be reasonable-at-law where a police officer saw a man violently rape a woman, where the unarmed man then ignored officer commands to move away from the victim, and the man then lunged at the officer: even though the officer had not identified himself as an officer and did not give a shoot warning); *accord Acosta v. City & County of San Francisco*, 83 F.3d 1143, 1145 n.3 (9th Cir. 1996) (observing that deadly force is lawful to protect against "great bodily injury"); *Edson v. City of Anaheim* (1998) 63 Cal.App.4th 1269, 1272 (approving jury instruction that officer deadly force is reasonable where evidence shows that the officer "reasonably believed" a suspect "posed an immediate threat of great bodily injury or death"); *Munoz v. City of Union City* (2004) 120 Cal.App.4th 1077, 1105-1106 (concluding that officers' deadly force is authorized to prevent "great bodily injury"); *People v. Morales* (2021) 69 Cal.App.5th 978, 994 (holding that self-defense by deadly force is lawful when the person is facing "imminent attack that might result in death or great bodily injury"); *see also Graham v. Connor*, 490 U.S. 386, 396-397 (1989).

73 *Compare Washington, supra*, 210 Cal.App.4th at pp. 1047-1048 ("some physical pain or damage, such as lacerations, bruises, or abrasions" constitutes great bodily injury under Cal. Pen. Code, § 12022.7(f)) *with Palm, supra*, 1998 U.S. App. LEXIS 7939 at pp. *5-6 ("A police officer has a right to use...deadly force[] as is necessary under the circumstances to protect himself and other from what he reasonably believes to be a threat of great bodily injury or harm.").

<u>GBI In Police Use Of Force & Its Consistency With CPRA Legislative Intent: The Narrow Definition</u>. By contrast, the **narrow definition** of GBI arguably rests largely in the <u>Government Code</u> and the case law associated with police use of force: and its narrower strictures are more consistent with the canons of statutory instruction and the apparent legislative history in revising and narrowing the scope of disclosability under SB 1421 & AB 748.

Under the narrow GBI approach, one looks first to the fact that, as previously observed herein, controlling California case law holds that GBI and SBI are essentially the same thing.[74]

Next, one looks to the fact that, in statutes relating to police use of force, such as those requiring annual reporting on officer-involved shootings and "incident[s] in which the use of force by a peace officer against a civilian results in serious bodily injury or death," SBI is defined as "**a bodily injury that involves a substantial risk of death, unconsciousness, protracted and obvious disfigurement, or protracted loss or impairment of the function of a bodily member or organ.**"[75]

Additionally, under the <u>narrow</u> GBI approach, one looks to fact that the non-shooting category of CPRA-discoverable force involves two types of force: one that results in death, and another that results in GBI. Particularly since rejected prior versions of the 2019 legislation were broader, and meant to include *all* uses of force, this pairing of GBI with death suggests that GBI is meant to be the kind of injury serious enough to be *comparable* to death. This would thus place the CPRA/Government Code definition of GBI/SBI in line with those authorities defining police-related "deadly force" as being "force that creates a substantial risk of causing death or serious bodily injury."[76]

---

74 *See Knoller*, *supra*, 41 Cal.4th at p 143 n.2; *Burroughs*, *supra*, 35 Cal.3d at p. 831; *Arnett*, *supra*, 139 Cal.App.4th at p. 1613 ("great bodily injury" and "serious bodily injury" "have substantially the same meaning"); *see also* Cal. Penal Code § 835a (an officer "is justified in using deadly force…when an officer reasonably believes, based on the totality of circumstances, that such force is necessary…to defend against an imminent threat of death or serious bodily injury to the officer or to another person.").

75 Cal. Gov. Code § 12525.2(d) (emphasis added).

76 Cal. Penal Code § 835a (amend. 2020); *Tennessee v. Garner* (1985) 471 U.S. 1, 9 n. 8; *Smith v. Hemet* (9th Cir. 2005) 394 F.3d 689, 706 ("deadly force" is "force employed [that] creates a substantial risk of causing death or serious bodily injury"); *accord Koussaya v. City of Stockton* (2020) 54 Cal.App.5th 902, 932-934 (explaining the 2020 amendments to Cal. Penal Code § 835a); *Long Beach Police Officers Assn. v. City of Long Beach* (1976) 61 Cal.App.3d 364, 368.

Notably, in terms of severity of injury, case authorities on deadly force always pair "death" and a definition of SBI/GBI that is more consistent with the Government Code definition of SBI: namely, in such authorities, SBI/GBI does *not* include less serious injuries like abrasions, bruises, punctures, physical pain, and the like – but, rather, **SBI/GBI only includes life-threatening and potentially permanent, disabling injuries.**[77]

In light of the fact that the CPRA is also housed in the Government Code where the narrower version of SBI/GBI can be found,[78] and since the Government Code and police force case law definitions of GBI/SBI are more consistent with the narrow definition, although there is as yet no controlling authority on point, the application of the narrow definition to the CPRA exception is more persuasive and likely to be accurate.

Significantly, the practical implications of the narrow definition of GBI, particularly in light of the legislative history of the 2019 amendments, also point to the narrow definition being the correct version for use in determining the scope of CPRA-discoverable officer police investigatory record and officer personnel file information.

To elaborate, if the Legislature meant to embrace a broader definition of GBI that, in effect, encompasses *any* use of force that causes any physical pain or leaves any marks at all, then why would the Legislature have adopted the limiting language about GBI, rather than its prior language that encompassed all uses of force? In such an event, if the broad definition of GBI were intended, then the GBI limiting language would have no meaning and would instead be redundant surplusage.

In other words, if the true legislative intent was to make *all* uses of force CPRA-discoverable, then it would be illogical to include specified categories of force incidents at all: especially when two of those specified categories, as demonstrated below, were subsequently removed prior to the bills' passage. It is thus contrary to the canons of statutory construction to view use of the term GBI as a green light to disclosure of all police force incidents: for such

77 *See id.*; *see also Thompson v. County of Los Angeles* (2006) 142 Cal.App.4th 154, 163-166 (use of a police dog – whose bite injuries typically result in punctures, lacerations, and contusions – does *not* constitute deadly force under California law).

78 Cal. Gov. Code § 7920.000, *et seq.* (formerly Cal. Gov. Code § 6250, *et seq.*)

construction would make the specific, restrictive categorizations into mere surplusage.[79]

Moreover, the **legislative history** of SB 1421 reveals that the broad Penal Code definition of GBI cannot be consistent with the definition of GBI used for purposes of determining disclosability of police uses of force under the CPRA.

Specifically, a precursor to SB 1421 was SB 1286. Introduced on February 19, 2016, the SB 1286 bill desired to "require…certain peace officer or custodial officer personnel records and records relating to complaints against peace officers and custodial officers to be available for public inspection" pursuant to the CPRA, including: "[any] record related to the investigation or assessment of any use of force by a peace officer that is likely to or does cause death or serious bodily injury, including but not limited to, the discharge of a firearm, use of an electronic control weapon or conducted energy device [TASER], and any strike with an impact weapon to a person's head."[80]

Significantly, as to TASERs, since at least 2010, courts have recognized that the TASER dart mode (the shoot-from-a-distance mode) can incapacitate a person temporarily, accompanied by significant pain; and that the types of injuries typically caused by TASER devices in dart mode include "puncture wounds or burns" and fall-related abrasions: injuries that courts have classified as "significant," while also holding that such injuries are *not* "serious" or "life-threatening" – unless a person is incapacitated from a high position, such that the fall causes death or paralysis.[81]

By contrast, also since at least 2010, courts have recognized that the types of injuries typically caused by TASER devices in drive-stun mode (the up-close/contact mode) include only pain or de minimis, insignificant, temporary

---

79 *See generally Commission on Peace Officer Standards & Training (POST) v. Superior Court*, 42 Cal.4th 278, 293 (2007) (holding that peace officer personnel records included only the types of information listed in the categories enumerated in the applicable statute).

80 Cal. Senate Committee on Public Safety, April 12, 2016 Hearing on SB 1286 at p. 6.

81 *See, e.g., Bryan v. MacPherson*, 630 F.3d 805, 813-814 (9th Cir. 2010); *Brooks v. City of Seattle*, 559 F.3d 1018, 1025, 1028 (9th Cir. 2010) (distinguishing dart mode as causing loss of muscle control and fall-related abrasions from drive-stun mode, which does not); *see generally Armatuni v. 5230 Hollywood*, 2022 Cal. Super. LEXIS 37762, *7-8 (Los Angeles Super. Ct. June 3, 2022) (restating plaintiffs' TASER allegations).

injuries: because the drive-stun mode "inflicts only transitory, localized pain" without "incapacitating muscle contractions or significant lasting injury."[82]

The case law detailing the nature of the injuries caused by TASERs is important to understanding the scope of the current law because, before 2019, the case law shows that the known non-deadly injuries typically caused by TASER devices included: puncture wounds and associated subdural hemorrhages; electrical burns; local (drive-stun) or significant/incapacitating (dart mode) pain; and, as to dart mode only, fall-related abrasions.[83]

However, this precursor bill to SB 1421 (SB 1286) – expanding the scope of disclosability to injuries associated with TASERs and batons – *died in committee.*[84]

On a related note, thereafter, the originally-introduced version of SB 1421 stated:

> *This bill* provides the public access, through the CPRA, to records related to: Reports, investigation, or findings of: Incidents involving the discharge of a firearm at a person by an officer. Incidents involving the discharge of an electronic control weapon at a person by an officer. Incidents involving the strike with an impact weapon or projectile to the head or neck of a person by an officer. Incidents involving use of force by an officer which results in death or serious bodily injury.[85]

However, the foregoing language – showing that TASER force and impact weapon/baton force incidents would be disclosable under SB 1421 – does *not* appear in the final statute: which, in turn, supports a narrower scope of

---

82 *See, e.g., Brooks, supra,* 559 F.3d at pp; 1025-1028; *Crowell v. Kirkpatrick,* 400 Fed. Appx. 592, 595 (2d Cir. 2010) (observing that TASER drive stun mode causes only pain, no permanent injury); *Brossart v. Janke,* 859 F.3d 616, 626 n. 6 (8th Cir. 2017) (TASER drive-stun mode causes only pain and "de minimis" injury); *see generally In re Brandon O,* 174 Cal.App.4th 637, 643 (2009); *In re M.S.,* 70 Cal.App.5th 728, 731 n. 2 (2021); *Fujikawa v. City of San Jose,* 2017 Cal.App. Unpub. LEXIS 7451, *7 n. 4 (2017) (distinguishing TASER dart mode from drive stun); *but see* Cal. R. Ct. 8.1115(a)-(b) (unpublished cases may not be cited).

83 *See, e.g., Brooks, supra,* 559 F.3d at pp; 1025-1028; *Bryan, supra,* 630 F.3d at pp. 813-814.

84 Cal. Senate Committee on Public Safety, Leg. Info., April 12, 2016, http://www.leginfo.ca.gov/pub/15-16/bill/sen/sb_1251-1300/sb_1286_cfa_20160412_170041_sen_comm.html.

85 Cal. Senate Committee on Public Safety, April 17, 2018 Hearing on SB 1421 at p. 6.

disclosability for SB 1421, excluding such force types, than some have otherwise suggested.[86]

Notably, even with this initially-proposed/later-rejected, much broader range of excepted/disclosable records than what was ultimately adopted, the Senate Floor Analysis repeatedly stated that "SB 1421 opens police officer personnel records in *very limited* cases, allowing local law enforcement agencies and law enforcement oversight agencies to provide greater transparency around **only the most serious police complaints**...[because the] public has a right to know all about *serious* police misconduct, as well as about officer-involved shootings and *other serious* uses of force."[87]

It should not escape notice here that the legislative history likens "other serious uses of force" to officer-involved shootings: suggesting that *only* uses of force comparable in seriousness to an OIS were intended to be disclosable under the CPRA.

It would thus be absurd to interpret the legislative intent as extending "the most serious police complaints" to those that, according to the Penal Code GBI definition, do no more than cause physical pain or abrasions (scrapes) and contusions (bruises).

Furthermore, embracing the precept that the incidents where disclosures should be permitted should be "very limited," the bill was then *further amended* by the Legislature to *remove* from the list of CPRA-disclosable force use of an electronic control weapons (*e.g.*, TASERs) as well as removing from the list of disclosable force strikes with impact weapons (*e.g.*, batons) or projectiles to the head or neck of a person.[88] This narrowing of the scope of disclosable force – removing TASERs and batons/impact weapons from the list – is key

86 *See* Cal. Penal Code § 832.7 (amend. 2019 by SB 1421).

87 Cal. Senate Rules Committee, Third Reading of SB 1421, at p. 7 (emphasis added); *First Amendment Coalition*, *supra*, 98 Cal.App.5th at pp. 610-610 (concluding that the "legislative history...confirm[s]" that Section 832.7(b) only "open[s] police officer personnel records [to CPRA disclosure] in very limited cases, allowing local law enforcement agencies and law enforcement oversight agencies to provide greater transparency around only the most serious police complaints." (emphasis added, interior quotations omitted). Thus, "[o]ur construction aligns with the legislative findings accompanying Section 832.7(b)...which emphasize...[that the] 'public has a right to know all about serious police misconduct, as well as about officer-involved shootings and other serious uses of force.'").

88 Cal. Senate Rules Committee, August 23, 2018 Unfinished Business, SB 1421 at p. 2.

to understanding how the *narrow* definition of GBI necessarily applies to the SB 1421 and AB 748 exceptions to the police investigatory records exemption from the CPRA.[89]

Specifically, as prefaced above, it is well known in the case law and otherwise that electronic control weapons ("ECWs" like TASERs) typically cause punctures in their probe or dart stun mode, and they cause burn-like dots or abrasions in their drive-stun mode.[90]

It is also well known in the case law and otherwise that impact weapons, like police batons and flashlights, typically cause contusions and possibly non-life-threatening fractures (except for baton blows to the head).[91] Whereas, it is also well known in the case law and otherwise that police K9 dog bites typically cause punctures and lacerations.[92]

Yet, under prevailing case law, **none of these uses of force are considered to be deadly force**: rather, like manual restraint, a TASER in drive-stun mode is considered to be non-deadly/low force; while a TASER in dart mode, impact weapons like police batons (to the body), pepper spray, and police K9

---

89 *See, e.g., Becerra v. Superior Ct.* (2020) 44 Cal.App.5th 897, 921 (holding that the legislative intent of SB 1421 was to make "significant force," *not* all force, disclosable).

90 *See, e.g., Carroll v. Ellington*, 800 F.3d 154, 166 (5th Cir. 2015) (acknowledging that puncture wounds on the chest and flank could be consistent with TASER probe deployments); *Willis v. Secor*, 2018 U.S. Dist. LEXIS 244687, *4 (C.D. Cal. 2018) (punctures were consistent with TASER darts); *Harris v. City of Tulare*, 2022 U.S. Dist. LEXIS 12799, *9 (E.D. Cal. 2022) (paired dots can be consistent with TASER drive stun application, while abrasions can be consistent with baton strikes); *Hesterberg v. United States*, 71 F.Supp.3d 1018, 1026 (N.D. Cal. 2014) (discussing TASER probes causing puncture injuries); *see also Mattos v. Agarano*, 661 F.3d 433, 443 (9th Cir. 2011 (distinguishing the neuromuscular full body incapacitation of TASERs in dart mode versus the pain-only effects of TASERs in drive stun to contact mode).

91 *See, e.g., People v. Odom* (2016) 244 Cal.App.4th 237, 241 (observing that parallel contusions could be consistent with being struck by a police baton); *Ervin v. Merced Police Dept.*, 2015 U.S. Dist. LEXIS 136655, *26-30 (E.D. Cal. 2015) (police baton use that fractured teeth evaluated by court as non-deadly force); *Valiavacharska v. Celaya*, 2011 U.S. Dist. LEXIS 109164, * 1-2 (N.D. Cal. 2011) (police baton fractured fingers).

92 *See, e.g., Hernandez v. Town of Gilbert*, 2019 U.S. Dist. LEXIS 61480, * 28-29 (D. Ariz. 2019) (police K9 dog bites caused lacerations and fractures to suspect's foot); *Vargas v. Whatcom Cty. Sheriff's Office*, 2021 U.S. Dist. LEXIS 29770, * 9 (W.D. Wash. 2021) (police K9 dog bites caused punctures to foot, nerve damage, and chronic pain); *Martus v. Terry*, 2011 U.S. Dist. LEXIS 36296, *4-5, 8-14 (D. Nev. 2011) (police K9 dog bites caused punctures to hip and loss of the tip of the suspect's index finger, but force still analyzed as non-deadly).

dog bites are all considered to be non-deadly/intermediate force under prevailing case law.[93]

Along related lines, under controlling case law, "deadly force" is force which, at the time it is used, creates a foreseeable and substantial risk of death or great bodily injury (or "serious bodily injury" in the California statutes), as adjudged based on the facts known to the officer using that force under the totality of the circumstances at the time.[94]

However, if the broader Penal Code definition of GBI were applied, because all of these force options are all likely to cause physical pain, all of these at-law non-deadly force options – TASERs, batons, pepper spray, K9s – would automatically become 'deadly force" – contrary to controlling case law precedent.

More importantly, if – in its revision of the CPRA – the Legislature intended the broader Penal Code definition of GBI to apply to police force, then the legislative history would not indicate (as it does) that the Legislature intended to *narrow* the scope of disclosability away from weapons that merely cause contusions, abrasions, lacerations, and punctures – as TASER and impact weapons do. It would be entirely inconsistent with the canons of statutory

93 *See Bryan v. MacPherson*, 630 F.3d 805, 825-826 (9th Cir. 2010) (TASERs are non-lethal force, but when used in dart mode, they are non-lethal intermediate force requiring the presence of a threat of harm to be justified; also noting that pepper spray and impact weapons are non-deadly force); *Brewer v. City of Napa*, 210 F.3d 1093, 1098 (9th Cir. 2000) (police K9 dogs' bites are non-deadly intermediate force); *Thomson v. Salt Lake County*, 584 F.3d 1304, 1316 (10th Cir. 2009) (potential for greater harm does not transform use of a police dog into deadly force); *Young v. County of Los Angeles*, 655 F.3d 1156, 1161 (9th Cir. 2011)(pepper spray and baton strikes are non-deadly intermediate force); *Forrester v. City of San Diego*, 25 F.3d 804, 806-808 (pain compliance techniques such as firm grip restraint, pressure holds, and arm/wrist twisting are non-deadly force); *Centeno v. City of Fresno*, 2016 U.S. Dist. LEXIS 180013, *25 (E.D. Cal. 2016) (manual restraint is non-deadly force); *Deorle v. Rutherford*, 272 F.3d 1272, 1279-1280 (9th Cir. 2001) (impact weapon, including cloth-cased shot akin to a rubber bullet, was non-deadly force as a matter of law); *Estate of Phillips v. City of Milwaukee*, 123 F.3d 586, 593-594 (7th Cir. 1992) (holding that prone restraint is non-deadly force).

94 *See. e.g.*, Cal. Penal Code § 835a ("deadly force" is "force that creates a substantial risk of causing death or serious bodily injury"); *accord Tennessee v. Garner*, 471 U.S. 1, 9 n.8 (1985); *Smith v. Hemet*, 394 F.3d 689, 701, 706 (9th Cir. 2005) ("deadly force" is "force employed [that] creates a substantial risk of causing death of serious bodily injury"); *see also Thompson v. County of Los Angeles* (2006) 142 Cal.App.4th 154, 163-166 (use of a police dog – whose bite injuries typically result in punctures, lacerations ,and contusions – does *not* constitute deadly force under California law); *Luchtel v. Hagemann*, 623 F.3d 975, 980 (9th Cir. 2010); *Tekle v. United States*, 511 F.3d 839, 844-845 (9th Cir. 2007); *Bryan, supra*, 630 F.3d at pp. 825-826.

construction to believe that, in its attempt to *narrow* the scope of CPRA disclosability under the SB 1421 and AB 748 exception, the Legislature adopted a term, GBI, that instead broadened the scope of disclosure to include, effectively, *all* uses of force.

As a result, since the broad Penal Code definition of GBI is both inconsistent with how GBI is defined in the context of police use of force, and since the broad version of GBI leads to absurd results, the broad version cannot be the legally correct version. This is particularly true considering the fact that California police chiefs' acquiescence to then-bills SB 1421 and AB 748 was reportedly contingent upon the Legislature's addition of the limiting GBI language.[95] There thus seems to be less support for the notion that the broader definition of GBI was the true legislative intent here: for it is unlikely that the police community would have embraced a definition of GBI relative to use of force that is wholly alien to and broader than their understanding of GBI/SBI as a fatal or near-fatal/permanent injury situation in the context of police use of force.[96]

Because the broad GBI interpretation would lead to absurd results that appear contrary to the legislative intent, the narrow GBI interpretation is better supported by common notions of **statutory construction**. To elaborate, under the canons of statutory construction for courts: "When we interpret a statute, [o]ur fundamental task…is to determine the Legislature's intent so as to effectuate the law's purpose. We first examine the statutory language, giving it a plain and commonsense meaning. We do not examine that language in isolation, but in the context of the statutory framework as a whole in order to determine its scope and purpose and to harmonize the various parts of the enactment. If the language is clear, courts must generally follow its plain meaning unless a literal interpretation would result in absurd consequences the Legislature did not intend. If the statutory language permits more than one reasonable

95 "California Legislature Passes Major Police Transparency Measures On Internal Investigations and Body Cameras," Los Angeles Times, published on Sept. 1, 2018, www.latimes.com/politics/la-pol-ca-police-transparency-bill-passes-20180831-story.html (reporting that the California Police Chiefs Association had approved the final draft of the bill a week before passage).

96 *See id.*; *see generally* Cal. Code Civ. Proc. § 1859; *In re Williamson* (1954) 43 Cal.2d 651, 654 ("It is the general rule [of statutory construction] that where the general statute standing alone would include the same matter [conduct] as the special [specific] act, and thus conflict with it, the special act will be considered as an exception to the general statute whether it was passed before or after such general enactment."); *accord People v. Murphy* (2011) 52 Cal.4th 81, 86; *Morton v. Mancari* (1974) 417 U.S. 535, 550 ("where there is no clear intention otherwise, a specific statute will not be controlled or nullified by a general one regardless of the priority of enactment"); *Townsend v. Little* (1883) 109 U.S. 504, 512; *Collandrez, supra*, 61 Cal.App.5th at p. 1052.

interpretation, courts may consider other aids, such as the statute's purpose, legislative history, and public policy. Furthermore, we consider portions of a statute in the context of the entire statute and the statutory scheme of which it is a part, giving significance to every word, phrase, sentence, and part of an act in pursuance of the legislative purpose."[97]

Along these lines, "whenever possible, significance must be given to every word [in a statute] in pursuing legislative purpose, and the court should avoid a construction that makes some words surplusage."[98] Thus, under the canons of statutory construction, a "statute should be interpreted to avoid an absurd result."[99]

As a result, given the fact that applying the broad Penal Code construction of GBI, to police use force would result in obliterating the case law distinctions between deadly force and non-deadly force, while also lowering the threshold for use of deadly force (increasing officer shootings); and given that the broad construction of GBI would also effectively eliminate the *Pitchess* and other guardrails the Legislature had imposed to keep the scope of the SB 1421 exception's disclosability "very limited"; and given the legislative history showing that the scope of the 2019+ exception was intended to be *narrowed* by the amendments, not broadened, it would be absurd to interpret the SB 1421-AB 748 use of the term "great bodily injury" (GBI) to be consistent with the Penal Code definition of GBI, as such has been expanded by case law.

As such, in light of the foregoing, the only reasonable statutory construction available here is that when the Legislature adopted the term "great bodily injury" (GBI) in the context of police uses of force that would become disclosable under the CPRA, the Legislature meant to embrace the interpretation of

---

97 *See Collandrez, supra*, 61 Cal.App.5th at p. 1052 (citing *Becerra v. Superior Ct.* (2020) 44 Cal.App.5th 897, 917 and *Weiss v. City of Del Mar* (2019) 39 Cal.App.5th 609, 618 (internal citations and quotation marks omitted)); *see also In re Williamson, supra*, 43 Cal.2d 651; *People v. Murphy, supra*, 52 Cal.4th 81.

98 *See Agnew v. State Bd. of Equalization* (1999) 21 Cal.4th 310, 330; *accord Collandrez, supra*, 61 Cal.App.5th at p. 1052; *Office of Inspector General v. Superior Ct.* (2010) 189 Cal.App.4th 695, 708 (quoting *Arnett v. Dal Cielo* (1996) 14 Cal.4th 4, 22).

99 *Wasatch Property Management v. Degrate* (2005) 35 Cal.4th 1111, 1122 (a "statute should be interpreted to avoid an absurd result"); *Newark Unif. Sch. Dist. v. Superior Ct.* (2015) 245 Cal.App.4th 887, 899 (Courts "may reject a literal construction that is contrary to the legislative intent apparent in the statute or that would lead to absurd results.") (cleaned up) (quoting *Riverside County Sheriff's Department v. Stiglitz* (2014) 60 Cal.4th 624, 630).

GBI that officers are trained to use when evaluating various types of force and distinguishing deadly force from non-deadly force. Thus, namely, for purposes of determining whether police force incidents are disclosable under the 2019+ amendments to the CPRA, the weight of the authorities clearly supports the *narrow* definition of GBI: that only force that causes death or a life-threatening and potentially permanent, disabling injury is CPRA disclosable under the applicable exception.

In other words, when applying all of these statutory construction principles here, the proper definition of GBI for purposes of determining the disclosability of police force under the CPRA is more consistent with the Government Code definition of SBI (which case law treats as interchangeable with GBI in the context of analyzing police use of force): namely, force that involves a substantial risk of death, unconsciousness, protracted and obvious disfigurement, or protracted loss or impairment of the function of a bodily member or organ is disclosable; while lesser force – such as non-deadly force that causes merely minor fractures, lacerations, punctures, contusions, abrasions or physical pain – is *not* disclosable.

However, it must be emphasized that, while the canons of statutory construction support the narrow definition of GBI when it comes to CPRA disclosability of police force, **there is as yet no controlling authority on point**. One hopes that future case law will decide this debate favorably and with more clarity. [100]

In the meantime, while what specifically constitutes "great bodily injury" will likely be a <u>question of fact for a jury,</u>[101] it seems probable that, for CPRA purposes, GBI will be construed to refer to physical injuries that are likely to

100 *NOTE*: One trial court level case might serve as a bellwether. In *Howey v. City of Fresno*, Fresno Super. Ct. case no. 23CECG01468 (Nov. 1, 2023) (J. Whalen), during the subject incident, the suspect had been TASERed in both drive-stun/contact mode and dart/probe mode: resulting in 11 TASER puncture wounds and 4 TASER abrasions to the groin – one of which had slight charring. However, the undisputed cause of the suspect's death was cocaine-related toxicity, *not* the TASERing. In denying a writ petition to compel CPRA disclosure of associated police investigatory records, the *Howey* Court held that since TASERs typically only leave superficial skin marks and cause only temporary pain, since they were meant to prevent more serious injuries (such as from other force options), and since – absent a fall from a great height – no case had found TASERs to cause significant/substantial injury, as opposed to a moderate harm or trivial/insignificant injury, standard TASER related injuries were *not* GBI under the CPRA: and associated police records were thus *not* disclosable public records. *Id.*

101 *See Escobar*, *supra*, 3 Cal.4th at pp. 745-750.

lead to death or that could result in death or permanent and substantial physical impairment akin to death.[102]

a. The Debate Over "Resulted In": Causation Versus Sequence, Where Causation May Be An Issue.

One of the unintended complications of the poor draftsmanship of the 2019 and 2022 statutes is its use of unusual and/or vague phrases, without any corresponding definition in the statutes or case law, that lead to bizarre or absurd results.

Under the 2019 and 2022 statutes, one of the categories of disclosable incidents includes uses of force that "resulted in" a death or GBI.[103] But the phrase "resulted in" remains undefined. However, the definition of "resulted in" is important: because it determines whether or not an incident's otherwise-exempt public records fall under the 2019/2022 exception to become disclosable – for if there was a use of force that did *not* "result in" a death or GBI, such records would remain exempt from disclosure.

Broad Construction – Resulted In = Sequential Event. Under the broad construction, "resulted in" has no relationship to causation; and it is thus merely fungible with "followed by." Under such a broad construction, where death or GBI followed the use of force, the records at issue would fall under the aforementioned exception.

While the broad construction has simplicity and the policy goals of the CPRA to support its interpretation, without some causation tied to the meaning of "resulted in," the broad construction arguably founders immediately due to the problem of line-drawing. Specifically, if proximate causation is not read into the phrase "resulted in," then *all* uses of force would become CPRA-disclosable. This is because, unless force is applied to someone who is immortal, removing causation from the equation, all uses of force are eventually followed by the death of the subject – whether that occurs days, months, years, or decades later.

---

102 *See generally Escobar*, *supra*, 3 Cal.4th at pp. 745-750; *see also People v. Cross* (2008) 45 Cal.4th 58, 63-64; Cal. Gov. Code § 12525.2(d); Cal. Penal Code § 243(f)(4).

103 *See, e.g.*, Cal. Penal Code § 832.7(b)(1)(A)(ii) (amend. 2019 & 2022); Cal. Gov. Code § 7923.625(e)(2) (formerly Cal. Gov. Code § 6254(f)(4)(C)(ii).

Similarly, while some might be tempted to argue that "but for" causation can be read into the phrase "resulted in," such a broad causation argument is functionally indistinguishable from the absence of any temporal or logical restrictions that transform "resulted in" into "followed by." For example, under "but for" causation analysis, but for the fact that a person's mother gave birth to the person, and but for the fact that all people breathe, that person would never have existed so as to inhale the toxic fumes expelled by a polluting factory; and, thus, under "but for" causation analysis, a "but for" (or "actual") cause of that person's pollution-related health problems must include his mother's birthing decision.

Without the temporal and logical limitations imposed by proximate causation analysis, the broad construction of "resulted in" thus transforms that phrase into a term that violates the canons of statutory construction. As noted above in the GBI debate section, statutory construction steers us away from interpretations that are: (a) unsupported by legislative history/intent; (b) contradicted by other provisions of the statute in question; and/or (c) lead to absurd results. The broad construction of "resulted in" accomplishes all three of these abhorrent outcomes.

First, as noted in the GBI debate section above, the legislative history of SB 1421 and AB 748 reveals that while broader versions of the bill that would have made all use of force incidents CPRA-disclosable were considered, they were rejected by the Legislature. Second, if the true legislative intent was to make all uses of force CPRA-discoverable (which it was not), then it would be illogical to include specified categories of incident which, alone, would escape the law enforcement investigations exemption from disclosure; and it is contrary to statutory construction to view the statutes' inclusions of specified, limited categories of discoverable police force incidents as a green light to the disclosure of all police force incidents because such would cause this broad version of "resulted in" to contradict the narrow, specified categories, as well as the other provisions that tell us that the 2019 and 2022 statutes were meant to create narrow exceptions to the otherwise-broad police investigatory records exemption. Third, the broad construction leads to absurd results: because it would force an agency to produce records pertaining to a use of force where death or GBI followed the use of force, perhaps even decades later, but had no real role in that death or GBI.[104]

---

104 *Wasatch Property Mgmt., supra,* 35 Cal.4th at p. 1122; *Newark Unif. Sch. Dist., supra,* 245 Cal.App.4th at p. 899.

As such, while there is as yet no known controlling authority on the issue, the broad construction of "resulted in" seems unlikely to be the legally correct version.

Narrow Construction – Resulted In = Proximately Caused. Under the narrow construction of "resulted in" a death or GBI, public records of officers' uses of force would only fall under the SB 1421/AB 748 (and SB 16) exceptions to the law enforcement investigatory records exemption where the custodial government agency's investigation determined that the officer's use of force was the proximate cause of the subject's death or GBI.

For the same reasons that the broad construction is contrary to the doctrine of statutory construction, the narrow construction is *consistent* with statutory construction canon. Specifically, the temporal and logistical restrictions that come with proximate causation analysis mean that the apparent intent of the 2019 and 2022 statutes is better served: to make CPRA-disclosable only those police records pertaining to the statute-specified incidents of interest – here, including uses of force that proximately cause a death or GBI; rather than all uses of force.

However, while the narrow construction has the obvious favorable factor of restricting or limiting the amount of records that agencies would need to disclose-produce under the CPRA, the narrow construction of "resulting in" comes with two significant drawbacks. First, the narrow construction means that agencies in receipt of CPRA requests tied to in-custody deaths are likely going to need to wait until their cause-of-death investigations are completed before they can determine whether requested records fall into the applicable exception and must be disclosed-produced: because determining if the police use of force proximately caused the death or GBI is key to determining an agency's CPRA disclosure duties.[105] Second, until courts provide us with

---

105 PRACTICE TIP (**The Related Disconnect Between Some Forensic Pathologists' Definition Of "Homicide" And The Common Understanding**). Particularly for incidents where a drug-intoxicated person is restrained and then dies, ostensibly from the drug overdose, there are often issues of disputed causation of death, particularly in associated civil lawsuits against the police.

However, a problem arises from a difference in terminology: and that difference is increasingly affecting CPRA disclosure decision-making. The common understanding of the term "homicide" is a reference to murder: intentionally and unlawfully causing the death of someone. *See, e.g.*, Cal. Penal Code § 187. By contrast, in forensic pathology (the medical science associated with autopsies and cause of death determinations), there are five "manners of death" that are used to broadly classify certain causes of death. One of those forensic pathology manners of death is "homicide": which

controlling case law on point, agencies are likely to be confronted with CPRA litigation for applying the narrow construction: litigation which could help or hurt all government agencies.

Thus, while the narrow construction of "resulted in" is likely the better-reasoned and more legally correct construction, agencies should consult with legal counsel before deciding which interpretive path to follow on this issue.

10. *Key Detail: When Must CPRA-Discoverable Officer Personnel File Records, or Critical Incident Recordings, Be Produced In Full, And When/How May They Be WITHHELD Or REDACTED?*

The most specific, and complicated, aspect of the 2019-amended statutes is that they set very detailed deadlines, and conditional extensions of deadlines, for different types of records and recordings based on a variety of circumstances;

---

that profession specifically and specially defines as "death at the hands of another." *See, e.g.*, "Guide for Manner of Death Classification," Nat'l Ass'n of Med. Examiners, 1st ed., Feb. 2002 (https://name.memberclicks.net/assets/docs/MANNEROFDEATH.pdf).

However, in part because some forensic pathologists apply "but for" causation analysis when determining manner of death, in many cases, even where the medical examiner has concluded that a person's death was proximately caused exclusively by the drugs and/or that deceased person's actions, if other persons (such as police officers) were present and/or making physical contact with that person at the time, even though the "main line" or "top" or proximate cause of death had nothing to do with other persons'/officers' actions, forensic pathologists belonging to the school of thought that embraces a broader construction of the "homicide" manner of death will classify such an in-custody drug overdose as a "homicide"; even though the medical examiner agrees that officer action did *not* proximately cause the death.

By contrast, other forensic pathologists believe that, unless the actions of someone else proximately caused the death, such a death should be classified as the manner of death "accident."

The broad construction by some pathologists/medical examiners of the homicide manner of death thus creates a CPRA disclosure issue for some agencies. This is because the autopsy report and associated cause of death investigation might decide that officer action did not proximately cause the subject's death, but the manner of death might still be classified as a homicide, possibly including as "other significant conditions" or "contributing factors" things like law enforcement arrest or restraint action. In such an event, a police agency embracing the narrow construction of "resulted in" will likely be pressed to defend why its broader construction of "homicide" manner of death should not be evidence that, contrary to the agency's withholding decision, the agency "knows" that the officer use of force "caused" or "resulted in" the death at issue, and thus improperly withheld requested records.

In sum, agencies are likely to find that the debate over the proper definition of the term "resulted in" may, at some point, intersect with a debate within the forensic pathology field as to whether "homicide" manners of death should be attached to in-custody deaths where officer action is *not* found to be the proximate cause of death.

and they also set specific limits on when and what may be withheld or redacted from such records/recordings if CPRA-discoverable.

Significantly, the rules are somewhat different for records of complaints/investigations than they are for incident audio/video recordings: not only in terms of the timing, but in terms of the availability/bases for withholding and/or redaction. Given their complexity, it would be prudent for every police agency to read the new statutes, verbatim, in their entirety. However, in essence, the revisions to the Penal Code and Government Code effectively render the now-public portions of officer personnel file records at least temporarily confidential again under very narrow circumstances where withholding or redaction is authorized under the new laws.

11. *Key Detail: The Debate Over Whether SB 1421, Or AB 748, Applies To Recordings. (IS IT A "RECORD" OR A "RECORDING"?)*

There is unlikely to be any significant debate among legal scholars that, as to SB 1421 [codified into amended versions of Penal Code sections 832.7 and 832.8] and AB 748 [codified into an amended version of Government Code section 6254(f)(4) and then recodified in Government Code sections 7923.600-7923.625], the 2019 amendments are unartfully and ambiguously drafted: containing complications and conflicts with existing law that were unnecessary to achieve their legislative objectives.

Significantly, the two bills adopted by the California Legislature appear to conflict, depending on how one construes their respective provisions. Specifically, if as its language asserts, SB 1421 was held to also apply to critical incident recordings, rather than just records and administrative recordings, like personnel appraisal/officer disciplinary interviews, because SB 1421 and AB 748 have completely different requirements for when, why, and for how long materials under their respective jurisdictions can be withheld or redacted (as explained more fully below regarding the different rules and deadlines for "records" versus "recordings"), these two related laws would fatally conflict.

To elaborate, on its face, SB 1421's provisions appear to apply to *all* otherwise-protected personnel file records in *all* mediums: however, because of ambiguous draftsmanship, some subsections thereof do not clearly limit their provisions to *personnel* file records/recordings.[106] Thus, an overly-broad literal reading of SB 1421 could construe its provisions to extend to *critical incident recordings* as well as administrative investigation files and recordings: thereby setting up the fatal conflict with AB 748 — whose language is narrowly drawn to apply *only* to critical incident recordings.[107]

The simplest resolution to this potential conflict between SB 1421 and AB 748 can be found in distinguishing *critical incident* recordings and comparable police investigative records from *administrative* investigation audio/video recordings and other such personnel file records.

To elaborate, regarding administrative investigations of certain officer uses of force, while it is common among police agencies to include critical incident recordings in the administrative investigation file, and thus in the officer personnel file — and thereby attempt to raise the *inference* that such critical incident videos fall under the officer personnel file protections of the *Pitchess* privilege — this practice does *not* transform critical incident videos into *Pitchess*-protected matter: and thus such videos would *not* fall under SB 1421.

To elaborate, the case law holds that recordings that were *not* created *during* the administrative investigation against the subject officer, but were instead created *before* such investigation (and thus are *not* for purposes related to the advancement, appraisal, or discipline of an officer), such pre-administrative investigation recordings are not *Pitchess*-protected officer personnel file records, *even when placed into the officer's personnel file.*[108]

This precept is important to understanding whether SB 1421 or AB 748 applies to the recording in question. By its language, SB 1421 appears *primarily* concerned with securing conditional and limited access to officer *personnel file* records: even though *some* of its language also seems to extend to selected police investigatory records pertaining to its specified categories of police misconduct. To the extent that SB 1421 governs limited, non-*Pitchess* access *only* to officer personnel file records, since critical incident videos are *not* officer personnel

106 *See* Cal. Penal Code § 832.7(b)(3) (amend. 2022; including subjecting "all…photographic, audio, and video evidence" to its jurisdiction).

107 *Compare* Cal. Penal Code § 832.7(b)(3) (amend. 2019 & 2022) *with* Cal. Gov. Code §§ 7923.600-7923.625 (formerly Gov. Code § 6254(f)). Notably, SB 16, which housed the 2022 revisions, did *not* cure the defects at issue.

108 *City of Eureka v. Superior Ct.* (2016) 1 Cal.App.5th 755, 763-764.

file records, arguably, SB 1421's provisions would *not* apply to critical incident recordings: *only* the provisions of AB 748 would apply to such recordings.

This interpretation — that SB 1421 applies *primarily* to personnel file "records" (which would include interview-type recordings, unless the recordings were specified in the statute but were *not* critical incident recordings), and *not* to critical incident recordings covered by AB 748 — may also be supported under the doctrine of statutory construction.

Under the **doctrine of statutory construction**, where a specific reference in one statute and a vaguer reference in another statute would cause the two statutes to be materially contradictory, case law will construe the terms of the more-specific statute to control over the conflicting terms of the vaguer statute.[109]

Thus, because AB 748 specifically applies to *critical incident recordings*, the vaguer references of SB 1421 to "recordings" must be deemed to be subordinate to the more specific references of AB 748: as a result, under statutory construction doctrine, AB 748's provisions would be deemed to control as to critical incident recordings, while SB 1421 would be deemed to control as to every other type of record or recording listed therein. Therefore, under statutory construction, even though SB 1421's definition of "records" seems to extend to non-administrative critical incident recordings, because SB 1421's definition is vaguer and broader than AB 748's definition of "recordings" thereunder, the terms of the narrower statute — AB 748 — would control over the recordings subject to its jurisdiction where those terms conflict with SB 1421: as they do in many of the statute's withholding and redaction rules.

While the complexities of the conflict between SB 1421 and AB 748 may seem baffling at first, for *records* of complaints/investigations into critical incidents and sustained specified officer misconduct (as detailed above), and for *recordings* of critical incidents, the new conditional rules for limited

---

109 *See* Cal. Code Civ. Proc. § 1859; *In re Williamson, supra*, 43 Cal.2d at p. 654 ("It is the general rule [of statutory construction] that where the general statute standing alone would include the same matter [conduct] as the special [specific] act, and thus conflict with it, the special act will be considered as an exception to the general statute whether it was passed before or after such general enactment."); *accord Murphy, supra*, 52 Cal.4th at p. 86; *Morton, supra*, 417 U.S. at p. 550 ("where there is no clear intention otherwise, a specific statute will not be controlled or nullified by a general one regardless of the priority of enactment"); *Townsend, supra*, 109 U.S. at p. 512.

withholding or redaction can thus be summarized and harmonized as explained below.[110] (For purposes of clarity herein, we refer to SB 1421 records and recordings as merely "records"; while we refer to AB 748 critical incident recordings as merely "recordings" — so as to avoid undue confusion.)

a. Resolving The Confusing Status Of Non-Administrative Interview Recordings.

As noted above, among the many needless complications arising from the unartful draftsmanship of SB 1421, and its failure to meaningfully consider how law enforcement investigations — both criminal and administrative — actually work, the language of the 2019 statutory revisions creates an ambiguity as to the status of witness/officer interviews that were created solely for the criminal investigation related to a critical incident.

On the one hand, as briefly noted above, witness interviews that were *not* conducted, and associated recordings that were *not* created for, the administrative investigation of an incident, but were, instead, created for the criminal investigation (i.e., before the administrative investigation) are *not* officer personnel file records, even if they are added to the officer's personnel file.[111] Nor are such witness interviews recordings of a critical incident event itself.

So the question remains: are they "records" under SB 1421 or "recordings" under AB 748 or neither?

If non-administrative witness interviews were neither personnel file records subject to SB 1421 nor critical incident recordings subject to AB 748, one would be tempted to say that they thus retain their full CPRA Section 6254(f) exemption from public records disclosure.

However, AB 748 defines a "critical incident video" as "a video or audio recording that *relates* to a critical incident.[112] Thus, since a recorded witness

110 For purposes of clarity in this book, when referring to "records" that are potentially discoverable under SB 1421, the term "records" must be construed to include recordings that are made as part of the officer performance appraisal process, such as administrative interview audio/video recordings. By contrast, where in this book we refer to "recordings" in the context of the new CPRA exception to *Pitchess*, we mean to reference critical incident video recordings only.

111 *City of Eureka, supra*, 1 Cal.App.5th at pp. 763-764.

112 *See* Cal. Gov. Code § 7923.625 (formerly Gov. Code § 6254(f)(4)(A)(i); emphasis added).

interview about a critical incident certainly "relates" to that incident, **witness/officer interviews from the criminal investigation of a critical incident likely fall under AB 748's jurisdiction.**

Notwithstanding the foregoing, the pertinent language of SB 1421 defines a "record[]" subject to its provisions as "all...audio, and video evidence; transcripts or recordings of interviews [and] all materials...presented for review to... any person or body charged with determining whether to file criminal charges against an officer in connection with any incident, or whether the officer's action was consistent with law and agency policy for purposes of discipline or administrative action...."[113] Thus, at first blush, a recorded witness interview about any incident subject to the CPRA-disclosable categories (OIS, UOF causing death, etc.) would also seem to fall under SB 1421's and SB 16's jurisdiction, <u>even if that recording was *not* made as part of an officer administrative review and even if that recording would *not* otherwise be deemed an officer personnel file record</u>.[114]

Because AB 748 and SB 1421/SB 16 thus both lay claim to such recordings, their conflicting language raises a problem: which deadlines for withholding and redaction control?

Again, at present, we can only turn to the doctrine of statutory construction for an answer. By its terms, AB 748 *only* applies to "critical incident recordings"; and AB 748 defines a "critical incident" to be *only* the first two of the eight categories of incident that are also disclosable under SB 1421 and SB 16: namely, officer-involved shootings ("OIS") and officer uses of force ("UOF") resulting in death or great bodily injury ("GBI").[115]

---

113 *See* Cal. Penal Code § 832.7(b)(3) (amend. 2022) (a disclosable "record[]" is "all investigative reports; photographic, audio, and video evidence; transcripts or recordings of interviews; autopsy reports; all materials compiled and presented for review to the district attorney or to any person or body charged with determining whether to file criminal charges against an officer in connection with an incident, or whether the officer's action was consistent with law and agency policy for purposes of discipline or administrative action, or what discipline to impose or corrective action to take; documents setting forth findings or recommended findings; and copies of disciplinary records relating to the incident, including any letters of intent to impose discipline, any documents reflecting modifications of discipline due to the Skelly or grievance process, and letters indicating final imposition of discipline or other documentation reflecting implementation of corrective action" — including such records where the officer resigned before the investigating agency completed its investigation).

114 *Compare* Cal. Penal Code § 832.7(b)(3) (amend. 2022) *with City of Eureka, supra*, 1 Cal.App.5th at pp. 763-764.

115 *Compare* Cal. Gov. Code § 7923.625(e)(1)-(2) (formerly Cal. Gov. Code § 6254(f)(4)(C)(i)-(ii)) *with* Cal. Penal Code § 832.7(b)(1)(A)-(E) (amend. 2022).

Thus, under the doctrine of statutory construction, **critical incident recordings — likely including non-administrative witness/officer interviews — would be subject to AB 748's jurisdictional system**: because such statute is more specific/narrower than SB 1421/SB 16.[116] However, ***other* disclosable recordings — e.g., non-administrative witness/officer interviews pertaining to sustained officer sex assaults on members of the public and sustained officer dishonesty in law enforcement, etc. — would be subject to SB 1421/SB 16's jurisdictional system.**[117]

By contrast, if an administrative interview recording did *not* pertain to one of the SB 1421/SB 16 disclosable categories of incidents, it would likely remain subject to the full *Pitchess* privilege. Likewise, if a non-administrative (*e.g.*, purely criminal investigative) witness/officer interview recording did *not* pertain to one of the SB 1421/SB 16 disclosable categories of incidents, it would likely remain subject to the full investigative records protection of the CPRA Section 6254(f) exemption.

In other words, for purposes of determining whether a recording is a "record" under SB 1421's/SB 16's jurisdiction or a "recording" under AB 748's jurisdiction, the deciding factor is likely to be: does the recording "relate" to a critical incident? If so, the recording is likely an AB 748 "recording"; if not, and if the recording pertains to one of the categories described above, then the recording is likely an SB 1421/SB 16 "record" — even if such recording is not otherwise an officer personnel file record.

12. *Key Detail: RECORDS — CPRA-Discoverable Complaints/ Investigations: Withholding & Redactions Available.*

In light of the foregoing, for clarity below, this book uses the term "records" to refer to records and recordings that are subject to SB 1421/SB 16 disclosure; whereas this book uses the term "recordings" to refer to critical incident recordings that are subject to AB 748 disclosure.

---

116 *Id.*; Cal. Code Civ. Proc. § 1859; *In re Williamson, supra*, 43 Cal.2d at p. 654 ("It is the general rule [of statutory construction] that where the general statute standing alone would include the same matter [conduct] as the special [specific] act, and thus conflict with it, the special act will be considered as an exception to the general statute whether it was passed before or after such general enactment."); *accord Murphy, supra*, 52 Cal.4th at p. 86; *Morton, supra*, 417 U.S. at p. 550 ("where there is no clear intention otherwise, a specific statute will not be controlled or nullified by a general one regardless of the priority of enactment"); *Townsend, supra*, 109 U.S. at p. 512.

117 *See id.*

Under the 2019 laws (revised again in 2022), although officer personnel file records of complaints/investigations of OIS v. person events, UOF v. person events where death or great bodily injury results, and sustained investigations of specified officer misconduct are now no longer presumed confidential — and are, instead, CPRA-discoverable and thus presumed to be matters of public record — there are several limited and conditional circumstances where such records may still be temporarily or (in narrow cases) indefinitely withheld, or produced with specified redactions.[118]

The withholding and redaction provisions of the 2019 and 2022 statutes are thus explained below.

WITHHOLDING Available: CPRA-Discoverable RECORDS.

- **During A Criminal Investigation Related To The UOF Incident — *Where The Interest In Withholding Clearly Outweighs The Public Interest In Disclosure*:** CPRA-discoverable officer personnel file records **may be withheld** from the CPRA-requestor for **up to 60 days** from the UOF incident date (or until the prosecutor decides whether or not to file criminal charges for the officer's UOF, whichever is *sooner*), **but only if** (a) the custodial police agency **explains in writing** to the requestor **its specific basis** — based upon specific, articulable, particularized facts — for believing the interest in withholding the records clearly outweighs the public interest in disclosure in that specific case; **and** (b) that writing includes an **estimated date for production** when the withholding interest is expected to be resolved and the requested records can be produced to the requestor.[119]

- **During A Criminal Investigation Related To The UOF Incident — *Where The Disclosure Would Interfere With That Investigation*:** CPRA-discoverable officer personnel file records **may be withheld** from the CPRA-requestor for **more than 60 days** from the UOF incident date (**but no more than 18 months**, or when the criminal investigation or associated criminal proceeding is no longer active, whichever is *sooner*), **but only if**

118 PRACTICE TIP: It is important to remember that portions of the officer's personnel file records which are not CPRA-discoverable remain presumed confidential: typically discoverable only under the traditional *Pitchess* procedure.

119 Cal. Penal Code § 832.7(b)(8)(A)(i) (amend. 2022); *see also* Cal. Gov. § 6254(f) (amend. 2019). Notably, this is *not* a basis for withholding a critical incident recording. *See* Cal. Gov. § 6254(f) (amend. 2019).

(a) *every 180 days*, the custodial police agency **explains in writing** to the requestor **its specific basis** — based upon specific, articulable, particularized facts — for believing the disclosure would interfere with that investigation, including but not limited to endangering the safety of a witness or confidential source, in that specific case; **and** (b) that writing includes an **estimated date for production** when the withholding interest is expected to be resolved and the requested records can be produced to the requestor.[120]

- **During A Criminal Investigation Related To The UOF Incident** — ***Where Clear And Convincing Evidence Shows The Disclosure Would Interfere With That Investigation (And The UOF Officer Is Not A Subject Of The Investigation)***: CPRA-discoverable officer personnel file records **may be withheld** from the CPRA-requestor for **more than 18 months** from the UOF incident date (or until the criminal investigation or associated criminal proceeding is no longer active), **but only if** (a) *every 180 days*, the custodial police agency **explains in writing** to the requestor **its specific basis** — based upon specific, articulable, particularized facts — for believing the disclosure would prejudice that ongoing criminal investigation, including but not limited to endangering the safety of a witness or confidential source in that specific case, in a manner that clearly outweighs the public interest in disclosure; (b) that basis is supported by **clear and convincing evidence**; **and** (c) that writing includes an **estimated date for production** when the withholding interest is expected to be resolved and the requested records can be produced to the requestor.[121]

- **After Criminal Charges Related To The UOF Incident Are *Filed* Against Any Person**: CPRA-discoverable officer personnel file records **may be withheld** from the CPRA-requestor if criminal charges have been filed against any person and those charges arise from the same incident where the UOF occurred: and, in that case, the records may be withheld **until there is a verdict or a guilty/no-contest plea** is entered and the time for withdrawing that plea has expired.[122] Unlike other withholding provisions that are tied to the criminal investigation being one where the UOF officer is a subject, this withholding provision is worded to apply to criminal charges against *any* person, as long as they arise from the UOF incident. Additionally,

120 Cal. Penal Code § 832.7(b)(8)(A)(ii) (amend. 2022).

121 Cal. Penal Code § 832.7(b)(8)(A)(ii) (amend. 2022).

122 Cal. Penal Code § 832.7(b)(8)(B) (amend. 2022).

unlike the other withholding provisions, there is no written-explanation requirement or periodic reporting requirement for this option.[123]

- **<u>During An Administrative Investigation Related To The UOF Incident</u>**: CPRA-discoverable officer personnel file records **may be withheld** from the CPRA-requestor for **<u>up to 180 days</u>** from the UOF incident date (or up to 30 days after any criminal investigation related to the UOF incident has closed, whichever is *later* — not sooner) during the pendency of an administrative investigation by the agency into the UOF incident (*e.g.*, where UOF officers are the subjects of the investigation).[124] Notably, unlike the other withholding provisions, there is no written-explanation requirement or periodic reporting requirement this this option.[125]

- **<u>When An Investigation Reveals A Civilian Complaint To Be Unfounded Or Frivolous</u>**: CPRA-discoverable officer personnel file records **may be withheld** from the CPRA-requestor indefinitely where the agency's investigation revealed the complaint to be unfounded (see above definition) or "frivolous" as defined by California Code of Civil Procedure section 128.5.[126] California law defines a "frivolous" complaint as "totally and completely without merit or for the sole purpose of harassing an opposing party."[127]

    - ► **<u>Practical Implications</u>**. Significantly, the unfounded/frivolous complaint withholding option is not at all limited by subject matter. This means that, arguably, even for a fatal OIS of a person, where a civilian submitted a complaint to the agency about that OIS, if the agency determined the complaint to be unfounded or frivolous, the agency would be excused from CPRA-disclosure of the associated officer personnel file investigative records: and such would remain *Pitchess* confidential. By contrast, this provision also means that where *no* civilian complaint was submitted about the OIS or UOF, this indefinite withholding provision would *not* apply.

---

123 *See id.* PRACTICE NOTE: However, as a best practice, the agency should consider at least issuing some kind of writing to the requestor advising of the pending criminal case after charges have been filed.

124 Cal. Penal Code § 832.7(b)(8)(C) (amend. 2022).

125 *See id.* PRACTICE NOTE: However, as a best practice, the agency should consider at least issuing some kind of writing to the requestor advising of the pending administrative investigation.

126 Cal. Penal Code § 832.7(b)(9) (amend. 2022).

127 Cal. Code Civ. Proc. § 128.5(b)(2).

- **Litigation & Civilian Complaints Withholding & Practical Implications**. It is important to note that the 2019 statutory revisions do *not* alter the exemption from CPRA-disclosure for police records pertaining to a pending litigation where the custodial agency is a party.[128] In other words, particularly when the Government Code exemption is read in conjunction with this Penal Code exemption, records pertaining to a **pending litigation** — arguably including the otherwise-public officer personnel file records that constitute CPRA-discoverable records (as specified above) — remain *Pitchess* confidential.[129] Thus, another way to think about this exemption from CPRA-discoverability is that **once someone submits a tort claim** to the agency about the UOF incident **or files a lawsuit** about such against the agency, the CPRA-discoverability of the associated officer personnel file records essentially becomes void: and **the records regain their *Pitchess* confidentiality protections.**[130]

REDACTION Available: CPRA-Discoverable RECORDS.

- **Officer & Third-Party Privacy**: Regardless of whether CPRA-discoverable officer personnel file records may or may not be withheld altogether, when produced to a CPRA requestor, portions of those records **may be redacted** to protect the following categories of private information: (1) **Personal Data** — such as an officer's or other person's home address, phone numbers, and/or the identities of his or her family members — but the "names and work-related information of peace and custodial officers" may *not* be redacted[131]; (2) **Complainant, Victim, Whistleblower & Witness Identifying Information** — information that would otherwise breach the anonymity of whistleblowers, complainants, victims, or witnesses, so as

128 Cal. Gov. Code § 7927.200(a) (formerly Cal. Gov. Code § 6254(b)).

129 *Compare* Cal. Gov. Code § 7927.200(a) (formerly Cal. Gov. Code § 6254(b)) ("[T]his division does not require the disclosure of…[r]ecords pertaining to pending litigation to which the public agency is a party,…[or] to a claim made pursuant to [the Tort Claims Act] (commencing with Section 810), until the pending [litigation or] claim has been finally adjudicated or otherwise settled.") *with* Cal. Penal Code § 832.7(b)(9) (amend. 2022) ("A record of a civilian complaint, or the investigations, findings, or dispositions of that complaint, shall not be released pursuant to this section if the complaint is frivolous, as defined in Section 128.5 of the Code of Civil Procedure, or if the complaint is unfounded.").

130 PRACTICE NOTE: Agencies should be mindful of this limited exemption. Clever requestors can be expected to pursue CPRA-discovery of the discoverable officer personnel file records before filing a suit or submitting a complaint: when only the more limited options for withholding apply.

131 Cal. Penal Code § 832.7(b)(6)(A) (amend. 2022).

"to preserve the[ir] anonymity"[132]; (3) **Confidential Medical, Financial, or Federally-Protected Information** — *e.g.*, information the disclosure of which is "prohibited by federal law"[133]; *and* (4) **Privacy Balancing Catch-All** — redactions are also permitted where disclosure "would cause an unwarranted invasion of personal privacy that clearly outweighs the strong public interest in records about possible misconduct" by officers.[134]

<u>Limits of Privacy – Officer Names May Not Be Redacted</u>: Even before the SB 1421 revolution began in 2019, case law held that the names of officers who used deadly force were disclosable under the CPRA.[135]

However, some of the provisions of SB 1421 and its sibling statutes caused some analysts to believe that while the names of *involved* officers (*e.g.*, officers who used force) were CPRA-disclosable, the names of *uninvolved/witness* officers (*e.g.*, officers who were just bystanders to the use of force and/or merely witnessed the alleged misconduct) could be withheld/redacted on privacy grounds.

Unfortunately, recent case law suggests that this is *not* the case: rather, **such case law has held that even the names of bystander/witness officers *are* CPRA-disclosable**, and may *not* be redacted, where the police records fall into an otherwise disclosable exception.[136] While such authority is not yet dispositive, as it has not yet been tested before the California Supreme Court, it is at least strongly persuasive and will likely have controlling effects.

- **<u>Physical Safety & Public Interest</u>**: Regardless of whether CPRA-discoverable officer personnel file records may or may not be withheld

---

132 Cal. Penal Code § 832.7(b)(6)(B) (amend. 2022). NOTE: The term "witnesses" arguably extends to protect the anonymity of non-subject officers. However, the 2022 revision stating that the names and work-related information and names of officers may not be redacted may cancel what many believed was a privacy protection for non-subject "witness" officers.

133 Cal. Penal Code § 832.7(b)(6)(C) (amend. 2022).

134 Cal. Penal Code § 832.7(b)(6)(C) (amend. 2022).

135 *See, e.g., Long Beach Police Officers Assn v. City of Long Beach* (2014) 59 Cal.4th 58, 73 (which held that the names of officers involved in a shooting use of force could *not* be withheld from CPRA disclosure).

136 *See, e.g., BondGraham v. Superior Ct.* (2023) 95 Cal.App.5th 1006, 1019-1020 (rejecting the trial court's conclusion that uninvolved, witness officers did not lose their right to privacy merely by witnessing a CPRA-disclosable event, the *BondGraham* Court ruled that the names of witness officers are also CPRA-disclosable and, thus, may *not* be redacted).

altogether, when produced to a CPRA requestor, portions of those records **may be redacted**: (1) **Physical Safety** — where a specific, articulable, particularized reason exists to believe that disclosure of the information in a record would pose a significant danger to the physical safety of an officer or other person, the information at issue may be redacted from a record produced under the CPRA; and (2) **Public Interest Catch-All** — where, in a particular case, the public interest in the redaction clearly outweighs the public interest in the disclosure, the information may be redacted.[137]

The Duty To Redact. As noted elsewhere, the preference of California law is that where exempt information is contained in a non-exempt, CPRA-disclosable record, and where that information can be reasonably segregated within that record, the custodial government agency has a duty to redact the exempt/privileged information, rather than to withhold the entire record. This is because "a public agency remains otherwise obligated to redact exempt information from a nonexempt record when the exempt and nonexempt materials are not 'inextricably intertwined' and are 'otherwise reasonably segregable.'"[138]

13. *Key Detail: RECORDINGS — CPRA-Discoverable Critical Incident Recordings: Withholding & Redactions Available.*

WITHHOLDING Available: Critical Incident RECORDINGS.

- **[*45 Days*] During A Criminal Or Administrative Investigation Related To The UOF Incident — *Where The Disclosure Would Interfere With That Investigation***: CPRA-discoverable critical incident audio and video recordings **may be withheld** from the CPRA-requestor for **up to 45 days** from the UOF incident date, **but only if** (a) the custodial police agency **explains in writing** to the requestor **its specific basis** — based upon specific, articulable, particularized facts — for believing the disclosure would substantially interfere with that investigation, including but not limited to endangering the safety of a witness or confidential source, in that specific case; **and** (b) that writing includes an **estimated date for production** when the withholding interest is expected to be resolved and the requested

137 Cal. Penal Code § 832.7(b)(7) (amend. 2022).

138 *See BondGraham*, *supra*, 95 Cal.App.5th at pp. 1017-1018 (citing *Becerra*, *supra*, 44 Cal.App.5th at p. 929; and holding that "assessments" of incidents that were CPRA disclosable are also disclosable, including related policy/training recommendations).

recording can be produced to the requestor.[139] Notably, this withholding exception for critical incident recordings applies regardless of whether the ongoing investigation at issue is a criminal investigation or an administrative investigation.[140]

- **[*Up To 1 Year*] During A Criminal Or Administrative Investigation Related To The UOF Incident — *Where The Disclosure Would Interfere With That Investigation (With Monthly Reporting)*:** CPRA-discoverable critical incident audio and video recordings **may be withheld** from the CPRA-requestor for **more than 45 days** from the UOF incident date (**but *only* until the criminal or administrative investigation at issue resolves/ends, or up to 1 year**, whichever is *sooner*), **but only if** (a) *every 30 days*, the custodial police agency **explains in writing** to the requestor **its specific basis** — based upon specific, articulable, particularized facts — for believing the disclosure would substantially interfere with that investigation, including but not limited to endangering the safety of a witness or confidential source, in that specific case; **and** (b) that writing includes an **estimated date for production** when the withholding interest is expected to be resolved and the requested recording can be produced to the requestor.[141] Notably, this withholding exception for critical incident recordings also applies regardless of whether the ongoing investigation at issue is a criminal investigation or an administrative investigation.[142]

- **[*More Than 1 Year*] During A Criminal Or Administrative Investigation Related To The UOF Incident — *Where The Disclosure Would Interfere With That Investigation (With Monthly Reporting and Clear and Convincing Evidence)*:** CPRA-discoverable critical incident audio and video recordings **may be withheld** from the CPRA-requestor for **more than 1 year** from the UOF incident date (but ***only* until the criminal or administrative investigation at issue resolves/ends**), **but only if** (a) *every 30 days*, the custodial police agency **explains in writing** to the requestor **its specific basis** — based upon specific, articulable, particularized facts — for believing the disclosure would substantially interfere with that investigation, including but not limited to endangering the safety of a witness or

139 Cal. Gov. Code § 7923.625(a)(1) (formerly Cal. Gov. Code § 6254(f)(4)(A)(i)).

140 *See id.*

141 Cal. Gov. Code § 7923.625(a)(2) (formerly Cal. Gov. Code § 6254(f)(4)(A)(ii)).

142 *See id.*

confidential source, in that specific case; (b) that basis is supported by **clear and convincing evidence; and** (c) that writing includes an **estimated date for production** when the withholding interest is expected to be resolved and the requested recording can be produced to the requestor.[143] Notably, this withholding exception for critical incident recordings also applies regardless of whether the ongoing investigation at issue is a criminal investigation or an administrative investigation.[144]

- **[*Indefinitely, Except To Subject-Requestor*] Where The Disclosure Would Violate A Recording-Subject's Privacy Interest In A Way That Cannot Be Cured By Redaction**: CPRA-discoverable critical incident audio and video recordings **may be withheld** from the CPRA-requestor **indefinitely if**: (1) the **reasonable expectation of privacy** of one of the subjects of the recording **cannot be adequately protected through redaction** — such as by blurring or obscuring technology; (2) from any CPRA-requestor *except* (a) where the requestor is the **subject** whose privacy is at issue, or (b) if the subject is a minor, the subject's requestor parents/legal guardians, or (c) if deceased, the subject's requestor "heir, beneficiary, designated immediate family member, or authorized legal representative"; **but only if** (3) the custodial police agency **explains in writing** to the requestor **its specific basis** — based upon specific, articulable, particularized facts — for believing that redaction cannot adequately protect the privacy of the subject at issue.[145] However, a catch-all provision applies, even when the subject is the CPRA-requestor: and **the catch-all permits the recording to be withheld, even from the subject-requestor, where disclosure would substantially interfere with the agency's criminal or administrative investigation.**[146] Under those circumstances, the 45-day, 46-day-to-1-year, and more-than-1-year withholding options and restrictions detailed above would apply, even to the subject-requestor.[147]

---

143 Cal. Gov. Code § 7923.625(a)(2) (formerly Cal. Gov. Code § 6254(f)(4)(A)(ii)).

144 *See id.*

145 Cal. Gov. Code § 7923.625(b)(2) (formerly Cal. Gov. Code § 6254(f)(4)(B)(ii)).

146 Cal. Gov. Code § 7923.625(b)(3) (formerly Cal. Gov. Code § 6254(f)(4)(B)(iii)).

147 *See id.* (referencing the withholding provisions of Cal. Gov. Code § 7923.625(a)(2) (formerly Cal. Gov. Code § 6254(f)(4)(A)(ii))). PRACTICE NOTE: The wording of the statutes strongly suggest that withholding recordings on this basis is disfavored and that redaction of recordings is the preferred course.

REDACTION Available: Critical Incident RECORDINGS.

- **Where The Disclosure Would Violate A Recording-Subject's Privacy Interest**: CPRA-discoverable critical incident audio and video recordings **may be redacted** to protect the **reasonable expectation of privacy of a subject** depicted in the recording, **but only if** (1) the custodial police agency **explains in writing** to the requestor **its specific basis** — based upon specific, articulable, particularized facts — for believing that the **subject's privacy interest clearly outweighs the public interest** in disclosure; (2) the **redaction** — such as by blurring or obscuring technology — **does not impair the viewer/listener from comprehending the incident events** depicted in the recording; **and** (3) aside from the permitted redaction, **no other alterations or edits to the recording are made.**[148] Notably, the language of the statute strongly suggests that privacy redactions of critical incident recordings are *preferred* over privacy-based withholding of such recordings.
    - ► It is also worth noting that, although physical safety redactions are not specifically authorized by the statutory revisions, they arguably remain available under the general withholding provisions of the Government Code.[149]

In an attempt to simplify the requirements and conditions, the 2019 laws for withholding and redaction of CPRA-discoverable records/recordings are summarized on the tables below.[150]

---

148 Cal. Gov. Code § 7923.625(b)(1) (formerly Cal. Gov. Code § 6254(f)(4)(B)(i)).

149 *Compare* Cal. Gov. Code § 7923.625(b)(1) (formerly Cal. Gov. Code § 6254(f)(4)(B)(i)) *with* Cal. Gov. Code § 7923.600(a) (formerly Cal. Gov. Code § 6254(f)): "[T]his division does not require disclosure of . . .any investigatory or security files compiled by any other state or local agency for correctional [or] law enforcement...purposes."), Cal. Gov. Code § 7923.515(a)(1) ("Notwithstanding any other provision of this article, a state or local law enforcement agency shall make public...information...except to the extent that disclosure of a particular item of information would endanger the safety of a person involved in an investigation or would endanger the successful completion of the investigation or a related investigation.") *and* Cal. Gov. Code § 7923.625(a)-(b)(2) (formerly Cal. Gov. Code § 6254(f)(4)(A)-(B)(ii); permitting withholding of critical incident audio/video recordings for witness safety and investigation-protection reasons).

150 PRACTICE NOTE: It is worth noting here that for police records/recordings that do *not* involve critical incidents, or for records that do *not* involve sustained officer sexual assault/dishonesty, several other CPRA exemptions from "disclosure" (production in response to a CPRA request) remain intact under the new laws. For example, the CPRA retains its general exemption from disclosure where disclosure would **endanger the safety of a person (civilian or officer) or endanger the successful completion of an investigation** related to the incident at issue. *See* Cal. Gov. Code § 7923.615(a)(1) (formerly Cal. Gov. § 6254(f) (the section before subsection (f)(1))).

14. *Table: Withholding Available Of CPRA-Discoverable Officer Personnel File Investigations Or Critical Incident Recordings – Requirements & Deadlines.*

a. WITHHOLDING C.P.R.A. Discoverable Records/ Recordings (Summary Chart).

Item	*Max. Time (Unless Basis Ends)*	*Standard of Proof for Basis*	*Writing Requirements*
Event: Privacy Concern - Only			
RECORDINGS – Critical Incidents	**45 Days**	Privacy of Subject Cannot Be Adequately Protected by Redaction	**Basis** for Withholding
Event: Criminal Investigation Ongoing			
RECORDS = Complaints-Investigations (CPRA-Discoverable)	**60 Days**	Withholding Interest **Clearly Outweighs** Public Interest	**Basis** for Withholding + **Estimate** On Production Date
RECORDS = Complaints-Investigations (CPRA-Discoverable)	**61 Days to 18 Months**	Disclosure Would **Substantially Interfere** With Investigation, Based on Specific-Articulable Facts	**Basis** for Withholding + **Estimate** On Production Date + **Regular (Every 180 Days) Updates** On Basis/Status

---

However, the CPRA also continues to mandate disclosure/production: (1) to a crime victim, or an insurer, the names/addresses and statements of involved persons and witnesses (except confidential informants, or where to do so would endanger such persons), all investigation diagrams, and the date, time, location, and description of the property involved in the incident; (2) to any person, including a victim (but excluding an arresting or criminal defendant), an arrestee's information (name, occupation, date of birth, physical description, time/date/factual circumstances of arrest and booking, bail amount, manner of release or location of incarceration, and all charges/warrants against the arrestee; (3) to any person, including a victim (but excluding an arresting or criminal defendant), basic police reports on criminal investigations and responses to calls for service; and (4) to journalists, government officials, and scholars, with the support of a sword declaration regarding the proper purpose of such request, the names and addresses of criminal arrestees or victims. *See* Cal. Gov. Code §§ 7923.600-7923.625 (formerly Cal. Gov. Code § 6254(f)).

It is also important to note that while Cal. Penal Code § 841.5 generally bars arrestees and criminal defendants from obtaining CPRA-discoverable records, Cal. Gov. Code § 7923.625 (formerly Gov. Code § 6254(f)) is specifically worded to *allow* criminal arrestees/defendants to have CPRA access to critical incident recordings.

Item	*Max. Time (Unless Basis Ends)*	*Standard of Proof for Basis*	*Writing Requirements*
RECORDS = Complaints-Investigations (CPRA-Discoverable)	**>18 Months**	Disclosure Would **Substantially Interfere** With Investigation, Based on Specific-Articulable Facts + **Clear & Convincing Evidence** Proof That Withholding Interest **Clearly Outweighs** Public Interest	**Basis** for Withholding + **Estimate** On Production Date + **Regular (Every 180 Days) Updates** On Basis/Status
RECORDINGS – Critical Incidents	**45 Days to 1 Year**	Disclosure Would **Substantially Interfere** With Investigation	**Basis** for Withholding + **Estimate** On Production Date + **Monthly (Every 30 Days) Updates** On Basis/Status
RECORDINGS – Critical Incidents	**>1 Year**	Disclosure Would **Substantially Interfere** With Investigation, Based on Specific-Articulable Facts + **Clear & Convincing Evidence** Proof That Withholding Interest **Clearly Outweighs** Public Interest	**Basis** for Withholding + **Estimate** On Production Date + **Monthly (Every 30 Days) Updates** On Basis/Status
Event: After Criminal Charges Filed Against *Any* Person re Incident			
RECORDS = Complaints-Investigations (CPRA-Discoverable)	Until A **Jury Verdict** – OR The Defendant(s) Enter A Non-Withdrawable **Guilty Plea** (Or No Contest Plea)	None	None

Item	***Max. Time (Unless Basis Ends)***	***Standard of Proof for Basis***	***Writing Requirements***
Event: Administrative Investigation Ongoing			
RECORDS = Complaints-Investigations (CPRA-Discoverable)	**180 Days OR 30 Days After Close Of Related Criminal Investigation** – Whichever is LATER	None	None
RECORDINGS – Critical Incidents	**45 Days to 1 Year**	Disclosure Would **Substantially Interfere** With Investigation	**Basis** for Withholding + **Estimate** On Production Date + **Monthly (Every 30 Days) Updates** On Basis/Status
RECORDINGS – Critical Incidents	**>1 Year**	Disclosure Would **Substantially Interfere** With Investigation, Based on Specific-Articulable Facts + **Clear & Convincing Evidence** Proof That Withholding Interest **Clearly Outweighs** Public Interest	**Basis** for Withholding + **Estimate** On Production Date + **Monthly (Every 30 Days) Updates** On Basis/Status
Event: Complaint Deemed Unfounded or Frivolous			
RECORDS = Complaints-Investigations (CPRA-Discoverable)	**Indefinitely**	None	None

b. Extended Withholding Chart.

Record Type	*Phase (When)*	*Timing Issues*	*Restrictions*
Reason-Basis: Withholding Interest Clearly Outweighs Public's Disclosure Interest			
Records: CPRA-Discoverable Investigations-Complaints	**During Ongoing Criminal Investigation**	For **Up To 60 Days** From the UOF Incident Date; – OR When The Prosecutor Decides Whether To File Criminal Charges Regarding The Officer's UOF; Whichever Is Sooner.	*Requirements*: • Writing-Basis: Agency Must Explain To The Requester **Why Interest In Delaying Disclosure Clearly Outweighs Public Interest In Disclosure.** • Estimate: Agency's Writing Must Provide An Estimated Date Of When It Will Produce The Withheld Records.[151]
Recordings: Critical Incident	**During Ongoing Criminal Investigation**	Not Applicable.	Withholding Not Available On This Basis.
Reason-Basis: Disclosure Would Interfere With The Incident Investigation			
Records: CPRA-Discoverable Investigations-Complaints	**During Ongoing Criminal Investigation**	For **More Than 60 Days** From the UOF Incident Date; – **BUT No More Than 18 Months** From the UOF Incident Date – OR When The Criminal Investigation Or Proceeding Is No Longer Active; Whichever Is Sooner.	*Requirements*: • Writing-Basis: *Every 180 Days*, Agency Must Explain To The Requester **How Disclosure Would Interfere With The Investigation, Such As By Endangering Witness Or Confidential Source Safety** › **Basis Must Rely Upon Specific, Articulable Facts.** • Estimate: Agency's Writing Must Provide An Estimated Date Of When It Will Produce The Withheld Records.[152]

151 Cal. Penal Code § 832.7(b)(8)(A)(i) (amend. 2022).

152 Cal. Penal Code § 832.7(b)(8)(A)(ii) (amend. 2022).

Record Type	*Phase (When)*	*Timing Issues*	*Restrictions*
Recordings: Critical Incident	**During Ongoing Criminal Or Admin. Investigation**	(1) For **Up To 45 Days** From the UOF Incident Date. OR (2) OR For **More Than 45 Days,** BUT **No More Than 1 Year.**	(1) *Requirements*: • Writing-Basis: Agency Must Explain To The Requester How Disclosure Would *Substantially* Interfere With The Investigation, Such As By Endangering Witness Or Confidential Source Safety ➤ Basis Must Rely Upon Specific, Articulable Facts. • Estimate: Agency's Writing Must Provide An Estimated Date Of When It Will Produce The Withheld Records.[153] (2) *Requirements*: • Writing-Basis: *Every 30 Days,* Agency Must Explain To The Requester How Disclosure Would *Substantially* Interfere With The Investigation, Such As By Endangering Witness Or Confidential Source Safety ➤ Basis Must Rely Upon Specific, Articulable Facts. • Estimate: Agency's Writing Must Provide An Estimated Date Of When It Will Produce The Withheld Records. • Resolution: Once The Basis For Withholding Resolves-Ends, The Recording Must Be Produced To The Requestor.[154]

153 Cal. Gov. Code § 7923.625(a)(1) (formerly Cal. Gov. Code § 6254(f)(4)(A)(i)).

154 Cal. Gov. Code § 7923.625(a)(2) (formerly Cal. Gov. Code § 6254(f)(4)(A)(ii)).

Record Type	*Phase (When)*	*Timing Issues*	*Restrictions*
Reason-Basis: Disclosure Would Interfere With The Incident Investigation – By *Clear & Convincing Evidence*			

Records: CPRA-Discoverable Investigations-Complaints	**During Ongoing Criminal Investigation**	For **More Than 18 Months** From The UOF Incident Date.	<u>*Requirements*</u>:
			• <u>Writing-Basis</u>: *Every 180 Days*, Agency Must Explain How Interest In Preventing Prejudice To The Ongoing Criminal Investigation Or Proceeding Clearly Outweighs Public Interest In Disclosure
			  ➤ Basis Must Rely Upon Specific, Articulable Facts.
			  ➤ Basis Must Be Shown By Clear & Convincing Evidence.
			• <u>Estimate</u>: Agency's Writing Must Provide An Estimated Date Of When It Will Produce The Withheld Records.
			• <u>Subject-Target:</u> The Subject Of The Criminal Investigation *Cannot* Be The Officer Who Used Force For This Extension Option To Be Available.[155]

155 Cal. Penal Code § 832.7(b)(8)(A)(ii) (amend. 2022).

Record Type	*Phase (When)*	*Timing Issues*	*Restrictions*
Recordings: Critical Incident	**During Ongoing Criminal Or Admin. Investigation**	For **More Than 1 Year** From The UOF Incident Date.	Requirements: • Writing-Basis: *Every 30 Days,* Agency Must Explain To The Requester How Disclosure Would *Substantially* Interfere With The Investigation, Such As By Endangering Witness Or Confidential Source Safety (and How Such Substantially Outweighs The Public Interest In Disclosure) › Basis Must Rely Upon Specific, Articulable Facts. › Basis Must Be Shown By Clear & Convincing Evidence. • Estimate: Agency's Writing Must Provide An Estimated Date Of When It Will Produce The Withheld Records. • Resolution: Once The Basis For Withholding Ends, The Recording Must Be Produced To Requestor.[156]

156 Cal. Gov. Code § 7923.625(a)(2) (formerly Cal. Gov. Code § 6254(f)(4)(A)(ii)).

Record Type	*Phase (When)*	*Timing Issues*	*Restrictions*
Reason-Basis: Criminal Charges Filed			
Records: CPRA-Discoverable Investigations-Complaints	**After Criminal Charges Related To UOF Incident Are Filed Against Any Person**	Until A **Jury Verdict** – OR The Defendant(s) Enter A **Non-Withdrawable Guilty Plea** (Or No Contest Plea).	*Requirements*: • Incident Related Criminal Charges Related To The Incident Must Be Filed. • NOTE: Unlike Other Provisions, The Withholding On This Basis Is Not Limited To Criminal Charges Against The UOF Officer.[157] • NOTE: This is not a specific basis for withholding critical incident recordings.
Reason-Basis: Admin. Investig. Ongoing			
Records: CPRA-Discoverable Investigations-Complaints	**During An Admin. Investigation Of The Incident**	For **Up To 180 Days** From the UOF Incident Date; – OR No More Than 30 Days After The Close Of Any Criminal Investigation Related To The UOF Incident – Whichever Is LATER.[158]	NOTE: The Withholding Rules For Critical Incident Recordings Apply Equally To Ongoing Criminal And Ongoing Administrative Investigations.[159]

157 Cal. Penal Code § 832.7(b)(8)(B) (amend. 2022).

158 Cal. Penal Code § 832.7(b)(8)(C) (amend. 2022).

159 Cal. Gov. Code § 7923.625(a)(1)-(2) (formerly Cal. Gov. Code § 6254(f)(4)(A)(i)-(ii)).

Record Type	*Phase (When)*	*Timing Issues*	*Restrictions*
Reason-Basis: Subject Privacy			
Recordings: Critical Incident	Any	**Up To 45 Days**, Subject To Same Extensions As Other Recordings – Where Investigation Protection Is Also At Issue	To **Protect Privacy Of The Subject Of The Recording**, Where Redaction Cannot Adequately Do So. *Requirements & Restrictions*: • Writing-Basis: Agency Must Explain To The Requester How **Redaction Of The Recording Cannot Adequately Protect The Subject's Privacy** – Such As By Blurring Of Face, Distortion Of Voice, Etc.[160] • Scope-Limits: Even If Public Disclosure Would Interfere With Investigation, Where Subject Whose Privacy Is At Issue Requests The Recording, **The Privacy Subject Must Be Provided With The Recording Upon Request**. • The Agency Can Also The Recording From A Subject-Requestor For Up To 45 Days – Subject To Extensions – Where Disclosure Would Prejudice An Ongoing Investigation.[161] • NOTE: This is *not* a basis for withholding personnel file records.
Reason-Basis: Unfounded Or Frivolous Complaints			
Records: CPRA-Discoverable Investigations-Complaints	Any	Indefinitely.	*Requirements & Restrictions*: Basis: Where The Investigation Revealed The Civilian Complaint To Be Unfounded, Or Frivolous (Per Cal. Code Civ. Proc. § 128.5), The Investigative/Complaint Records Remain *Pitchess* Confidential.[162]

160 Cal. Gov. Code § 7923.625(b)(2) (formerly Cal. Gov. Code § 6254(f)(4)(B)(ii)).

161 Cal. Gov. Code § 7923.625(b)(3) (formerly Cal. Gov. Code § 6254(f)(4)(B)(iii)).

PRACTICE NOTE: If a minor, the privacy subject's parents can also request production of the recording under this provision. If deceased, the privacy subject's heirs or legal representatives can also request production of the recording under this provision. *Id.*

162 Cal. Penal Code § 832.7(b)(9) (amend. 2022).

15. *Table: Redaction Available Of CPRA-Discoverable Officer Personnel File Investigations Or Critical Incident Recordings – Requirements & Deadlines.*

a. REDACTION C.P.R.A. Discoverable Records/ Recordings (Summary Chart).

Item	*Max. Time (Unless Basis Ends)*	*Standard of Proof for Basis*	*Writing Requirements*
Event: Privacy Concern - Only			
RECORDS = Complaints-Investigations (CPRA-Discoverable)	**Indefinitely**	(1) Officer Personal Data; (2) Complainant, Whistleblower, Victim & Witness Identity; (3) Medical, Financial, or Federally-Protected Info; or (4) Privacy Balancing = Privacy Interest Clearly Outweighs Public Interest in Disclosure	None
RECORDINGS – Critical Incidents	**Indefinitely**	Privacy Interest Clearly Outweighs Public Interest in Disclosure	**Basis** for Redacting + Redactions **Cannot Obscure Incident**
Event: Public Safety Concern (or Superior Public Interest In Redaction)			
RECORDS = Complaints-Investigations (CPRA-Discoverable)	**Indefinitely**	**Safety** = Specific-Articulable Facts Show **Physical Danger To Officer Or Civilian** By Disclosure; **Public Interest** = Public Interest Served By Redaction Clearly Outweighs Public Interest in Disclosure	None

b. Extended Redaction Chart.

Record Type	*Phase (When)*	*Timing Issues*	*Restrictions*
Reason-Basis: Subject Privacy			
Records: CPRA-Discoverable Investigations-Complaints	**Any**	Indefinitely.	*Restrictions On Permitted Redactions*: • Officer Personal Data: Officer Home Addres Phone Numbers, & Family Member Identiti May Be Redacted – But *Not* The Officers' Names Or Work-Related Information.[163] • Complainant, Whistleblower, Victim & Witness Names & Identifying Information May Be Redacted To Preserve Their Anonymity.[164] • Confidential Medical, Financial, Or Federally-Protected Information: May Be Redacted.[165] • Privacy Balancing Catch-All: Where An Interest In Preventing An Unwarranted Invasion Of Personal Privacy Clearly Outweighs The Strong Public Interest In Disclosure Of Records Of Officer Misconduct, Such Private Information Ma Be Redacted.[166]
Recordings: Critical Incident.	**Any**	Indefinitely.	*Requirements & Restrictions On Permitted Redactions:* • Writing-Basis: Agency Must Explain To Th Requester How The Recording Subject's **Privacy Interest Clearly Outweighs Publi Interest In Disclosure.**[167] • Permitted Redactions: Blurring Or Obscuring Of The Subject's Identity Is Permitted, BUT Only If The Redaction Does Not Impair The Recipient From Comprehending The Incident Events Depicted. • Prohibited Redactions: Aside From The Permitted Redactions, Recordings May No Be Otherwise Altered Or Edited.[168]

163 Cal. Penal Code § 832.7(b)(6)(A) (amend. 2022).

164 Cal. Penal Code § 832.7(b)(6)(B) (amend. 2022).

165 Cal. Penal Code § 832.7(b)(6)(C) (amend. 2022).

166 Cal. Penal Code § 832.7(b)(6)(C) (amend. 2022).

167 Cal. Gov. Code § 7923.625(b)(1) (formerly Cal. Gov. Code § 6254(f)(4)(B)(i)).

168 Cal. Gov. Code § 7923.625(b)(1) (formerly Cal. Gov. Code § 6254(f)(4)(B)(i)).

Record Type	*Phase (When)*	*Timing Issues*	*Restrictions*
Reason-Basis: Safety Or Public Interest			
Records: CPRA-Discoverable Investigations-Complaints	**Any**	Indefinitely.	*Requirements & Restrictions*: • Safety Basis: Where A Specific, Articulable, Particularized Reason Exists To Believe Disclosure Of Information In A Record Would Pose A Significant Danger To The Physical Safety Of An Officer Or Other Person, It May Be Redacted.[169] • Public Interest Catch-All: Where, In A Particular Case, The Public Interest In Redaction Clearly Outweighs The Public Interest In Disclosure, The Information May Be Redacted.[170] • NOTE: Recording redaction is *not* available on this basis.

Given the complexities of the new rules, police agencies would be wise to retain and consult with outside counsel to ensure proper compliance before producing, withholding, or redacting records and recordings that are discoverable under the new laws.

c. Sealing of Basis for Withholding or Redaction.

It is also worth noting that where an agency believes that a privilege would be impaired, or an investigation compromised, by stating its basis in a writing submitted to the CPRA requesting party, in response to an action to compel CPRA disclosure (pursuant to Cal. Gov. Code § 7923.000 (formerly Cal Gov. Code § 6258)), the agency is permitted to file an **application to seal the basis for its withholding** (pursuant to Cal. R. Ct. 2.550).[171] Notably, on its face, the amended statute does *not* appear to limit the availability of sealing to investigative records: as such, sealing is arguably available to protect the basis of withholding critical incident video as well.

169 Cal. Penal Code § 832.7(b)(6)(D) (amend. 2022).

170 Cal. Penal Code § 832.7(b)(7) (amend. 2022).

171 *See* Cal. Penal Code § 832.7(b)(8)(A)(iv) (amend. 2022).

16. *Internet Posting Requirement for Police Policies, Procedures, and Training Materials-Manuals.*

The California Legislature also imposed a mandatory Internet posting requirement for police policies, procedures and training manuals/educational materials. To elaborate, SB 978 added a statutory Internet posting requirement as to police procedures, policies, and training manuals. Specifically, beginning January 1, 2020, "each local law enforcement agency shall conspicuously post on their Internet Web sites all current standards, policies, practices, operating procedures, and education and training materials that would otherwise be available to the public if a request was made pursuant to the California Public Records Act…."[172] In other words, where a law enforcement agency's police procedures, policies, or training manuals/educational materials are otherwise discoverable under the California Public Records Act, those public records must be "conspicuously post[ed]" on the agency's website.

17. *Other Grounds For Withholding: The Debate Over Whether the CPRA Exemptions Still Apply After SB 1421.*

As implicated above, and as will be explained more fully in the CPRA chapter, there are a number of exemptions from CPRA disclosure. Some practitioners erroneously contend that SB 1421 effectively negated or repealed the CPRA's explicit exemptions from disclosure, and restricted CPRA exemptions for officer personnel file records only to the categories and for the reasons stated in SB 1421. In support of this broad construction of SB 1421, proponents cite to the opening sentence of Penal Code section 832.7(b) (emphasis added): "Notwithstanding subdivision (a), subdivision (f) of Section 6254 of the Government Code, or any other law, the following peace officer personnel records or records maintained by any state or local agency shall not be confidential and shall be made available for public inspection pursuant to the California Public Records Act."

However, this broad contention — that SB 1421 voids the CPRA exemptions for things like drafts or attorney-client privileged materials and so forth — runs afoul of the case authority regarding the **doctrine of statutory construction**. As explained above, that doctrine holds that where two statutes appear to be materially contradictory, the more specific statute will be deemed

172 *See* Cal. Penal Code § 13650 (eff. Jan. 1, 2019).

to control over the vaguer/more general statute.[173] Here, for several reasons, the doctrine of statutory construction reveals that the contention that SB 1421 negates the exemptions of Government Code §§ 7923.600-7923.625 (formerly Government Code § 6254) is fatally flawed.

First, here, by its own terms, SB 1421 *only* proposes to modify Penal Code sections 832.7 and 832.8: it does *not* modify any provisions of the Government Code or Evidence Code.[174] By contrast, by its own terms, AB 748 *only* proposes to modify former Government Code section 6254(f): it does *not* modify any provisions of the Penal Code or Evidence Code.[175] Since the CPRA exemptions *not* contained in former Government Code section 6254(f) are *not* covered by SB 1421 or AB 748, the other exemptions from CPRA disclosure have *not* been modified by these adopted bills — including but not limited to those exempted in Section 6254(a) (drafts), 6254(c) (personnel and medical files), and Section 6254(k) (statutorily privileged or protected materials).

Second, SB 1421/SB 16 specifically incorporates language adopting the *Pitchess* privilege. For example, by its own terms, SB 1421/SB 16 states that peace officer personnel file records "are confidential and shall not be disclosed in any criminal or civil proceeding except by discovery pursuant to Sections 1043 and 1046 of the Evidence Code..."[176] It also states that the *Pitchess* privilege motion-order system remains unchanged: "This section does not affect the discovery or disclosure of information contained in a peace or custodial officer's personnel file pursuant to Section 1043 of the Evidence Code."[177] It also contains a catch-all for "redaction" of information where the non-disclosure interest outweighs the public disclosure interest: "an agency may redact a record disclosed pursuant to this section, including personal identifying

173 *See* Cal. Code Civ. Proc. § 1859; *In re Williamson, supra*, 43 Cal.2d at p. 654 ("It is the general rule [of statutory construction] that where the general statute standing alone would include the same matter [conduct] as the special [specific] act, and thus conflict with it, the special act will be considered as an exception to the general statute whether it was passed before or after such general enactment."); *accord Murphy, supra*, 52 Cal.4th at p. 86; *Morton, supra*, 417 U.S. at p. 550 ("where there is no clear intention otherwise, a specific statute will not be controlled or nullified by a general one regardless of the priority of enactment"); *Townsend, supra*, 109 U.S. at p. 512.

174 *See* Senate Bill no. 1421 (2017-2018 Reg. Sess.; adopted as 2019 amendments to Cal. Penal Code §§ 832.7-832).

175 *See* Assembly Bill no. 748 (2017-2018 Reg. Sess.; adopted as 2018 amendment to Cal. Gov. Code § 6254(f); recodified as Cal. Gov. Code §§ 7923.600-7923.625 as of January 1, 2023).

176 Cal. Penal Code § 832.7(a).

177 Cal. Penal Code § 832.7(g).

information, where, on the facts of the particular case, the public interest served by not disclosing the information clearly outweighs the public interest served by disclosure of the information."[178] These references and incorporation negate the idea that "any other law" is broadly invalidated by SB 1421/SB 16, particularly as to *Pitchess* or comparable privileges. In other words, the broad construction of "any other law" must fail where, as here, more specific language shows that a narrower construction is proper.

Finally, there is nothing in the legislative history that suggests that, by adopting SB 1421 or SB 16, the Legislature intended to revoke sacrosanct privileges like the attorney-client privilege: which would the necessary and unavoidable result if the broad construction of "any other law" were adopted here.

As a result of the foregoing, the more persuasive and supported (narrow) construction of the authorities and statutes leads to the conclusion, that *in addition* to the bases for withholding and redaction afforded under SB 1421/SB 16 and/or AB 748, police agencies retain their right to withhold from CPRA disclosures personnel file records and/or critical incident recordings that remain subject to the other CPRA exemptions: such as the **CPRA exemption** for **drafts**, for information subject to a statutory privilege (like the **attorney-client privilege**), for information specifically created for **pending litigation**, for information protected by **federal records/information confidentiality**, and for information **exempt from disclosure orders issued under the *Pitchess* system.**[179]

Similarly, the narrow construction of SB 1421/SB 16 is more consistent with the apparent legislative intent that, where officer personnel file records and information were *unrelated* to critical incidents or sustained investigations of officer sexual assault on members of the public or sustained investigations of officer on-the-job dishonesty, those records retain their full *Pitchess* privilege protection, and such are thus exempt from CPRA disclosure.[180]

---

178 Cal. Penal Code § 832.7(b)(7).

179 Cal. Gov. Code § 7927.500 (formerly Cal. Gov. Code § 6254(a); drafts); Cal. Gov. Code § 7927.705 (formerly Cal. Gov. Code § 6254(k); statutory privilege; *e.g.*, Cal. Evid. Code § 952, *et seq.*); Cal. Gov. Code § 7927.700 (formerly Cal. Gov. Code § 6254(c); personnel or medical information-records); Cal. Gov. Code § 7923.805 (formerly Cal. Gov. Code § 6254(u)(2)-(3); officer and criminal system personal addresses and phone numbers); Cal. Evid. Code §§ 1043-1045.

180 Cal. Penal Code § 832.7(a)-(b) (amend. 2019).

Fortunately, so far, the narrow construction has been embraced by controlling authority.[181]

Absent An Express Exemption From CPRA Disclosure, The 2019+ Laws Make Covered Police Records Disclosable. While there has been much debate about whether the CPRA exemptions survived SB 1421 and its siblings, this debate has largely been resolved: the exemptions appear to have survived.[182]

However, where there is ambiguity between an older statute and the 2019+ CPRA disclosure laws, and the laws appear to directly conflict with the amended CPRA, absent an express or clear exemption, the 2019+ CPRA disclosure laws will likely be deemed to preempt and supersede the other laws.[183]

For example, in *First Amendment Coalition v. Superior Ct.* (2023) 98 Cal.App.5th 593, the appellate court analyzed whether the statute that makes disclosure of government subpoenaed records a crime (and grounds for government job disqualification) [Cal. Gov. Code § 11183] was superseded by the 2019+ CPRA disclosure statutes [*e.g.*, Cal. Penal Code § 832.7(b)].

In its analysis, the *First Amendment Coalition* Court held that although, under Cal. Penal Code § 832.7(b), "officer-related records falling within its scope are deemed nonconfidential and open to public inspection"; because that statute's "phrase '[n]otwithstanding…any other law' is a 'term of art'… that declares the legislative intent to override all contrary law…"[184]; **where exemptions do not conflict with Section 832.7(b), they remain in force**. In other words:

---

181 *Becerra v. Superior Ct.* (2020) 44 Cal.App.5th 897, 914-918, 920-921, 923-929 (holding that the "[n]otwithstanding…any other law" language of Section 832.7(b)(1) "cannot reasonably be read to do away with the entire CPRA" and that, as a result, the CPRA categorical exemptions remain in effect, except as to records that specifically fall into the SB 1421 categories of disclosable police personnel file records); *see also Ass'n for L.A. Deputy Sheriffs (ALADS) v. Superior Ct.* (2019) 8 Cal. 5th 28, 36-37, 50 n. 5, 56 (holding that a law enforcement agency does not violate Cal. Penal Code section 832.7 by disclosing to a prosecutor — such as by a *Brady* alert list or otherwise — the fact an officer of that agency who is a witness in a pending criminal prosecution may have information in the officer's personnel file that tends to exonerate the criminal defendant); *see also id.* at p. 50 n. 5 (2019 amendments emphasize that *Pitchess* protections intended to shield confidentiality of peace officer personnel file information from public, *not* from government agencies).

182 *See, e.g., ALADS, supra,* 8 Cal. 5th at pp. 39-57; *Becerra, supra,* 44 Cal.App.5th at pp. 914-918, 920-921, 923-92.

183 *See First Amendment Coalition, supra,* 98 Cal.App.5th at pp. 603-604, 610.

184 *Id.* at pp. 603-604.

> [L]ike the catchall exemption addressed in *Becerra* [*v. Superior Ct.* (2020) 44 Cal.App.5th 897], other statutory disclosure exemptions that do not pose a direct conflict with Section 832.7(b) – whether mentioned by name within the CPRA or incorporated into the CPRA by [Cal. Gov. Code § 7927.705 – making Evidence Code privileged information and information prohibited from disclosure by state or federal law exempt from CPRA disclosure] – may continue to operate. Again, whether a statutory exemption directly conflicts with Section 832.7(b) does not turn on the mere circumstance that application of the exemption would result in withholding of responsive records. Here, we may reasonably infer from the entire text of Section 832.7(b)(1) that its call for disclosure is intended to supersede, at a minimum, those exemptions like Section 832.7(a) and [Cal. Gov. Code § 7923.600 – the law enforcement investigatory records exemption] that would "nullify" its application to a wide or significant swath of officer-related records.[185]

Thus, the *First Amendment Coalition* Court held that where a statute required non-disclosure of government-subpoenaed records [Cal. Gov. Code § 11183 – which makes disclosure both a misdemeanor crime and a basis for disqualification from acting on behalf of a state agency], that statute directly conflicted with Section 832.7(b) when the subpoenaed records fall within those CPRA exceptions for disclosability: and Section 11183 thus does *not* operate to bar CPRA disclosure of such covered records.[186]

However, by way of contrast, where an inspector general report and related records were *expressly* exempted from the CPRA ("the Legislature has proclaimed they 'are not public records subject to [the CPRA]'"), Section 832.7(b) did *not* make those records CPRA disclosable: because Section 6126 caused such records to "exist outside that [CPRA] universe."[187] This thus contrasts with Cal. Gov. Code § 11183, which lacked an express legislative exemption from the CPRA: and thus caused Penal Code § 832.7(b) to trump its non-disclosure provisions.[188]

---

185 *Id.* at p. 610.

186 *Id.* at p. 609.

187 *Id.* at pp. 614-615; *see also* Cal. Penal Code § 6126.3(c)(1).

188 *Id.* at pp. 616-617.

Limitation Of Attorney-Client Privilege For Public Entity Attorneys. Notwithstanding the foregoing, the 2022 statutory revisions do contain one potentially-disturbing "clarification" that, on its face, mirrors controlling case law; but that, in its poor execution, could result in confusion and, ultimately, litigation.

Consistent with controlling authority, pure facts relayed to a public entity's attorney are expressly exempt from the attorney-client privilege, at least as it pertains to CPRA-disclosure of otherwise *Pitchess*-protected information.[189]

However, as it pertains to whether the information is CPRA-disclosable, after the section stating that "[f]actual information provided by the public entity to its attorney" shall be disclosable under the CPRA, notwithstanding an assertion of the lawyer-client privilege, the 2022 revisions go on to state that "factual information discovered in any investigation conducted by, or on behalf of, the public entity's attorney" is *also* CPRA-disclosable, notwithstanding the attorney-client privilege.[190]

While the 2022 revisions do go on to state that bases for non-disclosure from CPRA available under state and federal law *other* than the attorney-client privilege may be asserted as a basis for withholding such privileged public records[191], presumably including the attorney work product protection, depending on how the term "investigation" by a public entity's attorney is construed by the courts, as well as how diligent courts are in enforcing other bases for withholding attorney-related public records, if construed in an absurdly overbroad manner, this vague language could effectively void confidentiality for all documented non-work product factual communications between a public entity and its attorney.

Public Entity Attorney Billing Records. It should also be noted that such a broad construction of this limitation of privilege in the CPRA disclosure context may be undermined by the 2022 statute's provisions on the disclosure of public entity attorney's billing records.

While the new statute clarifies that the "[b]illing records related to the work done by the [public entity's] attorney" are generally CPRA-disclosable, such billing records remain exempt from disclosure if: (1) "the records…relate to active and ongoing litigation"; or (2) "disclose information [sic] for the

189 Cal. Penal Code § 832.7(b)(12)(A)(i) (amend. 2022).

190 *See id.*

191 Cal. Penal Code § 832.7(b)(12)(B) (amend. 2022).

purpose of legal consultation between the public entity and its attorney."[192] This last, poorly-worded phrase suggests that public entity attorney billing records that contain opinion attorney work product likely remain exempt from CPRA disclosure: as such writings would contain information *shared* (the missing word in the statute) for the purpose of legal consultation.

As a result, the billing records disclosure limitation suggests that the broader construction of public entity attorney "investigations" is *not* valid; and, thus, that the 2022 revisions should *not* be construed so as to void a public entity's right to confidentiality in its attorneys' advice and opinion work product.

However, the poor draftsmanship of this new language will likely need to be clarified by future court review.

F. Implications of the Statutory Exceptions.

Notably, absent the operation of one of these explicit exceptions to the *Pitchess* procedure, in state court cases, the *Pitchess* procedure is mandatory and the *exclusive* means for obtaining (discovery) or publishing (disclosure) of officer personnel file records and information.

However, developing case law has revealed that there is also an implicit exception to the *Pitchess* "discovery" procedures that is addressed in the next chapter.

That said, there is also an additional implication to the 2019+ CPRA exceptions to the *Pitchess* privilege: as predicted, courts are beginning to evaluate the operation and/or scope of the privilege in conjunction with an analysis of the CPRA disclosure requirements – evaluating them hand-in-hand.

Thus, for example, where the officer personnel file records at issue in a *Pitchess* motion concerned a sustained finding of officer dishonesty, the Court held that because Penal Code § 832.7(b) made such information CPRA-disclosable public records, and thus non-confidential, the trial court erred by subjecting such officer personnel file records to a standard *Pitchess* protective order because "[a] protective order issued under [Cal. Evid. Code § 1045(e)] is intended to protect [only] 'confidential' law enforcement personnel records."[193]

---

192 Cal. Penal Code § 832.7(b)(12)(A)(2) (amend. 2022).

193 *See Banuelos v. Superior Ct.* (2024) 2024 Cal.App.LEXIS 705, *8-9.

10. CUSTODIAN EXEMPTION: The Emerging Exception from *Pitchess* "Discovery" Procedures for the Custodial Government Agency (and the Impact of the *Michael* Cases).

In addition to the explicit statutory exemptions from the requirements of the *Pitchess* procedure, there is an implicit limitation to the *Pitchess* privilege that can arise in the context of litigation between a peace officer and his government agency employer, such as in employment cases between an officer and his employer law enforcement agency (or where the officer is an adverse witness to the custodial government agency). Specifically, in civil litigation, some peace officers improperly attempt to preclude discovery or deposition *by their government employer* of information contained in their personnel file — asserting the *Pitchess* privilege against the custodian of the personnel file in question.

However, **where the party seeking "discovery"** regarding information contained in a peace officer's personnel file **is the officer's employer and custodian of such personnel file records**, the **peace officer employer is *not* required to go through the *Pitchess* procedures regarding "discovery" of such information.**[1] This exemption from the "discovery" procedures for the custodial government entity as to peace officer personnel file information in that agency's custody was first expressly recognized in the case of *Michael v. Gates* (1995) 38 Cal.App.4th 737.

---

1 *See Michael v. Gates* (1995) 38 Cal.App.4th 737, 745; *see also* 79 Ops. Cal. Atty. Gen. 185, 193-195 (1996); *Gonzalez v. Spencer* (9th Cir. 2003) 336 F.3d 832, 837-838; *accord* Bender, Cal. Dep. & Discovery Practices 26.13 at [2]; *Zanone v. City of Whittier* (2008) 162 Cal.App.4th 174, 187.

To elaborate, under California law, the government agency that has custody and control of the officer's personnel file at issue is *not* required to go through the *Pitchess* process before its counsel *may*: (a) review that officer's personnel file (which the custodian already possesses), and/or (b) use the information in that file to aid the agency's defense — including as impeachment of the officer at issue during testimony under oath. In other words, the *Michael* cases generally stand for the proposition that **an officer cannot use the *Pitchess* privileges to stop the custodial public agency of that officer's personnel file from using those personnel records/information of that officer to defend itself against allegations raised by that officer.**[2]

A. The *Michael* Case and Rationale of the Custodial Government Entity Exception.

The operation of the custodial government agency exception to *Pitchess* "discovery" procedures is best understood by a review of the facts of the *Michael* case. In *Michael*, the Court of Appeal specifically addressed this issue in an action where a police officer asserted that his public entity former employer must go through the *Pitchess* procedures before the public entity's attorney could review his personnel records for the purposes of gathering impeachment evidence against that officer in a case where that officer was set to testify against the public entity on behalf of another party at trial. In reviewing that case, the *Michael* Court stated:

> Specifically, we are asked to determine whether, when a former police officer testifies against a police department in a lawsuit, the law enforcement agency which employed the officer may allow its lawyer to review the officer's personnel records in order to evaluate their use as impeachment at trial, without compliance with the [*Pitchess*] procedural requirements of Evidence Code sections 1043 and 1045. We determine that the Evidence Code's procedural requirements are not applicable to the facts just described, and that under those circumstances, inspection of records by the law enforcement agency and its attorney violates no statutory or constitutional right.[3]

---

2 *See Michael, supra*, 38 Cal.App.4th at pp. 743-745; *see also People v. Superior Ct (Gremminger)* (1997) 58 Cal.App.4th 397, 404-407.

3 *Michael, supra*, 38 Cal.App.4th at p. 740.

In other words, under the law, the public entity and its counsel is/are thus exempted from the *Pitchess* procedural requirements as to "discovery" of such personnel file records/information because:

> In ordinary legal usage, "discovery" refers to the inspection of documents and other materials in the possession or control of an adverse party in litigation, a process which has as its principal purpose the elimination of the "game" element of litigation.... [However, an] agency which reviews its own records with its attorneys has not engaged in discovery.... [Furthermore, the] statutory scheme is designed to protect peace officers' "just claim to confidentiality" and to regulate the use of peace officer personnel records in civil and criminal proceedings. [Citation] It was not intended to, and does not, create substantive or procedural obstacles to a police agency's review of its own files.... The privilege created by Evidence Code section 1043 is a conditional privilege [citation] and the statutory scheme makes it clear that the right to privacy in the records is limited.[4]

Accordingly, where a peace officer's personnel file records document the information at issue in litigation between the peace officer and the officer's government agency employer, the government agency and its agents *cannot* be required to seek through the *Pitchess* procedure discovery of information that has already been disclosed to the agency by being placed into the officer's personnel file, which is already in the government agency's custody.[5]

---

4 *Michael, supra*, 38 Cal.App.4th at pp. 744-745; *see also* 79 Ops. Cal. Atty. Gen. 185, 193-195 (1996); *Gonzalez, supra*, 336 F.3d at pp. 837-838 (analyzing the public entity's *Pitchess* procedural requirements in comparison to procedural requirements protecting juvenile criminal information); *accord Rosales v. City of Los Angeles* (2000) 82 Cal.App.4th 419, 425; *Bradshaw v. City of Los Angeles* (1990) 221 Cal.App.3d 908, 918-919 (holding that an officer does not have a private right of action on a negligence *per se* basis against his police employer for failure to follow the *Pitchess* procedures and that the plaintiff officer did not state a valid claim for invasion of the constitutional right to privacy where the information at issue was publicly available before the disclosure at issue), *overruled in part by Copley Press, Inc. v. Superior Ct.* (2006) 39 Cal.4th 1272, 1286 (overruling *Bradshaw* to the extent that *Bradshaw* asserted that the *Pitchess* privilege applied *only* in criminal and civil actions); Bender, Cal. Dep. & Discovery Practices 26.13 at [2].

5 *See Michael, supra*, 38 Cal.App.4th at pp. 744-745 (however, the court implied that a *Pitchess* motion may be needed for the agency to seek disclosure to the jury of the *Pitchess*-privileged matter in its possession at the time of trial); *accord People v. Superior Ct. (Gremminger)* (1997) 58 Cal.App.4th 397, 404-407.

Put simply, the rationale of this emergent exception to the *Pitchess* procedural requirement rests largely on the notion that "discovery" by the custodial government agency of protected personnel file material is *not* barred because the agency already has possession or custody — and thus "has not engaged in discovery" of — the otherwise protected information at issue.[6]

Accordingly:

> [a]n examination of the statutory scheme reveals that rather than forbidding a governmental agency which has custody and control of peace officer personnel records from reviewing those records with its attorney, the scheme contemplates, even demands, that a governmental agency and its lawyer will review those records, without noticed motion or court order.[7]

Indeed, in evaluating the proposition that a public entity should be required to go through the *Pitchess* procedure to review personnel file records/information in its custody, the *Michael* Court held that "[t]o read such a requirement into the statute would be to construct an <u>absurd result</u>. We construe statutes to avoid, not create, such results."[8]

B. <u>The *Michael* Case Rationale Extends to Personnel File Information Subject to the Agency's *Custody*, Even If Such Is *Not* In the Agency's *Possession*, or If Contained in the Officer's Mind (and the Implications of the Custodial Public Entity Possessing Superior *Pitchess* Privilege Rights Over the Officer and Waiver).</u>

Along these lines, where the information at issue in the litigation is either contained in the peace officer's personnel file, or protected personnel

---

6 *See Michael, supra,* 38 Cal.App.4th at p. 745 ("An agency which reviews its own records with its attorney has not engaged in discovery.")

7 *See Michael, supra,* 38 Cal.App.4th at p. 744; *accord People v. Superior Ct. (Johnson)* (2015) 61 Cal.4th 696, 713-714, 719-720 (approving and distinguishing *Michael* and *Gremminger*); *see generally People v. Superior Ct. (Johnson)* (2014) 228 Cal.App.4th 1046, 1068-1074 (citing *Michael* for the proposition that "'[a]n agency which reviews its own records [officer personnel files in its custody] with its attorney has not engaged in discovery'" that would otherwise warrant a *Pitchess* motion).

8 *Michael, supra,* 38 Cal.App.4th at p. 745 (emphasis added); *see also* 79 Ops. Cal. Atty Gen. 185, 193-195 (1996); *Gonzalez, supra,* 336 F.3d at pp. 837-838; *Zanone, supra,* 162 Cal.App.4th at p. 187 n. 14.

file information subject to the agency's custody, the *Pitchess* privilege cannot operate to bar discovery and *deposition* of that officer about that information, because the same rationale that would bar an officer from being forced to testify about *Pitchess*-privileged information *operates in the reverse* where the information at issue is *not* privileged from the party querying or questioning the peace officer about such personnel file information.[9]

To elaborate, it is true that the *outermost* scope of the custodial government entity's exemption from the *Pitchess* discovery procedural requirements remains an open question. Specifically, the rationale of the exception clearly supports a public entity questioning or even deposing one of its officers so as to "review" protected personnel file information *already in its possession*, without resort to the *Pitchess* procedure, as long as there is no disclosure of such information to persons/entities outside the privilege.[10] However, there is no authority *directly* on point on the question of whether a custodial public entity may question or depose one of its officers *seeking to obtain* protected personnel file information from one of its officers that is *not* already in the agency's possession, without resort to the *Pitchess* "discovery" procedure.

Notwithstanding this narrow gray area, it is reasonable to anticipate that courts applying the *Michael* cases will conclude that such information-seeking by the custodial government entity still does not constitute "discovery" subject to mandatory *Pitchess* procedures for two reasons.

First, the *Pitchess* privilege rules apply wherever the protected information is stored: the corollary of this rule is that the public entity acts as the custodian of such information, regardless of where it is stored — <u>even if it is stored in the officer's mind</u>: thus, the entity's lack of possession over the protected information at issue does *not* affect its legal custody over such information.[11]

---

9 *Compare Michael, supra,* 38 Cal.App.4th at pp. 740-745 *with Davis v. City of Sacramento* (1994) 24 Cal.App.4th 393, 401 *and City of San Diego v. Superior Ct.* (1981) 136 Cal.App.3d 236, 239.

PRACTICE NOTE: The rationale permitting <u>discovery</u> of such personnel file information by the custodial government agency does *not* appear to extend to <u>disclosure</u> of such information by the custodial government agency to others. *See Michael, supra,* 38 Cal.App.4th at pp. 740-745.

10 *See Johnson, supra,* 61 Cal.4th at pp. 713-721; *Michael, supra,* 38 Cal.App.4th at pp. 740-745; *Gremminger, supra,* 58 Cal.App.4th at pp. 404-407; *Zanone, supra,* 162 Cal.App.4th at p. 187; *City of San Diego, supra,* 136 Cal.App.3d at p. 239; *Hackett v. Superior Ct.* (1993) 13 Cal.App.4th 96, 99-101.

11 *See Johnson, supra,* 61 Cal.4th at pp. 713-721; *Michael, supra,* 38 Cal.App.4th at pp. 740-745; *Gremminger, supra,* 58 Cal.App.4th at pp. 404-407; *Zanone, supra,* 162 Cal.App.4th at p. 187; *City of San Diego, supra,* 136 Cal.App.3d at p. 239; *Hackett, supra,* 13 Cal.App.4th at pp. 99-101.

Second, as between the two joint *Pitchess* privilege holders — the public entity and the peace officer — the public entity has superior rights of access to the *Pitchess*-privileged information: thus, in a conflict or dispute between the entity and the officer over *Pitchess*-protected information, it does not stand to reason that the *Pitchess* procedure should be any bar to the *public entity* from obtaining access to protected information that the entity does not yet possess, but for which it is the legal custodian — as long as the public entity does not disclose such privileged information to persons outside the privilege.[12]

However, the definitive answer to this question must await future case law developments.

That said, it is worth noting that there are **multiple examples of the superior *Pitchess* rights of the custodial government agency in officer personnel files over the police officer.** One example is that the custodial government agency has the right to waive the hearing on *Pitchess* motion good cause determination, and proceed straight to the *in camera* review, even if the officer objects.[13]

Another example is that, during an ongoing administrative investigation of officer misconduct, for which the public agency may temporarily deem related records confidential (under Cal. Gov. Code § 3303), the officer's right to review his personnel file for adverse comments (under Cal. Gov. Code §§ 3305-3306) does *not* apply while the investigation is still active/ongoing; however, once the investigation is completed, the officer's right-to-review may be

---

12 *See Johnson, supra*, 61 Cal.4th 696 at pp. 714-715, 719-721; *Michael, supra*, 38 Cal. App.4th at pp. 740-745; *Gremminger, supra*, 58 Cal.App.4th at pp. 404-407; *Zanone, supra*, 162 Cal. App.4th at p. 187; *City of San Diego, supra*, 136 Cal.App.3d at p. 239; *Hackett, supra*, 13 Cal.App.4th at pp. 99-101; *Davis, supra*, 24 Cal.App.4th at pp. 401, 401 n. 2; *McMahon, supra*, 172 Cal.App.4th at pp. 1335-1337; *Sacramento Police Officers Assn. v. Venegas* (2002) 101 Cal.App.4th 916, 924-930; *People v. Mooc* (2001) 26 Cal.4th 1216, 1226-1229; *Haggerty v. Superior Ct.* (2004) 117 Cal.App.4th 1079, 1086; *see also* Cal. Evid. Code § 1043(c); Cal. Gov. Code §§ 3305, 3306, 3306.5.

13 *See* Cal. Evid. Code § 1043(d) ("No hearing upon a motion for discovery or disclosure shall be held without full compliance with the notice provisions of this section except upon a showing by the moving party of good cause for noncompliance, *or upon a waiver of the hearing by the governmental agency identified as having the records.*" (emphasis added); *see also Michael, supra*, 38 Cal.App.4th at p. 744 ("Notably, while the privilege against disclosure is held by both the individual officer and the police department…, the statute gives the authority to waive a hearing only to the agency, and not to the individual officer."; citing *Davis v. City of Sacramento* (1994) 24 Cal. App. 4th 393, 401).

effective.[14] Yet another example is the fact that, even under the Government Code, an officer is only entitled to inspect the records in his personnel file which constitute/contain adverse comments: the underlying supporting or investigative materials upon which such comments are based are *not* subject to the officer's Government Code inspection right, particularly where they are stored separately from the officer's personnel file, such as in an internal affairs file.[15]

Additionally, it is also worth noting that the custodial government agency exception is only an exemption to the *Pitchess* discovery (production to a litigant) procedures as to peace officer personnel file records/information subject to that agency's possession, custody, or control: the exception has no effect on the *Pitchess* restrictions on a public entity's disclosure (publication) of protected officer personnel file information to persons outside the scope of the privilege, such as to a trial jury. Indeed, California law even holds that when a government official/agency exceeds its lawful authority, disclosing police personnel file information in violation of statutes like Cal. Penal Code § 832.7, such disclosure can be a **misdemeanor crime.**[16]

Notwithstanding the developing nature of the outermost limits of this emerging exception to the *Pitchess* discovery procedures, it is thus clear that, under the *Michael* cases, in a civil case between the officer and the custodial

---

14 *See Oakland Police Officer's Assn v. City of Oakland* (2021) 63 Cal.App.5th 503, 522-523.

15 *See* Cal. Gov. Code §§ 3305, 3306, 3306.5; *Barber, supra*, 203 Cal.App.4th at pp. 651-655 (§ 3306.5 only applies prior to the officer's termination); *McMahon, supra*, 172 Cal.App.4th at pp. 1335-1337 (holding that Gov. Code § 3306.5 did not permit the officer to inspect internal affairs file materials that were not used in making adverse comments in the officer's personnel file and were stored separately from the personnel file); *Brutsch, supra*, 3 Cal.App.4th at p. 360 (holding that the inspection regime of Gov. Code § 3305 applies to information that might affect the officer's status of employment, such as information that could be used to discipline the officer, and did not include a right to inspect unfavorable comments made in connection with a promotional exam); *Sacramento Police Officers Assn., supra*, 101 Cal.App.4th at pp. 924-930 (holding that while Gov. Code § 3306.5 gives an officer the right to inspect internal investigation records kept separately from the officer's personnel file where such investigation records were used to impose discipline against him or constitute comparable adverse comments that could result in discipline, an officer does not have the right to inspect the entirety of the Department's investigative record where it is not stored within the officer's personnel file or does not constitute adverse comments affecting the status of the officer's employment); *cf. Aguilar v. Johnson* (1988) 202 Cal.App.3d 241, 249 (evaluating comparable limits under the Government Code).*cf.* Cal. Penal Code § 832.5(b)-(c) (regarding storage of complaints and related investigations in separate files from the officer's personnel file).

16 *See Towner v. County of Ventura* (2021) 63 Cal.App.5th 761, 772-773 (holding that intentional disclosure by a government official/officer of confidential officer personnel files in violation of Penal Code § 832.7 is a misdemeanor crime under Cal. Gov. Code § 1222).

government agency, because the peace officer does *not* have a *Pitchess* procedural privilege barring *discovery* of information in the peace officer records already in the custodial government agency's possession (because the *Pitchess* statutes shall not be construed to require absurd results), or subject to the agency's custody, the custodial government agency is *not* required to obtain a court order via a *Pitchess* motion before deposing or seeking other authorized *discovery* from that peace officer about such otherwise-protected material or information.[17] As long as the custodial agency conducts written discovery (as defined under the Code of Civil Procedure) or deposition of the officer about information the custodial agency already possesses in that officer's personnel file, or about information that is already subject to the agency's custody, the agency is *not* conducting "discovery" that would require a *Pitchess* motion or order.

Waiver. However, while the officer and the agency may have different rights to the officer personnel files, when both privilege holders act in concert, they can effect a powerful waiver that can facilitate the public interest in such information. Specifically, where *both* an officer and the custodial government entity waive the *Pitchess* protections as to otherwise-confidential specific peace officer personnel file information, *that specific information is no longer confidential.*

Thus, for example, where the Los Angeles Police Department ("LAPD") had voluntarily published-disclosed some of a peace officer's protected personnel file information to the *Los Angeles Times*, without any objection by (and with the implicit consent of) the involved officer, such information was no

---

17 *Compare Michael, supra*, 38 Cal.App.4th at pp. 740-745 *with Davis, supra*, 24 Cal. App.4th at p. 401 *and City of San Diego, supra*, 136 Cal.App.3d at p. 239; *see also Johnson, supra*, 2015 Cal. LEXIS 4647 at p. *23 (effectively concluding that a custodial government entity's criminal prosecutor was not in possession-custody of personnel files for investigating officers also employed by that entity because, in the criminal case, the prosecuting attorney "does not represent the agency" that was the custodian of such personnel records).

PRACTICE NOTE: The custodial agency should be cautious when California Code of Civil Procedure ("CCP") discovery requests or deposition questions seek "personnel file" information that is related to but not contained in the officer personnel file that the agency already possesses. If the officer refuses to provide a substantive response to the written request or deposition question at issue, the custodial agency should consider framing any motion to compel as a *Pitchess* motion particularly where the agency is trying to fill in any blanks in the personnel file it possesses.

longer confidential: and thus no longer restricted by the *Pitchess* protections of Cal. Penal Code § 832.7, *et al.*[18]

In sum then, where a government agency is the custodian of a peace officer's personnel file, that government agency is **not** required to go through the *Pitchess* "discovery" procedure in order to ask plaintiff-officer about personnel file information that may be at issue in the action simply because such information is or may be contained in that officer's personnel file, even if the agency does not already possess such information.

1. *The Emerging Exception Applies to Public Employees and Public Entities' Contract Attorneys Alike.*

Moreover, this emerging exception to the *Pitchess* "discovery" procedure applies regardless of whether the agent of the custodial government agency is a public employee or a contract or "private" attorney. This is because whether an attorney is a civil servant employee of a government client or a contract agent thereof has no bearing on the legal duties of confidentiality and loyalty that apply to all attorneys.[19] Nor does any of the authority related to the relevant *Pitchess* case law distinguish a public entity's attorney on the basis of whether that attorney is paid with taxpayer/public funds as an employee or as a contractor.

Indeed, in a discerning review of the analogous question of whether a private-contract employee representing a public entity could be entitled to qualified immunity (a right to which government employees were entitled), the U.S. Supreme Court reversed a circuit court that held that only government-employees were entitled to the protection of the qualified immunity right; in doing so, the Supreme Court reasoned that:

> Affording immunity not only to public employees but also to others acting on behalf of the government similarly serves to ensure that talented candidates [are] not deterred by the threat of damages suits

---

18 *See Rail v. Tribune* (2019) 43 Cal.App.5th 638, 657.

19 *See, e.g.*, Cal. Bus. & Prof. Code §§ 6067, 6068; *Gafcon, Inc. v. Ponsor & Assoc.* (2002) 98 Cal.App.4th 1388, 1411-1412 (holding that whether an attorney represents a government, a corporate entity, or otherwise, the attorney has essentially the same ethical duties to the client).

> from entering public service.... The government's need to attract talented individuals is not limited to full-time public employees. Indeed, it is often when there is a particular need for specialized knowledge or expertise that the government must look outside its permanent work force to secure the services of private individuals.... To the extent such private individuals do not depend on the government for their livelihood, they have freedom to select other work — work that will not expose them to liability for government actions. This makes it more likely that the most talented candidates will decline public engagements if they do not receive the same immunity enjoyed by their public employee counterparts.... The public interest in ensuring performance of government duties free from the distractions that can accompany even routine lawsuits is also implicated when individuals other than permanent government employees discharge these duties.... Not only will such individuals' performance of any ongoing government responsibilities suffer from the distraction of lawsuits, but such distractions will also often affect any public employees with whom they work by embroiling those employees in litigation.... Distinguishing among those who carry out the public's business based on the nature of their particular [employment] relationship with the government also creates significant line-drawing problems.... Such questions deprive state actors of the ability to "reasonably anticipate when their conduct may give rise to liability for damages".... frustrating the purposes immunity is meant to serve. An uncertain immunity is little better than no immunity at all.[20]

Moreover, it is important to note that in an action between a peace officer and the custodial government agency, it is the *public entity*, *not* the agency's attorney (private or otherwise), that is the party to this action, and **that it is the *party* to this action that is seeking and entitled to discovery**

---

20 *Filarsky v. Delia* (2012) 132 S.Ct. 1657, 1665-1666 (holding that on the issue of whether a contractor agent of a public entity should be entitled to the immunity otherwise afforded to publicly-employed agents of the public entity, in this case qualified immunity in § 1983 civil rights cases, it was irrelevant whether that agent was a government employee of that public entity or a private contractor of that public entity and refusing to distinguish between public employees and private agents of the government entity in determining the availability of the immunity right at issue); *Johnson*, *supra*, 61 Cal.4th at pp. 713-715 (implicitly holding that, unlike a criminal prosecutor, the attorney representing the custodial government agency is *not* required obtain a *Pitchess* order to review personnel file records-information in the agency's custody).

through such discovery devices such as written requests, interrogatories, and deposition questions.[21] Like any entity party, a government agency can only act through other natural persons: and whether the counsel retained by that public entity to take depositions or conduct discovery on its behalf is paid as an employee or an independent contractor, that attorney still represents the agency, a party to the action.[22]

Along these lines, when the *Michael* Court examined this issue, it concluded that though it was an *attorney* representing the public entity that reviewed the police personnel file of the officer in question, for purposes of impeachment at trial in a case where that officer was designated to testify against that public entity, that attorney was *not* required to follow the *Pitchess* procedures to discover/review the information contained in that officer's personnel file because the public entity that such attorney represented was the custodian of such officer's personnel records.[23]

Indeed, as to the notion that a public entity or its attorney should be required to go through the *Pitchess* procedure to obtain *discovery* as to personnel file records/information in its custody, the *Michael* Court held that "[t]o read such a requirement into the statute would be to construct an absurd result. We construe statutes to avoid, not create, such results."[24]

C. The Red Line of *Disclosure* to Persons or Entities Outside the Scope of the *Pitchess* Privilege: the Emerging Limits of the Custodial Government Agency Exception to the *Pitchess* Procedural Requirements.

However, as noted in above, although the question has not been *expressly* decided, despite the fact that *both* the agency and the officer are *Pitchess*-privilege holders, it should be noted that even a custodial agency must to go through the *Pitchess* procedure before seeking to ***disclose Pitchess-privileged***

21 *See, e.g.*, Cal. Code Civ. Proc. § 2025.220(a) ("A *party* desiring to take the oral deposition of any person shall give notice in writing." (emphasis added)); *cf.* Cal. Code Civ. Proc. §§ 2030.010 *et seq.*, 2031.010 *et seq.*, 2033.010 *et seq.*, 2034.010 *et seq.*

22 *See, e.g.*, Cal. Code Civ. Proc. § 2025.230; *see also Johnson*, *supra*, 61 Cal.4th at pp. 713-715.

23 *See Michael*, *supra*, 38 Cal.App.4th at pp. 743-745.

24 *Michael*, *supra*, 38 Cal.App.4th at p. 745; *see also* 79 Ops. Cal. Atty. Gen. 185, 193-195 (1996); *Gonzalez*, *supra*, 336 F.3d at pp. 837-838; *Zanone*, *supra*, 162 Cal.App.4th at p. 187 n. 14.

matters** to the jury **at trial of a civil action, or to the public absent the application of one of the aforementioned exceptions.[25] While the rationale underlying the *Pitchess* statutory procedure does not bar "discovery" regarding an officer's personnel records by those records' custodial public agency, that same rationale would prohibit *disclosure* of that presumed-confidential information to the public (*i.e.*, on the public record to a jury or to third parties).[26]

To elaborate, although the *Pitchess* statutes give the governmental agency (alone) the right to waive the *hearing* on a *Pitchess* motion, that power of waiver is *not* expressly extended to a power to waive the requirements of *filing* a *Pitchess motion* for disclosure altogether.[27]

Indeed, as noted above, the language of the *Pitchess* statutes indicates that there is a difference between *discovery* of protected matter and *disclosure* thereof. For example, a government agency may use an officer's personnel file information in litigation against that officer without such use constituting "discovery" under the *Pitchess* procedures — such as by reviewing such records or engaging in related evaluation/investigation of the records and related facts that does *not* involve disclosure thereof to persons or entities other than the officer or custodial government agency at issue; however, *disclosure* of such protected information at trial or to the public could establish grounds for an action for invasion of privacy or comparable torts, where the invasive effects of the personnel file information disclosure are "sufficiently serious in their

---

25 *See id.* at pp. 740-746 (resting part of its rationale on the fact that although the personnel files had been reviewed by the agency's attorneys, "the trial court did not allow [the former officer's] records to be used at trial"); *Zanone, supra*, 162 Cal.App.4th at p. 187 n. 14; *Gremminger, supra*, 58 Cal.App.4th at pp. 404-407 (observing that disclosure of peace officer records in violation of the *Pitchess* procedures may "constitute an unwarranted invasion of personal privacy").

26 *See* Cal. Evid. Code §§ 1040, 1042, 1043; Cal. Penal Code §§ 832.5, 832.7, 832.8; *Fagan, supra*, 111 Cal.App.4th at p. 618; 66 Ops. Cal. Atty. Gen. 128, 128-130 (1983).

27 *Compare* Cal. Evid. Code § 1043(c) *and Michael, supra*, 38 Cal.App.4th at pp. 744-745 *with* Cal. Evid. Code § 1043(a) ("In any case where discovery or disclosure is sought of peace…officer personnel records…the party seeking the discovery or disclosure shall file a written motion with the appropriate court…upon written notice…. Upon receipt of the notice the governmental agency served shall immediately notify the individual whose records are sought [for discovery or disclosure]."); *see also Johnson, supra*, 61 Cal.4th at pp. 713-715 (holding that the criminal prosecutor, like the criminal defense attorney, must comply with *Pitchess* motion requirements before seeking discovery or disclosure of protected officer personnel file information).

nature, scope, and actual or potential impact [to the officer so as] to constitute an egregious breach of the social norms underlying the privacy right."[28]

Significantly, and by way of contrast, the emerging trend conflicts somewhat with some prior precedent about what information custodial public entities can disclose to the news media without a *Pitchess* disclosure order. In a 1990 case, in observing that the *Pitchess* privilege codified under Penal Code sections 832.5, 832.7, and 832.8 and Evidence Code sections 1043 and 1045 (formerly known as 1978's Senate Bill no. 1436) "was intended 'to curtail the practice of record shredding and discovery abuses which allegedly occurred in the wake of [the *Pitchess* decision],'" one appellate court concluded that a custodial government agency could disclose at a news conference portions of an officer's administrative review board disciplinary hearing transcript without a *Pitchess* order because the *Pitchess* privilege "was not intended to abrogate a police department's right to disseminate information" under the California Public Records Act.[29]

However, it must be noted that such case (*Bradshaw*) was decided before the key *Michael*, *Johnson*, and *ALADS* cases: all of which appear to embrace the distinction that there are *Pitchess* statutory restrictions on public *disclosure* of officer personnel file information, notwithstanding the CPRA or the interests in public access to information.[30]

---

28 *See Michael, supra*, 38 Cal.App.4th at pp. 745-746 (resting its rejection of the officer's claims for invasion of privacy by violation of the *Pitchess* procedures on the grounds that mere review of personnel file information by the governmental agency's attorney, without public disclosure, was too minimal an invasion of privacy to be actionable); *Zanone, supra*, 162 Cal.App.4th at p. 187 n. 14 (observing that the question remains undecided as to whether a party that "legitimately obtains personnel records subject to such protection without first filing a *Pitchess* motion (for example, by receiving copies from the involved officer) is nonetheless precluded from offering that information into evidence or using it in cross-examination: that is, whether the *Pitchess* procedures affect not only discovery of personnel information but also its admissibility"); *Gremminger, supra*, 58 Cal.App.4th at p. 404-405 (observing that disclosure of peace officer records in violation of the *Pitchess* procedures may "constitute an unwarranted invasion of personal privacy"); *Johnson, supra*, 61 Cal.4th at pp. 713-715 (approving and distinguishing *Michael* and *Gremminger*).

29 *See Bradshaw, supra*, 221 Cal.App.3d at pp. 913-914, 916-917, 918 (holding that POBR only limits custodial government agency's right to disclose the officer's home address and photo to the news media, but that POBR and the Pitchess privilege and CPRA exemptions otherwise provide no other restrictions on agency media release of administrative hearing and related incident information).

30 *Compare Bradshaw, supra*, 221 Cal.App.3d at pp. 916-918 *with Michael, supra*, 38 Cal.App.4th at pp. 745-746 and *Johnson, supra*, 61 Cal.4th at pp. 713-715 *and Ass'n for L.A. Deputy Sheriffs (ALADS) v. Superior Ct.* (2019) 8 Cal. 5th 28, 36-37, 50 n. 5, 56.

Therefore, in light of the foregoing, as referenced above, there are three emergent trends in the case law and authorities which indicate that in order to *disclose Pitchess*-protected matter to outside parties in ways not specifically authorized by the *Pitchess* statutes, the governmental agency must at least file a noticed *Pitchess motion* with the court and immediately notify the affected officer of such motion (such as by service upon an officer-party).

First, the emerging case law indicates that while a custodial governmental agency may review peace officer personnel records or evaluate the facts therein without such conduct constituting "discovery" that would require a *Pitchess* motion (including related civil discovery in litigation between the officer and the custodial agency), where the government agency seeks to *use* such *Pitchess*-protected material in a way that would result in disclosure to the "public" (*i.e.*, to persons or entities other than the involved officer or the custodial government agency), even the prosecutor or governmental agency must (likely) obtain a court order via a *Pitchess* motion before engaging in such disclosure.[31]

Second, the emerging authorities underscore that *only* the custodial government agency, and *not* the officer, may waive the requirement of a *Pitchess* motion *hearing* (effectively vacating the hearing, since the *Pitchess* statute bars the court from holding a hearing on the motion upon defective notice by the moving party or waiver by the agency); however, such authorities do *not* state that the government agency may waive the requirement of *filing* a *Pitchess motion* altogether.[32]

Third, the emerging authorities indicate that a peace officer *might* have a private right of action, such as for invasion of privacy, where a governmental

---

31 *See* Cal. Evid. Code § 1043(a) ("[i]n any case in which...disclosure is sought of peace or custodial officer personnel records...the party seeking the...disclosure shall file a written motion with the appropriate court.... Upon receipt of the notice the governmental agency...shall immediately notify the individual whose records are sought [for disclosure]."); *Michael, supra*, 38 Cal.App.4th at pp. 745-746; *Zanone, supra*, 162 Cal.App.4th at p. 187 n. 14; *Gremminger, supra*, 58 Cal.App.4th at p. 404-407; *People v. Gwillim* (1990) 223 Cal.App.3d 1254, 1269-1270; 66 Ops. Cal. Atty. Gen. 128, 128-130.

32 *See* Cal. Evid. Code § 1043(c) ("No hearing upon a motion for discovery or disclosure shall be held without full compliance with the notice provisions of this section except upon...a waiver of the hearing by the governmental agency identified as having the records."); *Michael, supra*, 38 Cal.App.4th at pp. 745-746; *Zanone, supra*, 162 Cal.App.4th at p. 187 n. 14; *Gwillim, supra*, 223 Cal.App.3d at pp. 1269-1270; *cf.* Cal. Evid. Code § 1043(a) ("[i]n any case in which...disclosure is sought of peace or custodial officer personnel records...the party seeking the...disclosure shall file a written motion with the appropriate court").

agency violates the *Pitchess* procedures through unauthorized/un-excepted discovery or disclosure.[33]

Accordingly, where a custodial governmental agency seeks to *disclose* *Pitchess*-protected material to the public — *e.g.*, to persons or entities outside the scope of the *Pitchess*-privilege (i.e., to anyone other than the officer or custodial government agency at issue), such as for publication in a civil trial or otherwise — the emergent case law and authorities indicate that the safest practice for the agency to follow is to:

(1) immediately serve a notice of *Pitchess* motion on the affected peace officer;

(2) file a *Pitchess* motion for a court order authorizing such disclosure (but distinguishing that the agency does *not* require court authority for "discovery" of such matter); and

(3) await the entry of the Court's authorizing *Pitchess* order before making the disclosure of *Pitchess*-protected material at trial in California state court, or to the public (where such disclosure is not otherwise exempted).

It should also be noted that, under such circumstances, since waiver of the *Pitchess hearing* rests with the custodial governmental agency *alone*, it appears that the governmental agency would be able to avoid a hearing on its own motion — presumably by permitting the court to decide the *Pitchess* disclosure motion solely on the papers, and proceed straight to the *in camera*

---

33 *See Michael, supra*, 38 Cal.App.4th at pp. 745-746; *Zanone, supra*, 162 Cal.App.4th at p. 187 n. 14; *Gremminger, supra*, 58 Cal.App.4th at p. 404-407; *Rosales v. City of Los Angeles* (2000) 82 Cal.App.4th 419, 428-429 (holding that the officer did not state a cause of action for invasion of privacy because the officer did not have a reasonable expectation of privacy in his peace officer personnel files where discovery or disclosure thereof did not violate the *Pitchess* procedures or where such procedures were inapplicable); *see also* Cal. Evid. Code §1043(c); *Marken v. Santa Monica-Malibu Unif. Sch. Dist.* (2012) 202 Cal.App.4th 1250, 1266 (holding that mandamus relief is available to a public employee to "prevent a public agency from acting in an unlawful manner by releasing information the disclosure of which is prohibited by law"); *but see Bradshaw, supra*, 221 Cal.App.3d at pp. 918-920 (holding that an officer does not have a private right of action on a negligence *per se* basis against his police employer for failure to follow the *Pitchess* procedures and that the plaintiff officer did not state a valid claim for invasion of the constitutional right to privacy where the information at issue was publicly available before the disclosure at issue), *overruled in part by Copley Press, Inc. v. Superior Ct.* (2006) 39 Cal.4th 1272, 1286 (overruling *Bradshaw* to the extent that *Bradshaw* asserted that the *Pitchess* privilege applied *only* in criminal and civil actions).

review.[34] In such circumstances, however, the governmental agency would likely need to carefully consider the pros and cons of such waiver, and would likely need to clarify that it was only waiving (and arguably vacating) the *Pitchess* motion *hearing*, but *not* its right or duty to attend the mandatory *in camera* review session by the court.[35]

D. The Supreme Court's *Johnson* Decision and Its Implications.

In July 2015, the California Supreme Court unanimously decided a criminal case appeal that also had unexpectedly significant implications for public entities' administrative operations and their defense of civil actions: *People v. Superior Ct. (Johnson)* (2015) 61 Cal.4th 696. In reaching its decision — balancing a criminal defendant's Due Process/*Brady* disclosure rights with peace officers' *Pitchess* personnel record privacy rights and the practical needs of criminal prosecutors — the **Supreme Court effectively confirmed that public entities serving as custodians of their peace officers' personnel files are *not* required to obtain a *Pitchess* order from a court before reviewing such personnel file information.**

(Notably, before *Johnson*, California's Supreme Court had never even touched upon the *Michael* line of cases identifying the custodial government agency exception to the *Pitchess* discovery requirements.)

34 *See* Cal. Evid. Code § 1043(c); *Michael, supra*, 38 Cal.App.4th at pp. 743-744; *cf.* Cal. R. Ct. 3.1304(c).

PRACTICE NOTE: Although a governmental agency has the right to waive a hearing of the Pitchess motion, given the *in camera* review requirement of the *Pitchess* procedure, and given the fact that *only* the custodial government agency (and its counsel) has a right to participate in the *in camera* review, the governmental agency should consider whether the court considering the motion would constitute the waiver of *Pitchess* hearing so as to amount to a waiver of attendance at the *in camera* review session. The governmental agency should also consider that the advantages that could flow from a hearing — persuading a reluctant court, clarifying issues raised in the papers — may be lost by waiving a hearing; on the other hand, if the hearing is waived, but the court understands that the custodial agency is *not* waiving its right to attend the *in camera* review session, such a constrained audience with the court may present its own opportunities, while also raising grounds for challenge on appeal, potentially including on Due Process grounds. Accordingly, the governmental agency should proceed with caution before waiving (and arguably *de facto* vacating) a *Pitchess* hearing.

35 *See* Cal. Evid. Code § 915(b) (only the person authorized to claim the privilege, or the person from whom the disclosure of privileged matter is sought (or both) under Cal. Evid. Code § 1040 *et seq.*, "and any other persons as the person authorized to claim the privilege is willing to have present" may be in chambers when a court is ruling on a claim of privilege).

The *Johnson* case thus effectively approved the *Michael* line of cases that held that, in state court cases, where a custodial government agency is sifting through peace officer information already subject to its custody, the agency is *not* conducting "discovery" that would otherwise require a *Pitchess* motion and order; but where that custodial government agency seeks to "disclose" that protected personnel file information to someone outside of the privilege, it must obtain a *Pitchess* order.

1. *The Johnson Case Procedural History.*

The background of the *Johnson* case is particularly illuminating on the *Pitchess* procedural issues, and the inadvertent importance of the *Johnson* case to police administration and civil litigation defense.

The City and County of San Francisco, a single public entity, was prosecuting criminal defendant Johnson through its District Attorney's Office ("SF-DA") based on an investigation conducted by police officers of that same entity's San Francisco Police Department ("SFPD").[36] To fulfill its *Brady* disclosures duty about potentially exculpatory material in the investigating officers' personnel files, the SF-DA chose to file a *Pitchess* motion for the trial court to conduct an *in camera* review so as to determine if *Brady* material must be disclosed to the defendant.[37]

However, at defendant Johnson's request, the trial court held that the *Pitchess* procedures do not apply, and were contradictory, to the constitutional duty to make *Brady* disclosures — and therefore unconstitutional: the trial court thus ordered the SFPD to give the SF-DA access to the investigating officers' personnel files, and the SF-DA to then disclose *Brady* material found therein to defendant Johnson — without *any* court review, except on a showing of necessity.[38]

---

36 *People v. Superior Ct. (Johnson)* (2015) 61 Cal.4th 696, 705-709.

37 *See Johnson, supra*, 61 Cal.4th at pp. *705-709; *Martin v. Board of Election Exam'rs.* (1899) 126 Cal. 404, 409-410 (holding that under special legislative rules, the City of San Francisco and the County of San Francisco were merged into a single public entity); *cf.* Cal. Gov. Code §§ 945, 23000-23004, 34100-34102, 34501 (on organization and legal existence of cities and counties); *see also* Cal. Penal Code § 1054.1 (re statutory *Brady*-style disclosure duty of prosecutors).

38 *Johnson, supra*, 61 Cal.4th at pp. 707-709.

On appeal, the City and County of San Francisco argued that the SF-DA, one of its constituent departments, was *not* in possession of the investigating officers' personnel files because the SFPD, another constituent department, held onto those files, and the City and County of San Francisco had strict separation protocols between the SF-DA and the SFPD when it came to officer personnel files; the public entity appellant also argued that the criminal prosecutor's exception to the *Pitchess* requirements did not apply because the investigating officers were not the subject of the criminal investigation resulting in prosecution.[39]

In sum then, the public entity argued on appeal that because its own criminal prosecutor was *internally* barred from accessing that entity's peace officer personnel files without a *Pitchess* order or valid exception, the peace officer personnel files were thus equally available to defendant Johnson as to the SF-DA: and there was thus no *Brady* disclosure duty by the public entity's prosecutor.[40]

[Historically, the separate departments of the same public entity do *not* have any separate legal existence.[41] As a result, it should have been irrelevant for purposes of determining possession or custody that one department of the San Francisco government was prosecuting the criminal case while another department of that same government entity had actual possession of the officers' personnel files. On a separate note, the public entity appellant also

39 *Johnson, supra*, 61 Cal.4th at pp. 707-709; *see also People v. Superior Ct. (Johnson)* (2014) 228 Cal.App.4th 1046, 1056-1063 (the Court of Appeal opinion).

40 *Johnson, supra*, 61 Cal.4th at pp. 707-709; *see also Johnson, supra*, 228 Cal.App.4th at pp. 1056-1063.

41 *See, e.g., Bauer v. County of Ventura* (1955) 45 Cal. 2d 276, 288-289 (where plaintiffs sued a county's water agency, the California Supreme Court affirmed the dismissal of the water agency as a defendant, holding that an agency of a county is *not* a legal entity separate from the county itself, and thus a county's constituent agency was *not* a proper party to the lawsuit); *Talbot v. City of Pasadena* (1938) 28 Cal. App. 2d 271, 274, *overruled on other grounds by Dillon v. Board of Pension Commissioners* (1941) 18 Cal. 2d 427, 431 (where a city police agency and comparable official-capacity defendants were named in a suit against the municipality, the court affirmed dismissal of the city's police agency and comparable defendants on the grounds that the city's police agency could not be sued as a separate party in addition to suit against the municipality); *accord Sheehan v. Board of Police Commissioners* (1925) 197 Cal. 70, 75, 78 (holding that a municipal police board has no separate legal existence apart from the municipality itself and thus such police agency is thus incapable of suing or being sued, except in mandamus or injunction proceedings regarding compulsory performance or bar of its official duties), *overruled on other grounds by Mass v. Board of Educ.* (1964) 61 Cal. 2d 612, 627.

successfully argued that the *Pitchess* procedural requirements were consistent with the *Brady* duty, and therefore constitutional.]

On review, the Court of Appeal held that because the public entity's prosecutor was part of a "prosecution team" with that public entity's police department, and because the prosecutor's criminal investigation exception applied, the prosecutor should not be required to go through the *Pitchess* procedure before reviewing the investigating officers' personnel files — and thus the prosecutor had a duty to conduct such review for *Brady* disclosure purposes.[42] (Notably, the appellate court also implied that a court's *in camera* review under the *Pitchess* procedure *might* be consistent with the *Brady* duty, as long as the prosecutor did its *Brady* review of officer personnel files before bringing its *Pitchess* motion.[43])

However, in reaching its decision about the "prosecution team" duty, the appellate court relied heavily on the *Michael* line of cases: whose rationale about exemption from the *Pitchess* "discovery" procedures rests on the fact that where a public entity is already the custodian of protected peace officer personnel file information, it would be "absurd" to require that custodian to obtain a *Pitchess* order from a court before using that information — unless the entity planned on disclosing that information to someone outside the privilege limits, like to a trial jury.[44]

The appellate court thus implicitly held that *all* criminal prosecutors should be deemed to be in constructive possession-custody of the personnel files of all investigating officers who form part of the "prosecution team": presumably, even where the prosecutor and the officers are employed by *different* public entities. Notably, the appellate court and the appellant did not focus on the unusual fact that, in the *Johnson* case, the public entity prosecuting the case was the *same* public entity that had possession-custody of the officers' personnel files. As a result, on appeal, one of the issues indirectly before the Supreme Court was the same issue that arose in *Michael*: whether a custodial

42 *Johnson, supra*, 61 Cal.4th at pp. 707-709; *see also Johnson, supra*, 228 Cal.App.4th at pp. 1068-1076.

43 *Johnson, supra*, 61 Cal.4th at pp. 707-709; *see also Johnson, supra*, 228 Cal.App.4th at pp. 1076-1079.

44 *See Michael, supra*, 38 Cal.App.4th at pp. 740-745; *Gremminger, supra*, 58 Cal.App.4th at pp. 404-407; *Zanone, supra*, 162 Cal.App.4th at p. 187.

government agency must obtain a *Pitchess* order before reviewing officer pe sonnel file record information already in its possession-custody.[45]

2. *The Supreme Court's Johnson Decision and Its Impact.*

In *Johnson*, the California Supreme Court's unanimous decision approve but distinguished *Michael* and its progeny, observing that the *Michael* ca correctly held that while:

> a governmental agency may allow its own attorney to review [officer] personnel records in its possession in some situations without complying with the *Pitchess* procedures. It does not stand for the proposition that the prosecution, which does not represent the agency, may routinely review those records.[46]

Accordingly, the *Johnson* Court held that "prosecutors, as well as defe dants, must comply with the *Pitchess* procedures if they seek informatio from confidential [peace officer] personnel records."[47] The *Johnson* Cou also observed that a litigant could "employ the *Pitchess* procedures in the fir instance if it wishes to obtain the information" it was lacking.[48]

[The *Johnson* Court also held that the prosecutorial exception to *Pitche* only applies where the officer is the *subject* of the criminal investigation, an that the *Pitchess* procedure is constitutionally compatible with the *Brady* di closure duty, including the *Pitchess* requirement of a court's *in camera* revie prior to disclosure.[49] The *Johnson* Court thus held that, to satisfy its *Brad* duty, all a criminal prosecutor needs to do is alert the criminal defendant tha certain investigating officers are expected to be called as witnesses, and the it is up to the defendant to bring a *Pitchess* motion if the he wants to plum the records for *Brady* exculpatory material.[50]]

---

45 *Johnson, supra*, 61 Cal.4th at pp. 707-709; *cf. Johnson, supra*, 228 Cal.App.4th at p 1064-1074.

46 *Johnson, supra*, 61 Cal.4th at pp. 713-714.

47 *Johnson, supra*, 61 Cal.4th at pp. 714-715.

48 *Johnson, supra*, 61 Cal.4th at pp. 720-721.

49 *Johnson, supra*, 61 Cal.4th at pp. 718-723.

50 *Johnson, supra*, 61 Cal.4th at pp. 718-723.

Significantly for police administrators and public entity civil litigation defenders, the *Johnson* Court's holding, rationale, and effective adoption of the *Michael* cases means that — *except* when a public entity's attorney is representing the People of the State of California in a criminal proceeding, instead of representing that public entity — **a public entity remains exempt from the *Pitchess* "discovery" procedures for officer personnel file information in its possession-custody.**[51] Thus, for example, where a public entity's attorney reviews a peace officer's personnel file records in preparation for defense of a civil case against that officer, or a public entity police supervisor reviews such for administrative purposes, the public entity is <u>not</u> required to obtain a *Pitchess* order before conducting such review because such review by the custodial government entity is not "discovery" under the *Pitchess* procedures.[52]

The *Johnson* Court's quiet adoption of the *Michael* cases also means that where the public entity seeks to publish the protected peace officer personnel file information to someone outside the scope of the *Pitchess* privilege, such as to a trial jury, because such "disclosure" is governed by statute, even the custodial public entity must obtain a *Pitchess* order before making such disclosure.[53]

In sum then, the *Johnson* case effectively affirms the custodial government entity exception to the *Pitchess* **discovery** procedures, while implicitly approving earlier lower court cases (of the *Michael* line) holding that even custodial government entities are <u>not</u> exempt from the *Pitchess* **disclosure**-publication procedures.

Notably, the California Supreme Court has recently indirectly confirmed its reasoning on this issue: observing that the *Pitchess* privilege system is meant

---

51 *Johnson, supra*, 61 Cal.4th at pp. 709-715, 718-721; *see Michael, supra*, 38 Cal.App.4th at pp. 740-745; *Gremminger, supra*, 58 Cal.App.4th at pp. 404-407; *Zanone, supra*, 162 Cal.App.4th at p. 187; *Gwillim, supra*, 223 Cal.App.3d at pp. 1269-1270.

52 *See Johnson, supra*, 61 Cal.4th at pp. 718-723; *Michael, supra*, 38 Cal.App.4th at pp. 740-745; *Gremminger, supra*, 58 Cal.App.4th at pp. 404-407; *Zanone, supra*, 162 Cal.App.4th at p. 187.

53 *See Johnson, supra*, 2015 Cal. LEXIS 4647 at pp. 23-24, 33-37; *Michael, supra*, 38 Cal. App.4th at pp. 740-745; *Gremminger, supra*, 58 Cal.App.4th at pp. 404-407; *Zanone, supra*, 162 Cal. App.4th at p. 187; *Gwillim, supra*, 223 Cal.App.3d at pp. 1269-1270 (holding that a prosecutor may review an officer's personnel file, such as an immunized statement made regarding on-duty conduct, without resort to the *Pitchess* procedures because of the investigative exception of the *Pitchess* statutes, but also reasoning that *use* of such personnel file records during the prosecution, such as at trial, may *not* be permitted by Cal. Penal Code § 832.7 — and thus implying that a *Pitchess* motion may be required where the prosecution seeks to use protected material at trial, even if a court order was not necessary to discover/obtain such material from the governmental agency).

to shield officer personnel file information from the *public*, *not* from government agencies.[54]

3. *The Significance of a Public Entity's Possession or Custody of the Personnel File Records-Information as a Party to the Action: and the Related Limits of Constructive Possession in Criminal Cases.*

In addition to the foregoing, one significant subtlety emerged from the *Johnson* case procedural history. In their opinions reaching opposite results on unexpectedly comparable rationales touching upon the *Pitchess* issues, the Court of Appeal and the California Supreme Court devoted little to no attention to the fact that, in *Johnson*, both the department prosecuting the criminal case and the department with actual possession of the investigating officers' personnel files were constituent parts of the *same public entity*.[55] But the question of which public entity is the custodian and/or in possession of the officer personnel file is *crucial* to the evaluation of *Pitchess* privileges and procedural requirements.[56]

---

54 *See Ass'n for L.A. Deputy Sheriffs (ALADS) v. Superior Ct.* (2019) 8 Cal. 5th 28, 36-37, 50 n. 5, 56 (holding that a law enforcement agency does not violated Cal. Penal Code § 832.7 by disclosing to a prosecutor (such as by a *Brady* alert list or otherwise) the fact an officer of that agency who is a witness in a pending criminal prosecution may have information in the officer's personnel file that tends to exonerate the criminal defendant); *see also id.* at pp. 46-47 ("Senate Bill 1421 does not 'affect the discovery or disclosure of information contained in a peace or custodial officer's personnel file pursuant to Section 1043 of the Evidence Code [citing Cal. Penal Code § 832.7(g)]. Nor does it 'supersede or affect the criminal discovery process outlined in…[Evidence Code] Section 1054 [et seq.]…, or the admissibility of records pursuant to [Cal. Penal Code § 832.7(a), which codifies the court decision in *Pitchess v. Superior Court* (1974) 11 Cal.3d 531…."); *see also id.* ("[E]ven if Senate Bill 1421 does not increase the amount of information that a defendant [or moving party] can *compel* an agency to disclose, the bill, by making certain records nonconfidential, reduces the amount of information that agencies are *forbidden* from disclosing voluntarily…. [O]ur conclusion that records described in section 832.7(b) are 'not confidential' does not mean that they are invariably open for public inspection over the agency's objection.") (emphasis in original); *see also id.* at p. 50 n. 5 (holding that the 2019 amendments emphasize that *Pitchess* protections are intended to shield confidentiality of peace officer personnel file information from the *public*, *not* from government agencies).

55 *See Martin v. Board of Election Exam'rs.* (1899) 126 Cal. 404, 409-410 (holding that under special legislative rules, the City of San Francisco and the County of San Francisco were merged into a single public entity); *cf.* Cal. Gov. Code §§ 945, 23000-23004, 34100-34102, 34501 (on organization and legal existence of cities and counties); *compare Johnson, supra*, 2015 Cal. LEXIS 4647 at pp. *22-24, 33 *with Johnson, supra*, 228 Cal.App.4th at pp. 1064-1074.

56 *See, e.g., Chambers v. Superior Ct.* (2007) 42 Cal.4th 673, 679; *People v. Mooc* (2001) 26 Cal.4th 1216, 1229; *see also* Cal. Evid. Code § 1045.

Before *Johnson*, the courts had rejected the notion proffered by the *Johnson* prosecution-appellant: rather, prior court cases had held that where the prosecutor was part of the same public entity as the department in possession of confidential records, or where the separate public entity gathered evidence for that criminal prosecutor in that separate entity's files, the prosecutor was deemed to be in constructive possession of the records at issue (the same team theory of constructive possession).[57]

In the lower court version of *Johnson*, although the Court of Appeal did not use the words "constructive possession" in its opinion, the Court of Appeal's "prosecution team" rationale rested on an extension of earlier precedents so as to effectively deem *all* prosecutors — even those employed by *separate* public entities (and not just separate departments of the *same* public entity, as was the case in *Johnson*) — to be in constructive possession of the personnel files of the law enforcement officers who conducted the criminal

---

57 *See, e.g., In re Brown* (1998) 17 Cal.4th 873, 878 (holding that exculpatory evidence held by county crime lab should have been disclosed by county prosecutor under *Brady* even though the prosecutor was actually unaware of it); *People v. Sims* (1982) 32 Cal.3d 468, 474-474, 486-487 (where a welfare beneficiary was the subject of an administrative action by a Sonoma County Social Services Department wherein the County sought to reduce the beneficiary's payments on grounds of fraud: but, in that administrative proceeding, the beneficiary was effectively exonerated; and where the Sonoma County District Attorney, representing the People of the State of California, then sought to prosecute the beneficiary for welfare fraud; when, on motion by the defendant beneficiary, the courts held that because there was such a unity of interests (or "privity") between the "People of the State of California" (as represented by the Sonoma County District Attorney) and the Sonoma County Social Services Department that had lost the administrative action, the administrative action's exoneration had issue preclusive collateral estoppel effect on the District Attorney's prosecution that, under res judicata principles, necessitated dismissal of the criminal charges — holding that "privity" is a shorthand for describing between two separate parties that have such a unity of interests that the two separate parties should be treated as one party — and applying res judicata collateral estoppel to the criminal charges); *Barnett v. Superior Ct.* (2010) 50 Cal.4th 890, 903 (holding that prosecutors are not responsible for disclosing evidence in other agencies' files unless such evidence was gathered by that separate entity in connection with the investigation of the case being prosecuted); *People v. Gutierrez* (2003) 112 Cal.App.4th 1463, 1475 (citing *Alford v. Superior Ct.* (2003) 29 Cal.4th 1033 to distinguish the obligations of a prosecutor in possession of *Pitchess* material and a prosecutor lacking possession, and observing that the *Pitchess in camera* review and disclosure procedure is constitutionally compatible with the *Brady* disclosure duty even where the prosecutor possesses potentially exculpatory *Pitchess*-privileged matter); *In re Steele* (2004) 32 Cal.4th 682, 697 (the penumbral "possession" of a prosecutor that extends to information held by the police investigator only extends to "information possessed by others acting in the government's behalf that w[as] **gathered in connection with the investigation**"; accordingly, a "prosecutor does not have a duty [under *Brady*] to disclose exculpatory evidence or information" that is *not* in the prosecutor's possession, even if such is in the possession of the police investigating agency, where that information "has no connection to the investigation or prosecution of the criminal charge against the defendant": this is because, the "prosecutor does not have the duty to search for or to disclose such information" not in its possession).

investigation upon which the prosecution relied, at least for *Brady* purposes.[58] Thus, applying *Michael*, the Court of Appeal concluded that since the *Johnson* prosecutors should be deemed to already be in constructive possession of their investigating officers' personnel files, the criminal prosecution had no *Pitchess* procedural bar to reviewing such personnel records: and thus had a *Brady* duty to conduct such review.[59]

In contrast, in the dispositive *Johnson* case, the California Supreme Court distinguished *all* criminal prosecutors from the government attorneys at issue in the *Michael* case by noting that, unlike attorneys who represent the custodial public entity, the "prosecution...does not represent the agency" that is the custodian of the investigating officers' personnel files.[60] While the Supreme Court does not *expressly* reverse prior cases following the constructive possession rationale for criminal prosecutors, in reaching its unanimous holding that *no* criminal prosecutors have a *Brady* duty to review/produce investigating officers' personnel files (even the *Johnson* prosecutors, who were part of the *same public entity* as the investigating officers), the *Johnson* Court's entire rationale necessarily rests on the notion that **because criminal prosecutors do *not* represent the custodial public entity in the criminal case, criminal prosecutors *never* possess — constructively or otherwise — officer personnel file information.**[61]

Put another way, the *Johnson* Court's holding means that because the public entity is *not* a *party* to the criminal action — since the prosecuting party is the People of the State of California, *not* the city or county that employs the criminal prosecutors — and because the public entity is *not* represented by the prosecutor in that criminal action, the prosecuting attorney *cannot* be deemed to possess the investigating officers' personnel file records, even when the prosecuting attorney is actually employed by the custodial public entity in actual possession of such files.[62] Thus, applying *Johnson* and distinguishing *Michael*, the Supreme Court held that a criminal prosecutor has the same access to the

58 *See Johnson, supra*, 228 Cal.App.4th at pp. 1064-1068.

59 *See Johnson, supra*, 228 Cal.App.4th at pp. 1064-1074.

60 *Johnson, supra*, 61 Cal.4th at pp. 713-715.

61 *Johnson, supra*, 61 Cal.4th at pp. 713-715, 719.

62 *See Johnson, supra*, 61 Cal.4th at pp. 713-715, 719.

investigating officers' personnel files as the criminal defense, and that both must bring a *Pitchess* motion prior to obtaining discovery or disclosure thereof.[63]

The inevitable contrapositive of the *Johnson* Court's rationale is that **where the custodial public entity *is* a party to the action, and where the attorney at issue *does* represent the custodial public entity, under *Johnson* and *Michael, as re-affirmed in the ALADS case,* the custodial public entity is *not* required to obtain a *Pitchess* order before reviewing the officer personnel file records-information in its possession or subject to its custody.**[64]

Thus, the *Johnson* case has the unique effect of subjecting *all* criminal prosecutors to *Pitchess* discovery and disclosure procedures, even when the prosecuting attorneys are employed by the custodial government entity (because the custodial public entity is *not* a represented party to the criminal action), while also effectively affirming the exemption in civil cases from *Pitchess* discovery requirements for the custodial government entity.

E. The Custodial Government Entity Exception in Brief.

In sum then, while the emergent authority exempts the custodial government agency from being required to comply with the *Pitchess* discovery procedures — i.e., the exception permits the custodial entity to review officer personnel records/information or to question an officer under oath about information already contained in that officers personnel file or subject to that agency's custody — where the government agency seeks to disclose such *Pitchess*-protected matter to the jury or the public, even the government agency is required to (and certainly should, as a best practice), file a *Pitchess* motion for a court order authorizing the disclosure sought by the government agency.

In other words, under the emergent case law, a custodial public agency does *not* need a *Pitchess* motion or order to review an officer's personnel file information, or to depose or otherwise query the officer about such personnel file information already in the agency's custody, because such is *not* "discovery" subject to the *Pitchess* procedural requirements; however, where the

63 *See Johnson, supra,* 61 Cal.4th at pp. 713-715, 718-721.

64 *See Johnson, supra,* 61 Cal.4th at pp. 713-715, 718-721; *Ass'n for L.A. Deputy Sheriffs (ALADS), supra,* 8 Cal. 5th at pp. 36-56; *Michael, supra,* 38 Cal.App.4th at pp. 740-745; *Gremminger, supra,* 58 Cal.App.4th at pp. 404-407; *Zanone, supra,* 162 Cal.App.4th at p. 187; *Gwillim, supra,* 223 Cal.App.3d at pp. 1269-1270.

custodial public agency seeks to *disclose* that personnel file information t other unauthorized persons (such as to a jury at trial), a *Pitchess* motion an order is likely required.

1. *Implications of the 2019 Statutory Revisions.*

It is also worth noting that, as it pertains to CPRA-discoverable office personnel files and critical incident recordings, their general lack of *Pitche* confidentiality means that either the prosecutor or the criminal defense attorne can obtain sought-after records/recordings through the CPRA. Otherwise, th 2019 amendments appear to have no impact on the emerging exception fror *Pitchess* discovery procedures for the custodial government agency.

11. CIVIL DISCOVERY: The Complex Intersection Between the *Pitchess* Procedure and the California State Civil Discovery Procedures.

While the *Pitchess* procedure is the *exclusive* means for *obtaining* discovery-disclosure of peace officer personnel file records under California law, there is authority indicating that use of other discovery procedures to attempt to obtain *Pitchess*-privileged materials will impose *additional* limits that otherwise would likely be inapplicable.

To elaborate, while California courts have ruled that "Evidence Code section 1043 *et seq*. constitutes the exclusive means for discovery of [peace officer personnel file] records by a litigant in a civil action," this does *not* mean that all other applicable limitations and requirements potentially affecting a *Pitchess* discovery motion are ignored in a civil case.[1] Rather, "the specific Evidence Code procedures relating to discovery of peace officer personnel records take **precedence** over the general discovery rules outlined in the Code of Civil Procedure."[2]

Thus, where otherwise applicable laws — such as the Civil Discovery Act — do *not* conflict with the Evidence Code discovery procedure, those other laws may remain applicable to *Pitchess* discovery.[3] In other words, the Evidence

---

1 *See New York Times Co. v. Superior Ct.* (1997) 52 Cal.App.4th 97, 102, *overruled on other grounds by Copley Press, Inc. v. Superior Ct.* (2006) 39 Cal.4th 1272, 1298.

2 *See County of Los Angeles v. Superior Ct.* (1990) 219 Cal.App.3d 1605, 1611 (emphasis added); *accord City of Fresno v. Superior Ct.* (1988) 205 Cal.App.3d 1459, 1476-1477 (holding that, where it is more specific, Evid. Code § 1043 overrides former Code Civ. Proc. § 2031).

3 *See generally County of Los Angeles, supra*, 219 Cal.App.3d at p. 1611 (holding that where plaintiff did not meet the more expansive requirements of Evidence Code § 1043, plaintiff

Code discovery-disclosure procedures constitute the *minimum* — but *not* the *only* — threshold a moving party must meet when seeking *Pitchess* discovery or disclosures.[4]

This interaction between the requirements of the *Pitchess* procedures and the requirements of the Code of Civil Procedure presents its most problematic application when a party first attempts to obtain *Pitchess*-privileged materials by written discovery under the Civil Discovery Act and then seeks to obtain those same materials through a *Pitchess* motion seeking to compel production-discovery of those materials.

Under the non-*Pitchess* discovery procedures, where a party in a civil case seeks a court order to compel further responses-production to any of its written discovery requests, including any document demands, "[u]nless notice of this motion is given within 45 days of the service of the response, or any supplemental response [to the demand at issue], or on or before any specific later date to which the demanding party and the responding party have agreed in writing, the demanding party waives any right to compel a further response to the demand."[5] Additionally, the law requires that any civil motion to compel production also include a meet-and-confer declaration stating "facts showing a reasonable and good faith attempt at an informal resolution of each issue presented by the motion."[6]

In other words, under the Code of Civil Procedure requirements, where a party responds to written discovery requests, including document demands, but the responding party withholds production-disclosure of responsive documents or information (including on grounds of privilege), in order to be

---

was *not* entitled to officer personnel files); *Hall v. Superior Ct.* (2005) 133 Cal.App.4th 908, 916-918 (where Code of Civil Procedure and California Rules of Court procedures for filing motions were *not* overridden by Evidence Code § 1043, those procedural provisions remained in force and overrode a conflicting local rule); *cf. County of Los Angeles v. Superior Ct.* (1993) 18 Cal.App.4th 588, 600-602 (analyzing Evidence Code § 1043 in conjunction with Government Code § 6254).

4 *See, e.g.*, *Hall*, *supra*, 133 Cal.App.4th at pp. 917-918 (holding that the motion format and notice rules still applied to *Pitchess* motions because they were not superseded by more specific Evidence Code requirements).

5 Cal. Code Civ. Proc. § 2031.310(c); *accord Sinaiko Healthcare Consulting, Inc. v. Pacific Healthcare Consultants, Inc.* (2007) 148 Cal.App.4th 403-404 (evaluating Code Civ. Proc. § 2031.310); *Sexton v. Superior Ct.* (1997) 58 Cal.App.4th 1403, 1410 (under former Code Civ. Proc § 2031(l), the court lacks jurisdiction to rule upon an untimely motion to compel).

6 *See, e.g.*, Cal. Code Civ. Proc. §§ 2016.040, 2031.310(b)(2).

able to file and serve a motion to compel production-disclosure of that matter, the propounding-moving party must first: (1) meet and confer with the responding party and try to work out any dispute over the materials sought; (2) include a declaration documenting that effort with the motion to compel; and (3) notice that motion to compel further production-responses within 45 days of the service date of the disputed response.[7]

By contrast, the *Pitchess* statutes have no conflicting requirements about submitting any request for the records sought to the officer or agency, or about conferring with opposing counsel before filing a motion, or regarding a time limit for submitting a *Pitchess* motion: under the *Pitchess* procedure, in order to obtain discovery of the records sought, all a moving party needs to do is to file their *Pitchess* motion and let the process work its way through the court system.[8]

Thus, it appears that where a party first elects to seek discovery of *Pitchess*-privileged materials and information through written discovery requests pursuant to the Code of Civil Procedure, because the aforementioned civil discovery requirements do *not* conflict with — and are thus *not* superseded by — the *Pitchess* statutory procedures, by using discovery vehicles available under the Code of Civil Procedure, the party seeking discovery is imposing *additional* restrictions on that propounding party's ability to obtain the *Pitchess* matter.

Accordingly, with regard to attempted discovery of *Pitchess*-protected materials in a civil case, it may be a safer and less cumbersome practice for a civil litigator to *exclude* such materials and information from their other discovery requests and simply file and serve a *Pitchess* motion as to the privileged matters. Moreover, to reduce the potential costs of such motion, the moving party could provide much more than the minimum notice of motion hearing so that, while the motion was pending, the moving party could confer with the opposing party with the aim of removing from the court's hearing any matters for which there was no genuine dispute — *i.e.*, as to matter about which both the subject officer and the governmental agency were willing to waive the *Pitchess* privilege.

---

7 *See, e.g.*, Cal. Code Civ. Proc. §§ 2016.040, 2031.310.

8 *See, e.g.*, Cal. Evid. Code § 1043.

In any event, a party seeking discovery of *Pitchess*-privileged matter in a civil case should tread cautiously in its discovery attempts so as to avoid needlessly increasing the burdens of discovery when it comes to protected personnel records and information.

Furthermore, in light of the amended Government Code and Penal Code sections, where officer personnel files and/or critical incident recordings are CPRA-discoverable, the party seeking such records/recordings will have that route available, rather than proceeding through the civil discovery procedures.[9]

9 *See* Cal. Gov. Code §§ 7923.600-7923.625 (formerly Cal. Gov. Code § 6254(f)), Cal. Penal Code §§ 832.7-832.8 (amend. 2019).

12. *BRADY*: A Brief Overview of the Tense Balancing Between the *Pitchess* Privilege and the Constitutional *Brady* Disclosure Duty in Criminal Cases.

One of the frequent clashes in law arises between the *Pitchess* privilege and the *Brady* disclosure duty in criminal cases and the tension that results.

A. A Brief Review of the *Brady* Disclosure Rule.

Under the Fourteenth Amendment to the U.S. Constitution, which bars states from denying any person due process of law, criminal defendants' rights to a fair trial imposes on the states certain obligations consistent with their sovereign duty to ensure that "'justice shall be done.'"[1] As agents of the sovereign, prosecutors must honor these obligations: thus, they must refrain from using evidence they know to be false, to correct false evidence when it appears; and they must disclose to the defense potentially exculpatory evidence.[2]

Most famously enunciated in *Brady v. Maryland*, this *Brady* duty to disclose potentially exculpatory evidence is an obligation to disclose to the criminal defense evidence that is favorable to the accused and material either to guilt or punishment.[3]

---

1 *Brady v. Maryland* (1963) 373 U.S. 83; *Cone v. Bell* (2009) 556 U.S. 449, 451; *Ass'n for L.A. Deputy Sheriffs (ALADS) v. Superior Ct.* (2019) 8 Cal. 5th 28, 39-41; *City of Los Angeles v. Superior Ct.* (2002) 29 Cal.4th 1, 7-10.

2 *ALADS, supra*, 8 Cal. 5th at pp. 39-41; *Mooney v. Holohan* (1935) 294 U.S. 103, 112–113; *Kyles v. Whitley* (1995) 514 U.S. 419, 437-438; *Pyle v. Kansas* (1942) 317 U.S. 213, 216; *Napue v. Illinois* (1959) 360 U.S. 264, 269.

3 *ALADS, supra*, 8 Cal. 5th at pp. 39-41; *Brady, supra*, 373 U.S. at p. 87.

For *Brady* purposes, evidence is favorable where it helps the defense or hurts the prosecution, such as by impeaching a prosecution witness.[4]

Under *Brady*, evidence is material where there is a reasonable probability that, had the evidence been disclosed to the defense, the result of the proceeding would have been different.[5]

To evaluate materiality, one must consider the collective significance of the undisclosed evidence, as well as the effect of the non-disclosure on defense investigations and trial strategies.[6] In evaluating materiality, there is a reasonable probability that the result of the proceeding would have been different where that likelihood is great enough to undermine confidence in the outcome of the trial: it is *not* necessary to show that it would have been more likely that defendant would have received a different result if the disclosure had been made.[7]

The materiality standard applies both after judgment, when evaluating whether *Brady* was violated, and before judgment, when evaluating whether evidence favorable to the defense must be disclosed.[8] Before judgment, it may be difficult to know what evidence will ultimately prove material: accordingly, as a result, a prosecutor should resolve doubtful *Brady* disclosure questions in favor of disclosure.[9]

Where implicated, the *Brady* disclosure duty thus encompasses an obligation to disclose to the defense all evidence in its possession, custody, or control that would tend to help the accused: including information that would tend to impeach or undermine the credibility of an involved law enforcement officer.[10]

---

4 *ALADS, supra*, 8 Cal. 5th at pp. 39-41; *People v. Zambrano* (2007) 41 Cal.4th 1082, 1132; *see also United States v. Bagley* (1985) 473 U.S. 667, 676.

5 *Kyles, supra*, 514 U.S. at pp. 433–434.

6 *ALADS, supra*, 8 Cal. 5th at pp. 39-41; *Zambrano*, supra, 41 Cal.4th at p. 1132; *Kyles, supra*, 514 U.S. at p. 436.

7 *ALADS, supra*, 8 Cal. 5th at pp. 39-41; *Smith v. Cain* (2012) 565 U.S. 73, 75.

8 *ALADS, supra*, 8 Cal. 5th at pp. 39-41; *Kyles, supra*, 514 U.S. at pp. 437-438; *United States v. Agurs* (1976) 427 U.S. 97, 108.

9 *ALADS, supra*, 8 Cal. 5th at pp. 39-41; *Agurs, supra*, 427 U.S. at p. 108; *see also Kyles, supra*, 514 U.S. at pp. 438–439; Pen. Code, § 1054.1(d)–(e) (statutory disclosure obligation); Cal. R. Prof. Conduct, rule 3.8(d) & cmt. 3 (ethical disclosure obligation).

10 *ALADS, supra*, 8 Cal. 5th at pp. 47-54; Cal. Penal Code § 1054.1.

The *Brady* disclosure duty also extends to information that is not personally known to the prosecuting attorney: this means that the *Brady* duty carries with it a constitutional obligation to try to learn of any defense-favorable evidence known to others acting on the government's behalf in that same case (the "prosecution team"), including the police; but it does *not* extend to obtaining information from agencies or state actors who are not directly involved in that criminal prosecution.[11]

B. The Tension Between the Brady and the *Pitchess* Privilege.

From a practical perspective, this *Brady* disclosure duty of a prosecutor tends to collide with the *Pitchess* privilege rights: as prosecutors are accused of failing to disclose exculpatory evidence in the personnel files of officers who form part of the prosecution team or are prosecution witnesses.

A good example in how this tension plays out can be found in: *Association of Los Angeles Deputy Sheriffs (ALADS) v. Superior Court* (2019) 8 Cal.5th 28.

In *ALADS*, the California Supreme Court grappled with the aftershocks that the Legislature's 2018 adoption of the sometimes byzantine provisions of SB 1421 and AB 748 (effective January and July 2019, respectively) had upon long-established principles of *Pitchess* privilege and California Public Records Act ("CPRA") law.[12] As explained more fully in a preceding chapter, with conflicting exceptions, complex temporary withholding provisions, and overlapping and ambiguous procedures, SB 1421 and AB 748 are best harmonized to require that police records and recordings, including those normally protected from CPRA disclosure by Penal Code §§ 832.7-832.8 or Government Code §§ 7923.600-7923.625 (former Government Code § 6254(f)), must be disclosed upon CPRA request when such records and recordings pertain to one of the four categories specified in the 2019 amendments to those statutes.

In *ALADS*, the deputies' union argued that *Pitchess* privileges barred their law enforcement agency employer from disclosing to prosecutors the names and identifying information of officers on the Sheriff's Department's *Brady* list, including the fact that the officers may have *Brady*-disclosable

---

11 *ALADS*, *supra*, 8 Cal. 5th at pp. 39-41; *Kyles*, *supra*, 514 U.S. at pp. 437-438.

12 *ALADS*, *supra*, 8 Cal. 5th at pp. 39-57; Cal. Penal Code §§ 832.7-832.8; Cal. Gov. Code §§ 7923.600-7923.625 (formerly Cal. Gov. Code § 6254(f)).

information in their personnel files.[13] Notably, the union argument ignored the superior *Pitchess* privilege and waiver rights available to the custodial government entity.[14]

In considering the issues, the trial court held that, as to deputies who were involved as potential witnesses in the pending criminal case at issue, *Brady* lists could be produced to the prosecutor without violating *Pitchess*. The appellate court reversed, citing the *Pitchess* privilege as grounds to bar *Brady* lists' disclosure to prosecutors.

On review by the Supreme Court, the *ALADS* Court affirmed the *Pitchess* privilege, but harmonized it against the *Brady* disclosure duty in deciding that *Brady* list production did not violate the *Pitchess* privilege.

The *ALADS* Court reasoned that because a prosecutor has an affirmative constitutional duty not only to disclose exculpatory evidence in its possession, but also to seek out such information from other agencies participating in the criminal investigation at issue, and because a *Brady* list only reveals that specified officers *may* have *Brady*-disclosable information in their personnel files — *not* what that information specifically is — disclosure of *Brady* alert lists to prosecutors is permitted without seeking a *Pitchess* order.[15]

Notably, the *ALADS* Court underscored that, prosecutors in receipt of such a *Brady* list would still be required to obtain the relevant personnel file information by the *Pitchess* motion-order system. Under *ALADS*, the only exception for the prosecutor from the *Pitchess* privilege system for confidential officer personnel file records-information would be where the prosecutorial exception applies: namely, where the officer at issue is the *subject*, *not* just a witness, of the criminal investigation-prosecution.[16]

---

13 *ALADS*, *supra*, 8 Cal. 5th at pp. 39-57.

14 *Davis v. City of Sacramento* (1994) 24 Cal.App.4th 393; *McMahon v. City of Los Angeles* (2009) 172 Cal.App.4th 1324.

15 *ALADS*, *supra*, 8 Cal. 5th at pp. 39-57.

16 *ALADS*, *supra*, 8 Cal. 5th at pp. 39-57; *People v. Superior Ct. (Johnson)* (2015) 61 Cal.4th 696, 714-723.

Furthermore, as *Johnson* makes clear, the prosecutor is *not* required under *Brady* to bring a *Pitchess* motion to obtain such exculpatory officer personnel file information: though the prosecution, like the defense, is *permitted* to do so.[17]

Significantly, however, while, in *ALADS* and *Johnson*, the Supreme Court has repeatedly stated that law enforcement agencies' preparation of a *Brady* alert list is "laudable" — because such lists aid prosecutors in fulfilling their *Brady* disclosure constitutional duties — the Court held that law enforcement agencies are *not* required to maintain *Brady* lists.[18] Indeed, the *ALADS* Court was explicit, by clarifying that its ruling "is not to imply that *Brady* alerts are a constitutionally required means of ensuring *Brady* compliance; only that disclosure of *Brady* material is required, and that *Brady* alerts help to ensure satisfaction of that requirement."[19] This lack of duty as to maintaining *Brady* lists accords with the *ALADS* Court's recognition that many agencies do not maintain *Brady* lists, and with the absence of any mandate for doing so in the Court's key opinions on point, such as *ALADS* or *Johnson*.

Thus, the *ALADS* Court specifically held that a police department's "*Brady* list is confidential to the extent it was derived from confidential records"; but that any *Pitchess* confidentiality therein did *not* bar the police department from sharing such list with the prosecutor.[20] Along related lines, referencing the SB 1421 and AB 748 legislation that was still going into effect at the time, the *ALADS* Court also noted that where California law makes officer personnel file information non-confidential, such as under the 2019 CPRA exceptions, then *Brady* lists based on that non-confidential information are not confidential at all.[21]

This tension between *Brady* and *Pitchess* is thus something one may expect to recur in criminal cases.

---

17 *See ALADS, supra,* 8 Cal. 5th at pp. 39-57; *Johnson, supra,* 61 Cal.4th at 714-723.

18 *See ALADS, supra,* 8 Cal. 5th at pp. 39-57; *Johnson, supra,* 61 Cal.4th at 714-723.

19 *ALADS, supra,* 8 Cal. 5th at p. 52.

20 *ALADS, supra,* 8 Cal. 5th at pp. 43-44.

21 *See id.*

13. C.P.R.A.: A Primer on the California Public Records Acts and its Complex Intersection With *Pitchess* Privilege Law.

As explained in a preceding chapter on the exceptions from *Pitchess* ("STATUTORY EXEMPTIONS to the Otherwise Mandatory *Pitchess* Procedure"), the 2019 and 2022 amendments of SB 1421, SB 16 and AB 748 are most effectively viewed as a new California Public Records Act ("CPRA") statutory exception to the *Pitchess* privilege or, alternatively, as creating a new exception to some of the statutory exemptions from CPRA: somewhat narrowing the scope of some of the CPRA exemptions for *Pitchess*-privileged matter and for police investigatory records.[1]

However, since there is an increasingly complex relationship between the two competing legal impulses — one (*Pitchess*) presuming confidentiality, and the other (CPRA) presuming public access — a comprehensive understanding of the scope and operation of the *Pitchess* privilege warrants a deeper exploration of the California Public Records Act.[2]

---

1 *See* Cal. Penal Code §§ 832.7-832.8 (amend. 2019, 2022); Cal. Gov. Code §§ 7923.600-7923.625 (formerly Cal. Gov. Code § 6254(f)).

2 This chapter is intended to be only a brief overview of the CPRA. For a more extensive exploration of the CPRA, please see Additional Resources, such as below.

ADDITIONAL RESOURCES: *The People's Business: A Guide to the California Public Records Act*, League of California Cities, Apr. 2017 (a comprehensive review of the CPRA). Another excellent resource can be found at: James Chadwick/Sheppard Mullin, "First Amendment Coalition's California Public Records Act Primer," *Resources: Access to Records*, circa 2020 (a convenient short guide on the CPRA).

PRACTICE TIP: Many practitioners reference the CPRA as merely the Public Records Act (or "PRA"). *See, e.g., The People's Business: A Guide to the California Public Records Act*, League of California Cities, Apr. 2017; James Chadwick/Sheppard Mullin, "First Amendment Coalition's California Public Records Act Primer," *Resources: Access to Records*, circa 2020. However, for

A. The Policy Objectives of the CPRA.

Enacted in 1968 in response to California legislators' impatience with opacity in government, the CPRA is modeled on the federal Freedom of Information Act ("FOIA"): and the CPRA's rationale and purposes are often analyzed in tandem with the language, precedents, and history of the federal FOIA.[3]

The policy objectives of the CPRA are stated at the outset of the Act: "In enacting this chapter, the Legislature, mindful of the right of individuals to privacy, finds and declares that access to information concerning the conduct of the people's business is a fundamental and necessary right of every person in this state."[4] In explaining this rationale, courts often quote James Madison: who stated that knowledge "'will forever govern ignorance and a people who mean to be their own governors [] must arm themselves with the power knowledge gives. A popular government without popular information[,] or the means of acquiring it, is but a prologue to a farce or a tragedy or perhaps both.'"[5]

It thus should come as no surprise that, in 2004, the CPRA was effectively incorporated into the California Constitution itself, which held (as a general proposition) that: "[t]he people have the right of access to information concerning the conduct of the people's business, and, therefore, the meetings of public bodies and the writings of public officials and agencies shall be open to public scrutiny"; and making state and local agency compliance with the CPRA a constitutional mandate (subject to legal limits specified elsewhere).[6]

---

practitioners who practice in both California state and federal courts, omitting the state origin from the Act name can lead to confusion. Moreover, **the Act itself announces its name as the "*California* Public Records Act."** Cal. Gov. Code § 7920.000 (formerly Cal. Gov. Code § 6251; emphasis added). Hence, here, CPRA is the norm; *not* PRA. Cal. Gov. Code §§ 7920.000-7931.000 (formerly Cal. Gov. Code §§ 6250-6277) (CPRA).

3 *See American Civ. Liberties Union Found'n v. Deukmejian* (1982) 32 Cal.3d 440, 447-449; *accord San Gabriel Tribune v. Superior Ct.* (1983) 143 Cal.App.3d 762, 771-773 ("James Madison stated...[that knowledge] 'will forever govern ignorance and a people who mean to be their own governors [] must arm themselves with the power knowledge gives. A popular government without popular information[,] or the means of acquiring it, is but a prologue to a farce or a tragedy or perhaps both.'").

4 Cal. Gov. Code § 7921.000 (formerly Cal. Gov. Code § 6250).

5 *See, e.g., San Gabriel Tribune, supra,* 143 Cal.App.3d at pp. 771-773.

6 *See* Cal. Const., art. I, § 3(b)(1); *see also* Cal. Const., art. I, § 3(b)(7) (mandating state and local agency compliance with the CPRA and the Ralph M. Brown Act, Cal. Gov. Code § 54950, *et seq.*).

B. Public Entities Subject to the CPRA.

In summary, **except the California state Legislature and the state Judiciary, *every public entity* in California is subject to the CPRA's requirements**, including every: state agency (including the State Bar of California), state officer, county, city (whether general law or chartered), city and county (like the unified public entity that is San Francisco), school district, municipal corporation, district, political subdivision, board, commission or agency thereof, or other local or public agency available under Government Code section 54952.[7]

By contrast, state *legislative* records are *not* subject to CPRA requests; but such state legislative records *are* available under an alternative public access provision, the Legislative Records Act.[8]

C. CPRA Definition of Public Records.

Under the CPRA, a "public record" is "any writing containing information relating to the conduct of the public's business [that was or is] prepared, owned, used, or retained by any state or local agency[,] regardless of physical form or characteristics."[9]

As a foundation to establishing its disclosure requirements, the CPRA broadly defines a "writing" as basically any kind of record, in any medium stored or recorded, including: "any handwriting, typewriting, printing, photostating, photographing, photocopying, transmitting by electronic mail or facsimile, and every other means of recording upon any tangible thing any communication or representation, including letters, words, pictures, sounds, or symbols, or combinations thereof, and any record thereby created, regardless of the manner in which the record has been stored."[10]

---

7 Cal. Gov. Code § 7920.510 (formerly Cal. Gov. Code § 6252).

8 Cal. Gov. Code §§ 9070-9080 (Legislative Records Act); *see also* Cal. Gov. Code § 9073, *et seq.* (legislative record request procedures).

9 Cal. Gov. Code §§ 7920.530, 7920.545 (formerly Cal. Gov. Code § 6252(e), (g)) (but excluding from the "public records" definition records that are in the custody of the Governor's Office that were created on or before January 5, 1975); *California State Univ. Fresno v. Superior Ct.* (2001) 90 Cal.App.4th 810, 824-825.

10 Cal. Gov. Code § 7920.545 (formerly Cal. Gov. Code § 6252(g)); *see also* Cal. Gov Code §§ 7928.700 (formerly Cal. Gov. Code § 6253.31) (making private entity agency audit-review

Although some sister-state courts have construed similar definitions of public records to include metadata that is part of an underlying public document, it is unclear if such is the rule under the CPRA.[11]

All told, the definition of "public record" is broadly construed.[12] Indeed, particularly in light of the constitutional incorporation, courts construe the CPRA *disclosure duty broadly*, but the *exemptions* from CPRA disclosure *narrowly*.[13]

1. *Government Records Prepared, Owned, Used, or Retained By A State Or Local Agency Are Public Records.*

In order to be subject to the CPRA as public records, the requested records must be: (1) "related to the conduct of the public's business"; and (2) "prepared, owned, used or retained by any state or local agency."[14] Significantly, **the definition of "public records" only applies to eligible records in existence *at the time of the request.***[15]

Where a record is possessed by a public entity's consultant or agent/employee, but where the public entity has the legal or contractual right of

---

contracts public records), 7924.510 (formerly Cal. Gov. Code § 6254.7) (making pollution monitoring data and reports public records), 7928.400 (formerly Gov. Code § 6254.8) (making public employee contracts public records — *but see Versaci v. Superior Ct.* (2005) 127 Cal.App.4th 805, 817 (exempting from disclosure employee personal performance goals included in public employee contracts)), 6261 (itemized statements of judicial expenditures are public records).

11 *Compare Lake v. City of Phoenix* (Ariz. S. Ct. 2009) 218 P.3d 1004, 1007-1008 (where a public record document is created in electronic format, the underlying metadata is as much a part of the document as the visible portion, and such must therefore be disclosed under Arizona's public records laws) *and O'Neill v. City of Shoreline* (Wa. S. Ct. 2010) 240 P.3d 1149, 1154 (because metadata could show how and potentially why a public record document has been altered, metadata falls within the kind of public record information subject to disclosure under Washington's public records laws) *with* Cal. Gov. Code §§ 7922.570, 7922.680, 7922.585 (formerly Cal. Gov. Code §§ 6253.9, 6253.10, 6254.9(a)-(d), respectively) (exempting proprietary computer software from public records disclosure).

12 *California State Univ. Fresno, supra*, 90 Cal.App.4th at pp. 824-825.

13 *See Commission on Peace Officer Standards & Training (POST) v. Superior Ct.* (2007) 42 Cal.4th 278, 305-306; *Sierra Club v. Superior Ct.* (2013) 57 Cal.4th 157, 175-176; *Sutter's Place v. Superior Ct.* (2008) 1616 Cal.App.4th 1370, 1378-1381.

14 Cal. Gov. Code § 7920.530 (formerly Cal. Gov. Code § 6252(e)); *cf.* Cal. Gov. Code §§ 7924.110, 7924.005 (formerly Cal. Gov. Code §§6253.5-6253.6) (making certain election petitions and related materials, but not requests for bilingual ballots, public records).

15 Cal. Gov. Code §§ 7920.530, 7920.545, 7922.525, 7929.000 (formerly Cal. Gov. Code §§ 6252(e), (g), 6253, 6254(d)(3)).

ownership over such records, such records are deemed to be within the constructive possession of the public entity; by contrast, where there is no such legal right of ownership, records in the possession or control of a public entity's agent are *not* deemed to be within the constructive possession of the public agency.[16]

Thus, for example, where a public employee was conducting public business using his personal email account, those emails were subject to CPRA disclosure as public records.[17] However, by contrast, where a city consultant's files were *not* contractually owned by the city, and where the consultant was an independent contractor, even though the consultant's work regarded public business, the records in the consultant's possession were *not* public records subject to CPRA disclosure.[18]

However, **just because the government has *custody* of some record, that custody does *not* transform the record into a public record**; rather, to be a public record, it must be a "record [that] is kept by an officer [of the government] because it is necessary or convenient to the discharge of his official duty, [then] it is a public record."[19] Thus, even if a record is in the possession of a public entity, if the record contains mostly *personal* information, like an employee's residential address or personal to-do lists for grocery shopping or personal messages that are **unrelated to the public employee's government activities**, such records are *not* public records.[20]

---

16 *See, e.g., City of San Jose v. Superior Ct.* (2017) 2 Cal.5th 608, 623-629 (records of public employees conducting public business are public records subject to the CPRA, even if stored in private accounts); *Consolidated Irrigation Dist. v. Superior Ct.* (2013) 205 Cal.App.4th 697, 710-711 (because city did not have ownership or legal control over files in the possession of its independent contractor consultant, the consultant's records were *not* public records); *Community Youth Athletic Ctr. v. City of Nat'l City* (2013) 220 Cal.App.4th 1385, 1428-1429 (where city contract with survey consultant gave it contractual ownership over related files in consultant's possession, those files were public records subject to the CPRA; but the city was not required to forward the CRPA request to the contractor verbatim).

17 *City of San Jose, supra,* 2 Cal.5th at pp. 623-629.

18 *Consolidated Irrigation Dist., supra,* 205 Cal.App.4th at pp. 710-711.

19 *Id.*; *San Gabriel Tribune, supra,* 143 Cal.App.3d at p. 774.

20 *San Gabriel Tribune, supra,* 143 Cal.App.3d at p. 774 (home/personal shopping list, friend's letter to public officer unrelated to government activities, and comparable personal records are *not* public records, even when in the possession of a public entity); *accord Braun v. City of Taft* (1984) 154 Cal.App.3d 332, 340; *see Regents of the Univ. of Cal. v. Superior Ct.* (2013) 222 Cal.App.4th 383, 399-405 (financial investment records not prepared, owned, used or retained by the public entity are *not* public records).

The definition of "public records" is thus key to understanding the CPRA disclosure duty: the CPRA effectively presumes that all government-held records are disclosable public records; but then the CPRA specifically carves out numerous exemptions and, more recently, exceptions to those exemptions — as will be detailed more fully below.

D. C.P.R.A. REQUEST PROCEDURE: Making a Public Records Request Under the CPRA.

1. *WHO May Request Public Entity Records.*

Generally, any "person" who is a "member of the public" may request disclosure-publication of public entity records.[21]

Under the CPRA, a "person" is "any natural person, corporation, partnership, limited liability company, firm, or association; *but* a "member of the public" is "any person except a member, agent, officer, or employee of a federal, state, or local agency acting within the scope of his or her membership, agency, office, or employment."[22] In other words, under a literal reading of Section 6252, governments and government actors working in the course and scope of their duties would *not* be proper CPRA requesters.[23]

Fortunately, Section 6252.5 and associated case law clarifies that, notwithstanding Section 6252's definition of "member of the public," elected officials and officers of any state or local agency do have standing to make CPRA requests, just like anyone else.[24]

---

21 Cal. Gov. Code §§ 7920.515, 7920.520 (formerly Cal. Gov. Code § 6252(b)-(c)); Cal. Gov. Code § 7922.525 (formerly Cal. Gov. Code § 6253).

22 Cal. Gov. Code §§ 7920.515, 7920.520 (formerly Cal. Gov. Code § 6252(b)-(c)) (emphasis added).

23 *See id.*; *see also National Conf. of Black Mayors v. Chino Cmty. Publishing, Inc.* (2018) 25 Cal.App.5th 570, 586-587 (impliedly distinguishing a "public officer" from a "member of the public").

24 Cal. Gov. Code § 7921.305(a) (formerly Cal. Gov. Code § 6252.5); *Los Angeles Unif. Sch. Dist. v. Superior Ct.* (2007) 151 Cal.App.4th 759, 763-764, 766-767, 772-773 (where a school district denied a city attorney's CPRA request on grounds that the city attorney was not a member of the public under the CPRA, the court affirmed the city attorney's right to the requested records and impliedly affirmed the city's CPRA right to fees).

Significantly, the requester's *purpose* in seeking the public records is *irrelevant*: as long as the records are CPRA-disclosable, the public agency has a duty to disclose such; and a government entity may *not* impose restrictions upon access to public records based upon the requester's purpose.[25]

2. *HOW Public Records Requests May Be Made.*

The CPRA envisions four ways by which CPRA requesters may obtain access to public records: (1) by personal inspection at a government agency; (2) by requesting and obtaining copies of public records; (3) by the agency posting public records on its website; or (4) by an alternative procedure designed by the government agency, as long as such complies with the minimum standards imposed by the CPRA.[26]

The CPRA request must "reasonably describe an identifiable record" in order to trigger the CPRA disclosure duty.[27] However, notably, there is *no* express requirement in the CPRA that the CPRA request be in writing: unless a reasonable agency procedure requires otherwise, a CPRA request can be made orally, in person or by phone.[28]

a. In Person Public Records Inspections.

Government agencies must make public records available for in person inspection during their regular office hours, except those portions that are exempt from CPRA disclosure.[29] The CPRA thus presumes that, on verbal or written request, a CPRA requester can come in to a government office, and just start poking away through the public records requested: with some reasonable limitations, as explained more fully below.

---

25 Cal. Gov. Code § 7921.300 (formerly Cal. Gov. Code § 6257.5).

26 Cal. Gov. Code §§ 7922.525, 7922.530(a), 7922.535, 7922.500, 7922.505, 7922.545 (formerly Cal. Gov. Code § 6253(a)-(f)).

27 Cal. Gov. Code §§ 7922.525, 7922.530(a) (formerly Cal. Gov. Code § 6253(a)-(b)).

28 *See, e.g.*, Cal. Gov. Code § 7922.525 (formerly Cal. Gov. Code § 6253); Cal. Gov. Code § 7922.600 (formerly Cal. Gov. Code § 6253.1); *Los Angeles Times v. Alameda Corridor Transp. Auth.* (2001) 88 Cal.App.4th 1381, 1392.

29 Cal. Gov. Code §§ 7922.525, 7922.530(a) (formerly Cal. Gov. Code § 6253(a)-(b)).

b. Requests For Copies Of Public Records.

Where a CPRA requester seeks to have the custodial government agency produce copies of requested public records, the agency is required to do so either: (1) by producing hardcopies, upon the requester's payment of direct copying costs; *or* (2) by posting the requested records to the agency's website and directing the requester to the specific web page where such records are posted — unless the requester makes a subsequent conditional request for record hardcopies, which then forces the agency to re-disclose the records as hardcopies.[30]

As explained more fully below, while the in-person inspection request presumes more or less same-day *access* to the requested records, *without* copying by the custodial agency, a request for public record copies permits the agency to take up to 10 days to respond to the request, with various extensions of time available under the CPRA — as explained more fully below.[31]

c. Website Posting Of Public Records.

Either preemptively or in response to a CPRA request, a public agency can also satisfy the CPRA by posting the requested record on its website: in the case of a CPRA request, the agency must then also direct the requester to the specific "location on the internet website" where the requested public record is posted.[32] The CPRA thus presumes that when pointing the requester to a website, the requester will be able to view the requested documents directly, without substantial additional searching or research.[33]

However, where an agency responds to a CPRA request by directing the requester to public records on its website, such web-pointing does *not* necessarily absolve the agency of any hardcopy production duty: where, *after* a website posting referral by the agency, the requester then claims an inability to access the public record on the website, or an inability to "reproduce" (*e.g.*,

30 Cal. Gov. Code §§ 7922.535, 7922.500 (formerly Cal. Gov. Code § 6253(c)-(d)).

31 *See, e.g.*, Cal. Gov. Code § 7922.535 (formerly Cal. Gov. Code § 6253(c)).

32 Cal. Gov. Code § 7922.545 (formerly Cal. Gov. Code § 6253(f)); *see also* Cal. Gov. Code § 7924.900 (formerly Cal. Gov. Code § 6253.8) (mandating specified state agency enforcement orders to be posted on the agency's website).

33 *See id.*; *see also* Cal. Gov. Code § 7922.600(a) (formerly Cal. Gov. Code § 6253.1(a) (agency's duty to assist the requester to identify specific documents responsive to the request).

print) the public record(s) at issue from the website, the requester's subsequent modified request for public record copies triggers the agency's duty to produce those same public records via the hardcopy CPRA disclosure-production provisions of Government Code section 7922.530(a) (formerly Government Code section 6253(b)).[34]

d. Agency-Customized Public Record Access Procedures: Limits.

The CPRA also allows public agencies to devise their own custom procedures for CPRA requests and production: provided that such alternative or supplemental procedures comply with the CPRA's minimum standards in a way that "allow[s] for faster, more efficient, or greater access to [public] records" than would otherwise be available under the CPRA's procedures.[35]

This includes agency-customized procedures that constitute "reasonable limits on the use of the requester's equipment that are necessary to protect the safety of the records" or that are needed to "ensure the long-term preservation [or integrity] of historic or high-value records"; as well as custom procedures that are designed to "prevent the copying of records from being an unreasonable burden to the orderly function of the agency and its employees."[36]

As a general rule, agencies are strongly encouraged to develop clear, written procedures and forms for submitting and responding to CPRA requests.

---

34 Cal. Gov. Code §§ 7922.530(a), 7922.545 (formerly Cal. Gov. Code § 6253(b), (f)).

35 Cal. Gov. Code §§ 7922.530(c), 7922.505 (formerly Cal. Gov. Code § 6253(d)(2), (e)); *see also* Cal. Gov. Code § 7922.630 (formerly Cal. Gov. Code § 6253.4(a)) ("Every agency may adopt regulations in accordance with this article stating the procedures to be followed when making its records available."); Cal. Gov. Code § 7922.640(a) (formerly Cal. Gov. Code § 6253.4(c)) (requiring agency-customized procedures to be consistent with the CPRA and its underlying legislative intent).

PRACTICE TIP: Every public entity should establish a straightforward, clear set of publicly-available procedural rules and forms for submitting CPRA requests, in consultation with experienced counsel. As to a web-based form that allows requesters to give the agency the kind of information it needs to evaluate the agency needs, such forms tend to reduce the need for clarification and time-consuming disputes with requesters. In consultation with experienced counsel, agencies should also establish a standard form for responses to CPRA requests, both for disclosures and denials, to ensure that the agency's responses are uniform and in full compliance with the CPRA.

36 Cal. Gov. Code §§ 7922.530(c), 7922.505 (formerly Cal. Gov. Code § 6253(d)(2), (e))

E. C.P.R.A. RESPONSES: Due Dates, Determining What Is Responsive, and Logistical Issues for Responding To A CPRA Request.

1. *Deadlines For A Response To A CPRA Request: Agency's Production of COPIES of Public Records.*

a. 10 Day Response To CPRA Request For Copies.

Somewhat distinguished from the in person public records inspection request, where the CPRA requester is seeking **agency-made copies** of the requested public records, the CPRA clearly holds that, in general, the agency has 10 days to respond to the request, as measured by the receipt date: by either "promptly" producing the requested records with *or* subsequent to the response or, if public records are being withheld, by stating the agency's reasons for such withholding — such as the applicability of a Section 6254 exemption.[37]

As explained more fully below, for a CPRA request for copies, the CPRA does *not* require disclosure-production of public records on the same day that the agency gives its response to the request.

b. Additional 14 Day Extended Response.

However, in "unusual circumstances," through the agency's head or agency's designee, the agency can automatically extend its time to respond to the CPRA request by an additional 14 days (i.e., up to 24 days from the date the request was received), provided that:

(1) [**Written Notice of Extension**] the agency provides written notice to the requester of its invocation of the 14-day extension; *and*

(2) [**Estimated Date of Production**] the agency provides a written estimate as to the date and time when the requested records will be made available; *and*

(3) [**Need to Search Separate Archive**] the "unusual circumstance" at issue involves the agency's need to search agency facilities that are separate

---

37 Cal. Gov. Code §§ 7922.530(a), 7922.535 (formerly Cal. Gov. Code § 6253(b)-(c)).

from the facility where the request was received, and to collect responsive records therefrom; *or*

(4) [**Need to Search Voluminous Records**] the "unusual circumstance" at issue involves the agency's need to search through "a voluminous amount of separate and distinct records that are demanded in a single request"; *or*

(5) [**Need to Consult With Another Agency or Department**] the "unusual circumstance" at issue involves the need to consult with another agency or department with a "substantial interest in the determination of the request"; *or*

(6) [**Need to Compile Computer Data**] the "unusual circumstance" at issue involves the agency's need to compile computerized data, including construction of a data abstract, or customized computer programming in order to satisfy the request.[38]

2. *Deadlines For Response to CPRA Request: Requester's IN PERSON Inspection of Public Records.*

The CPRA presumes that a request for **in person inspection** of public records, without agency copying, must be satisfied on or about the same day as the request, *if* the request is made during regular office hours and the records can be easily compiled; otherwise, even for in-person requests, the CPRA presumes that the requester can come back to the agency's office during regular office hours so the agency can "promptly" satisfy the inspection request after the responsive records have been located and compiled.[39]

Notwithstanding the foregoing, some practitioners construe the CPRA to mean that, in order to permit the agency to have adequate time to examine, identify, collect, and produce responsive records — and to redact such, if necessary — even for in person inspections, the 10 day rule that applies to responding to a request for copies *also* applies to responding to a request for in person inspection.[40]

---

38 Cal. Gov. Code §§ 7922.535 (formerly Cal. Gov. Code § 6253(c)).

39 *See Rosenthal v. Hansen* (1973) 34 Cal.App.3d 754, 761.

40 *See generally* Cal. Gov. Code §§ 7922.525, 7922.530(a), 7922.505, 7922.500 (formerly Cal. Gov. Code § 6253(a)-(d)); 88 Ops. Cal. Atty. Gen. 153 (2005).

Given the lack of clear authority on point, for in person inspections, **the safest practice is for public entities to presume that a response to a request must be provided as close in time to the request as is allowed by the agency's office hours and its need to review, identify, compile, and possibly redact the requested public records**. As explained more fully below, even for an in person CPRA request, the CPRA does *not* require disclosure-production of public records on the same day that the agency gives its response to the request.

a. Agency May Impose Reasonable Restrictions On Disclosure.

However, in any case, the in person inspection option presumes that the agency may impose reasonable restrictions: (a) to prevent the requester from taking possession of the public records made available for inspection; and/or (b) to prevent the requester from so monopolizing the records at issue that he or she (1) unduly interferes with the work of that public agency, or (2) impairs other requesters' equal access to such public records.[41]

Thus, a public entity is entitled to devise and enforce reasonable rules and restrictions for public inspections of records where such rules are designed "to protect the safety of the records against theft, mutilation or accidental damage, to prevent inspection from interfering with the orderly function of [its] office and its employees, and generally to avoid chaos in the records archives."[42]

Notably, as long as the requester seeks to make copies himself or herself of such records by using a device that does *not* involve physical contact with the records, and as long as the requester's copying methods will *not* result in document destruction or access to secure computer databases, under the CPRA, the requester *is* allowed to make his or her own copies, such as by photographing each page.[43] The requester is also allowed to use the agency's own equipment to do make copies, free of charge and within reasonable restrictions:

---

41 *Bruce v. Gregory* (1967) 65 Cal.2d 666, 676-678 (holding that Cal. Gov. Code § 1227 and Cal. Code Civ. Proc. § 1892 empower agencies to impose reasonable restrictions on in person inspections of public records "to protect the safety of the records against theft, mutilation or accidental damage, to prevent inspection from interfering with the orderly function of [its] office and its employees, and generally to avoid chaos in the records archives.").

42 *Bruce, supra*, 65 Cal.2d at pp. 676-678; *accord Rosenthal, supra*, 34 Cal.App.3d at p. 761.

43 Cal. Gov. Code § 7922.530(b)-(c) (formerly Cal. Gov. Code § 6253(d)(1)-(2)).

provided that the agency's equipment also does not physically touch or damage the public records at issue.[44]

Given these restrictions on in person inspection, it is perhaps no surprise that most requesters simply request agency-made copies of the public records sought.

3. *Deadlines: Reasonable Timeliness of Response and Production Suffice.*

Notably, while the CPRA includes no penalty for untimely responses or production, at a certain point, courts will treat unreasonable delays in responses or production as a failure to comply with the CPRA.[45] Thus, while there is no specific authority under the CPRA defining what constitutes an *un*timely response or *un*timely production, courts often treat CPRA responses as *timely* under the Act where "an agency…makes a 'good faith effort[] to fully and timely respond to a records request,' and produces all requested records in a 'reasonably timely fashion' or in a 'reasonably prompt' manner given the breadth of the particular request."[46]

For example, in one pertinent case, a requester made an "informal" CPRA request to a public agency on March 24 and 30, 1992, and then a "formal" CPRA request on April 12, 1992; the agency then produced responsive records, first on April 17, 1992, and then again on May 11, 1992; then, when

44 Cal. Gov. Code § 7922.530(b)-(c) (formerly Cal. Gov. Code § 6253(d)(1)-(2)).

PRACTICE TIP: It is difficult to imagine a copying machine that does not touch the documents it copies. As a result, this "restriction" may operate in practice more like a prohibition on free copying by the agency.

45 *See Motorola Comm'n & Elec., Inc. v. Department of Gen. Serv.* (1997) 55 Cal.App.4th 1340, 1345 (where CPRA disclosures were made only after a CPRA lawsuit had been noticed, the delayed disclosures were untimely); *Found v. Regents of the Univ. of Cal.* (Los Angeles Super. Ct. 2019) 2019 Cal. Super. LEXIS 10578, *3-5 (rejecting the Regents' argument that there could never be a penalty for an untimely response, and concluding that where the responding agency demonstrates bad faith delay or a lack of unusual circumstances affecting the promptness of a CPRA response, courts have power to enforce the CPRA against the responding agency); *Wilder v. Superior Ct.* (1998) 66 Cal.App.4th 77, 84 (the "timeliness of disclosure is often of crucial importance in actions brought under the Public Records Act"); *but see Rogers v. Superior Ct.* (1993) 19 Cal.App.4th 469, 483 ("The Act provides no remedy for failure to timely comply with a request for records.").

46 *Mahan v. California Air. Res. Control Bd.* (Sacramento Super. Ct. 2017) 2017 Cal. Super. LEXIS 14856, *31 (citing *Pacific Merchant Ship. Assn. v. Board of Pilot Comm.* (2015) 242 Cal. App.4th 1043, 1059).

the requester then made a further CPRA request on May 21, 1992, the agency produced records in response to those requests on June 8, 1992, and again on July 1, 1992 — more than 3 months after the initial request, and about 6 seeks after the last request: in that case, the reviewing court held that there was no actionable CPRA violation by the agency because the government entity had produced its responsive records in a "reasonably timely manner…."[47]

Similarly, where a business requested contract information from a state agency on June 27, 1995 via a mailed and faxed CPRA request, and where the agency notified that business requester on July 5, 1995 that it was compiling the requested records; and where the agency then produced some of the requested records on July 7 or July 10, as well as a substantial amount of responsive records in binders produced on July 11; and where the agency then notified the CPRA requester on July 13 that one contract was being withheld due to proprietary information therein; although the reviewing court had held that *some* of the response was untimely, for purposes of evaluating whether the CPRA requester was a "prevailing party" entitled to recover attorneys' fees, the reviewing court held that *the state agency substantially complied with the request*, and that thus, as to the CPRA lawsuit filed July 14, 1995, the state agency was the prevailing party.[48]

In other words, although the CPRA specifies that a response to a request is due 10 days from the request's receipt date, with an available 14-day extension, as long as the public entity makes a good faith effort to fully and timely respond to the request in a reasonably timely manner and to produce disclosable records in a reasonably prompt fashion, there should be no penalty to the agency that misses those 10-day or 24-day (10+14) deadlines.[49]

47 *Rogers, supra*, 19 Cal.App.4th at p. 483.

48 *Motorola, supra*, 55 Cal.App.4th at pp. 1342, 1348-1351.

49 *Motorola, supra*, 55 Cal.App.4th at p. 1349 ("[The CPRA] requires an agency, upon receipt of a request for public records, to determine within 10 days whether to comply [with the request] and to notify the requesting party of its decision. **It does not require the production within 10 days**…. The Public Records Act does not specify when records must be produced to a requesting party." (emphasis added).)

PRACTICE TIP: Additionally, the time to respond to a CPRA request is automatically extended to the next business day where the response deadline would otherwise fall on a weekend or holiday. *See* Cal. Civ. Code §§ 10-11.

While also endeavoring to come as close as practicable to the statutory response deadlines in both their response and their post-response production-disclosure of records, agencies should keep this legal leeway in mind.

4. *Deadlines: Calculated From Receipt Date, Not Service Date.*

Where the CPRA references the deadlines for responding to a CPRA request, it says that the response is due "within 10 days from **receipt** of the request…."[50] However, the date a request is *received* is *not* necessarily the same as the date the request was *made or served.*[51]

The difference between the two dates — service date versus receipt date — is a matter of hornbook law that arises most frequently in civil litigation regarding the calculation of when a response is due to a summons/complaint, and/or to a discovery request, served by mail, as opposed to served/delivered in person.

Service. Under the Code of Civil Procedure, the infamous "mailbox rule" holds that a pleading or discovery request is deemed to have been "served" on the recipient party on the date such pleading or discovery was placed into the mail; *not* on the date upon which it was actually received by the recipient.[52] Thus, any deadlines for the recipient to respond to that served document are calculated from the mail-deposit date, *not* the mail-receipt date — with an automatic extension of 5 days' response time because the document requiring a response was mailed to the recipient, rather than delivered in person (personal service).[53]

However, other areas of California law do *not* automatically embrace the principles of the mailbox rule for deadline calculation. For example,

---

50 Cal. Gov. Code § 7922.535(a) (formerly Cal. Gov. Code § 6253(c)) (emphasis added).

51 *See generally Motorola, supra,* 55 Cal.App.4th at p. 1349; *Mahan, supra,* 2017 Cal. Super. LEXIS 14856 at pp. 26-27 (citing *Motorola* and Section 6253).

52 *See* Cal. Code Civ. Proc. § 1013(a); *McKeon v. Sambrano* (1927) 200 Cal. 739, 741 ("'service is complete at the time of the deposit' in the mail"); *Cole v. Los Angeles Unif. Sch. Dist.* (1986) 177 Cal.App.3d 1, 4 (the extension available under Section 1013 does *not* apply to a public entity's deadline to respond to a Tort Claims Act demand).

53 *See* Cal. Code Civ. Proc. § 1013(a); *McKeon, supra,* 200 Cal. at p. 741; *Cole, supra,* 177 Cal.App.3d at p. 4.

ail-service of a Government Code tort claim does *not* extend the time for : public entity to serve its claim response.[54]

Receipt. Here, the CPRA does *not* state that a public agency's response due within 10 days (or up to 24 days) from the date the CPRA request is ade or served; rather, the CPRA specifically starts the deadline clock from e date upon which the agency *received* the request.[55]

Thus, where a CPRA request is made in person, and when the agency's fice is open, the request date and the receipt date will be the same day; as ould also generally be the case, barring technical problems impairing timely ceipt, where the request was emailed or faxed to the recipient public agency.

However, significantly, where a CPRA request is mailed, the request may ot be received for *days* after the mail-deposit/service date.

Thus, for example, in the case of a mailed CPRA request, since the CPRA ases its deadlines upon agency *receipt*, and *not* upon service, for example, if ie CPRA request was mailed on July 29 but not received until August 5, the)-day response deadline would be calculated from August 5: as August 15 of iat same year.

As a result, in calculating their CPRA response deadlines and CPRA roduction-disclosure deadlines, public entities should use the CPRA request's *ceipt* date, *not* the date on the which the request appears to have been made, or the apparent service date of the request.

5. *CPRA Response v. CPRA Disclosure-Production.*

Notably, when the CPRA request is for *copies* of public records, **the CPRA mandates that the response-determination be made *in writing*.**[56] The uthority does not specify that such is required for *in person* CPRA requests or inspection; but agencies would be wise to presume that a written response o a CPRA request is always the best practice.

---

54 *See Cole, supra*, 177 Cal.App.3d at p. 4.

55 *Compare* Cal. Code Civ. Proc. § 1013(a) *with* Cal. Gov. Code § 7922.535(a) (formerly Cal. Gov. Code § 6253(c)).

56 Cal. Gov. Code § 7922.540(a) (formerly Cal. Gov. Code § 6255(b)).

On a related note, many practitioners erroneously presume that the deadline for responding to the CPRA request with the agency's disclosure determination is the same date as the deadline for making any CPRA disclosures-production itself: but the authorities provide more leeway on this issue than one would presume — in a way that underscores that an agency's *response* to a CPRA request is *not* necessarily the same thing as its *disclosure-production.*

Specifically, in reference to making a "response" to a CPRA request, Section 6253(c) of the CPRA states that, after making its determination within 10 days as to whether the request seeks disclosable records, the public agency "shall promptly notify the person making the request of the [agency's] determination and the reasons therefor"; then, "when the agency dispatches the determination, and if the agency determines that the request seeks disclosable public records, the agency shall state the estimated date and time when the records will be made available."[57]

In other words, the CPRA's statutory language contemplates that a public agency's determination-response to a CPRA request is *not* necessarily the same thing as its disclosure-production of records responsive to that request; rather, the statute presumes that the agency's response-determination to the CPRA request *precedes* and is *separate* from its production of records responsive to that request.[58]

Such statutory construction necessarily implies that, whereas the common presumption is that disclosure-production is due within 10 to 24 days of the request (10 days, plus the 14-day extension, where applicable), this presumption is perhaps misleading and incorrect. Rather, **as long as the disclosure-production is made "promptly available" to the requester after the response is made, a deadline which authority indicates to be production in a "reasonably timely manner" after the request and response, then the public agency should be in compliance with the CPRA.**[59]

---

57 *See* Cal. Gov. Code § 7922.535(a) (formerly Cal. Gov. Code § 6253(c)).

58 *Id.* (also presuming that a CPRA response-determination is in writing); *see generally Rogers, supra,* 19 Cal.App.4th at p. 483.

59 *See* Cal. Gov. Code §§ 7922.530(a), 7922.535(a) (formerly Cal. Gov. Code § 6253(b)-(c)); *Motorola, supra,* 55 Cal.App.4th at p. 1349 ("[The CPRA] requires an agency, upon receipt of a request for public records, to determine within 10 days whether to comply [with the request] and to notify the requesting party of its decision. It does *not* require the production within 10 days… The Public Records Act does not specify when records must be produced to a requesting party.");

In sum, in most cases, the CPRA does *not* require a public agency to produce responsive records within 10 to 24 days of the receiving the CPRA request; rather, the agency is required to transmit a response-determination generally within the 10 to 24 day deadline, or within a reasonably timely manner, and thereafter the agency is required to disclose-produce the responsive, non-exempt public records to the requester, also within a reasonably timely manner after the response and request-receipt dates.[60]

The New 45 Day Production Deadline For Specified Officer Misconduct. However, effective January 1, 2022, through SB 16, the California Legislature has imposed a specific deadline for disclosure-production of public records that are not being withheld — where the records pertain to specified instances of officer misconduct.

To elaborate, where the public records sought pertain to one of the eight categories of officer misconduct for which police investigative and officer personnel file records are now CPRA-disclosable, under SB 16, unless the agency is withholding the records under an operative exemption or caveat that negates or delays its duty of disclosure, the agency is now required to disclose-produce public records "at the earliest possible time and no later than 45 days from the date of the request for their disclosure."[61]

This means that, unless an exemption or caveat applies that authorizes the custodial public entity to permanently or temporarily withhold the requested records, where the requested public records pertain to (1) an OIS of/at a person, (2) a UOF causing D/GBI, or a sustained finding of (3) officer excessive force, (4) officer failure to intervene to stop excessive force, (5) sexual assault on a member of the public (specially defined), (6) officer dishonesty in law enforcement duties, (7) officer discrimination, or (8) unlawful arrest or unlawful search, the custodial government entity is required to produce such public records to the requester **no later than 45 days from the date of receipt of the request**.

Rogers, supra, 19 Cal.App.4th at p. 483 (emphasis added); *Mahan, supra*, 2017 Cal. Super. LEXIS 14856 at p. *31.

60 *See id.*

61 Cal. Penal Code § 832.7(b)(11) (amend. 2022).

6. ***Requests For Clarification Are Due Before The Agency's Response-Determination.***

As explained more fully below, public entities have a legal duty to assist the CPRA requester in making a disclosable request.[62] From this agency duty to assist arises a duty to seek clarification of vague/ambiguous CPRA requests. Essentially, "[a] public agency has a duty to make 'a reasonable effort to elicit additional clarifying information from the requester that will help identify the record or records'" sought.[63] Moreover, the CPRA presumes that such a request for clarification will come *before* the response-determination is made.[64]

Thus, for example, where a CPRA requester sought certain city-related emails for the private accounts of a specific public employee (the city attorney), but the request did not specify whether it sought emails conducting city business on the private accounts of the public employee or private emails on the private account, when the city responded on the assumption that the CPRA request sought only that public employee's *private* emails, and thereby refused the request in its response-determination, because the city had *not* sought clarification *before* making its response, and because public records stored in public employees' private accounts (but *not* private records stored in the private account) *are* CPRA-disclosable, the reviewing court held that the city had violated the CPRA, and that the CPRA requester was thus entitled to attorneys' fees as a result of the CPRA lawsuit that followed.[65]

---

62 *See* Cal. Gov. Code § 7922.600(b) (formerly Cal. Gov. Code § 6253.1(b)).

63 *San Diegans for Open Gov. v. City of San Diego* (2016) 247 Cal.App.4th 1306, 1321 (citing Cal. Gov. Code § 6253.1(b) (now codified as Cal. Gov. Code § 7922.600(b)); *accord Community Youth Athletic Ctr., supra*, 220 Cal.App.4th at pp. 1417-1418.

64 *Compare San Diegans for Open Gov., supra*, 247 Cal.App.4th at pp. 1321-1323 *and* Cal. Gov. Code § 7922.600(b) (formerly Cal. Gov. Code § 6253.1(b)) *with* Cal. Gov. Code §§ 7922.530(a), 7922.535(a) (formerly Cal. Gov. Code § 6253(b)-(c)) *and Community Youth Athletic Ctr., supra*, 220 Cal.App.4th at pp. 1417-1418.

65 *San Diegans for Open Gov., supra*, 247 Cal.App.4th at pp. 1312, 1322-1323; *accord Community Youth Athletic Ctr., supra*, 220 Cal.App.4th at pp. 1417-1418 (where city failed to produce raw data from property field surveys and property-by-property crime data, because the city presumed in its response — without seeking clarification from the CPRA requester — that such data was not specifically included in the broadly-worded request, the reviewing court affirmed that the city had violated the CPRA and was liable for attorneys' fees).

Thus, **public entities should treat their request for clarification as being due *before* their response-determination is due**: i.e., sometime *less than* the 10 to 24 day window available under Section 6253.

As a practical matter, the earlier the request for clarification is made, the more likely the agency will have an answer that makes preparing its response-determination more effective and more likely to withstand challenge.

Notably, there is no express provision of the CPRA that extends the deadline for responding to a CPRA request with the agency's determination by reason of requesting clarification of the request.[66] In fact, the organization and language of the CPRA appears to presume that a request for clarification is a normal part of timely responding to a CPRA request under the 10 or 24 day deadlines.[67]

Thus, as a best practice, public agencies should presume that making a request for clarification does *not* extend the deadline for responding to a CPRA request with the agency's determination: however, given the pertinent case law, a mixed response — featuring a partial determination along with a request for clarification — does appear likely to satisfy the CPRA response deadlines without significant risk.[68]

---

66 *Compare* Cal. Gov. Code § 7922.600(b) (formerly Cal. Gov. Code § 6253.1(b)) *and* Cal. Gov. Code §§ 7922.530(a), 7922.535(a) (formerly Cal. Gov. Code § 6253(b)-(c)) *with San Diegans for Open Gov., supra*, 247 Cal.App.4th at p. 1321 (implicitly presuming the request for clarification does *not* extend the response deadline) *and Community Youth Athletic Ctr., supra*, 220 Cal.App.4th at pp. 1417-1418 (same).

67 *See id.*; *see also* Cal. Gov. Code § 7922.525(a) (formerly Cal. Gov. Code §6253(c)) (omitting requests for clarification as a basis for extending the response deadline by 14 days).

68 *See* Cal. Gov. Code § 7922.600(b) (formerly Cal. Gov. Code § 6253.1(b)); Cal. Gov. Code §§ 7922.530(a), 7922.535(a) (formerly Cal. Gov. Code § 6253(b)-(c)); *San Diegans for Open Gov., supra*, 247 Cal.App.4th at p. 1321; *Community Youth Athletic Ctr., supra*, 220 Cal.App.4th at pp. 1417-1418.

7. *Chart: CPRA Response & Disclosure-Production Deadlines.*

The following is thus a chart briefly summarizing the foregoing CPRA deadlines, calculated from the receipt date (*not* the service date) of the CPRA request.

CPRA Request Is For:	***Request For CLARIFICATION Due:***	***RESPONSE-Determination Due (Normal):***	***RESPONSE-Determination Due (Unusual Circumstances):***	***DISCLOSURE-Production Due:***
In Person Inspection	***Before* Response-** Determination (*< 10 Days*)	Up to **10 Days***	Up to **24 Days*** (*10 Days + 14 Day Extension*)	"Promptly" & Reasonably Timely Manner After Response-Determination OR Up to **45 Days** If Specified Officer Misconduct**
Agency-Made Copies (*Hardcopies or Website Posting*)	***Before* Response-** Determination (*< 10 Days*)	Up to **10 Days***	Up to **24 Days*** (*10 Days + 14 Day Extension*)	"Promptly" & Reasonably Timely Manner After Response-Determination OR Up to **45 Days** If Specified Officer Misconduct**

* All deadlines are subject to: (a) CPRA prohibitions on public agency delays or obstruction of disclosures; *and* (b) CPRA presumptions that, depending on the case-specific circumstances affecting the agency's ability to make its determination and/or to disclose records, "reasonably timely" compliance with the CPRA is sufficient, even if exact compliance with the deadlines is not accomplished.[69]

** PRACTICE TIP: It is in the best interests of the public agency for the public entity to adopt, as a best practice, a custom of disclosing-producing disclosable public records as close in time to the response-determination date as practicality allows under the circumstances. Many agencies treat the 10 day deadline as their production deadline: while this is *not* strictly required, it is a wise goal to pursue, when feasible. As a practical matter, agencies should treat the new 45 day deadline as their target for production, even where the records at issue do not pertain to the specified categories of officer misconduct: as courts might increasingly look to that deadline as they try to determine what constitutes prompt/reasonably timely disclosure.

69 *See id.*

8. *Response: Agency's Diligent Search for Requested Public Records v. Undue Burden.*

The courts recognize that CPRA requests "invariably impose some burden on public agencies."[70] Thus, "[u]nless a records request is overbroad or unduly burdensome, agencies are obliged to disclose all [public] records they can locate with 'reasonable effort.'"[71]

"Reasonable efforts do not require that agencies undertake extraordinarily extensive or intrusive searches, however"; and the courts "do not hold that any particular search method is required or necessarily adequate...."[72] This is because a "clearly framed request which requires an agency to search an enormous volume of data for a 'needle in a haystack' or, conversely, a request which compels the production of a huge volume of material may be objectionable as unduly burdensome."[73] In this vein, the "size of the request is not the measure,...but whether the records can be located with reasonable effort."[74]

Thus, as an example of the range of reasonable effort versus undue burden, courts have held that a request that required the agency to comb through 80,000 documents to prepare an index to aid the requester in identifying documents for disclosure would be unduly burdensome, and thus outside the enforceable scope of the CPRA; but that a CPRA request that required the agency to comb through only 2,100 documents to accomplish the same end would *not* be unduly burdensome: and, as part of its duty to assist the requester to identify responsive records, the agency would thus be required under the CPRA to review and index such records.[75]

---

70 *City of San Jose, supra*, 2 Cal.5th at p. 627.

71 *Id.*; *California 1st Amend. Coalition v. Superior Ct.* (1998) 67 Cal.App.4th 159, 166.

72 *Id.*

73 *California 1st Amend. Coalition, supra*, 67 Cal.App.4th at p. 166; *see generally American Civ. Liberties Union Found'n (Deukmejian), supra*, 32 Cal.3d at pp. 452-454 (where the burden is too great, the interest in non-disclosure may outweigh the interest in disclosure); Cal. Gov. Code § 7922.000 (formerly Cal. Gov. Code § 6255(a)).

74 *State Bd. of Equalization v. Superior Ct.* (1992) 10 Cal.App.4th 1177, 1186; *see also California 1st Amend. Coalition, supra*, 67 Cal.App.4th at p. 166.

75 *See, e.g., State Bd. of Equalization, supra*, 10 Cal.App.4th at p. 1192 (distinguishing *Rosenthal, supra*, 34 Cal.App.3d at pp. 756-758 and holding that forcing agencies to create indexes of documents in response to CPRA requests is permissible because it "puts part of the responsibility for identifying records with the agency itself."); *see also* Cal. Gov. Code § 7922.600 (formerly Cal. Gov. Code § 6253.1).

As long as the employee who conducts the search for public records has been properly trained on public records identification, and particularly where the public entity adopts measures designed to *reduce* the likelihood that public records are stored only on or in public employee's private accounts or files, a reasonable effort search by that entity's trained employee should satisfy the requirements of the CPRA.[76]

In other words, in general, a public entity satisfies its CPRA diligent-search duty when the agency's trained employee conducts a reasonable effort to locate responsive records in the agency's possession, custody, or control.[77]

9. *Agency's Constructive Possession: Public Employees' Private Files.*

Where the public records are in the *constructive* possession of the public entity, as opposed to the *actual* possession of the agency, such as where the entity-owned public records are possessed by a contractor or employee, the entity should communicate the substance of the request to the contractor or employee: however, in that event, as long as the agency's query to the contractor or employee is "reasonably calculated to locate responsive documents," the agency may "reasonably rely" on the contractor or employee to search their own files, accounts, and devices for potentially responsive public records and materials.[78] In such a case, the contractor or employee may need to support the results of their records search by sworn affidavit/declaration.[79]

In other words, to satisfy the CPRA's diligent-search duty, a public entity employee charged with identifying and compiling CPRA-request responsive records should not only hunt through the agency-possessed/controlled archives, but — particularly where the agency permits or suspects that its employees may store agency-owned public records on or in private files — the custodial employee should also communicate the substance of the CPRA to such employees or contractors; and, in that event, the custodial employee conducting the

---

76 *See, e.g.*, Cal. Gov. Code §§ 7922.530(a), 7922.535(a), 7922.600, 7921.055 (formerly Cal. Gov. Code §§ 6253(b)-(c), 6253.1, 6253.3); *American Small Bus. League v. United States S.B.A.* (9th Cir. 2010) 623 F.3d 1052, 1053-1054.

77 *See id.*

78 *City of San Jose, supra*, 2 Cal.5th at pp. 628-629; *Consolidated Irrigation Dist., supra*, 205 Cal.App.4th at pp. 710-711.

79 *See, e.g.*, *Grand Cent. Partnership, Inc. v. Cuomo* (2d Cir. 1999) 166 F.3d 473, 481.

search may reasonably rely on the other employees or contractors to conduct their own search for responsive records in their private files.[80]

As detailed above, **where a record is possessed by a public entity's consultant or agent/employee, but where the public entity has the legal or contractual right of ownership over such records, such records are deemed to be within the constructive possession of the public entity**; *by contrast*, where there is no such legal right of ownership, records in the possession of a public entity's agent are *not* deemed to be within the constructive possession of the public agency.[81]

Thus, as summarized in the example above, where a public employee was conducting public business using his personal email account, those emails were subject to CPRA disclosure as public records, even though they were on the employee's private account.[82]

However, again by contrast, where a city consultant's files were *not* contractually owned by the city, and where the consultant was an independent contractor, even though the consultant's work regarded public business, the records in the consultant's possession were *not* public records subject to CPRA disclosure.[83]

10. *Response: The Agency's Duty To Assist The CPRA Requester.*

Generally, the government agency also has a legal duty to try to assist the CPRA requester in "mak[ing] a focused and effective request that reasonably describes an identifiable [public] record or records...."[84]

80 *See generally City of San Jose, supra*, 2 Cal.5th at pp. 628-629; *Consolidated Irrigation Dist., supra*, 205 Cal.App.4th at pp. 710-711.

81 *See, e.g., City of San Jose, supra*, 2 Cal.5th at pp. 623-629 (records of public employees conducting public business are public records subject to the CPRA, even if stored in private accounts); *Consolidated Irrigation Dist.*, supra, 205 Cal.App.4th at pp. 710-711 (because city did not have ownership or legal control over files in the possession of its independent contractor consultant, the consultant's records were *not* public records); *Community Youth Athletic Ctr., supra*, 220 Cal. App.4th at pp. 1428-1429 (where city contract with survey consultant gave it contractual ownership over related files in consultant's possession, those files were public records subject to the CPRA; but the city was not required to forward the CRPA request to the contractor verbatim).

82 *City of San Jose, supra*, 2 Cal.5th at pp. 623-629.

83 *Consolidated Irrigation Dist.*, supra, 205 Cal.App.4th at pp. 710-711.

84 *See* Cal. Gov. Code § 7922.600(a) (formerly Cal. Gov. Code § 6253.1(a)).

The agency may fulfill this duty to assist by doing *all* of the following "to the extent reasonable under the circumstances":

(1) assisting the CPRA requester to more clearly identify the records or information that are sought by and responsive to the request;

(2) describing the information technology and location where the identified records exist/are located; *and*

(3) "providing suggestions for overcoming any practical basis for denying access to the records or information sought."[85]

However, under certain circumstances, the agency is *not* obliged to assist the requester, such as: (1) where it has determined that the request should be denied based on an exemption available under Government Code section 7920.000 *et seq.* (formerly included in Government Code section 6254); *or* (2) where it has made "a reasonable effort to elicit additional clarifying information from the requester that will help identify the record or records" and yet, thereafter, the agency is still "unable to identify the requested information" sought.[86]

In other words, if the subject records are exempt from CPRA disclosure, or if — after a diligent effort to figure out/clarify what the requester is requesting — the agency just cannot comprehend what records the CPRA requester seeks via the request, then the agency's duty to assist the requester reaches its end.

11. *Response: Denial of a Public Records Request and Identification of the Deniers and Basis.*

Notably, the CPRA statutes require that where a CPRA request is denied, the names and titles of each person responsible for the denial must be included in the denial communication.[87] Additionally, when denying a CPRA request, **the public agency must specify which exemption(s) it believes support the**

85 Cal. Gov. Code § 7922.600(a)(1)-(3) (formerly Cal. Gov. Code § 6253.1(a)(1)-(3)).

86 Cal. Gov. Code § 7922.600(b) (formerly Cal. Gov. Code § 6253.1(b)).

87 *See, e.g.*, Cal. Gov. Code §§ 7922.540(b), 7922.000 (formerly Cal. Gov. Code §§ 6253(d)(3), 6255).

refusal to disclose-produce the requested records.[88] Along related lines, when an agency denies a CPRA request, its determination supporting the denial must be in writing.[89]

12. *Response: Redactions In General (Partial Denial).*

The CPRA presumes that some parts of public records will contain non-disclosable parts: thus, where the non-disclosable portions are "reasonably segregable" from the disclosable portions, the agency may withhold or redact the non-disclosable portions while producing the disclosable portions; in other words, *redactions are permitted* under the CPRA so as to foster the larger goals of public records disclosures, as long as the basis for the redaction (specified exemption) is identified in the agency's response.[90] However, where non-disclosable/exempt information *cannot* be reasonably segregated from the disclosable portions, such as where the two are inextricably intertwined, then the entire record may be withheld, rather than redacted.[91]

F. Miscellaneous CPRA Provisions.

There are more than a few CPRA provisions that have little to no bearing on law enforcement work.

For example, after the death of a minor foster child, the name, date of birth, and date of death shall be reported to the county child welfare agency.[92] Similarly, if a local agency makes certain records accessible to some members of that agency's legislative body (like a city council or county board of supervisors), it must share the same record, to the same extent, with the rest of that body's members: it may not discriminate among members.[93]

---

88 *See* Cal. Gov. Code § 7922.000 (formerly Cal. Gov. Code § 6255(a)); *Long Beach Police Officers Assn. v. City of Long Beach* (2014) 59 Cal.4th 59, 67.

89 Cal. Gov. Code § 7922.540(a) (formerly Cal. Gov. Code § 6255(b)).

90 *See* Cal. Gov. Code § 7922.525 (formerly Cal. Gov. Code § 6253(a)); *American Civ. Liberties Union Found'n, supra*, 32 Cal.3d at pp. 452-454; *see generally International Fed. of Prof. & Tech. Eng'rs., Local 21 v. Superior Ct.* (2007) 42 Cal.4th 319, 329.

91 *See id.*

92 Cal. Gov. Code § 7927.420 (formerly Cal. Gov. Code § 6252.6).

93 Cal. Gov. Code § 7921.310 (formerly Cal. Gov. Code § 6252.7).

However, a handful of the miscellaneous CPRA provisions bear brief mention here.

1. *The Ban On Outsourcing CPRA Disclosure Decisions & Ban On CPRA Evasion By Privatization.*

For example, one seemingly miscellaneous provision is noteworthy: public entities are prohibited from selling, exchanging, furnishing, or otherwise providing public records to a private entity in a manner that prevents the public entity from disclosing such records under the CPRA.[94] In other words, public entities cannot get around the CPRA's requirements by turning over their public records to a private entity not subject to the Act.

A public entity is also barred from outsourcing "control" of the "disclosure of information" to any other party.[95] Thus, where public records have been placed in the custody of a private entity, the *public* entity, *not* the private entity, is responsible for ensuring full compliance with the CPRA, notwithstanding any private entity restrictions or interpretations: in other words, the public entity *cannot* hand over its government-owned records to a private company and then stand behind that company's decisions as to what records to disclose in response to a CPRA request; nor may the public entity evade its duty to directly produce CPRA-disclosable records to the requestor by such outsourcing CPRA disclosures to a private entity.[96]

2. *The CPRA Allows Public Entities To Disclose More Than The Minimum; Limited Waiver Of CPRA Exemptions By Willful Disclosure.*

Most exemptions from the CPRA are permissive, *not* mandatory; the custodial government agency can disclose records that are otherwise exempt from CPRA disclosure *if it chooses*, as long as such disclosure is not

---

94 Cal. Gov. Code § 7921.010 (formerly Cal. Gov. Code § 6270).

95 Cal. Gov. Code § 7921.005 (formerly Cal. Gov. Code § 6253.3); *see also Regents of the Univ. of Cal., supra*, 222 Cal.App.4th at p. 405 (where financial investment data regarding a public entity's investments was prepared by a private entity, those investment records were not public records, nor did the entity violated Section 6253.3 by engaging in such investment activity).

96 Cal. Gov. Code § 7921.005 (formerly Cal. Gov. Code § 6253.3); *see also Community Youth Athletic Ctr., supra*, 220 Cal.App.4th at pp. 1422-1423, 1428-1429; *see generally Regents of the Univ. of Cal., supra*, 222 Cal.App.4th at p. 405.

otherwise restricted by law; thus, the agency is *not required* to invoke the CPRA exemptions.[97]

Thus, for example, although the CPRA and *Pitchess* exempted officer personnel file information from disclosure, where, at a news conference about a city police officer holding two uniformed, on-duty Sheriff's deputies at gunpoint without cause, a police chief and sheriff elected to read part of the officer's administrative review board hearing transcript and disclose certain incident facts to the public; on review, the court held that because the CPRA exemptions were permissive, not mandatory, and because the information shared was within the scope of information disclosable under the Peace Officers' Bill of Rights ("POBR" or "POBAR") by the custodial government entity, there was no violation of the CPRA or *Pitchess*, and thus no grounds for the officer's associated invasion of privacy lawsuit.[98]

However, where the public entity elects to disclose an otherwise-exempt public record, it waives the exemptions as to that voluntarily-disclosed record unless:

(1) the disclosure was made pursuant to the Information Practices Act (Cal. Civ. Code § 1798) or discovery proceedings;

(2) the disclosure was made through a legal proceeding or otherwise required by law;

(3) the disclosure was within the scope of a statute that allows disclosure for limited purposes;

(4) the disclosure was *not* required by law and otherwise barred from publication by a local agency's legislative body;

---

97 Cal. Gov. Code § 7921.505 (formerly Cal. Gov. Code § 6254.5); *Black Panther Party v. Kehoe* (1974) 42 Cal.App.3d 645, 656 (the **CPRA exemptions are permissive, *not* mandatory**; in general, they permit disclosure where, in the exercise of its discretion, the custodial public entity determines that the public interest favors disclosure over non-disclosure).

98 *See Bradshaw v. City of L.A.* (1990) 221 Cal.App.3d 908, 913-914, 916-917 (holding that POBR only limits custodial government agency's right to disclose the officer's home address and photo to the news media, but that POBR otherwise provides no other restrictions on a public agency's media release); *see also Black Panther Party*, supra, 42 Cal.App.3d at p. 656.

(5) the disclosure was made to a government agency that agrees to treat the information as confidential;

(6) state agency records were disclosed to a financial institution or affiliate thereof in the agency's regulatory or supervisory capacity; and/or

(6) in the case of specialized disclosures made under the Department of Business Oversight and/or Department of Managed Health Care.[99]

Thus, for example, where a district attorney disclosed to a police department a non-public letter explaining its decision to charge a police officer, and where the district attorney delivered such letter with the understanding that it would remain confidential, the district attorney did *not* waive its Section 6254(f) exemption from CPRA disclosure of that letter.[100]

Significantly, however, the inadvertent disclosure of attorney-client privileged matter in a CPRA production does *not* constitute a waiver of the attorney-client privilege.[101]

G. C.P.R.A. EXEMPTIONS: Exclusions and Privileges, Temporary Withholding, and Redactions.

Given the broad scope and operation of the CPRA, aside from litigation over whether requested records were "public records" in the first place, most of the disputes regarding CPRA responses and production arise from application of the various CPRA exemptions from disclosure. Under the CPRA, "[t]he people's right to know, however, is not absolute"; accordingly, the CPRA provides many specific exemptions from disclosure, plus the catch-all exemption.[102] However, "[s]pecific exemptions from this general requirement

99 Cal. Gov. Code § 7921.505 (formerly Cal. Gov. Code § 6254.5).

100 *Rackauckas v. Superior Ct.* (2002) 104 Cal.App.4th 169, 178-179.

101 *Ardon v. City of Los Angeles* (2016) 62 Cal.4th 1176, 1182-1189, 1191 (waiver of CPRA exemptions only applies to voluntary-knowing disclosure of exempted material, not to inadvertent disclosures of exempted material, and holding that the attorney-client privileged matter and attorney work product protected matter were not public records and must be returned); *cf. generally Newark Sch. Dist. v. Superior Ct.* (2015) 245 Cal.App.4th 887, 896-898 (holding that inadvertent disclosure does not waive privilege, despite language to the contrary in the opinion).

102 *Regents, supra,* 222 Cal.App.4th at p. 400.

disclosure...are construed narrowly to ensure maximum disclosure of the onduct of governmental operations."[103]

Along related lines, it must be noted that **the CPRA exemptions do <u>not</u> pply to discovery conducted in civil litigation, authorized administrative roceedings, or criminal matters.**[104] Rather, they operate *only* to limit CPRA isclosures, *not* to limit civil or criminal discovery: even though courts will ften examine whether a document is a public record in evaluating whether r not such record is discoverable in a related civil lawsuit.[105]

Therefore, **to better understand the *Pitchess* privilege's intersection vith the CPRA, we must explore the core exemptions in turn, *as they apply o police-related records*,** along with some brief review of other potentially olice-pertinent exemptions.[106]

---

103 *New York Times v. Superior Ct.* (1990) 218 Cal.App.3d 1579, 1584-1585 (citing, among others, *CBS Inc. v. Block* (1986) 42 Cal.3d 646, 651-652).

104 *See* Cal. Gov. Code § 7920.200 (formerly Cal. Gov. Code § 6260) (the CPRA does not limit civil litigants' rights to discovery in civil actions, or in administrative actions, nor does it affect the parties' discovery rights in criminal cases); *accord Cal. ex rel. Div. of Indus. Safety v. Superior Ct.* (1974) 43 Cal.App.3d 778, 784-785; *see generally City of Los Angeles v. Superior Ct.* (1973) 33 Cal. App.3d 778, 783-785 (citing Gov. Code § 6254(f) and Cal. Evid. Code § 1040 in support of the precept that, in a civil battery/assault case against a law enforcement officer, "[t]he character or reputation of a defendant is not an issue in a civil action for assault [or battery], and evidence of other specific instances of misconduct is not admissible to prove misconduct on the particular occasion."; and holding that pre-incident officer misconduct not directly related to the incident was not discoverable).

105 *See id.*; *see also, e.g.*, *City of Los Angeles*, *supra*, 33 Cal.App.3d at pp. 783-785 (in a civil battery case against a police officer, holding that information sought by civil litigant's interrogatories was not discoverable, in part, because of Section 6254(f) and the Evidence Code official information privilege and reversing lower court order mandating production of the officer's personnel file information).

106 NOTE: While there are a great many exemptions from the CPRA, *only* those likely to arise in cases related to police records are addressed in this book. Please see Additional Resources if a more comprehensive of the other CPRA exemptions is desired.

ADDITIONAL RESOURCES: *The People's Business: A Guide to the California Public Records Act*, League of California Cities, Apr. 2017 (a comprehensive review of the CPRA). Another excellent resource can be found at: James Chadwick/Sheppard Mullin, "First Amendment Coalition's California Public Records Act Primer," *Resources: Access to Records*, circa 2020 (a convenient short guide on the CPRA).

1. *The CPRA Exemption For DRAFTS (The EXECUTIVE-DELIBERATIVE PROCESSES Exemption).*

Government Code section 7927.500 (formerly Government Code section 6254(a)) features an exemption from CPRA disclosure for: "preliminary drafts, notes, or inter-agency or intra-agency memoranda that are not retained by the public agency in the ordinary course of business, if the public interest in withholding those records clearly outweighs the public interest in disclosure."[107] Modeled on and often analyzed in conjunction with the federal Freedom of Information Act ("FOIA")[108], in reality, the "drafts" exemption is a CPRA exemption "to protect communications to the decisionmaker before the decision is made…."[109]

The primary purpose of the CPRA's drafts/executive deliberative process exemption is "to prevent injury to the quality of executive decisions" by protecting "'frank discussion of legal or policy matters'" from being "inhibited" and, thereby, to prevent "'efficiency of Government'" from being "'greatly hampered'" by having such pre-decisional discussions subjected to public scrutiny.[110] This is because "'Human experience teaches that those who expect public dissemination of their remarks may well temper candor with a concern for appearances… to the detriment of the decisionmaking process.'"[111]

To fall under this exemption, the record(s) at issue must meet three conditions:

(1) the record(s) must be **pre-decisional in nature** — i.e., a "draft" or "note" or "memorandum" created *before* the decision has been made that is used as part of the policy decision-making process;

---

107 Cal. Gov. Code § 7927.500 (formerly Cal. Gov. Code § 6254(a)).

108 *See, e.g.*, 5 U.S.C. § 552(b)(5); *Times Mirror Co. v. Superior Ct.* (1991) 53 Cal.3d 1325, 1339-1341.

109 *See Times Mirror Co., supra*, 53 Cal.3d at p. 1341.

110 *See Times Mirror Co., supra*, 53 Cal.3d at pp. 1340-1341.

111 *See Times Mirror Co., supra*, 53 Cal.3d at p. 1341 (citing *United States v. Nixon*, 418 U.S. 683, 705 (1974) and *Environmental Prot. Agency v. Mink*, 410 U.S. 73, 87 (1973) (admonishing against forcing executive decisions to be made in a "'fishbowl'"); *Citizens for a Better Env. v. Department of Food & Agriculture* (1985) 171 Cal.App.3d 704, 712 (regarding Section 6254(a), "The purpose of the exemption is to provide a measure of agency privacy for written discourse concerning matters pending administrative action.").

(2) the record(s) must be of a kind that are ***not* normally retained by the public agency** in the regular course of business; *and*

(3) the public **interest in non-disclosure must clearly outweigh the public interest in disclosure.**[112]

Significantly, the policy need underlying the drafts/deliberative process exemption "is even stronger if the [CPRA] demand comes while policy is still being developed"; but the drafts exemption still applies "with respect to past decisions...."[113]

Regarding the first condition, the record(s) at issue must be as to *pre*-decisional matters; post-decisional matters are *not* exempt from CPRA disclosure: in other words, records created *after* the decision was made would *not* fall under this exemption.[114] As to the second condition, the burden is on the public agency to prove that it does not normally retain the record(s) requested: but where it does normally retain such drafts, they would be disclosable even if they tended to reveal pre-decisional deliberative processes.[115] Notably, the whether the last condition applies tends to be a case-specific inquiry.[116]

---

112 *See* Cal. Gov. Code § 7927.500 (formerly Cal. Gov. Code § 6254(a)); *Times Mirror Co., supra*, 53 Cal.3d at pp. 1340-1342; *Citizens for a Better Env., supra*, 171 Cal.App.3d at pp. 711-712.

113 *Times Mirror Co., supra*, 53 Cal.3d at p. 1341.

114 *See Times Mirror Co., supra*, 53 Cal.3d at pp. 1340-1342; *Citizens for a Better Env., supra*, 171 Cal.App.3d at pp. 711-712; *see also National Lab. Rel. Bd. v. Sears, Roebuck & Co.*, 421 U.S. 132, 150-152 (1975) (reaching same finding on same rationale regarding executive-deliberative process exemption from FOIA).

115 *See Citizens for a Better Env., supra*, 171 Cal.App.3d at p. 714; *Golden Door Prop., LLC v. Superior Ct.* (2020) 53 Cal.App.5th 733, 769-773 (where agency failed to show how the withheld records were relied upon in an executive-deliberative process, it failed to meet its burden that the records were exempt under Section 6254(a)); *San Diego Police Officers Assn. v. City of San Diego* (2002) 98 Cal.App.4th 779, 784-786 (holding that, while there is no duty to preserve an investigator's raw notes and draft reports, if such *are* routinely preserved, Section 6254(a) does *not* exempt them from CPRA disclosure).

PRACTICE TIP: Agencies that have clear retention and document-destruction policies regarding such records have an easier time proving that they do not normally retain the draft records at issue.

116 *Compare Times Mirror Co., supra*, 53 Cal.3d at pp. 13444-1346 (holding that the governor's private calendar was exempt from CPRA disclosure, even though it contained some purely factual entries, because it tended to show what facts were important to his decision-making) *with Citizens for a Better Env., supra*, 171 Cal.App.3d at pp. 713-718 (holding that where the county compiled records as part of an internal review to determine whether it was in compliance with state pesticide laws, as part of a review about whether to make any administrative changes, the purely factual records, but not necessarily the records reflecting opinions or recommendations, were CPRA-disclosable).

However, when these conditions are met, such "drafts" are *exempt* from CPRA disclosure "[e]ven if the content of a document is purely factual, it is nonetheless exempt from public scrutiny if it is 'actually...related to the process by which policies are formulated'...or [it is] 'inextricably intertwined' with 'policy-making processes.'"[117]

Thus, for example, the California Governor's private calendar was exempt from CPRA disclosure under the drafts exemption because, even the identities of the persons he was meeting with would disclose which facts he found to be significant in his decision-making process: and thus disclosure of his private calendar would necessarily disclose his pre-decisional decision-making processes; and therefore the public interest in non-disclosure clearly outweighed the public interest in disclosure regarding such calendar, even though the private calendar contained some matters that were purely factual.[118]

a. Other Deliberative Process Exemptions: The CPRA Exemption For Agency Training To Non-Union Public Employees and Regarding Health Care Service Negotiations.

Government Code sections 7928.410, 7926.220 (formerly Government Code sections 6254(p)-(q)) also feature a more-specific exemption from CPRA disclosure for local and state agency records "that reveal" the "agency's deliberative processes, impressions, evaluations, opinions, recommendations, meeting minutes, research, work products, theories, or strategy" or communications pertaining to two subject matters: (1) "instruction, advice, or training to employees who do not have full collective bargaining and representation rights" under Gov. Code § 3500, *et seq.* or Educ. Code § 8430, *et seq.*; or (2) "negotiations with providers of health care services" to public employees, including related "instruction, advice, or training to employees" — with the caveat that the executed contracts themselves can be inspected up to one year later, if the

---

117 *See Times Mirror Co., supra*, 53 Cal.3d at p. 1342 (citing *Ryan v. Department of Justice*, 617 F.2d 781, 790 (D.C. Cir. 1980) and *Soucie v. David*, 448 F.2d 1067, 1077-1078 (D.C. Cir. 1971)).

118 *See Times Mirror Co., supra*, 53 Cal.3d at pp. 1344-1346; *accord California 1st Amend. Coalition, supra*, 67 Cal.App.4th at pp. 167-174 (holding that, although supervisory applications contained purely factual matter, because disclosure of those facts would tend to reveal what was significant in the decision-making process of policy-makers hiring such supervisors, the applications were *exempt* from CPRA disclosure under Section 6254(a) and Section 6255).

rates are redacted, and in full up to three years later.[119] The CPRA also extends similar exemptions to deliberative processes regarding Medi-Cal, the Managed Risk Insurance Board, and the State Compensation Insurance Fund.[120]

However, these union and health care deliberations exemptions are unlikely to arise in police-related CPRA record requests or civil discovery.

2. *The CPRA PENDING LITIGATION Records Exemption.*

Government Code section 7927.200 (formerly Government Code section 6254(b)) features an exemption from CPRA disclosure for: "[r]ecords pertaining to pending litigation to which the public agency is a party" — or records pertaining to claims made under the Tort Claims Act (Government Code section 810, *et seq.*) — "until the pending litigation or claim has been finally adjudicated or otherwise settled."[121]

However, as a result of the case law, the pending litigation/claim exemption is narrowly construed to apply *only* to records **specifically prepared *by* the public agency**, or at its direction, **for use in anticipated or existing litigation** *where the agency is a party.*[122]

On a related note, where the purpose underlying the document's preparation is dual, then the "'dominant purpose'" underlying the record's preparation

---

119 Cal. Gov. Code §§ 7928.410, 7926.220 (formerly Cal. Gov. Code § 6254(p)-(q)); *see also* Cal. Gov. Code §§ 7926.225, 7926.235, 7926.230, 7929.400-7929.430 (formerly Cal. Gov. Code § 6254(v), (w), (y), (ad)) (extending the deliberative process protections to records regarding Medi-Cal, the Managed Risk Insurance Board, and the State Compensation Insurance Fund.

120 *See* Cal. Gov. Code §§ 7928.410, 7926.220, 7926.225, 7926.235, 7926.230, 7929.400-7929.430 (formerly Cal. Gov. Code § 6254(p)-(q), (v), (w), (y), (ad)); *Humane Soc'y of U.S. v. Superior Ct.* (2013) 214 Cal.App.4th 1233, 1254 n. 20 ("[S]ection 6254 specifically exempts research and deliberative processes for specified records involving employer/employee relations (§ 6254, subd. (p)), Medi-Cal, (§ 6254, subd. (q)), the Managed Risk Insurance Board (§ 6254, subds. (v), (w), (y)), and the State Compensation Insurance Fund (§ 6254, subd. (ad)).").

121 Cal. Gov. Code § 7927.200(a) (formerly Cal. Gov. Code § 6254(b)).

122 *Fairley v. Superior Ct.* (1998) 66 Cal.App.4th 1414, 1420-1421; *see generally City of Hemet* (1995) 37 Cal.App.4th 1411, 1419-1420 (in dicta); *County of Los Angeles v. Superior Ct. (Axelrad)* (2000) 82 Cal.App.4th 819, 830-832 ("A document is protected from disclosure under the pending litigation exemption only if the document was specifically prepared for use in litigation."; and holding that the trial court needed to conduct an *in camera* review to determine if the over-detention reports, logs, and task force reports at issue in the CPRA request were specifically prepared for use in anticipated litigation).

will determine whether the pending litigation exemption applies.[123] By contrast, where a document was *not* created by the agency with the dominant purpose of anticipated litigation in which the agency is a party, the agency's post-litigation reliance on such document in such litigation does *not* extend the pending litigation exemption to that document.[124]

Attorney Billing Records. Thus, for example, attorney billing records are *not* protected by the pending litigation exemption of CPRA Section 6254(b) because they are *not* created by the agency or at its direction with the *primary purpose* of being *used* in a pending or existing litigation in which the public entity is a party.[125]

However, it should be noted here that such attorney-client billing records are widely construed to be protected from disclosure by the attorney-client communications privilege and/or the attorney work product protection under the CPRA: where such attorney invoices "reveal anything about legal consultation or provide insight into litigation strategy" — as most industry-standard narrative legal bills tend to do.[126] Thus, for example, where attorney invoices stated only the amounts of legal fees incurred, neither the pending litigation nor the attorney-client privilege exemptions would bar CPRA disclosure; but where those same invoices reflected litigation strategy or documented specific legal advice, then while the pending litigation exemption still would *not* apply, the attorney-client privilege and/or attorney work product CPRA exemption *would* likely apply.[127]

Attorney Correspondence. Another example that better illustrates the pending litigation exemption can be found in the case of attorney

---

123 *Fairley, supra*, 66 Cal.App.4th at pp. 1420-1421; *see also City of Hemet, supra*, 37 Cal. App.4th at pp. 1418-1420.

124 *See id.*

125 *County of Los Angeles v. Superior Ct.* (2012) 211 Cal.App.4th 57, 67.

126 *See County of Los Angeles v. Superior Ct.* (2017) 12 Cal.App.4th 1264, 1270-1277; *accord Los Angeles County v. Superior Ct.* (2016) 2 Cal.5th 282, 298-300 (holding that, under the CPRA, while there is no categorical privilege in attorney billing records, "the contents of an [attorney] invoice are privileged only if they either communicate information for the purpose of legal consultation or risk exposing information that was communicated for such purpose"); *Costco Wholesale Corp. v. Superior Ct.* (2009) 47 Cal.4th 725, 737-740; *see also* Cal. Gov. Code §§ 7927.705, 7930.110 (formerly Cal. Gov. Code §§ 6254(k), 6276.04) (incorporating attorney-client privilege and attorney work product protections into CPRA exemptions).

127 *See id.*

correspondence pertaining to a case. Specifically, where attorneys for a party public agency exchanged correspondence with attorneys for a non-party on the subject of anticipated litigation, even the correspondence from the *non-party* attorneys was exempt under the pending litigation exemption because it tended to reflect the party attorneys' impressions and because it was shared on the condition that it be kept confidential.[128]

Not Applicable To Pleadings & Tort Claims. Along related lines, the pending litigation exemption does *not* apply to the actual civil complaint filed and served, or the actual tort claim submitted: because those documents were *not* prepared by the public agency; but, rather, were prepared by the claimant.[129]

Notably, the fact that records may be obtainable via civil discovery in an active litigation does *not* prevent them from being disclosable under the CPRA, where the pending litigation exemption does not apply.[130]

Terminates When The Litigation Ends. However, even where the pending litigation exemption does apply, unless some other exemption applies, **once the litigation has concluded** (and thus is no longer "pending"), **the pending litigation exemption no longer shields otherwise-protected records from CPRA disclosure**: thus, depositions from *closed* cases and similar litigation records that might have been protected by this exemption during the litigation will no longer exempt the records from CPRA disclosure once the litigation is over.[131]

3. *The CPRA PERSONNEL FILES And MEDICAL FILES Exemption.*

Government Code section 7927.700 (formerly Government Code section 6254(c)) features an exemption from CPRA disclosure for: "personnel, medical, or similar files, the disclosure of which would constitute an unwarranted invasion of personal privacy."[132]

128 *Board of Trustees of Cal. State Univ. v. Superior Ct.* (2005) 132 Cal.App.4th 889, 899-900.

129 *Poway Unif. Sch. Dist. v. Superior Ct.* (1998) 62 Cal.App.4th 1496, 1502-1505; *see also City of Los Angeles v. Superior Ct.* (1996) 41 Cal.App.4th 1083, 1089, 1092 (where claimant includes medical records in a complaint or tort claim, claimant has likely waived privilege in such records).

130 *See Wilder, supra,* 66 Cal.App.4th at pp. 84-85.

131 *City of Los Angeles, supra,* 41 Cal.App.4th at p. 1089 ("the Legislature did not intend to cloak records of matters that were concluded").

132 Cal. Gov. Code § 7927.700 (formerly Cal. Gov. Code § 6254(c)).

Medical Records. This means that, as to medical records, the CPRA is essentially in accord with the California Constitutional right to privacy in one's medical records.[133] Namely, barring an applicable exception to their confidentiality, medical records are *not* CPRA-disclosable.[134]

Along related lines, records do not become exempt medical records simply because they contain some medical-related information. For example, where a physician was disciplined for violation of the Medical Practices Act due to drug abuse, regarding the state government's publication of the disciplinary disposition report, which included the fact that the doctor had been disciplined for drug abuse, the reviewing court held that the disposition report was *not* a medical record exempt from public records publication under CPRA Section 6254(c).[135]

Public Employee Personnel Records, Other Than Police Officers. By contrast, as to non-police-officer public employee or public-agency-held personnel files, courts read the last clause of this provision as a modifier: in other words, because CPRA exemptions are construed narrowly, public employee personnel files are generally held to be exempt from CPRA disclosure only to the extent that such disclosure would constitute an unwarranted invasion of personal property.[136]

The rationale underlying this narrowing of the exemption for non-officer public employee personnel files is that, on matters of particular public interest (*e.g.*, proved misconduct by a public employee who is not a law enforcement officer, convicted criminals taking care of children under state-granted exemptions from the ban on such, etc.), "public employee privacy must give way to the public's right to know."[137]

---

133 Cal. Const., Art. I, § 1.

134 *See id.*; Cal. Gov. Code § 7927.700 (formerly Cal. Gov. Code § 6254(c)).

135 *See Kayfetz v. Cal.* (1984) 156 Cal.App.3d 491, 497-499.

136 *See, e.g., Bakersfield City Sch. Dist. v. Superior Ct.* (2004) 118 Cal.App.4th 1041, 1043-1047.

137 *Bakersfield City Sch. Dist., supra*, 118 Cal.App.4th at pp. 1043-1047; *accord American Fed. of State etc. Employees v. Regents of the Univ. of Cal.* (1978) 80 Cal.App.3d 913, 918 (holding that CPRA does not exempt public school employees' personnel records from disclosure where such records show alleged misconduct of the employee to be true).

a. Examples Of Disclosable Public Employee Personnel Information.

Thus, for example, where a city council member obtained and displayed to the news media two letters showing that the city manager had appointed a firefighter to the senior post of transit administrator, and then that the firefighter's promotion had been rescinded and his original position reinstated just four days later, when the firefighter sued for breach of privacy, claiming such records were in his personnel file and thus exempt from CPRA disclosure, the reviewing court held that, although the letters displayed to the press had come from the plaintiff's personnel file as a public employee, and although the disclosed public records contained the firefighter's salary information, because the letters contained no personal information other than his name, salary, and position changes, the letters displayed were *not* subject to the Section 6254(c) exemption from CPRA disclosure.[138]

Similarly, where a news organization sought state records for a list of all persons employed by licensed child care facilities who had been granted an exemption under state law that otherwise would have barred such convicted persons from working in the child care facilities, due to such persons having criminal convictions, the reviewing court held that because the fact of a person's conviction of a crime is a public matter, even to the extent such licensure records were personnel file records for private employees that became public records by virtue of the government's routine maintenance and possession of such, the list of child care workers who had also been convicts was *not* exempt from CPRA disclosure under Section 6254(c).[139]

By contrast, where a news organization sought not just the position titles and associated salary information for a number of California cities' public employees, but also to have such information specified by public employee name (so that the list would include the name, position, and salary of each public employee), the reviewing court held that because the public interest in knowing how public funds are spent could be satisfied without specific

---

138 *See Braun v. City of Taft* (1984) 154 Cal.App.3d 332, 341-345; *accord Bakersfield City Sch. Dist., supra*, 118 Cal.App.4th at pp. 1043-1047 (where school employee's personnel records included records of discipline for confirmed wrongdoing, the records of wrongdoing were *not* exempt from CPRA disclosure under Section 6254(c) because that section "provided no exemption for records relevant to charges of misconduct which had administratively been found to be true").

139 *See CBS Broadcasting Inc. v. Superior Ct.* (2001) 91 Cal.App.4th 892, 907-909.

employees' names being matched to their salaries and positions, and because publication of such personal information could put the public employees at risk, such as by means of identity theft, Section 6254(c) exempted such personnel file information — the employee names matched to salary and position — from CPRA disclosure: even though the anonymous salary and position information was subject to CPRA disclosure.[140]

Along related lines, public employees' salary information, including the salary information of law enforcement officers *is* generally disclosable under the CPRA.[141]

Similarly, *except* for law enforcement officers personnel records regarding investigations-complaints-discipline, in general, particularly when the allegations are well founded, complaints or investigations against public employees *are* disclosable: including the discipline (if any) imposed against the public employee, as well as the information on which such discipline was based.[142] By contrast, where the allegations were found to be trivial or groundless, such public employee complaints and investigations are *not* CPRA-disclosable.[143]

In other words, **when it comes to public employees who are *not* law enforcement officers, and private employees whose personnel file records-information are public records, CPRA disclosure of their personnel file records-information depends upon a case-specific evaluation of the facts as to whether disclosure of the requested personnel information would constitute an unwarranted invasion of the employee's privacy, as balanced against the public interest in disclosure of such information.**

Significantly, this Section 6254(c) exemption effectively overlaps with the Section 6254(k) exemption for statutorily privileged records: since medical records are protected from CPRA exemption thereunder due to various state and federal laws, as are some personnel file records — including law enforcement officer

140 *See Teamsters Local 856 v. Priceless, LLC* (2003) 112 Cal.App.4th 1500, 1511-1523; but see also id. at pp. 1523-1525 (by contrast, as to *police officer* salary and position information, holding that such was *Pitchess* privileged and thus exempt from CPRA disclosure under Section 6254(k)).

141 *International Fed. of Prof. & Tech. Eng'rs., Local 21, AFL-CIO v. Superior Ct.* (2007) 42 Cal.4th 319, 340-346.

142 *See American Fed. of State, County, & Municipal Emp. v. Regents of the Univ. of Cal* (1978) 80 Cal.App.3d 913, 918; *Bakersfield City Sch. Dist., supra*, 118 Cal.App.4th at pp. 1045-1046

143 *See id.*

personnel file (*Pitchess* privileged) records-information.[144] Thus, for law enforcement officers, a weaker protection of their personnel file records-information is available under Section 6254(c); but officers will generally find a much stronger protection available under Section 6254(k)'s incorporation of the *Pitchess* privilege.

4. *The CPRA Exemption For LAW ENFORCEMENT INVESTIGATORY RECORDS.*

Generally shorthand-referenced as the CPRA exemption for police investigatory records, Government Code section 7923.600 (formerly included in Government Code section 6254(f)) features an exemption from CPRA disclosure for police-related documents and recordings that constitute records of, or records compiled by, "any state or local police agency"[145] — including but not limited to "any investigatory or security files," or records of complaints to such agencies, or records of investigations conducted by such agencies, where such records were generated for any "correctional, law enforcement, or licensing purposes" related to potential criminal action/prosecution.[146]

---

144 *See, e.g.*, Cal. Civ. Code § 56, *et seq.* (Confidentiality of Medical Information Act); Cal. Evid. Code § 990, *et seq.* (physician-patient privilege); Cal. Evid. Code §§ 1040-1047 *and* Cal. Penal Code § 832.7 (*Pitchess* privilege in officer personnel file records-information); Cal. Health & Safety Code § 128675, *et seq.* (Health Data & Advisory Council Consolidation Action); 42 U.S.C. § 1320d (Health Insurance Portability & Accountability Act; "HIPAA"); *see also Teamsters Local 856, supra*, 112 Cal.App.4th at pp. 1523-1525 (holding that because law enforcement officer salary information is *Pitchess*-protected officer personnel file information, Cal. Gov. Code § 6254(k) exempted such information from CPRA disclosure, and the exclusive means for discovery or disclosure of such information was the *Pitchess* system under Cal. Evid. Code §§ 1043 and 1045).

145 "Police agency" includes but is *not* limited to the California Attorney General, California Department of Justice, and the California Officer of Emergency Services. *See* Cal. Gov. Code §§ 7923.600-7923..625 (formerly Cal. Gov. Code § 6254(f)).

146 *See* Cal. Gov. Code § 7923.605 (formerly Cal. Gov. Code § 6254(f)) ("(a) Notwithstanding section 7923.600, state and local law enforcement agencies shall disclose the names and addresses of persons involved in, or witnesses other than confidential informants to, the incident, the description of any property involved, the date, time, and location of the incident, all diagrams, statements of the parties involved in the incident, the statements of all witnesses, other than confidential informants, to the victims of an incident, or an authorized representative thereof, an insurance carrier against which a claim has been or might be made, and any person suffering bodily injury or property damage or loss, as the result of the incident caused by arson, burglary, fire, explosion, larceny, robbery, carjacking, vandalism, vehicle theft, or a crime as defined by subdivision (b) of Section 13951, unless the disclosure would endanger either of the following: (1) The safety of a witness or other person involved in the investigation. (2) The successful completion of the investigation or a related investigation. (b) However, this article does not require the disclosure of that portion of those investigative files that reflects the analysis or conclusions of the investigating officer."); *see also State of Cal. ex rel. Div. of Indus. Safety v. Superior Ct.* (1974) 43 Cal.App.3d 778, 783-784 (holding that "[u]nless there is a concrete and definite prospect of...criminal law enforcement" regarding the code enforcement records, then

One of the **broader** of the CPRA exemptions[147], the police investigation records exemption thus <u>includes</u> (but is not limited to):

- **Autopsy Reports** and Coroner Photos[148];

- **Complaints** to Law Enforcement Agencies[149];

- **Confidential Informants**' Names or Addresses[150];

- **Dispatch Radio Recordings**[151];

- **Intelligence Information** Collected by Law Enforcement Agencies – including Drone Video Footage that is part of a police investigation[152];

Section 6254(f) does not apply to exempt such from CPRA disclosure because such a construction would cause the exemption to consume the rule favoring disclosure, since all public agencies are in some way pursuing compliance with or enforcement of the law; not just police agencies).

147 *See Rackauckas, supra*, 104 Cal.App.4th at p. 174 (referencing Section 6254(f) as the "'broad' investigation exemption").

148 *See* Cal. Gov. Code § 7930.180 (formerly Cal. Gov. Code § 6276.34) (post-mortem autopsy photos are exempt from disclosure); Cal. Code Civ. Proc. § 129 (autopsy photos shall not be disseminated or published, except in a criminal or civil action); *Dixon v. Superior Ct.* (2009) 170 Cal. App.4th 1271, 1276-1279 (coroner and autopsy reports related to deaths where potential criminality is being investigated are exempt from CPRA disclosure).

149 *See* Cal. Gov. Code § 7923.600(a) (formerly Cal. Gov. Code § 6254(f) (preceding sub-paragraph (1))).

150 *See* Cal. Gov. Code § 7923.605(a) (formerly Cal. Gov. Code § 6254(f)) (excluding the names and addresses of "confidential informants" from the exception to the police investigatory records exemption); *see also* Cal. Gov. Code § 7927.705 (formerly Cal. Gov. Code § 6254(k)) (incorporating statutory privileges into CPRA exemptions); Cal. Evid. Code § 1041 (public entity has a privilege to refuse to disclose identity of confidential informant re criminal violations where the need for preserving the confidentiality of the informant outweighs the need for disclosure in the interests of justice); *accord People v. Navarro* (2006) 138 Cal.App.4th 146, 160-161, 164-165 (affirming trial court's conduct of an *in camera* hearing, excluding the criminal defense, to determine if the interest in confidentiality of an informant's identity outweighed the need for disclosure where informant supplied information that led to other witnesses, and where those subsequent witnesses' information formed the basis of a search warrant that, in turn, led to incriminating evidence and conviction).

151 *Haynie v. Superior Ct.* (2001) 26 Cal.4th 1061, 1065-1072 (holding that the Section 6254(f) exemption barred disclosure where detainee requester sought witness interviews/statements and witness contact recordings, dispatch radio and police communication recordings, and other recordings pertaining to the incident leading to his detention, which necessarily would have included 9-1-1 call recordings).

152 *See* Cal. Gov. Code § 7923.600(a) (formerly Cal. Gov. Code § 6254(f) (preceding sub-paragraph (1)); *Castañares v. Superior Ct. of San Diego County* (*in re City of Chula Vista*) (2023) 98 Cal.App.5th 295, 310.

- **Investigation Reports and Records/Files** (but see exceptions for arrestee information and specified incidents)[153];

- **Security Procedures** of Law Enforcement Agencies[154];

- Suspect Photos (**Mug Shots**)[155];

- **Witness Interview Recordings and Statements**[156] (but see limited exception for specified CPRA requesters below); and

- **9-1-1 Type Call and/or Other Incident-Related Recordings.**[157]

Thus, for example, where the CPRA requester sought state Department of Justice cards and indexes that identified persons suspected of being or believed to be involved in organized crime — including identifying such persons by name, physical description, criminal history/records, known associates (criminal and non-criminal), occupation, and residence address — the California Supreme Court held that such law enforcement investigatory and criminal intelligence records were *exempt* from CPRA disclosure under Section 6254(f).[158]

Notably, however, records of **code enforcement actions** that are being prosecuted *administratively*, as opposed to criminally, are *not* law enforcement investigation records; and thus are *not* subject to the Section 6254(f)

---

153 *See* Cal. Gov. Code § 7923.600(a) (formerly Cal. Gov. Code § 6254(f) (preceding sub-paragraph (1)).

154 *See* Cal. Gov. Code § 7923.600(a) (formerly Cal. Gov. Code § 6254(f)) (preceding sub-paragraph (1)); *Northern Cal. Police Practices Project v. Craig* (1979) 90 Cal.App.3d 116, 121-122 (affirming that, where the records sought by the CPRA requester would disclose specific CHP security and safety procedures, Section 6254(f) authorized the CHP to refuse to disclose-produce such records).

155 *See* 86 Ops.Cal.Atty.Gen. 132, *9 (2003).

156 *Haynie, supra*, 26 Cal.4th at pp. 1065-1072 (holding that Section 6254(f) exemption barred disclosure where detainee requester sought witness interviews/statements and witness contact recordings, dispatch radio and police communication recordings, and other recordings pertaining to the incident leading to his detention, which necessarily would have included 9-1-1 call recordings).

157 *Haynie, supra*, 26 Cal.4th at pp. 1065-1072.

158 *American Civ. Lib. Union (Deukmejian), supra*, 32 Cal.3d at pp. 443-452; *see also id.* at p. 446 n. 5 (observing in dicta that the organized crime suspect-associate records were also potentially exempt under Section 6254(c) of the CPRA); *see generally Williams v. Superior Ct.* (1993) 5 Cal.4th 337, 350.

exemption: though they may be exempt under other provisions, such as the official information privilege, the catch-all public interest exemption, or other applicable CPRA exemptions.[159]

a. CPRA Disclosure of Police Drone Recordings.

Along related lines, recent case law has predictably clarified when audio/video recordings made by police drones (*e.g.*, miniature aerial remote-controlled drone helicopters, and comparable devices, used by law enforcement) are disclosable under the CPRA.

Drone Recordings Of *Criminal Activity Investigation* Are *Exempt* From Disclosure. Specifically, where the police drone audio/video footage was recorded/captured in furtherance of a law enforcement criminal investigation, whether or not such recording was made part of a police investigatory file, the drone video footage is exempt from CPRA disclosure as a law enforcement investigatory record (presumably unless an exception applies, such as drone video of an OIS).[160]

Drone Recordings *Unrelated To Criminal Activity* Are Likely *Disclosable*. However, by contrast, where the drone recording was made to investigate a non-criminal problem, *e.g.*, so as to see what kind of police assistance *might* be needed for some event that "do[es] not suggest a crime might have been committed or is in the process of being committed" – such as drone investigation related to a stranded motorist, or a dangerous/roaming wild animal, or a water leak – such drone recordings are *not* exempt under the law enforcement records exemption, and thus – unless otherwise exempt/

159 *State of Cal. ex rel. Div. of Indus. Safety*, *supra*, 43 Cal.App.3d at pp. 783-784 (holding that administrative code enforcement records are not police records subject to Section 6254(f) exemption); *see also Haynie*, *supra*, 26 Cal.4th at pp. 1068-1069 (for records pertaining to criminal law enforcement, the Section 6254(f) exemption applies even if the record is (a) not included in the investigative file, and (b) not a record prepared specifically for the investigation, as long as it is an unpublished record upon which the investigation relies); *San Jose v. Superior Ct.* (1999) 74 Cal.App.4th 1008, 1019-1025 (reviewing comparable cases and holding that where the information sought would disclose private citizens' identities regarding airport noise complainants, the Section 6255 catch-all exempted such records from CPRA disclosure).

160 *See Castañares v. Superior Ct. of San Diego County (in re City of Chula Vista)* (2023) 98 Cal.App.5th 295, 306, 310.

privileged (such as under the catchall or some other exemption) – such drone recordings are *disclosable* public records under the CPRA.[161]

This distinction is due to the court's rationale that "[t]he drone video footage should not be treated as a monolith, but rather, it can be divided into separate parts corresponding to each specific call. Then each distinct video can be evaluated under the CPRA in relation to the call triggering the drone dispatch."[162]

Non-Criminal Drone Recordings *Might* Still Be Exempt Under The Catchall. However, where drone footage is *not* exempt under the *law enforcement investigatory records exemption*, particularly where third-party privacy concerns might necessitate voluminous redactions, the recordings *might* still be exempt under the **catchall exemption**, on a case-by-case basis: and the law enforcement agency must then develop a specific factual record to show that the public interest in non-disclosure outweighs the public interest in disclosure.[163]

b. Rationale Underlying the Police Investigation Exemption.

The California Supreme Court has clarified that the purpose of the law enforcement investigation exemption is to prevent disclosure from "impair[ing]

---

161 *Id.* at pp. 306-312; *see also id.* at p. 310 ("The first category consists of drone video footage that is part of an investigatory file. As the parties agree, this footage would be exempt from disclosure under the CPRA per section 7923.600, subdivision (a). [¶] The second category consists of instances where officers used a drone to investigate whether a violation of law was occurring or had occurred but did not create a corresponding investigatory file. Examples of such use of drones include dispatching a drone to investigate a possible assault, a claim of someone causing a disturbance, or a suspected break-in; yet, the resultant video footage did not become part of an investigatory file. . . . [D]rone video footage investigating these and other claims of crimes being committed would fall under the records of investigations exceptions. The final category is any drone footage that does not fall under categories one or two. Such footage would consist of using a drone to make a factual inquiry to determine what kind of assistance is required, not to investigate a suspected violation of law. For example, a 911 call about a mountain lion roaming a neighborhood, a water leak, or stranded motorist on the freeway could warrant the use of a drone but do not suggest a crime might have been committed or is in the process of being committed.")

162 *Id.* at p. 312; *see also* Gov. Code § 7923.600(a); *Black Panther Party v. Kehoe* (1974) 42 Cal.App.3d 645, 654.

163 *See Castanares, supra,* 98 Cal.App.5th at pp. 313-314 (where the City had provided a declaration stating that such drone video redaction would take "1833.3 hours or 229.2 workdays to simply review and redact the footage without the additional legal review research, and quality control that would be necessary to evaluate privacy, safety, and legal concerns," the Court held that, had the City also clarified how much of that time applied to non-criminal-investigation drone footage, such might have triggered the catchall exemption).

'routine' investigations."[164] This is because disclosure of police investigation records would have dangerous effects whose public interest in avoidance outweighs the need for disclosure, namely that: "[c]omplainants and other witnesses whose identities were disclosed might disappear or refuse to cooperate. Suspects, who would be alerted to the investigation, might flee or threaten witnesses. Citizens would be reluctant to report suspicious activity. Evidence might be destroyed."[165]

Thus, in rejecting arguments that the nature, extent, importance, or quality of the law enforcement investigation should determine whether the Section 6254(f) exemption applies, the California Supreme Court underscored that the records for *any* police investigation into potential crime are exempt, *even if the investigation is cursory or hits a dead end*: this is because "[l]aw enforcement officers may not know whether a crime has been committed until an investigation of a complaint is undertaken. An investigation may be inconclusive either as to the cause of death or the circumstances in which the death occurred. A fire may be suspicious, but after investigation[,] be found to have an accidental or natural origin."[166] As a result, when it comes to the definition of police investigation records subject to the exemption, the police investigation exemption is more broadly construed.

c. Duration of the Police Investigation Exemption.

Significantly, although there is a definitive beginning to the exemption, in most cases, *there is no practical end to its operation* (unlike the pending litigation exemption). Specifically, the law enforcement investigation exemption begins to apply to related records "[o]nce an investigation…has come into being because there is a concrete and definite prospect of [criminal] enforcement proceedings at that time"; in such an event, as to records created at the time such prospect became concrete and definite, "materials that relate to the investigation and, thus, properly belong in the file, remain exempt…."[167]

However, once the law enforcement investigation exemption applies, **exempt items remain exempt from CPRA disclosure <u>even after the</u>**

---

164 *See Haynie, supra*, 26 Cal.4th at pp. 1070-1071.

165 *Id.*

166 *Id.*

167 *See Rackauckas, supra*, 104 Cal.App.4th at p. 174 (citing *Williams, supra*, 5 Cal.4th at pp. 361-362); *Office of the Inspector Gen. v. Superior Ct.* (2010) 189 Cal.App.4th 695, 709-710.

investigation ends — regardless of whether or not a criminal prosecution is brought.[168]

d. PRE-2019 EXCEPTIONS To The CPRA Exemption For Law Enforcement Investigatory Records.

Significantly, even *prior to the 2019 amendments*, under Government Code sections 7923.610-7923.620 (formerly Government Code section 6254(f)(1)-(3)), there were exceptions to the Section 7923.600 (formerly Section 6254(f)) exemption for police investigatory records and/or information: exceptions that effectively restored certain police investigatory records and information to disclosable public record status.

Specifically, even before 2019, the following police investigatory records and information are (and were) CPRA-disclosable public records:

1. Incident **Witnesses' Names and Addresses** (*Except* Confidential Informants)*;

2. Incident **Dates, Times, and Locations***;

3. Incident **Diagrams** (All)*;

4. Incident **Involved Parties' Statements** and **Witness Statements** (*Except* Confidential Informants)*;

5. **Customer Lists of Alarm or Security Companies** Provided to a Public Agency[169];

6. **Arrestee Identifying Information (Arrest Report Information)** — including (a) Full Name, (b) Occupation, (c) Date of Birth, (d) Hair and Eye Color, (e) Height and Weight, (f) Date and Time of Arrest, (g) Location of Arrest, (h) Date and Time of Booking, (i)

168 *See Rackauckas, supra*, 104 Cal.App.4th at pp. 174-175 (citing *Rivero v. Superior Ct.* (1997) 54 Cal.App.4th 1048, 1058-1059 and *Haynie, supra*, 26 Cal.4th at pp. 1065, 1070); *see also Williams, supra*, 5 Cal.4th at pp. 361-362, 361 n. 13.

169 *See* Cal. Gov. Code § 7923.600(a) (formerly Cal. Gov. Code § 6254(f) (preceding subsection (f)(1))). NOTE: Categories marked with an asterisk (*) have restricted categories of CPRA requesters to which such information is CPRA-discoverable.

Factual Circumstances Surrounding the Arrest, (j) Amount of Bail Set, (k) Time and Manner of Release OR Location Where Arrestee is Currently Being Held, (l) All Criminal Charges on Which the Arrestee is Being Held, (m) Any Outstanding Warrants From Other Jurisdictions, *and* (n) Any Parole or Probation Holds[170];

7. **Complaints and Requests for Assistance (Calls for Service Report Information re Crimes or Incidents Resulting in Police Investigation)** — including (a) Incident Date and Time, (b) Incident Location, (c) Report/Call Date and Time, (d) Victim Name, (e) Victim Age, (f) Factual Circumstances Surrounding the Crime or Incident, (g) General Description of Any Injuries, Property, or Weapons Involved, *and* (h) Time and Nature of the Agency's Response to the Call for Service (*Except* the Names of Sex or Hate Crime Victims or the Names and Images of Human Trafficking Victims or Immediate Family Until the Related Prosecution Ends)[171];

8. **Arrestee and Crime Victim Addresses** (*Not* Names) — **For Journalistic, Scholarly, or Political/Governmental Purposes *Only*,** Supported By Requester Declaration (*Except* the Addresses of Sex or Hate Crime Victims)[172];

---

170 *See* Cal. Gov. Code § 7923.610 (formerly Cal. Gov. Code § 6254(f)(1)). Notably, unlike the first four categories of information made disclosable under this exception to the police investigatory records CPRA exemption, the statute does *not* expressly limit the types of CPRA requester who may obtain arrest reports.

171 *See* Cal. Gov. Code § 7923.615 (formerly Cal. Gov. Code § 6254(f)(2)(A)-(B)). NOTE: **Victims of specified sex and hate crimes are entitled to have their names withheld from calls-for-service reports.** *See id.* (re Cal. Penal Code §§ 220, 236.1, 261, 261.5, 262, 264, 264.1, 265, 266, 266a, 266b, 266c, 266e, 266f, 266j, 267, 269, 273a, 273d, 273.5, 285, 286, 288, 288a, 288.2, 288.3, 288.4, 288.5, 288.7, 289, 422.6, 422.7, 422.75, 646.9, 647.6). Where the victim is a victim of human trafficking, *at the request of the victim*, the names and images of the victim, and of the victim's "immediate family" (as defined by Penal Code § 422.4, but *not* including any family members charged with a crime arising from the same incident) may also be withheld from disclosure until the investigation or any subsequent prosecution is completed. *See* Cal. Gov. Code § 7923.615(c) (formerly Cal. Gov. Code § 6254(f)(2)(B)).

172 *See* Cal. Gov. Code § 7923.620 (formerly Cal. Gov. Code § 6254(f)(3)). NOTE: **This paragraph also bars recipients using the addresses, either directly or indirectly, to sell a product or service of any kind.** To obtain information pursuant to this paragraph, the requester must execute a sworn declaration stating that the address information will not be used, either directly or indirectly, to sell a product or service of any kind. *See also* Cal. Penal Code § 841.5; *Los Angeles Police Dept. v. United Reporting Pub. Corp.* (1999) 528 U.S. 32, 35-41 (aff'g constitutionality of Cal Gov. Code § 6254(f)(3) re limited access and use re arrestee information).

and

9. **Traffic Accident Reports** — To Involved Persons or Parties Subject to Liability.[173]

(i) Restricted Requesters For Specified (*) Police Records.

However, as to the first four categories of CPRA-disclosable police investigatory records-information (see * above re witness names/addresses; incident dates, times, locations; diagrams; and witness statements), *on its face*, this statutory exception to the exemption (and, thereby, access to such police investigatory records) is *only* expressly available to:

(1) the victims of an incident;

(2) an authorized representative of a victim of an incident;

(3) an insurance carrier against which a claim has been made or might be made; and

(4) "any person suffering bodily injury or property damage or loss" as a result of the incident.[174]

However, even as to the above-specified eligible CPRA requesters for the first four categories of disclosable information, the statute expressly limited the *types* of incidents for which such records were disclosable to acts that would constitute crimes under California law, had such incidents occurred in California.[175]

---

173 Cal. Veh. Code § 20012.

174 *See* Cal. Gov. Code § 7923.605(a) (formerly Cal. Gov. Code § 6254(f)) (preceding subsection (f)(1) and stating that "law enforcement agencies shall disclose [the above-specified categories of information]...to the victims of an incident" and others identified thereafter); *see also* Cal. Gov. Code § 13951(b) (defining "crime" as applicable under Section 7923.605); Cal. Gov. Code § 7928.300 (formerly Cal. Gov. Code § 6254.30) (victim need not prove legal residency to be entitled to public records, and current driver's license or identification or passport is sufficient to establish identity, if required by the agency).

175 *See id.*

Thus, for example, as to these first four categories of disclosable information (see * above re witness names/addresses; incident dates, times, locations; diagrams; and witness statements), such would generally be *un*available to non-victim criminal suspects making CPRA requests.[176] In other words, as to the first four categories of police investigatory records, only specified CPRA requesters were entitled to the excepted disclosure, and only if the incident at issue constituted a crime under California law (regardless of whether the incident occurred within California).[177]

By contrast, the remaining categories of disclosable information (after the first four above) do *not* have any statutory restrictions upon the types of CPRA requesters for whom such information is disclosable under the pre-2019 exceptions to the police investigatory records exemption; or as to the types of incidents for which the information is disclosable.[178]

Moreover, as a practical matter, the restriction covering the first four categories is really only a restriction that applies to the third and fourth categories (diagrams and witness statements): this is because the information in the first two categories (witness names/addresses and incident date/time/location) is either completely (incident date/time/location) or partially (witness names/addresses, if the witness is a victim or an arrestee) available under that portion of the exception's provision that does *not* restrict the CPRA requesters who may access the excepted police records.

(ii) Excepted *Information* Must Be Produced, *Not* Necessarily Excepted Records.

Significantly, even where law enforcement investigation information *is* CPRA-disclosable, the custodial public agency is *not* required to produce the *actual records* containing such information: as long as the disclosable information itself is properly disclosed to the CPRA requester.[179]

176 *See id.*; *Buckheit v. Dennis*, 2012 U.S. Dist. LEXIS 49062, * 61 n. 10 (N.D. Cal. 2012).

177 *Id.*

178 *Compare* Cal. Gov. Code § 7923.605(a) (formerly Cal. Gov. Code § 6254(f) (preceding subsection (f)(1), *first* paragraph)) *with* Cal. Gov. Code § 7923.610 (formerly Cal. Gov. Code § 6254(f) (preceding subsection (f)(1), *third* paragraph)).

179 *See Haynie*, *supra*, 26 Cal.4th at pp. 1065-1067, 1071-1072.

Thus, for example, where a law enforcement agency produced certain CPRA-disclosable information to a detainee who then became a CPRA requester, and where the law enforcement agency disclosed such information via a *written summary* that detailed the date, time, location, involved persons, and basic factual circumstances of the incident at issue, including the involvement of any weapons or injuries, the reviewing court held that the agency had satisfied its CPRA burden and that the agency was *not* then required to disclose-produce the underlying reports and recordings themselves to the requester.[180]

(iii) The Caveats (Exceptions To The Exceptions) That Restore The Police Records Exemptions.

Even prior to 2019, there were two caveats, or exceptions to the exceptions that would, in effect, restore the law enforcement investigatory records exemption from CPRA disclosure:

(1) The **Ongoing Investigation Protection** (or Caveat) For Investigation, Investigator, and Witness Endangerment; and

(2) The **Investigator Analyses and Conclusions Protection** (or Caveat).

We will explore each in turn here.

(iv) Caveat: The Ongoing Investigation Protection & Witness/Investigator Protection.

Notwithstanding the foregoing, even as to the above-specified information excepted from the police investigative records exemption, under the pre-2019 system, law enforcement agencies remain exempt from CPRA disclosure of investigatory records **where the disclosure**:

(1) "**would endanger the safety of a witness or other person involved in the investigation**"; or

---

180 *Id.*; *see also Williams*, *supra*, 5 Cal.4th at pp. 349-350 ("The required disclosures of *information derived from the records* about incidents, arrests, and complaints need not, in most cases, entail disclosure of the records themselves." (emphasis in original)).

(2) "**would endanger the successful *completion* of the investigation or a related investigation.**"[181]

Part of the rationale underlying this limited restoration of the exemption where disclosure would endanger a witness/person or an investigation is the California Legislature's recognition of the need to protect the confidentiality of informants' identities and statements.[182]

When asserting witness/person or investigation endangerment, the custodial public entity bears the burden of demonstrating that disclosure would create such danger.[183]

Moreover, the trial court is obliged to review *in camera* the records for which the public agency claims disclosure would endanger the safety of a witness or other person or of an as-yet-incomplete investigation.[184]

Perhaps obviously, the ongoing investigation restoration of **the law enforcement investigative records exemption only applies while the investigation remains incomplete**: a public entity cannot validly assert that a disclosure would endanger an investigation that is already complete.[185]

Thus, for example, where a municipal police department's investigation had been pending for over 16 months, out of a customary 24 months, but where the police agency was no longer actively investigating the circumstances of the decedent's death, and the district attorney had already declined to file any criminal charges associated with the death, where the CPRA requester sought police reports related to the death, when a police agency sergeant asserted in a conclusory declaration that disclosure would endanger the still-officially-incomplete

---

181 *See* Cal. Gov. Code § 7923.605(a) (formerly Cal. Gov. Code § 6254(f) (preceding subsection (f)(1), emphasis added)).

182 *See, e.g., People v. Sotelo* (Cal. Ct. App. 1979) 153 Cal.Rptr. 348, 353 n. 6 (90 Cal. App.3d 200).

183 *See Fredericks v. Superior Ct.* (2015) 233 Cal.App.4th 209, 225, 235; *accord City of Santa Rosa v. Press Democrat* (1986) 187 Cal.App.3d 1315, 1320.

184 *See, e.g., Register Div. of Freedom Newspapers v. County of Orange* (1984) 158 Cal. App.3d 893, 904 (rev'g trial court for failure to conduct *in camera* review to assess factual merit of agency's assertion that disclosure would endanger a person/witness or a pending investigation).

185 *See, e.g., Estate of Rutman v. City & County of San Francisco* (San Francisco Super. Ct 2016) 2016 Cal.Super.LEXIS 1473, *1-2; *Estate of Amaro v. City of Oakland* (N.D. Cal. 2010) 2010 U.S. Dist. LEXIS 15573, * 37.

investigation, the court held that the public agency had failed to establish that the ongoing investigation provisions applied: and thus holding that the requested records were disclosable.[186]

Similarly, where a federal court was reviewing the propriety of a public entity's CPRA exemption claims, in order to assess whether the plaintiff's statute of limitations should be deemed tolled during the period of the public agency's "stonewall[ing]," where the mother of a decedent made a CPRA request after the investigation into her son's death was already complete, the reviewing court held that the ongoing investigation provision of Section 6254(d) did *not* apply: and thus that the decedent's mother should have her deadline to file suit extended.[187]

By contrast, for purposes of evaluating Eleventh Amendment sovereign immunity, where a federal court was reviewing whether or not a prison's public records coordinator was acting within his lawful authority and official capacity in refusing a CPRA request for records associated with a jailhouse murder while the murder case was still ongoing, the federal court inferred that the coordinator was acting within the lawful course and scope of his employment.[188]

(v) Caveat: The Investigator Analysis & Conclusions Protection.

Additionally, notwithstanding the foregoing, even as to the above-specified information excepted from the exemption, under the pre-2019 system, law enforcement agencies are/were remained exempt from CPRA disclosure where the disclosure would include "that portion of those investigative files that reflects the analysis or conclusions of the investigating officer."[189]

Thus, for example, where the custodial public entity withheld from CPRA disclosure-production a prosecutor's letter whose exclusive purpose and content was to document his investigatory thoughts, legal opinions, impressions/

---

186 *Estate of Rutman*, *supra*, 2016 Cal.Super.LEXIS 1473 at pp. *1-2.

187 *Estate of Amaro*, *supra*, 2010 U.S. Dist. LEXIS 15573 at p. * 37.

188 *See Bradley-Aboyade v. Crozier* (E.D. Cal. 2020) 2020 U.S. Dist. LEXIS 138936, *3-4, 20-23.

189 *See* Cal. Gov. Code § 7923.605(b) (formerly Cal. Gov. Code § 6254(f) (preceding subsection (f)(1))); *Rackauckas*, *supra*, 104 Cal.App.4th at p. 174.

analyses, and conclusions, the reviewing court held that such records retained their exemption under Section 6254(f).[190]

Similarly, in a case where no official incident reports were prepared, where a CPRA requester sought production of a police investigator's entire investigative file, including the investigators' analyses and conclusions, because such analyses and conclusions were exempt from CPRA disclosure, the requester's subsequent civil claim based on alleged CPRA violations regarding such file was held to be meritless.[191]

e. The 2019 And 2022 Exceptions To The CPRA Exemption For Law Enforcement Investigatory Records: Specified Officer Conduct.

As explained more fully in the foregoing chapter — "**STATUTORY EXEMPTIONS to the Otherwise Mandatory *Pitchess* Procedure**" under the section titled "The CPRA Exception for Recordings of Critical Incidents and for Complaint/Investigation Records of Officer-Involved Shootings, Serious Uses of Force, Officer Sexual Assault on Non-Officers, and Officer Dishonesty in Policing" — and as explained briefly below, effective 2019 and 2022, SB 1421 and SB 16 [codified in Cal. Penal Code §§ 832.7(b)-(i) and 832.8(b)-(c)] and AB 748 [codified in Cal. Gov. Code § 7923.625 (formerly Cal. Gov. Code § 6254(f)(4))] created an additional exception to this police investigation exemption from CPRA.

In summary, with a complicated system for withholding or redactions in specified circumstances, and with more than a few subtle carve-outs, the 2019/2022 amendments except from the CPRA police investigation records exemption those records and recordings pertaining to eight specific categories of officer-involved incidents and alleged misconduct (up from four categories in 2019): (1) officer-involved shootings/firearm discharges ("**OIS**") of or at persons; (2) officer uses of force **("UOF") resulting in death or great bodily injury ("GBI")**; (3) **sustained** investigations of **officers' excessive/unreasonable force**; (4) **sustained** investigations of **officers' failure to intervene to stop another officer's use of excessive/unreasonable force**; (5) **sustained** investigations of **officer sexual assaults against members of the public**, uniquely

190 *See Rackauckas, supra*, 104 Cal.App.4th at p. 176.

191 *See Shapiro v. Anderson* (C.D. Cal. 2016) 2016 U.S. Dist. LEXIS 55539, *22-23.

defined; (6) **sustained** investigations of **officer dishonesty** in the performance of the officer's **law enforcement duties**; (7) **sustained** investigations of **officers' discrimination against a protected class**; and (8) **sustained** investigations of **officers' unlawful arrests and/or unlawful searches**.

Please refer to the aforementioned chapter for a full exploration of the scope, operation, disputed interpretations, limits, and recent case law decisions and trends regarding this complex exception to the CPRA exemption for law enforcement investigatory records.

5. *The CPRA General Exemption For Information PRIVILEGED Or Protected By Federal Or State Law.*

Government Code section 7927.705 (former Government Code section 6254(k)) features an exemption from CPRA disclosure for: "Records, the disclosure of which is exempted or prohibited pursuant to federal or state law, including but not limited to, provisions of the Evidence Code related to privilege." The effect of this statutory provision is to incorporate both federal and state privileges into the CPRA exemptions: with some of the most pertinent to law enforcement records highlighted below.[192]

6. *CPRA's PRIVACY Privileged Information Catch-All.*

The effect of Government Code section 7927.705 (former Government Code section 6254(k)) is to incorporate privacy protections into the CPRA exemption where such protections are specifically embodied in federal or state law.[193] The rationale for such incorporation is based on the Legislature's balancing of the California constitutional right to privacy with the public's "right

---

192 *See, e.g.*, Cal. Gov. Code § 7927.705 (formerly Cal. Gov. Code § 6254(k)) (privileged matters exempt from disclosure); Cal. Evid. Code §§ 952-954; *see also National Conf. of Black Mayors*, *supra*, 25 Cal.App.5th at pp. 586-587 (holding that a public officer does not lose his or her right to privacy or to statutory privileges, like the attorney-client privilege, merely by entering public office; and ruling that where a city mayor used city emails to conduct business on behalf of an unaffiliated public interest group, because the business at issue was that of the public interest group, and not the city, even though city resources were used, the mayor and the public interest group retained their privacy rights and privileges in the related emails, which were deemed *not* be to be public records disclosable under the CPRA).

193 *See id.*; *see also, e.g.*, *New York Times*, *supra*, 218 Cal.App.3d at pp. 1584-1585 (citing, among others, *CBS Inc.*, *supra*, 42 Cal.3d at pp. 651-652).

to review the government's conduct of its business."[194] Thus, by means of this incorporation, various privacy protections under the law are transformed into CPRA exemptions.[195]

For example, the following privacy protections in California and federal law establish **privacy exemptions** under the CPRA: **child abuse/neglect reports; elder abuse records; mental health (§ 5150) detention records; library patron use/circulation reports; licensee financial information; juvenile custody records; medical records and communications; personal contact information** (in many, but not all, cases) — including the personal contact information of *elected or appointed officials on the internet* (without their written permission); and **workers' compensation benefits.**[196]

However, the operation of these CPRA statutory privacy exemptions does *not* mean that the records at issue are not discoverable: it just means that systems other than the CPRA must be used to obtain such exempted records. For example, outside of a limited group of government employees who are entitled to access to such records, although juvenile records are CPRA exempt,

---

194 *See New York Times, supra*, 218 Cal.App.3d at pp. 1584-1585 ("Article I, section 1, of the California Constitution guarantees all persons the inalienable right to privacy.... Nonetheless, the public and the press have a right to review the government's conduct of its business.... Consequently, in enacting the Public Records Act, the Legislature balanced the individual's privacy interest with the right to know about the conduct of public business. [citation] Specific exemptions from this general requirement of disclosure are listed in section 6254 [and elsewhere in the CPRA] and are construed narrowly to ensure maximum disclosure of the conduct of governmental operations.").

195 *See id.*; *see also* Cal. Gov. Code §§ 7927.700, 7923.625(b)(1), 7927.705 (formerly Cal. Gov. Code § 6254(c), (f)(4)(B)(i), (k)).

196 *See* Cal. Gov. Code § 7927.700 (formerly Cal. Gov. Code § 6254(c), (medical information and workers' compensation benefits exemption)), 7927.705 (formerly 6254(k)) (general privilege incorporation), 7927.100 (formerly 6254(j)) (library circulation exemption), 7925.005 (formerly 6254(n)) (licensee financial information exemption); Cal. Gov. Code §§ 7928.200-7928.230 (formerly Cal. Gov. Code § 6254.21) (barring posting of elected or appointed officials' home addresses or telephone numbers on internet, without their written permission, including but not limited to judges, prosecutors/public defenders, municipal executives and legislators, and police chiefs/sheriffs); Cal. Gov. Code § 7922.000 (formerly Cal. Gov. Code § 6255(a)) (public interest catch-all exemption); Cal. Gov. Code § 7927.105 (formerly Cal. Gov. Code § 6267) (library use exemption); Cal. Penal Code §§ 11165.6, 11165.7, 11167.5, 11169 (as to child abuse/neglect reports); Cal. Evid. Code §§ 990-1027 (physician/therapist and patient privileges); Cal. Civ. Code § 56, *et seq.* (Confidentiality of Medical Information Act); Cal. Health & Safety Code § 128675, *et seq.* (Health Data & Advisory Council Consolidation Act); Cal. Welf. & Inst. Code §§ 827, 827.9, 828, 5328, 5330, 15633; 42 U.S.C. § 1320d (Health Insurance Portability & Accountability Act, or "HIPAA"); *see also* Cal. Lab. Code § 138.7(a).

enile detention records are obtainable primarily through a court petition 1 order.[197]

a. CPRA Disclosure v. CPRA Exemption For Personal Contact Information.

When it comes to **personal contact information**, such as a person's name address or phone number, whether the person is a public employee or a pri- :e citizen whose contact information is possessed by a public agency, deter- ning the applicability of the CPRA privacy exemption requires a case-spe- ic inquiry. "In determining whether the public interest in nondisclosure of dividuals' names and addresses [and other contact information] outweighs ıe] public interest in disclosure of that information, courts have evaluated ıether disclosure would serve the legislative purpose of 'shed[ding] light on agency's performance of its statutory duties.'"[198]

Thus, "[w]here disclosure of names and addresses [or contact infor- ation] would not serve this purpose, denial of the request for disclosure ıs been upheld."[199] "Courts have also recognized that the public interest in sclosure [of persons' identities and contact information] is minimal, even hen the requester asserts that personal contact [information] is necessary to ınfirm government compliance with mandatory duties, where the requester ıs alternative, less intrusive means of obtaining the information sought."[200]

"However, where the disclosure of names and addresses [and contact ıformation] is necessary to allow the public to determine whether public fficials have properly exercised their duties by refraining from the arbitrary xercise of official power, disclosure has been upheld."[201]

Thus, for example, even when such persons were assured anonymity, the lentities of donors to public universities were held to be CPRA-disclosable[202];

197 *See, e.g.*, Cal. Welf. & Inst. Code §§ 827(a)(3), 827.9(d).

198 *City of San Jose v. Superior Ct.* (1999) 74 Cal.App.4th 1008, 1020.

199 *Id.*; *see generally Long Beach Police Officers Assn. v. City of Long Beach* (2014) 59 :al.4th 59, 74-75.

200 *Id.*

201 *Id.*

202 *California State Univ. of Fresno Assn. v. Superior Ct.* (2001) 90 Cal.App.4th 810, 834-835.

as were the identities of persons who were exceeding their water restrictions, so as to expose potential special treatment; as well as the identities and applications of concealed weapons permit applicants, except where to do so would jeopardize the applicants' safety or the privacy of medical/mental health information.[203]

OIS Officers' Names Are Generally Disclosable. Notably, among the identities that the CPRA holds to be disclosable are **the names of law enforcement officers who are involved in an on-duty shooting** — unless there is a particularized showing in a specific case as to why the public interest in nondisclosure outweighs the public interest in disclosure.[204]

By contrast, because disclosure of the identities of complainants about airport noise was determined to have a chilling effect on the government's ability to receive such complaints, the public interest in nondisclosure of those identities and contact information was held to outweigh the public disclosure interests: so that such identities were *not* disclosable.[205]

b. The CPRA Exemption For Officers' And Criminal System Officials' Home Addresses And Phone Numbers.

On a related note, Government Code section 7923.805 (formerly Government Code section 6254(u)) features a specific exemption from CPRA disclosure for: the home address or telephone number of prosecutors, public defenders, **peace officers**, judges, court commissioners, and magistrates as provided on firearms licenses applications or, pursuant to the Section 6255(a)

---

203 *New York Times, supra*, 218 Cal.App.3d at pp 1585-1586; *New York Times v. Superior Ct.* (1997) 52 Cal.App.4th 97, 104-105; *see also* Cal. Gov. Code § 7923.800 (formerly Cal. Gov. § 6254(u)(i)) (limiting disclosure of concealed weapons permit application information and identities).

204 *See* Cal. Penal Code § 832.7(b)(5)-(6), (i); *Long Beach Police Officers Assn., supra*, 59 Cal.4th at pp. 74-75 (holding that the CPRA requires the disclosure of the names of officers *involved* in an on-duty shooting, unless there is a particularized showing as to why the public interest in nondisclosure of the names of such officers outweighs the public interest in disclosure); *New York Times, supra*, 52 Cal.App.4th at pp. 104-105 (holding that the identities of shooting officers are disclosable); *see also City of San Jose, supra*, 74 Cal.App.4th at pp. 1019-1021; Cal. Penal Code § 832.7(b)(6)(A) (officer names and work-related information for officers involved in incidents falling within the eight excepted categories are CPRA-disclosable; though witness-officer names arguably might remain exempt from disclosure).

205 *City of San Jose, supra*, 74 Cal.App.4th at pp. 1022-1025; Cal. Penal Code § 832.7(b)(6)(B) (complainant, whistleblower, victim, and witness names and identifying information remain exempt from CPRA disclosure).

catch-all, otherwise.[206] This is because "Section 6254(u)…evidences California's recognition of the [law enforcement sector] applicant's interest in maintaining the confidentiality" of their home addresses and personal phone numbers.[207]

The CPRA also establishes a related exemption for law enforcement sector public employees' home addresses by incorporating a Vehicle Code confidentiality for the home addresses of peace officers, police employees and dispatchers, prosecutors and public defenders, city attorneys and county counsel, and other specified government employees.[208]

Thus, even if law enforcement officers' *names* might be disclosable in a specific case (*e.g.*, OIS), under Section 6254(k) and/or Section 6255, **police officers' personal addresses and personal phone numbers** (and presumably similar personal contact information) **remain exempt from CPRA disclosure,** under Section 6254(u) and Section 6276.24.[209]

However, as noted above, **the CPRA holds that the *names* of law enforcement officers who are involved in an on-duty shooting (OIS) *are* disclosable** — unless there is a particularized showing in a specific case as to why the public interest in nondisclosure outweighs the public interest in disclosure.[210]

---

206 *See* Cal. Gov. Code § 7923.805 (formerly Cal. Gov. Code § 6254(u)(2)-(3) (emphasis added); Cal. Gov. Code § 7922.000 (formerly Cal. Gov. Code § 6255(a)); *Coleman v. Brown*, 2018 U.S. Dist. LEXIS 183514, * 15 (E.D. Cal. 2018) (citing Cal. Gov. Code § 6254(u) for the proposition that public "employees' personal addresses and personal telephone numbers" are *not* matters of public record); *Birdt v. San Bernardino Sheriffs Dept.*, 2014 U.S. Dist. LEXIS 80481, * 2-3 (C.D. Cal. 2014) (citing Section 6254(u)(2)-(3) for the proposition that because peace officer personal phone numbers and personal addresses are exempt from CPRA disclosure, they were properly redacted in responses to civil discovery requests; as long as the officers' names were not redacted).

207 *See Mehl v. Blanas*, 241 F.R.D. 653, 657-659 (E.D. Cal. 2007).

208 *See* Cal. Gov. Code § 7927.705 (formerly Cal. Gov. Code § 6254(k)); Cal. Gov. Code § 7930.155 (formerly Cal. Gov. Code § 6276.24); Cal. Veh. Code § 1808.4.

209 *See id.*

210 *See* Cal. Penal Code § 832.7(b)(5)-(6), (i); *Long Beach Police Officers Assn.*, *supra*, 59 Cal.4th at pp. 74-75 (holding that the CPRA requires the disclosure of the names of officers involved in an on-duty shooting, unless there is a particularized showing as to why the public interest in nondisclosure of the names of such officers outweighs the public interest in disclosure); *New York Times*, *supra*, 52 Cal.App.4th at pp. 104-105 (holding that the identities of shooting officers are disclosable); *see also City of San Jose*, *supra*, 74 Cal.App.4th at pp. 1019-1021.

7. *CPRA's ATTORNEY-CLIENT PRIVILEGE & ATTORNEY WORK PRODUCT PROTECTION* ***Privileged Information Catch-All.***

By the aforementioned mechanism of privilege incorporation, effectively underscored by way of Section 6276.04, Section 6254(k) also establishes a CPRA exemption for attorney-client privileged matters and attorney work product protected information.[211]

While the scope of this book is *not* intended to embrace a full exploration of every privilege available to law enforcement agencies and officers, a *brief* recap of the attorney-client privilege and the attorney work product protection may assist the reader in evaluating whether or not police records are CPRA-disclosable, regardless of whether such are also *Pitchess*-privileged.[212]

a. Attorney-Client Privilege Recap.

To elaborate, under California law, confidential information transmitted between a client and the client's lawyer in the course of that attorney-client relationship, including communications and advice/counsel, are subject to the **attorney-client privilege** and, as a result, are exempt from disclosure: ***except* where the lawyer's services were sought or obtained to commit a crime or fraud; where the lawyer reasonably believes disclosure is necessary to**

---

211 *See* Cal. Gov. Code §§ 7927.705 (formerly Cal. Gov. Code § 6254(k)) (privileged matters exempt from disclosure), 7930.110 (formerly Cal. Gov. Code § 6276.04) (expressly incorporating by reference into the CPRA exemptions the attorney-client privilege and the attorney work product protection); Cal. Evid. Code §§ 952-954; Cal. Code Civ. Proc. § 2018.010, *et seq.*; *see also National Conf. of Black Mayors, supra*, 25 Cal.App.5th at pp. 586-587 (holding that a public officer does not lose his or her right to privacy or to statutory privileges, like the attorney-client privilege, merely by entering public office; and ruling that where a city mayor used city emails to conduct business on behalf of an unaffiliated public interest group, because the business at issue was that of the public interest group, and not the city, even though city resources were used, the mayor and the public interest group retained their privacy rights and privileges in the related emails, which were deemed *not* be to be public records disclosable under the CPRA).

212 *See generally Commodity Futures Trading Comm'n v. Weintraub*, 471 U.S. 343, 348 (1985); *In re Financial Corp. of Am.*, 119 B.R. 728, 736 (Bankr. C.D. Cal. 1990) (holding that the Federal Deposit Insurance Corporation, a federal quasi-agency, may assert the attorney-client privilege); *Ernestine Ching Young v. City & County of Honolulu*, 2008 U.S. Dist. LEXIS 110120, *20-21 (D. Haw. 2008) (holding that since the privilege belongs to the city-entity, a city council-member cannot waive that privilege without authorization from the city-entity); *see generally Upjohn Co. v. United States*, 449 U.S. 383, 389-390 (1980) (holding that corporate entities may assert the privilege); *Roberts v. City of Palmdale* (1993) 5 Cal.4th 363, 370 ("Ample authority acknowledges the right of public entities to assert the attorney-client privilege.").

prevent a crime likely to result in death or substantial bodily harm; where the client has died and testamentary intent is at issue, such as that regarding a property conveyance; or in a legal malpractice action between the lawyer and client.[213]

Confidential Forum Required. To be confidential, an attorney-client communication must be made "by a means which, so far as the client is aware, discloses the information to no third persons other than those who are present to further the interests of the client...or those to whom disclosure is reasonably necessary for the...accomplishment of the purpose for which the lawyer is consulted...."[214]

Thus, for example, where a private employee communicated with his personal attorney through his company's computer, and where that company's computer policy had previously warned the employee that it reserved the right to monitor all emails and that there was no confidentiality of communications sent via its system, because the employee had no reasonable expectation of confidentiality, his attorney-client emails sent via the company computer were *not* privileged.[215]

Purpose of the Privilege. The purpose of the attorney-client privilege is to preserve a relationship of confidentiality between an attorney and a client: and to avoid the harm of disruption to that relationship.[216] Where the party claiming the privilege shows that the dominant purpose of the relationship between the communicating parties was an attorney-client relationship, the

---

213 *See* Cal. Evid. Code §§ 950-962; *see also* Cal. Gov. Code §§ 7927.705, 7930.110 (formerly Cal. Gov. Code §§ 6254(k), 6276.04).

214 Cal. Evid. Code § 952.

215 *Holmes v. Petrovich Dev. Co. LLC* (2011) 191 Cal.App.4th 1047, 1071-1072.

216 *Costco Wholesale Corp, supra*, 47 Cal.4th at pp. 746-747; *Fireman's Fund Ins. Co. v. Superior Ct.* (2011) 196 Cal.App.4th 1263, 1272 (also observing that misapplication of the privilege is reviewed on appeal for abuse of discretion); *see also Upjohn Co. v. United States*, 449 U.S. 383, 390-391 (1980) (observing that the purpose of the attorney-client privilege is to promote candid communication between an attorney and his/her client, including the sharing of information with the attorney for the purpose of obtaining advice as well as the counsel's advice thereon, in order to preserve the interests of the client in obtaining the full benefits of our legal system and thereby promote our society's broader interests in the observance of law and the administration of justice); *accord Jaffee v. Redmond*, 518 U.S. 1, 11 (1996).

privilege thus applies; and there is no need for the party asserting privilege to show that any prejudice would result from disclosure.[217]

<u>Scope of Privilege Coverage</u>. The attorney-client privilege extends to the *entirety* of the communication, even if the communication includes unprivileged information.[218] Thus, the "'privilege covers the transmission of documents which are available to the public, and not merely information in the sole possession of the attorney or the client. In this regard, it is the actual fact of the transmission [of the communication] which merits protection, since discovery of the transmission of specific public documents might very well reveal the transmitter's intended strategy.'"[219]

However, this doctrine has limits because "'a client may be examined on deposition or at trial as to the facts of the case, whether or not he has communicated them to his attorney.... While the privilege fully covers communication as such, it does not extend to subject matter otherwise unprivileged merely because that subject matter has been communicated to the attorney.'"[220] This is because "'a litigant may not silence a witness by having him reveal his knowledge to the litigant's attorney.'"[221]

Thus for example, while the identity of specific case law or articles an attorney forwarded to his client would be privileged, the privilege would not bar another party from using the contents of those cases or articles, if obtained outside of the privileged relationship.[222]

---

217 *See Costco Wholesale Corp., supra,* 47 Cal.4th at p. 733-736 (also holding that a document does *not* need to be prepared in anticipation of litigation in order to be subject to the attorney-client privilege); *see also Clark v. Superior Ct.* (2011) 196 Cal.App.4th 37, 49-54.

218 *Costco Wholesale Corp., supra,* 47 Cal.4th at p. 734.

219 *Id.*; *accord Mitchell v. Superior Ct.* (1984) 37 Cal.3d 591, 600-601 (both factual matter transmitted between an attorney and client, as well as legal advice, are protected from disclosure by the privilege); *In re Jordan* (1974) 12 Cal.3d 575, 580 (the specific identity and copies of cases and law review articles forwarded by an attorney to the client were attorney-client privileged from disclosure).

220 *Costco Wholesale Corp., supra,* 47 Cal.4th at p. 735.

221 *Id.*

222 *Compare In re Jordan, supra,* 12 Cal.3d at p. 580 *with D.I. Chadbourne, Inc. v. Superior Ct.* (1964) 60 Cal.2d 723, 733-734.

Notably, the attorney-client privilege applies whether the attorneys are within a law firm communicating among themselves about the client's case or whether the attorneys are in-house employees of the client.[223]

Extension To Attorney Agents. Moreover, the privilege extends not only to attorney-client communications, but to communications between an attorney's non-lawyer agent and the client, where the agent is retained to assist with the representation: this necessarily includes client communications with an attorney's investigator.[224] Along related lines, attorney investigative files are subject to the attorney-client privilege where the client retained the attorney to provide legal advice regarding such investigation.[225]

Duration. Unlike the pending litigation exemption, the attorney-client privilege endures even after litigation has concluded related to the subject of the communication.[226]

Waiver Must Be Intentional. Additionally, the "'privilege is not waived in the absence of a manifest intent to waive'" it.[227] Thus, "inadvertent disclosures" of privileged materials will *not* waive or void the privilege where: (1) there was no subjective intent by the privilege holder to disclose privileged material; (2) the privilege holder took reasonable precautions to preserve the privilege before the inadvertent disclosure; and (3) after discovery of the inadvertent disclosure, the privilege holder promptly sought the return of the inadvertently disclosed/otherwise-privileged material.[228]

Restriction On Attorney-Client Privilege's Bar On Disclosure For Public Entity Attorneys. The 2022 revisions to the Penal Code appear to prevent lawyer-client privilege from being asserted as an exemption from

---

223 *Costco Wholesale Corp., supra*, 47 Cal.4th at p. 733-734; *Fireman's Fund Ins. Co., supra*, 196 Cal.App.4th at pp. 1272-1275; *Clark, supra*, 196 Cal.App.4th at pp. 49-54.

224 *Fireman's Fund Ins. Co., supra*, 196 Cal.App.4th at pp. 1274-1275.

225 *State Farm Fire & Cas. Co. v. Superior Ct.* (1988) 206 Cal.App.3d 1428, 1432; *People v. Meredith* (1981) 29 Cal.3d 682, 686; *Gonzalez v. Municipal Ct.* (1977) 67 Cal.App.3d 111, 119-120.

226 *Roberts, supra*, 5 Cal.4th at pp. 371-373; *but see* Cal. Evid. Code § 957; *Fletcher v. Superior Ct.* (1996) 44 Cal.App.4th 773, 778-779 (privilege does not cover deceased clients' communications regarding testamentary intent).

227 *McDermott Will & Emery LLP v. Superior Ct.* (2017) 10 Cal.App.5th 1083, 1101-1102.

228 *Id.*; *accord Ardon, supra*, 62 Cal.4th at pp. 1190-1191; *State Comp. Ins. Fund v. WPS, Inc.* (1999) 70 Cal.App.4th 644, 652-654.

CPRA disclosure under less-than-clear conditions as follows. Where the officer misconduct at issue pertains to one of the eight categories that constitute the CPRA exception to the *Pitchess* privilege (see 2019/2022 exceptions above), the new statutory revisions now render disclosable public records with the following information: (1) purely factual information provided by the public entity to its attorney; (2) factual information discovered in any investigation conducted by, or on behalf of, the public entity's attorney — presumably meaning that non-opinion attorney work product is now disclosable, even if otherwise shielded by the attorney-client privilege; and (3) public entity attorney billing records, *unless* (a) the billing records pertain to an ongoing litigation (in which case, the billing records remain exempt from disclosure), or (b) the billing records include information shared for the purpose of legal consultation between the public entity and its attorney — i.e., opinion attorney work product (as explained below).[229]

b. Attorney Work Product Protection Recap.

Under California law, there is also a privilege or protection for confidential **attorney work product**: with similar exceptions from its scope as the attorney-client privilege.[230]

<u>**Purpose**</u>. The purpose of the attorney work product protection is: (1) to "[p]reserve the rights of attorneys to prepare cases for trial with that degree of privacy necessary to encourage them to prepare their cases thoroughly and to investigate not only the favorable but the unfavorable aspects of those cases"; and (2) to "[p]revent attorneys from taking undue advantage of their adversary's industry and efforts."[231]

<u>**Scope & Definition Of Attorney Work Product**</u>. At its core, the attorney work product protection covers: (1) "writing[s] that reflect an attorney's impressions, conclusions, opinions, or legal research or theories" — which are "not discoverable under any circumstances"; and (2) other non-opinion attorney work product, "unless the court determines that denial of discovery will

229 Cal. Penal Code § 832.7(b)(12)(A)-(B) (amend. 2022).

230 Cal. Code Civ. Proc. §§ 2018.010-2018.080; *see also* Cal. Gov. Code §§ 7927.705 7930.110 (formerly Cal. Gov. Code §§ 6254(k), 6276.04.

231 Cal. Code Civ. Proc. § 2018.020; *Coito v. Superior Ct.* (2012) 54 Cal.4th 480, 496.

unfairly prejudice the party seeking discovery in preparing that party's claim or defense" or if non-disclosure "will result in injustice."[232]

These two types of attorney work product are commonly referenced as: (1) **opinion attorney work product**, which enjoys an absolute protection from disclosure or discovery; and (2) **non-opinion attorney work product**, which enjoys a conditional protection subject to *in camera* review and evaluation by a court.[233]

Opinion attorney work product is *not* disclosable under *any* circumstances, unless the work product falls under the crime-fraud, malpractice, or Bar discipline exceptions.[234]

Non-opinion attorney work product material, which includes factual information gathered by attorneys or their agents, may be discovered *only* where the propounding party has met two criteria: (1) that there is a substantial need for such material; and (2) that the propounding party is unable to otherwise obtain the material without undue hardship.[235]

---

232 Cal. Code Civ. Proc. § 2018.030.

233 *See* Cal. Code Civ. Proc. §§ 2018.030, 2018.060; *Williamson v. Superior Ct.* (1978) 21 Cal.3d 829, 835; *National Steel Prods. Co. v. Superior Ct.* (1985) 164 Cal.App.3d 476, 488-490; *Hernandez v. Superior Ct.* (2003) 112 Cal.App.4th 289, 297; *see also Holmgren v. State Farm Mut. Auto. Ins. Co.*, 976 F.2d 573, 576-577 (9th Cir. 1992); *see generally Hickman v. Taylor*, 329 U.S. 495, 509-512 (1947) (concluding that written statements made by attorneys, interviews conducted by attorneys, attorney-drafted materials such as private memoranda, briefs, and correspondence, as well as the personal recollections and mental impressions of counsel formed in the course of the attorney's legal duties were protected from disclosure by the attorney work product doctrine).

PRACTICE TIP: The scope of the attorney work product differs slightly in federal court from its California court counterpart. For example, in federal court cases, opinion work product is discoverable but only where (1) the mental impressions of the attorney are at issue in the case, such as in a bad faith litigation, and (2) the need for the material is compelling. *See Holmgren*, 976 F.2d at pp. 576-577; *South Yuba River Citizens League v. National Marine Fisheries Serv.*, 257 F.R.D. 607, 611-612 (E.D. Cal. 2009); *see also National Labor Relations Bd. v. Sears, Roebuck & Co.*, 421 U.S. 132, 154 (1975) ("Whatever the outer boundaries of the attorney's work-product rule are, the rule clearly applies to memoranda prepared by an attorney in contemplation of litigation which set forth the attorney's theory of the case and his litigation strategy.")

234 *See* Cal. Code Civ. Proc. §§ 2018.010-2018.080; *Williamson, supra*, 21 Cal.3d at p. 835; *National Steel Prods. Co., supra*, 164 Cal.App.3d at pp 488-490; *Hernandez, supra*, 112 Cal.App.4th at p. 297; *BP Alaska Exploration, Inc. v. Superior Ct.* (1988) 199 Cal.App.3d 1240, 1250-1253, 1271 (holding that opinion attorney work product, when delivered to the client, is absolutely protected from disclosure).

235 *See Carehouse Convalescent Hosp. v. Superior Ct.* (2006) 143 Cal.App.4th 1558, 1565-1566; *Pound v. DeMera DeMera Cameron* (2005) 135 Cal.App.4th 70, 79; *see also* Code Civ. Proc. §§

Thus, for example, witness statements — including recordings thereof — *collected by an attorney* are generally subject to the non-opinion attorney work product protection, which is also known as the qualified work product privilege; *unless* the specific statements reveal opinion attorney work product subjecting them to the unqualified privilege.[236]

The attorney work product protection likewise extends to the work product of non-testifying experts and consultants "so as to encourage litigants to receive expert guidance in formulating their strategies."[237] However, in general, once that expert/consultant is designated as a testifying witness for trial, the act of expert designation constitutes a partial waiver of the attorney work product protection regarding the expert's knowledge and opinions on a material matter in dispute between the parties on a claim or defense at issue in the action: with the purpose being to allow the opposing party to explore the nature, scope, bases, and subject of the expert's trial testimony and related opinions, even if the expert relies in part on otherwise-protected attorney work product.[238]

Warning: Consult Legal Counsel. Public entities should *always* **consult with their attorneys** when trying to determine if records or information are potentially privileged from disclosure under either the attorney-client privilege or the attorney work product protection: as such privilege law is complex and the risks of disclosure and waiver of privilege are otherwise unnecessarily great.

2018.050, 2018.070 (stating statutory work product exceptions in cases of crime-fraud and for Bar disciplinary proceedings); *see also* Fed. R. Civ. P. 26(b)(3); *Holmgren*, 976 F.2d at pp. 576-577; *South Yuba, supra*, 257 F.R.D. at pp. 611-612; *see also Hickman, supra*, 329 U.S. at pp. 510-511.

236 *Coito, supra*, 54 Cal.4th at pp. 494-497.

237 *South Yuba, supra*, 257 F.R.D. at p. 612; *accord National Steel Prods. Co., supra*, 164 Cal.App.3d at pp. 487-492; *see also* Fed. R. Civ. P. 26(b)(4) ("a party may not…discover facts known or opinions held by an expert who has been retained or specially employed by another party in anticipation of litigation or to prepare for trial and who is not expected to be called as a witness at trial"); *see generally Holmgren*, 976 F.2d 573.

238 *See* Cal. Evid. Code § 721; *Zellerino v. Brown* (1991) 235 Cal.App.3d 1097, 1117; *People v. Ledesma* (2006) 39 Cal.4th 641, 695; *see People v. Coddington* (2000) 23 Cal.4th 529, 605 (inferring that the scope of the work product protection is the same in both criminal and civil actions), *overruled in part on another ground in Price v. Superior Ct.* (2001) 25 Cal.4th 1046, 1069 n.13; *Bonds v. Roy* (1999) 20 Cal.4th 140, 148-149; *DePalma v. Rodriguez* (2007) 151 Cal.App.4th 159, 164-165 (holding that an expert may be precluded from testifying at trial on a subject that was not described in his expert witness declaration); *Jones v. Moore* (2000) 80 Cal.App.4th 557, 562-565 (precluding testimony where expert, at deposition, effectively narrowed the scope of his proposed trial testimony despite a broader designation in his expert-witness declaration); *People v. Combs* (2004) 34 Cal.4th 821, 864 (holding that the defense waived the attorney-client and work product privileges as to a non-testifying expert's report when its testifying expert relied upon that report in his trial testimony).

8. *CPRA's PITCHESS PRIVILEGE Incorporation.*

As a reminder of what is covered at the outset of this book, the definition of what constitutes a law enforcement officer's "personnel file" is specified under California law as "any file maintained under that individual's name by his or her employing agency and containing records related to any of the following" information: (a) personal data, including marital status, family members, educational and employment history, home addresses or similar information; (b) medical history; (c) election of employee benefits; (d) employee advancement, appraisal, or discipline; (e) complaints, or investigations of complaints, concerning an event or transaction in which he or she participated, or which he or she perceived and pertaining to the manner in which he or she performed his or her duties; or (f) any other information the disclosure of which would constitute an unwarranted invasion of personal privacy.[239]

By the CPRA's same mechanism of incorporation of other statutory privileges into its exemptions, effectively underscored by way of Penal Code section 832.7(a) and Government Code section 6276.34, Government Code section 7927.705 (formerly Government Code section 6254(k)) also incorporates a CPRA exemption for *Pitchess*-privileged officer personnel file records-information: *except* for the limited categories of information explained herein above (OIS, UOF resulting in death or GBI, and sustained investigations showing specified officer misconduct) that were excepted from the *Pitchess* exemption, effective 2019 and 2022.[240]

---

239 *See* Cal. Penal Code § 832.8; *Commission on Peace Officer Standards & Training [POST] v. Superior Ct.* (2007) 42 Cal.4th 278, 293 (holding that physical inclusion of a document in a peace officer's personnel file is insufficient to trigger the *Pitchess* privilege; rather, only those documents specifically identified in Cal. Penal Code § 832.8 as personnel records are entitled to *Pitchess* procedural protections); *see also* Cal. Penal Code § 832.5(b)-(c) (mandating that complaints and "any reports or findings related to these complaints" against a peace officer must be retained in a peace officer's personnel file, or a separate file designated by that department's policy, "for a period of at least five years" — unless the investigation results in a sustained finding of officer misconduct, at which point the fifteen-year retention requirement is triggered); *Zanone v. City of Whittier* (2008) 162 Cal. App.4th 174, 187-189 (holding that to trigger the *Pitchess* privilege, the "complaint or investigation of a complaint must both concern an event that involved the officer as a participant or witness *and* pertain to the officer's performance of his or her duties," and exempting from the *Pitchess* procedure a statement from a memorandum written by a witness officer about another officer's racial discrimination where that statement by that witness officer impeached his defense-favorable testimony in an employment discrimination case).

240 *See* Cal. Gov. Code §§ 7927.705 (formerly Cal. Gov. Code § 6254(k)) (privileged matters exempt from disclosure), 7930.180 (formerly 6276.34) (expressly incorporating by *reference* into the CPRA exemptions the *Pitchess* privilege system); Cal. Evid. Code §§ 1040-1047 (especially Sections 1043 and 1045).

The CPRA's exemption from disclosure for *Pitchess*-privileged matter arises in part from the fact that Section 6254(k) incorporates privileges embodied in other state and federal statutes, *including the California Evidence Code*: and, as explained in detail in the preceding chapters, the *Pitchess* privilege is embodied in the California Evidence Code and the California Penal Code, in addition to extensive case law explaining its operation and scope.[241]

Notably, even the 2019 statutory amendments from SB 1421 (and 2022 amendments from SB 16) underscore the continuation of the *Pitchess* privilege system: as underscored by the *express* incorporation of the amended version of Penal Code section 832.7 and the related key case law.[242]

The full scope of the *Pitchess* privilege is explained in detail in the preceding chapters. Indeed, the unique intersection of the *Pitchess* privilege, and the amended scope of the associated CPRA exemption and its new post-2019 narrow exception to that exemption, is explored in detail in the chapter titled "**STATUTORY EXEMPTIONS to the Otherwise Mandatory *Pitchess* Procedure**" in the section titled "The CPRA Exception for Recordings of Critical Incidents and for Complaint/Investigation Records of Officer-Involved Shootings, Serious Uses of Force, Officer Sexual Assault on Non-Officers, and Officer Dishonesty in Policing."

Please see the aforementioned preceding chapter and section for details on the operation of the *Pitchess* exemption to the CPRA, and the related 2019/2022 exceptions to that exemption.

a. A Brief Elaboration On California's Official Information Privilege.

Similar to its federal-law counterpart, as explained in a succeeding chapter, California embraces a privilege for official information.[243] By operation of Section 6254(k), this privilege is also incorporated into the CPRA as an exemption from disclosure.[244]

---

241 *See, e.g.*, Cal. Evid. Code §§ 1040-1047 (especially §§ 1043 and 1045); Cal. Penal Code §§ 832.7-832.8; *Ass'n for L.A. Deputy Sheriffs (ALADS) v. Superior Ct.* (2019) 8 Cal. 5th 28, 36-56.

242 *See* Cal. Penal Code § 832.7(g)-(i); *see also* Cal. Penal Code § 832.7(b)(7).

243 Cal. Evid. Code § 1040.

244 *See* Cal. Gov. Code § 7927.705 (formerly Cal. Gov.Code § 6254(k)).

Although, for purposes of evaluating whether officer personnel file records being sought for discovery or disclosure via a *Pitchess* motion are exempt from discovery or disclosure, there is no meaningful distinction between the officer personnel file aspect of the *Pitchess* privilege and the official information aspect of such.[245] However, since CPRA requests tend to be broader and routinely include requests for police records other than officer personnel file records, it is worthwhile to include here a brief recap of the California statutory official information privilege.

Definition Of Official Information. Under California law, "official information" is "information acquired in confidence by a public employee in the course of his or her duty and not open, or officially disclosed, to the public prior to the time the claim of privilege is made."[246] For example, courts treat police investigative files and medical information provided to a public agency as generally subject to the official information privilege.[247]

Significantly, the definition of "official information" also includes information or records for which "[d]isclosure is forbidden by an act of the Congress of the United States or a statute of this state": in other words, where there is a statutory privilege barring disclosure of the records-information, those

245 NOTE: In light of the fact that, for practical purposes, the official information privilege largely overlaps the officer personnel file records privilege, for purposes of analyzing the personnel file records privilege, this book has treated the *Pitchess* privilege as incorporating the official information privilege: because information sought via a *Pitchess* motion is likely to embrace official information within an officer's personnel file; thus negating any need to distinguish the official information privilege from the remainder of the *Pitchess* privilege vested in officer personnel file information. However, as a practical matter, CPRA requests often seek police records that are *not* officer personnel file records, but which may still be privileged official information. Thus, here, we explain the distinctions underlying the California-law version of the official information privilege.

246 Cal. Evid. Code § 1040(a).

247 *See, e.g., Department of Motor Veh. v. Superior Ct.* (2002) 100 Cal.App.4th 363, 373-374 (citing *Board of Med. Quality Ass. v. Gherardini* (1979) 93 Cal.App.3d 669, 678 and Cal. Veh. Code § 1808.5 for the proposition that since medical information is "'intrinsically confidential,'" medical information constitutes "official information" under Evidence Code § 1040); *see also County of Orange v. Superior Ct.* (2000) 79 Cal.App.4th 759, 767-770 (holding that, where a criminal investigation is pending, the investigative file is absolutely privileged official information necessitating that the trial court stay the civil action until the criminal investigation is complete; and thereafter only permitting limited production to the investigative file, after *in camera* review, as to those parts of the investigative file for which confidentiality may no longer be needed, under a *Pitchess*-analogous standard of materiality and good cause).

records-information are also treated as privileged "official information" under California law.[248]

As a practical matter then, in determining whether the official information privilege bars disclosure, only otherwise unprivileged confidential information is likely to be at issue; i.e., **where official information is restricted from disclosure, but *not* prohibited, only then is a substantive analysis of the official information privilege likely necessary.**[249]

Absolute Bar: Statutory Prohibition Makes Official Information Privilege Absolute. Where the statutory prohibition aspect of the official information applies (i.e., where federal or California law prohibits the specified records-information from being publicly disclosed), then the official information privilege is an absolute bar to disclosure.[250]

Conditional Bar: Restricted But Not Prohibited Disclosures. However, where there is no statutory prohibition on disclosure of the records-information at issue, the official information privileges becomes a conditional bar to disclosure that does *not* apply where: (1) "a person authorized to do so has consented that the information be disclosed in the proceeding"; *or* (2) after *in camera* review, a court fails to determine that, in evaluating the public interest in non-disclosure, "there is a necessity for preserving the confidentiality of the information that outweighs the necessity for disclosure in the interest of justice"; however, in balancing the interests of confidentiality versus disclosure, "the interest of the public entity as a party in the outcome of the proceeding may not be considered."[251]

In other words, where there is a statutory restriction, but *not* a prohibition, on disclosure of the specific official information at issue, the conditional

---

248 Cal. Evid. Code § 1040(b)(1); *White v. Superior Ct.* (2002) 100 Cal.App.4th Supp. 1, 6.

249 *See White, supra*, 100 Cal.App.4th Supp. at pp. 6-7 (holding that information whose disclosure is prohibited by federal or California law is subject to an absolute official information privilege; whereas information that is merely restricted by law, but where disclosure is permitted, such information is subject to a conditional official information privilege only where a court balances the need for confidentiality against the requester's interest in obtaining the information at issue).

250 *See White, supra*, 100 Cal.App.4th Supp. at pp. 6-7; *see also* Cal. Evid. Code § 1040(b)(1); Cal. Gov. Code § 7927.705 (formerly Cal. Gov. Code § 6254(k)).

251 *See White, supra*, 100 Cal.App.4th Supp. at pp. 6-7; *see also* Cal. Evid. Code § 1040(b)(2); Cal. Gov. Code §§ 7927.705, 7922.000 (formerly Cal. Gov. Code §§ 6254(k), 6255).

bar of the official information privilege only applies if: (1) there has been no consent to the disclosure; or (2) the court finds that the public interests in non-disclosure outweighs the public interests in disclosure[252] (a foreshadowing of the form of analysis for the generic public interest catch-all exemption).

***Public* Interests & Materiality Are Considered In Balancing, But Not The Entity's Interests**. Although the public entity's case-specific non-disclosure interest may *not* be considered in the court's balancing, the court *may* consider the public interest in non-disclosure by evaluating the potential "effect of the disclosure upon the integrity of public processes and procedures": and, in doing so, the court may weigh the non-disclosure interest against a materiality and good cause assessment of "the importance of the material sought to the fair presentation of the litigant's case, [and] the availability of the material to the litigant by other means" — including the "effectiveness and relative difficulty of such other means."[253]

In other words, for purposes of evaluating the official information privilege when the conditional bar applies, the court may balance the public interest in non-disclosure against the litigant's arguments for materiality/good cause need for the disclosure.[254]

Thus, for example, where a criminal defendant subpoenaed an inspector general's report that tended to show that, as to the officer who investigated his alleged assault on a correctional ward, the investigating officer had been dishonest in an unrelated investigation, because such report tended to undermine the credibility of the investigating officer's testimony about the incident assault, and because the report at issue was made confidential but *not* privileged by Cal. Penal Code § 6126.5(a), the defendant's interest in obtaining the report to mount his criminal defense outweighed the public interest in preserving the confidentiality of the report.[255]

---

252 *See id.*

253 *Compare* Cal. Evid. Code § 1040(b)(2) *with Shepherd v. Superior Ct.* (1976) 17 Cal.3d 107, 126 (remanding the case for trial court evaluation of the specific grand jury records sought to determine whether any were offered to the government in confidence, and excluding grand jury transcripts from any production order).

254 *See id.*

255 *See, e.g., White, supra*, 100 Cal.App.4th Supp. at pp. 3-7.

<u>Distinguishing Confidential Information From Privileged Information</u>. As the California Supreme Court has explained, while a statute may restrict who may receive certain information, such as by limiting the persons authorized to receive such information, or by preventing the information from being disclosed except in specified circumstances not requiring court intervention, in such an event, such information is merely confidential: to be truly privileged, as opposed to merely confidential, a statute must also exclude such information from being admitted into evidence and more definitively bar its disclosure.[256]

Where the official information privileges *does* apply, the "public entity has a privilege to refuse to disclose [such] official information, and to prevent another from disclosing" such.[257] Therefore, where the official information privilege applies to requested public records, such records are *exempt* from CPRA disclosure.[258]

9. *OFFICER TRAINING RECORDS: The Apparent CPRA Exemption For Officer Training Records, Logs, Certificates, and Materials.*

As noted in the preceding chapter on the statutory exemptions from the *Pitchess* privilege, and the new CPRA statutory *Pitchess* exemption (also known as the new exception to the *Pitchess* privilege exemption from the CPRA), while there is some authority suggesting that officer training records and materials — such as documents provided to officers in their training, or documentation of officer training including training logs or certificates — *might* be CPRA-disclosable in some cases, **the balance of authorities appears to tip in favor of construing *all* such training records and training materials as *Pitchess*-protected officer personnel file records that are exempt from CPRA disclosure** under Government Code section 7927.705 (formerly Government Code section 6254(k)).[259]

---

256 *See Davies v. Superior Ct.* (1984) 36 Cal.3d 291, 298-299; *see also White, supra*, 100 Cal.App.4th Supp. at pp. 3-7.

257 Cal. Evid. Code § 1040(b).

258 *See* Cal. Gov. Code § 7927.705 (formerly Cal. Gov. Code § 6254(k)).

259 *Compare* Cal. Gov. Code § 7928.40 (formerly Cal. Gov. Code § 6254(p)(2)) *and* Cal. Penal Code § 13650 *with* Cal. Penal Code §§ 832.7(a), 832.8(a)(1) (protected officer "personnel file" records include records "relating" to an officer's "educational…history") *and Commission on Peace Officer Standards & Training (POST), supra*, 42 Cal.4th at pp. 285-286, 293-295, 300-303 (holding that, absent case-specific security concerns, such as uncover officer status, identities and employer names of peace officers in POST's possession was not exempt from the CPRA because such was not within the enumerated categories of information specified in Cal. Penal Code § 832.8) *and*

In other words, notwithstanding 2019's addition of Penal Code section 13650 (mandating that where officer training materials are CPRA-disclosable, they must be posted on a law enforcement agency's website), officer training records — including training materials, training handouts/curriculum, training logs, training manuals, and training certificates — appear to constitute *Pitchess*-privileged officer personnel file records: and, as a result, such **officer training records appear to be exempt from CPRA disclosure.**[260]

10. *The CPRA TERRORISM RESPONSE PLAN Exemption.*

Government Code section 7929.200 (formerly Government Code section 6254(aa)) features an exemption from CPRA disclosure for: any "document prepared by or for a state or local agency that assesses its vulnerability to terrorist attack or other criminal acts intended to disrupt the public agency's operations and that is for distribution or consideration in a closed session."[261] The "exemption[] [is] designed to safeguard governmental interests concerning national security."[262]

However, this exemption has yet to be litigated to such a degree as to result in significant case law on point.

11. *The CPRA PUBLIC INTEREST IN NON-DISCLOSURE Catch-All Exemption.*

Generally shorthand-referenced as the public interest catch-all exemption, Government Code section 7922.000 (formerly Government Code section 6255(a)) features a generic exemption from CPRA disclosure where: "[t]he agency shall justify withholding any record by demonstrating…that[,] on the facts of the particular case[,] the public interest served by not disclosing

---

Northern Cal. Police Practices Project, supra, 90 Cal.App.3d at pp. 118-119, 123-124 (holding that CHP training manuals re law enforcement procedures, weapons tactical training, and related safety and security protocols were generally exempt from CPRA disclosure, but where the materials contained non-exempt information, such materials should be produced if the exempt material could be segregated from the non-exempt material) *and City of Fresno v. Superior Ct.* (1988) 205 Cal.App.3d 1459, 1465-1466 (on review of a *Pitchess* motion, presuming that policy manuals, training materials, training handouts and "other documents which have been used in the training of the police officers listed" in the motion were *Pitchess*-protected officer personnel file records).

260 *See id.*

261 Cal. Gov. Code § 7929.200 (formerly Cal. Gov. Code § 6254(aa)).

262 *Ardon, supra*, 62 Cal.4th at p. 1183.

the record clearly outweighs the public interest served by disclosure of the record."[263] In other words, where the public interest in non-disclosure clearly outweighs the public interest in disclosure, the catch-all exemption may apply.

Although the CPRA does not specify what public interest factors may weigh in the balance against disclosure, one non-exclusive benchmark courts use to determine whether the public interest in non-disclosure clearly outweighs the public interest in disclosure is the list of exemptions in Section 6254: to see if the record sought for the catch-all exemption is comparable to (or "similar in nature to") a record that is expressly exempted under Section 6254.[264]

However, "[w]hile the specific exemptions set forth in section 6254 may be helpful in identifying certain interests to be protected under section 6255, they are not exclusive."[265] This is because "[n]othing in the text or history of section 6255 limits its scope to specific categories of information or established exemptions or privileges."[266] Rather, "[e]ach request for records must be 'considered on the facts of the particular case' in light of the competing 'public interests'" between disclosure and non-disclosure.[267]

Burden Of Proof On Party Opposing Disclosure. However, to justify non-disclosure under Section 6255, the burden of proof is on the proponent of non-disclosure to show that, in the case-specific balancing of the interests of non-disclosure or confidentiality against the interests in disclosure, there is a "clear overbalance on the side of confidentiality."[268]

Only Public Interests, *Not* Litigant Interests, May Be Considered In Balancing. When weighing the interests of disclosure against the interests

---

263 Cal. Gov. Code § 7922.000 (formerly Cal. Gov. Code § 6255(a)).

264 *See Times Mirror Co., supra*, 53 Cal.3d at pp. 1337-1339 ("'[T]he provisions of section 6254 will provide appropriate indicia as to the nature of the public interest in nondisclosure and will thus aid the courts in determining the disclosability of a document under section 6255.'"); *accord American Civ. Liberties Union (Deukmejian), supra*, 32 Cal.3d at p. 462.

265 *Times Mirror Co., supra*, 53 Cal.3d at p. 1338; *accord City of Los Angeles*, supra, 41 Cal.App.4th at pp. 1089-1090.

266 *Times Mirror Co., supra*, 53 Cal.3d at p. 1338; *see also Wilson v. Superior Ct.* (1996) 51 Cal.App.4th 1136, 1139, 1142.

267 *Times Mirror Co., supra*, 53 Cal.3d at p. 1338.

268 *Michaelis, Montanari & Johnson v. Superior Ct.* (2006) 38 Cal.4th 1065, 1071; *accord Black Panther Party, supra*, 42 Cal.App.3d at p. 657.

of non-disclosure, the court must consider *only* the public interests: *not* the interests of the custodial public entity or of the CPRA requester.[269] Moreover, where the alleged public interest is minimal or hypothetical, such is insufficient to tip the balance: and a public interest in disclosure is also minimal where the requester has alternative, less-intrusive means for obtaining the underlying information in the requested records or in achieving the purpose underlying the request.[270]

Undue Burden May Be Weighed In Public Interest Balancing. Notwithstanding the foregoing, in weighing these competing interests under Section 6255, particularly where exempt information is so intertwined with non-exempt information that disclosure of the records, even with redactions, would defeat the utility of the disclosure, courts may consider whether the burden and expense of extracting exempt information from the records at issue is so great that such burden causes the public interest in non-disclosure to clearly outweigh the public interest in disclosure — i.e., the public interest in disclosure would not be served because what would be disclosed would be of little to no use, whereas the burden on the public entity in producing the information would be great, undermining public interests by impairing the entity's ability to perform its public service role.[271]

As intended by the California Legislature, the public interest catch-all exemption is thus open-ended and case-specific.[272]

---

269 *See Coronado Police Officers Assn. v. Carroll* (2003) 106 Cal.App.4th 1001, 1014-1016 (where public defender database contained client files and information on recurring issues such as police performance, because the database contained personal information and its sharing allowed public defenders to better defend their criminal clients without having to start every investigation from scratch, the court held that the public interest in non-disclosure clearly outweighed the public interest in disclosure); *accord Connell v. Superior Ct.* (1997) 56 Cal.App.4th 601, 616-617.

270 *See Los Angeles Unif. Sch. Dist. v. Superior Ct.* (2014) 228 Cal.App.4th 222, 248 (holding that the public interest of disclosure of a public employee's identity is minimal where knowing that identity would not appreciably further the public's right to monitor agency action); *City of San Jose, supra*, 74 Cal.App.4th at p. 1020.

271 *See, e.g., American Civ. Lib. Union (Deukmejian), supra*, 32 Cal.3d at pp. 444-453 (where index cards of organized crime suspects could only be redacted for exempt personal identifying information with substantial burden, and the redacted cards would contain only general information unsuited to the alleged public interest in disclosure, the entire cards were exempt from CPRA disclosure); *Michaelis, Montanari & Johnson, supra*, 38 Cal.4th at pp. 1072-1077 (where disclosure of proposed contracts still under negotiation would unduly burden the city's negotiations, Section 6255 exempted the contracts from disclosure at least until the negotiations were completed).

272 *See id.*; *see also City of Los Angeles v. Superior Ct.* (2017) 9 Cal.App.5th 272, 283.

Examples Where Balance Favored Non-Disclosure (Catch-All Applied). Some **non-disclosure *examples*** of records where courts have found the Section 6255 public interest exemption to *apply* include (but are not limited to):

Complainant personal information regarding complaints to the city about airport noise[273];

Criminal defense database information from the public defenders' office, including information about police officers[274];

Draft city contracts about airport land leasing while the negotiations were still ongoing[275];

Organized crime suspect index cards with suspect identifying and contact information, occupation and known associates[276]; and

Teacher test results, where teachers were identified by name, as part of a measure of teachers' effect on student performance on standardized testing[277];

Examples Where Balance Favored Disclosure (Catch-All Not Applicable). By contrast, some **disclosure *examples*** of records where, on balancing the public interests under Section 6255, courts have found the public interest exemption did *not apply* include (but are not limited to):

Concealed weapons permit applications, including applicant identities and reasons permit sought (unless a significant safety issue exists)[278];

Day care facility workers' identities where such workers were granted exemptions that otherwise would have barred them, as ex-convicts, from such employment — so as to facilitate evaluation of whether the exemptions were being unfairly granted[279];

---

273 *City of San Jose, supra*, 74 Cal.App.4th at pp. 1022-1025.

274 *Coronado Police Officers Assn., supra*, 106 Cal.App.4th at pp. 1014-1016.

275 *Michaelis, Montanari & Johnson, supra*, 38 Cal.4th at pp. 1072-1077.

276 *American Civ. Lib. Union v. Deukmejian, supra*, 32 Cal.3d at pp. 444-453.

277 *Los Angeles Unif. Sch. Dist., supra*, 228 Cal.App.4th at pp. 239-253.

278 *CBS Inc., supra*, 42 Cal.3d at pp. 652-657.

279 *CBS Broadcasting, Inc., supra*, 91 Cal.App.4th at pp. 908-909.

Donor identities and contributions or licensing fees paid to a public university arena for luxury accommodations[280];

Geographic Information System base map information with measurements of various public and private buildings to within about 1 foot[281];

Promotion letters first appointing a public employee to a supervisory city office and then rescinding that appointment days later[282];

Settlements regarding a school district and minor sexual assault victims[283]; and

Unpaid bills on state warrants.[284]

In asserting the public interest catch-all exemption, public entities would be well advised to consult experienced legal counsel to help the law enforcement agency craft a meritorious argument for why the case-specific facts justified non-disclosure under Section 6255.

12. *The 2019 (SB 1421 & AB 748) And 2022 (AB 1421) EXCEPTIONS to the CPRA Exemptions: Specified Officer Misconduct.*

As noted far more extensively in the preceding chapter about the statutory exceptions to the *Pitchess* privilege[285], and as summarized above, SB 1421 and AB 748 — respectively codified in Cal. Penal Code §§ 832.7(b)-(i), 832.8(b)-(c) and Cal. Gov. Code § 7923.625 (formerly Cal. Gov. Code § 6254(f)(4)) — in effect create some narrow exceptions to both: (1) the CPRA exemption for matter protected by the *Pitchess* privilege in officer personnel file records-information, but

---

280 *California State Univ., Fresno Assn., supra*, 90 Cal.App.4th at pp. 833-835.

281 *County of Santa Clara v. Superior Ct.* (2009) 170 Cal.App.4th 1301, 1320-1329.

282 *Braun, supra*, 154 Cal.App.3d at pp. 344-346.

283 *Copley Press, Inc. v. Superior Ct.* (1998) 63 Cal.App.4th 367, 376-377.

284 *Connell, supra*, 56 Cal.App.4th at pp. 616-617.

285 "**Statutory Exemptions to the Otherwise Mandatory *Pitchess* Procedure**" in the section titled "The CPRA Exception for Recordings of Critical Incidents and for Complaint/Investigation Records of Officer-Involved Shootings, Serious Uses of Force, Officer Sexual Assault on Non-Officers, and Officer Dishonesty in Policing."

also (2) in the police investigatory records exemption from CPRA that is stated in Government Code sections 7923.600-7923.625 (formerly section 6254(f)).

To recap what is covered more extensively in the aforementioned chapter and section, with byzantine temporary withholding and redaction rules applicable for a variety of reasons more fully explored in such prior chapter, including but not limited to the pending/open investigation temporary withholding/redaction provisions of the SB 1421/AB 748 exceptions to the exemptions, **the 2019 and 2022 statutory revisions create new exceptions to the CPRA exemptions from disclosure for *Pitchess* privileged matter and police investigatory records for eight categories of police-related records and recordings**:

(1) **[OIS] officer-involved shootings ("OIS")** of/at persons ("discharge of a firearm at a person"), regardless of injury, including incident audio/video recordings thereof[286];

(2) **[UOF-D/GBI] officer uses of force** ("UOF") on persons, **where death or great bodily injury ("D/GBI") resulted,**[287] including incident audio/video recordings thereof[288];

(3) **[Excessive Force] officer uses of unreasonable or excessive force**, but only where the agency's investigation resulted in a *sustained* finding[289];

(4) **[Failure to Intervene to Prevent Excessive Force] where officers fail to intervene against another officer using force that is clearly unreasonable or excessive,** but only where the agency's investigation resulted in a *sustained* finding[290];

---

286 Cal. Penal Code §§ 832.7(b)(1)(A)(i) (amend. 2022).

287 In the context of incident video/audio recordings, the new laws refer to OIS and death/great bodily injury uses of force as "critical incidents" or "serious" uses of force. *See, e.g.*, Cal. Penal Code §§ 832.7 cmt (2018); *cf.* Cal. Gov. Code § 7923.625 (formerly Cal. Gov. Code § 6254(f)(4)). NOTE: Even after the 2022 revisions, however, the definition of "great bodily injury" remains ambiguous, as explained more fully below.

288 Cal. Penal Code §§ 832.7(b)(1)(A)(ii) (amend. 2022).

289 Cal. Penal Code §§ 832.7(b)(1)(A)(iii) (amend. 2022).

290 Cal. Penal Code §§ 832.7(b)(1)(A)(iv) (amend. 2022).

(5) [**Sexual Assault — Specified**] **officer sexual assault on non-officers/non-employees,** with a customized definition of what constitutes officer sexual assault,[291] but only where the agency's investigation resulted in a *sustained* finding;

(6) [**Policing Dishonesty**] **officer dishonesty in law enforcement duties,**[292] but only where the agency's investigation resulted in a *sustained* finding;

(7) [**Discrimination**] **officer discriminatory conduct or writings against members of a protected class,** but only where the agency's investigation resulted in a *sustained* finding[293]; and

(8) [**Unlawful Arrest & Unlawful Search**] officers' unlawful arrests or unlawful searches, but only where the agency's investigation resulted in a *sustained* finding.[294]

For a more comprehensive discussion of the scope, limit, operations, and vagaries of the SB 1421 and AB 748 exceptions to these CPRA exemptions, please see the aforementioned chapter: "**STATUTORY EXEMPTIONS to the Otherwise Mandatory *Pitchess* Procedure**" under the section titled

291 Cal. Penal Code §§ 832.7(b)(1)(B)(i)-(iii) (amend. 2022). NOTE: The statute specifically *excludes* the employees/officers of the subject officer's agency from the scope of sexual assault investigations that may be CPRA-discoverable, where sustained; however, it specifically *includes* cadets, explorers, or other youth program members within the scope of CPRA-discoverable sexual assaults by the agency's officers, where sustained. *See* Cal. Penal Code § 832.7(b)(1)(B)(iii). Thus, for example, where a subject officer had a sustained finding of a sexual assault against an employee of that officer's employing agency, the associated investigation records would fall *outside* the scope of the new CPRA *Pitchess* exception: and would remain confidential and discoverable only by the traditional *Pitchess* process. Additionally, "sexual assault" for purposes of CPRA disclosure is defined as: the "commission or attempted initiation of a sexual act with a member of the public by means of force, threat, coercion, extortion, offer of leniency or other official favor, or under the color of authority. For purposes of this definition, the propositioning for[,] or commission of[,] any sexual act while on duty is considered a sexual assault." *See* Cal. Penal Code § 832.7(b)(1)(B)(ii). This arguably means that a sustained finding that an officer had *consensual* on-duty sex with a member of the public would be CPRA-disclosable. *See id.*

292 *See* Cal. Penal Code §§ 832.7(b)(1)(C) (amend. 2022), 832.8 (amend. Jan. 2019); Cal. Gov. Code §§ 7923.600-7923.625 (formerly Cal. Gov. Code § 6254). PRACTICE NOTE: The statute is clear that the new exemption applies only to acts of dishonesty by the officer in his/her official law enforcement function: such as false reporting, perjury as a police officer witness, and such. *See id.*

293 Cal. Penal Code §§ 832.7(b)(1)(D) (amend. 2022).

294 Cal. Penal Code §§ 832.7(b)(1)(E) (amend. 2022); *see also* Cal. Penal Code §§ 832.7-832.8 (amend. 2019); Cal. Gov. Code §§ 7923.600-7923.625 (formerly Cal. Gov. Code § 6254(f)).

"The CPRA Exception for Recordings of Critical Incidents and for Complaint/ Investigation Records of Officer-Involved Shootings, Serious Uses of Force, Officer Sexual Assault on Non-Officers, and Officer Dishonesty in Policing."

a. Reminder On The Pre-2019 EXCEPTIONS To CPRA's Law Enforcement Investigatory Exemption.

As noted in detail in the foregoing section on the law enforcement investigatory exemption, and exceptions thereto, even prior to 2019, there were numerous exceptions to that exemption (and caveats, or exceptions to those exceptions that effectively restored the exemption). Please see the preceding aforementioned section for additional details.

13. *EXOTIC CPRA Exemptions Less Likely To Arise In Requests Related to Police Records, But Still Appropriate For Reference Here.*

There are a number of additional CPRA exemptions which are unlikely to arise in the typical police-related civil case or in requests seeking police-related records, but which still bear brief reference herein.

While the CPRA incorporates into its exemptions literally dozens of exemptions embraced in specified statutes — ranging from various kinds of medical, psychological, agricultural, insurance/actuarial, and trade secrets[295] — there are only a handful of the more exotic CPRA exemptions that have a meaningful probability of arising in requests for police records.

Such exotic exemptions are listed here only in index form, to help the reader spot issues that may warrant further legal research. To better understand the key details of these exotic CPRA exemptions, one should consult the CPRA statutes and their incorporated reference statutes and definitions-scopes directly.

Agency Computer Software Exemption. The computer *software* a government agency uses is *not* itself a public record: thus, computer mapping systems, computer programs, computer graphics systems and comparable

---

295 *See* Cal. Gov. Code §§ 7930.000, 7930.005, 7930.105-7930.215 (formerly Cal. Gov. Code §§ 6275, 6276, and 6276.02-6276.48).

software are *exempt* from the CPRA — but this exemption does *not* mean that public records stored on a computer system are CPRA-exempt.[296]

Architectural Plans Of Official Buildings.[297]

Arrest Records Not Resulting In Conviction (Information To Employers) Exemption.[298]

Attorney-Client Communications Exemption (Specific Incorporation).[299]

Attorney Work Product Exemption (Specific Incorporation).[300]

Child Abuse Reports Exemption.[301]

Closed Sessions of Local Agency Legislative Bodies (*e.g.*, City Councils and Boards of Supervisors) Exemption.[302]

Computer/Information Technology System Security Records.[303]

Confidential Taxpayer Information Exemption.[304]

---

296 Cal. Gov. Code §§ 7922.570, 7922.585 (formerly Cal. Gov. Code §§ 6253.9, 6254.9).

297 *See* Cal. Gov. Code § 7927.705 (formerly Cal. Gov. Code § 6254(k)); 17 U.S.C. §§ 17, 101, 102(A)(8), 106, 107 (protecting trade secrets and original works of authorship); Cal. Health & Safety Code § 19851 (building plans may not be copied without written permission of signatory or current building owner).

298 Cal. Gov. Code § 7930.110 (formerly Cal. Gov. Code § 6276.04); *see also* Cal. Lab. Code § 432.7.

299 Cal. Gov. Code §§ 7927.705, 7930.110 (formerly Cal. Gov. Code §§ 6254(k), 6276.04); *see also* Cal. Evid. Code §§ 952-953; Cal. Bus. & Proc. Code § 6068.

300 Cal. Gov. Code § 7930.110 (formerly Cal. Gov. Code § 6276.04; *see also* Cal. Code Civ. Proc. § 2018.010 *et seq.*; Cal. Bus. & Prof. Code § 6202.

301 Cal. Gov. Code § 7930.125 (formerly Cal. Gov. Code § 6276.10); *see also* Cal. Penal Code §§ 11167, 11167.5.

302 Cal. Gov. Code § 7930.165 (formerly Cal. Gov. Code § 6276.28); *see also* Cal. Gov. Code § 54956.9.

303 Cal. Gov. Code § 7929.210 (formerly Cal. Gov. Code § 6254.19).

304 Cal. Gov. Code § 7925.000 (formerly Cal. Gov. Code § 6254(i)).

Criminal History Summary Information Exemption.[305]

Criminal Offender Records (Except As Needed By Public Agencies For Crime Control) Exemption.[306]

Critical Infrastructure Information.[307]

Death-Autopsy Reports Where Medical Negligence Was A Cause Of Death Exemption.[308]

Firearms License Applications Information Exemption.[309]

Home Addresses Of Peace Officers, Police Employees/Dispatchers, Prosecutors, City Attorneys And County Counsel, And Other Specified Government Employees Exemption.[310]

In-Home Support Services Provider Information Exemption. One of the more unusual conditional exemptions from the CPRA involves information provided to the state by persons who are providing in-home supportive services under Cal. Welfare & Inst. Code § 12300, *et seq.*: via the CPRA, the providers' contact information is available to an exclusive bargaining agent or labor organization, as defined by Cal. Welfare & Inst. Code § 12301.6 or § 12302.25; however, otherwise, such contact information is exempt from CPRA disclosure.[311]

---

305 Cal. Gov. Code § 7930.165 (formerly Cal. Gov. Code § 6276.28); *see also* Cal. Penal Code § 13300.

306 Cal. Gov. Code § 7930.130 (formerly Cal. Gov. Code § 6276.12); *see also* Cal. Penal Code §§ 11076, 13202.

307 Cal. Gov. Code § 7929.205 (formerly Cal. Gov. Code § 6254(ab)).

308 Cal. Gov. Code § 7930.135 (formerly Cal. Gov. Code § 6276.14); *see also* Cal. Bus. & Prof. Code § 802.5.

309 Cal. Gov. Code § 7923.800 (formerly Cal. Gov. Code § 6254(u)(1)) (where applicant is vulnerable to attack, etc.).

310 Cal. Gov. Code § 7930.155 (formerly Cal. Gov. Code § 6276.24); *see also* Cal. Veh Code § 1808.4.

311 Cal. Gov. Code § 7926.300 (formerly Cal. Gov. Code § 6253.2).

Jury Lists And Potential Juror Lists Exemption.[312]

Law Enforcement Vehicle And Exempt Vehicle Registration Exemption.[313]

Licensing Exam Tests, Scores, And Data Exemption.[314]

Marital Communications Exemption.[315]

Medical Information For Pre-Hospital Emergency Care By Peace Officers, Firefighters, And Other Specified Persons Exemption.[316]

Multi-Jurisdictional Drug Law Enforcement Closed Meetings To Discuss Criminal Investigations Exemption.[317]

Officer Personnel File Records-Information (*Pitchess* Privilege) Exemption.[318]

Post-Mortem Autopsy Photos Exemption.[319]

Safe Surrender Baby's Parent Information Exemption.[320]

---

312 Cal. Gov. Code § 7930.165 (formerly Cal. Gov. Code § 6276.28); *see also* Cal. Code Civ. Proc. § 197.

313 Cal. Gov. Code §§ 7930.165, 7930.190 (formerly Cal. Gov. Code §§ 6276.28, 6276.38); *see also* Cal. Veh. Code § 5003.

314 Cal. Gov. Code § 7929.605 (formerly Cal. Gov. Code § 6254(g)); *but see* Cal. Educ. Code § 99150, *et seq.*

315 Cal. Gov. Code § 7930.170 (formerly Cal. Gov. Code § 6276.30); *see also* Cal. Evid. Code §§ 980-987.

316 Cal. Gov. Code § 7930.185 (formerly Cal. Gov. Code § 6276.36); *see also* Cal. Health & Safety Code § 1797.188.

317 Cal. Gov. Code §§ 7930.170 (formerly Cal. Gov. Code § 6276.30), 54957.8.

318 Cal. Gov. Code § 7930.180 (formerly Cal. Gov. Code § 6276.34); *see also* Cal. Penal Code §§ 832.7-832.8.

319 Cal. Gov. Code § 7930.180 (formerly Cal. Gov. Code § 6276.34); *see also* Cal. Code Civ. Proc. § 129.

320 Cal. Gov. Code § 7930.190 (formerly Cal. Gov. Code § 6276.38); *see also* Cal. Health & Safety Code § 1255.7(k).

Sealed Arrest Records Exemption.[321]

Specified Civil Case Settlement Information (Limited) Exemption.[322]

Specified Sex Assault Victim's Information And Counseling Exemption.[323]

Social Security Numbers And Information Exemption.[324]

Trade Secrets Exemption.[325]

As noted above, either by operation of Section 6254(k), or by the express incorporation provisions of the CPRA, there are dozens of additional, specific, and often technical exemptions from the CPRA's public record disclosure requirements: most of which are designed to protect privacy in health care/medicine, child care, certain business dealings and innovations, and comparable governmental or private functions.[326]

However, a full exploration of all of the available CPRA exemptions would require a book of its own: and such exceeds the scope of this guidebook — whose focus is on law enforcement records/information and related privileges (specifically, the *Pitchess* privilege) and legal/practical issues assorted therewith.

The reader is thus encouraged to explore the more exotic CPRA exemptions on his or her own. (For additional resources, please see footnote below.[327])

---

321 Cal. Gov. Code § 7930.195 (formerly Cal. Gov. Code § 6276.40; *see also* Cal. Penal Code §§ 851.7, 851.8, 1203.45.

322 Cal. Gov. Code §§ 7930.165 (formerly Cal. Gov. Code § 6276.28), 68513.

323 Cal. Gov. Code §§ 7930.195, 7930.200 (formerly Cal. Gov. Code §§ 6276.40, 6276.42); *see also* Cal. Penal Code §§ 290.21, 13823.5; Cal. Evid. Code §§ 1035.2, 1035.4, 1035.8.

324 Cal. Gov. Code §§ 7922.200-7922.210, 7930.195 (formerly Cal. Gov. Code §§ 6254.27-6254.29, 6276.40); *see also* Cal. Veh. Code § 1653.5; Cal. Comm. Code § 9526.5.

325 Cal. Gov. Code § 7930.205 (formerly Cal. Gov. Code § 6276.44); *see also* Cal. Evid. Code § 1060.

326 *See* Cal. Gov. Code §§ 7930.000, 7930.005, 7930.105-7930.215 (formerly Cal. Gov. Code §§ 6275, 6276, 6276.02-6276.48).

327 ADDITIONAL RESOURCES: *The People's Business: A Guide to the California Public Records Act*, League of California Cities, Apr. 2017 (a comprehensive review of the CPRA). Another excellent resource can be found at: James Chadwick/Sheppard Mullin, "First Amendment Coalition's

14. *No Privilege Logs Required; No Duty to Create Records; Limited Duty to Retain Records Prior to Request.*

No Duty To Create Or Reconstruct Responsive Records. Generally speaking, a public entity has no duty to *create* records that are responsive to a CPRA request where such records do not exist at the time of the request.[328] Along related lines, a public entity is *not* required to reconstruct a public record that was lawfully discarded prior to receipt of the request.[329] However, a public entity could be subject to an attorneys' fee award if records were unreasonably discarded.[330]

No Privilege Log Required. Although there is a limited exception to this, in that the agency's duty to assist the CPRA requester can be construed as a duty to index voluminous responsive records to better clarify which disclosable records the requester is actually seeking,[331] where an agency has determined that requested records are exempt from CPRA disclosure, the public agency is *not* required to prepare an index or "privilege log" of responsive records that it is withholding from CPRA disclosure-production: as courts deem such log preparation to be too burdensome upon public entities.[332]

Conditional Duty To Index Voluminous Responsive Records. However, as noted above, where a CPRA request would otherwise seek records so voluminous as to support an undue burden defense, the public agency's *duty to*

California Public Records Act Primer," *Resources: Access to Records*, circa 2020 (a convenient short guide on the CPRA).

328 *See, e.g.*, Cal. Gov. Code § 7922.505 (formerly Cal. Gov. Code § 6253(e)); *Haynie, supra*, 26 Cal.4th at pp. 1074-1075.

329 *Compare, e.g.*, Cal. Penal Code § 832.5(b)-(c) (officer personnel file complaints and related records must only be retained for 5 years, unless findings of officer misconduct are sustained, then they must be retained for 15 years) *and* Cal. Evid. Code § 1045(b)(1) (personnel file information more than 5 years prior to the incident date is not *Pitchess* discoverable or *Pitchess* disclosable) *with Community Youth Athletic Ctr., supra*, 220 Cal.App.4th at pp. 1445-1447 (where responsive records from three years prior were destroyed by the agency, possibly due to neglect, the CPRA requester could be entitled to recover attorneys' fees for the agency's failure to produce the records).

330 *Id.*

331 *See State Bd. of Equalization, supra*, 10 Cal.App.4th at p. 1192 (distinguishing *Rosenthal, supra*, 34 Cal.App.3d at pp. 756-758 and holding that forcing agencies to create indexes of documents in response to CPRA requests is permissible because it "puts part of the responsibility for identifying records with the agency itself."); *see also* Cal. Gov. Code § 7922.600 (formerly Cal. Gov. Code § 6253.1).

332 *See Haynie, supra*, 26 Cal.4th at pp. 1074-1075.

assist the requester has been construed to include a duty to create an index o voluminous records: to better allow the requester to narrow its request an better identify which records may be responsive to its request.[333]

H. PRODUCTION: The Burden of Costs for Disclosures.

At first blush, the CPRA seems to hold that, in general, the custodia government agency bears the costs of copying public records.[334]

Thus, for example, if the CPRA requester comes to the agency for in-pe son public records inspection, the requester is generally entitled to make copies of the public records, "without being charged any fees or costs," using the agency's own equipment: but *only* as long as the copying method does no require the equipment to make physical contact with the record, does not resul in damage to the record, and such does *not* require requester access to secure technology/computer systems — and, where the agency's equipment is used for such no-charge, no-contact copying, the agency may impose reasonable limits on the equipment use to preserve the integrity of the records or to pro tect against undue burdens on agency operations.[335]

Requester Must Pay For Record Copying Costs. However, perhaps because virtually no form of record copying widely used today does *not* involve direct equipment contact with the document (*e.g.*, photocopying necessarily touches the document being copied), the CPRA also states that, upon a request for copying of public records, the public agency is *only* required to disclose-pro duce the records "upon payment of fees covering direct costs of duplication, or a statutory fee if applicable."[336] In other words, under the CPRA, **the public**

333 *See State Bd. of Equalization, supra*, 10 Cal.App.4th at p. 1192 (distinguishing *Rosenthal, supra*, 34 Cal.App.3d at pp. 756-758 and holding that forcing agencies to create indexes of documents in response to CPRA requests is permissible because it "puts part of the responsibility for identifying records with the agency itself."); *see also* Cal. Gov. Code § 7922.600 (formerly Cal. Gov. Code § 6253.1).

334 *See, e.g.*, Cal. Gov. Code § 7922.525 (formerly Cal. Gov. Code § 6253).

335 *See, e.g.*, Cal. Gov. Code § 7922.500 (formerly Cal. Gov. Code § 6253(d)).

336 Cal. Gov. Code §§ 7922.530(a), 7922.505 (formerly Cal. Gov. Code §§ 6253(b), (e)); Cal. Gov. Code §§ 54985, 81008; 85 Ops.Cal.Atty.Gen. 225 (2002).

agency is *not* required to produce public record copies unless and until it receives any copying cost charges.[337]

Requester Cannot Be Required To Pay For Redaction Or Retrieval, Unless Customized Software Is Developed For Specific Electronic Records Retrieval. However, while the agency can withhold production-disclosure of public records until the requester has paid the direct costs of copying-producing the records, namely the reasonable costs of running the copying machine and for supplying the paper (or comparable production expenses), **the agency may *not* require the requester to pay other ancillary costs of production**: such as inspection, retrieval, or redaction fees.[338] However, where the requester seeks electronic records, the agency is also permitted to charge the requester for customized computer programming or unusual computer data retrieval costs.[339] Notwithstanding the foregoing, 2022 revisions to California law expressly clarify that chargeable copying costs allowed under Government Code section 7922.530 (formerly Government Code section 6253) "shall not include the costs of searching for, editing, or redacting the records" requested under the CPRA.[340]

Waiver Of Copying Costs. The agency is also *permitted*, but *not* required, to waive the copying fees/costs: such as making waivers for indigent requesters.[341]

For Record Copy Requests, An Exact Copy Is Typically Required. Notably, unless it is "impracticable to do so," an "exact copy shall be provided…."[342]

1. *Production Of Electronic Format Records.*

Along related lines, where the public record is stored in electronic format, generally, it must be produced in the same "format [as the] one that has been used by the agency to create copies for its own use or for provision to other

---

337 Cal. Gov. Code §§ 7922.530(a), 7922.505 (formerly Cal. Gov. Code §§ 6253(b), (e)); Cal. Gov. Code §§ 54985, 81008; 85 Ops.Cal.Atty.Gen. 225 (2002).

338 *Id.*; *see also North County Parents Org. v. Department of Ed.* (1994) 23 Cal.App.4th 144, 146-148.

339 *See id.*; *see also* Cal. Gov. Code § 7922.570 (formerly Cal. Gov. Code § 6253.9).

340 Cal. Penal Code § 832.7(b)(10) (amend. 2022).

341 *See, e.g.*, Cal. Gov. Code § 7922.505 (formerly Cal. Gov. Code § 6253(e)); *North County Parents Org.*, *supra*, 23 Cal.App.4th at pp. 146-148.

342 Cal. Gov. Code § 7922.530(a) (formerly Cal. Gov. Code § 6253(b)).

agencies"; that is, unless production in the same electronic format "would jeopardize or compromise the security or integrity of the original record" or of any proprietary software, the electronic record must be produced in its native form and format.[343]

Electronic Record Production May Result In Special Copying Costs. Where public records are produced in electronic format, the requester bears the production costs for "the cost of programming and computer services necessary to produce a copy of the record" in electronic format, but only where: (1) Section 6253.9 mandates production in electronic format; *or* (2) production for the request would "require data compilation, extraction, or programming…."[344]

The Agency Cannot Force The Requester To Accept Electronic Versions Of Hardcopy Records. Notably, an agency cannot mandate that it will *only* produce records in electronic format: the CPRA appears to indicate that where a public record was stored in non-electronic format, the agency cannot force the requester to accept only an electronic format version of that record.[345]

2. *Recording Redactions Are Not Chargeable to the Requester.*

Until recently, one of the most contentious areas of the CPRA was the fact that it requires often extensive pre-disclosure redactions of information, particularly for critical incident recordings, but then imposes the costly burden of such redactions on the custodial public entity.

While many public agencies had sought to extend the CPRA's cost-shifting for complex data extractions to audio and video recording redactions (such as for costs incurred in obscuring videos to protect subject privacy), the California Supreme Court has been definitive on this issue.

Although custodial public entities may charge the requester for production and copying costs of *complex data* extracted from a database[346], **the time and equipment or related staff or software costs of making mere deletions or**

---

343 *Compare* Cal. Gov. Code § 7922.570 (formerly Cal. Gov. Code § 6253.9(a)) *with* Cal. Gov. Code § 7922.580(c) (formerly Cal. Gov. Code § 6253.9(f)).

344 Cal. Gov. Code § 7922.575(b) (formerly Cal. Gov. Code § 6253.9(b)).

345 Cal. Gov. Code § 7922.580(b) (formerly Cal. Gov. Code § 6253.9(e)).

346 Cal. Gov. Code § 7922.575(b)(2) (formerly Cal. Gov. Code § 6253.9(b)(2)).

redactions of information (such as those redactions involved in protecting the privacy of a person depicted thereon) are *not* something that government agencies can charge to the requester under California law: rather, the public entity must bear those redaction costs, even where the redactions are time-consuming, costly, and mandated by law.[347]

I. <u>CHECKLIST: Issue-Spotting For RESPONDING TO CPRA REQUESTS.</u>

In order to better assist public entities, and the records custodians thereof, in responding to CPRA requests, the below checklist is intended to summarize the above so as to help public agencies identify issues and otherwise troubleshoot their responses and/or disclosures to CPRA requests for public records.

1. FORM. Did The Request Comply With The Public Agency's CPRA Request Procedure (If Any)?

a. If Yes, proceed to next issue.

b. If No, The Agency Must Assist Requester — By Advising How To Comply With The Agency's Procedure.

c. *<u>Reminder</u>: Response Typically Due 10 Days After Request Receipt.*[348]

2. CLARITY. Is The Scope Of The Request Clear?

a. If Yes, proceed to next issue.

b. If No, The Agency Must Assist Requester — By Seeking Clarification As To The Specific Records Being Requested.

---

347 *Natl. Lawyers' Guild, S.F. v. City of Hayward* (2020) 9 Cal. 5th 488, 498-500 (holding that, pertaining to chargeable production-copying costs, the term "extraction" in Cal. Gov. Code § 6253.9(b)(2) refers to computer data extraction from a complex database, not deletions or redactions, and thus holding that the agency may not charge the requester for redaction times/costs, even when labor-intensive and even when the redactions are mandated or authorized by law).

348 PRACTICE TIP: For improper/procedure-violative CPRA requests, or unclear requests, the public agency should consider immediately invoking the 14 day extension on CPRA response time.

c. *<u>Reminder</u>: The Agency's Duty To Assist The Requester May Require The Agency To Prepare An <u>Index Of Potentially Responsive Documents</u> — Where The Request Is Overbroad & The Agency Is Trying To Clarify-Narrow Its Scope.*

3. **POSSESSION. Does The Public Agency Actually Possess Or Control Records Responsive To The CPRA Request?**

   a. If Yes, proceed to next issue.

   b. If No, Agency Must Inform Requester.

   c. *<u>Reminder (Constructive Possession)</u>: Public Records Stored In Public Employees' Private Files Are Disclosable; Public Records Controlled & Owned By A Public Agency's Private Contractors Are Likely <u>Not</u> Disclosable.*

   d. *(With Some Caveats.)*

4. **EXEMPTIONS. Are The Requested Public Records Exempt From CPRA Disclosure?**

   a. <u>Drafts & Deliberative Processes</u>. Is The Requested Public Record A Pre-Decisional Draft-Memorandum-Communication?

   b. <u>Pending Litigation Record</u>. Was The Requested Public Record Specifically Created In Anticipation Of And For Use In Litigation Where The Public Entity Is Expected To Be Or Is A Party?

   c. <u>Medical Records</u>. Is The Requested Public Record A Medical Record Or Contain Protected Medical Information Of A Public Employee Or Private Citizen?

   d. <u>Police Investigatory Records (Un-Excepted)</u>. Is The Requested Public Record A Law Enforcement Investigatory Record Or Report That Does <u>Not</u> Fall Under An *Exception* To The CPRA Exemption? *(See Exceptions Below.)*

i. *Consultation With Legal Counsel Recommended Before Asserting This Exemption.*
ii. *Reminder: Even For Excepted Police Investigatory Records, Investigator's Analyses & Conclusions Remain Exempt From Disclosure.*

e. Endangerment To Ongoing Police Investigation Or Crime Witness. Would Disclosure Of The Requested Public Record Endanger The Successful Completion Of An Ongoing Law Enforcement Investigation Or Endanger The Safety Of A Witness?

i. *Consultation With Legal Counsel Recommended Before Asserting This Exemption.*
ii. *Reminder: Even For Excepted Police Investigatory Records, Confidential Informant Identities & Contact Information Remain Exempt From Disclosure.*

f. Statutory Privacy Protection. Is The Requested Public Record Subject To Some Other Federal Or State *Specific* Privacy Protection?

i. *Consultation With Legal Counsel Recommended Before Asserting The Statutory Privacy Exemption.*
ii. *Reminder: Peace Officer, Judge, Prosecutor, & Public Defender Home Addresses, Phone Numbers, & Personal Contact Information Are Exempt From Disclosure.*
iii. *Except For The Aforementioned Persons, Public Employee & Private Citizen Names & Contact Information Might Be Exempt, Unless Such Disclosure Serves The Public Interest In Ensuring Government Compliance With Its Mandatory Duties.*

g. Privileged Records: Attorney-Client & Attorney Work Product. Does The Requested Public Record Contain Confidential Attorney-Client Communications Between The Agency And Its Attorneys Or Attorneys' Agents; *Or* Does It Contain Protected Attorney Opinions-Analyses Or Protected Attorney Factual Summary Or Attorneys' Factual Investigation?

h. Privileged Records: *Pitchess* — Officer Personnel Files. Does The Requested Public Record Contain Protected Officer Personnel File Information? (*See Exceptions Below.*)

   i. *Reminder: Peace Officer, Judge, Prosecutor, & Public Defender Home Addresses, Phone Numbers, & Personal Contact Information Are Exempt From Disclosure.*
   ii. *Reminder: The Names Of Officers Directly Involved In An Officer-Involved Shooting Are Not Exempt From Disclosure (Are Disclosable).*

i. Officer Training Logs & Materials. Do The Requested Public Records Constitute Law Enforcement Officer Training Logs, Training Certificates, Training Manuals, Or Training Curriculum Materials?

j. Terrorism Response Plans. Does The Requested Public Record Contain The Agency's Assessment Of Its Vulnerability To Terrorist/Mass Scale Attacks, And Related National Security Type Plans?

k. Public Interest In Non-Disclosure. Based On Prior Legal Precedents, Is There A Persuasive Argument That The Public's Interest (*Not* The Agency's Interest) In Non-Disclosure Outweighs The Public Interest (*Not* The Requester's Interest) In Disclosure?

   i. *Consultation With Legal Counsel Recommended Before Asserting The Public Interest Catch-All Exemption.*

l. Exotic Exemptions. Are The Requested Public Records Subject To One Of The Rarely-Applicable Exotic Exemptions?

   i. *Consultation With Legal Counsel Recommended Before Asserting An Exotic CPRA Exemption.*

m. If Yes to any of the above exemptions, proceed to next issue.

n. If No To All Of The Above Exemptions, Agency Must Disclose The Records & Produce In A Reasonably Timely Manner After The Response (*The Exceptions Below Are Likely Moot At This Point*).

i. *Reminder: Response Typically Due 10 Days After Request Receipt, But Production Is Due A Reasonable Amount Of Time Thereafter.*

5. **EXCEPTIONS To Exemptions. Do The Requested Public Records Fall Under An *Exception* To The Exemptions That Restores Them To Disclosable Status?**

a. OIS Involved Officer Names. Does The Public Records Request Merely Seek The Names And/Or Badge Numbers Of Law Enforcement Who Were Directly Involved In An Officer-Involved Shooting?

b. Criminal Witness Names & Addresses — To Specified Requesters. Is The Requester A Criminal Victim Or Victim's Authorized Representative, Insurer, Or Non-Criminal-Suspect Injured Party From A Crime Seeking Criminal Witness Names & Addresses (Except Those Of Confidential Informants)?

c. Criminal Incident Dates, Times & Locations — To Specified Requesters. Is The Requester A Criminal Victim Or Victim's Authorized Representative, Insurer, Or Non-Criminal-Suspect Injured Party From A Crime Seeking The Dates, Times, And/Or Locations Of Related Incidents?

d. Criminal Investigation Diagrams — To Specified Requesters. Is The Requester A Criminal Victim Or Victim's Authorized Representative, Insurer, Or Non-Criminal-Suspect Injured Party From A Crime Seeking Any Diagrams Prepared In That Criminal Investigation?

e. Criminal Witness & Involved Party Statements — To Specified Requesters. Is The Requester A Criminal Victim Or Victim's Authorized Representative, Insurer, Or Non-Criminal-Suspect Injured Party From A Crime Seeking The Witness Statements Or Involved Party Statements From A Criminal Investigation (Except Those Of Confidential Informants)?

f. Alarm Or Security Company Shared Information. Does The Request Seek Public Records Of Customer Lists Or Customer Information Provided By Alarm Or Security Companies To A Public Agency?

g. Arrestee Identifying Information/Arrest Report Information. Does The Request Seek Public Records Of Disclosable Arrest/Arrestee Information (*Disclosable Categories Below*)?

i. Arrestee Full Name;
ii. Arrestee Occupation;
iii. Arrestee Date Of Birth;
iv. Arrestee Hair & Eye Color;
v. Arrestee Height & Weight;
vi. Date & Time Of Arrest;
vii. Location Of Arrest;
viii. Date & Time Of Booking;
ix. Factual Circumstances Surrounding The Arrest;
x. Amount Of Bail Set;
xi. Time & Manner Of Release OR Location Where Arrestee Is Currently Being Held;
xii. All Criminal Charges On Which The Arrestee Was Held;
xiii. Any Outstanding Warrants Against The Arrestee From Other Jurisdictions; and
xiv. Any Probation Or Parole Holds Against The Arrestee.

h. Complaints & Requests For Police Assistance (Reports On Calls For Service). Does The Request Seek Public Records Of Disclosable Calls For Assistance/Service Information About Some Incident (*Disclosable Categories Below*)?

i. Incident Date & Time;
ii. Incident Location;
iii. Report/Request Call Date & Time;
iv. Victim Name (Except For Sex Assault, Human Trafficking, Or Hate Crime Victims);
v. Victim Age;
vi. Factual Circumstances Of Incident;
vii. General Description Of Any Injuries, Property, Or Weapons Involved; and
viii. Time & Nature Of Agency's Response To Call/Request/ Complaint.

i. Arrestee & Crime Victim Addresses Only — For Research Purposes. Has The Requester Sought Only The Addresses Of Arrestees And/Or Crime Victims Supported By A Declaration That Such Information Is To Be Used Only For Journalistic, Scholarly, Or Political/Governmental Purposes?

j. Traffic & Accident Reports — To Specified Requesters. Is The Requester A Person Involved In A Traffic Collision Or Accident, Or A Party Subject To Liability From Such Accident, Seeking The Related Reports?

k. Critical Incident Recordings & Records [SB 1421 & AB 748]. Does The Request Seek Public Records Of Disclosable Information About An Officer-Involved Shooting Of A Person, Or An Officer Use Of Force That Caused Death Or Great Bodily Injury? (*See Withholding & Redaction Provisions Below.*)

l. Sustained Officer Sexual Assault Records & Recordings [SB 1421]. Does The Request Seek Public Records Of Disclosable Information About A Sustained Investigation Of An Officer's Sexual Assault On A Member Of The Public? (*See Withholding & Redaction Provisions Below.*)

m. Sustained Officer Dishonesty In Law Enforcement Records & Recordings [SB 1421]. Does The Request Seek Public Records Of Disclosable Information About A Sustained Investigation Of An Officer's Dishonesty In The Performance Of The Officer's Law Enforcement Duties? (*See Withholding & Redaction Provisions Below.*)

   i. If Yes To Any Of The Above Exceptions, The Public Records-Information Are Very Probably Disclosable As Applicable Under The Exception To The Exemption; *but* proceed to the next issue.
   ii. If No To All Of The Above Exceptions, And One Of The Exemptions Applied Above, The Agency Remains Exempt From Disclosing Or Producing The Records.
   iii. *Reminder: Even For Excepted Police Investigatory Records, Confidential Informant Identities & Contact Information Remain Exempt From Disclosure.*

iv. *Reminder: Even For Excepted Police Investigatory Records, Investigator's Analyses & Conclusions Remain Exempt From Disclosure.*

v. *Reminder: Peace Officer, Judge, Prosecutor, & Public Defender Home Addresses, Phone Numbers, & Personal Contact Information Remain Exempt From Disclosure.*

vi. *Reminder: CPRA Determination-Response Is Typically Due 10 Days After Request Receipt, But Production Is Due A Reasonable Amount Of Time Thereafter.*

6. **WITHHOLDING & REDACTION (Caveats). Are The Disclosable Public Records Subject To Temporary Withholding Or Redaction?**

a. Withholding — Ongoing Criminal Investigation. Does The Request Seek Public Records From An Ongoing-Incomplete Criminal Or Homicide Investigation?

i. *Reminder: There Are Different Deadlines And Requirements For Withholding On This Basis, With Distinctions Over Whether The Records Are Critical Incident Recordings Or Not, And With Increasing Evidentiary Thresholds The Longer The Records Are Withheld. (See aforementioned chapter on the CPRA statutory exemption to the Pitchess privilege.)*

b. Withholding — Ongoing Administrative Investigation. Does The Request Seek Public Records From An Ongoing-Incomplete Administrative Or Personnel Investigation?

i. *Reminder: There Are Different Deadlines And Requirements For Withholding On This Basis, With Distinctions Over Whether The Records Are Critical Incident Recordings Or Not, And With Increasing Evidentiary Thresholds The Longer The Records Are Withheld. (See aforementioned chapter on the CPRA statutory exemption to the Pitchess privilege.)*

c. Withholding — Criminal Charges Filed. Have Criminal Charges Been Filed Regarding The Incident At Issue In The Request, But A Verdict Or Irrevocable Plea Has Not Yet Been Entered?

d. Withholding — Complaint Unfounded Or Frivolous. Does The Request Pertain To A Complaint Against An Officer That Was Deemed Unfounded Or Frivolous?

e. Withholding — Privacy Cannot Be Protected By Redaction. Does The Request Seek Disclosable Public Records Where The Privacy Interests Of Individuals Identified In Such Records Cannot Be Protected By Redaction?

   i. *Reminder: Redactions Are Preferred Over Withholding, So Proof Supporting Privacy Withholding Will Be Challenging.*

f. Redaction In General. Is Any Exempt Information In The Otherwise-Disclosable Public Record Reasonably Segregable From The Record Without Rendering The Record Useless To The Requester/Public?

   i. *Reminder: Redactions To Protect Officer Or Witness Safety From A Specific Threat Are Permitted.*

g. Redaction Of Critical Incident Recordings [AB 748]. Are Any Privacy-Protection Redactions To Recordings Made In A Way That Does Not Meaningfully Obscure A Viewer's (Or Listener's) Understanding Of The Incident Events Or Otherwise Alter The Incident Event Depiction?

   i. If Yes, the record may be temporarily withheld or redacted (as applicable above).
   ii. If No, The Agency Must Disclose The Records & Produce Without Temporary Withholding Or Redactions.

7. RESPONSE. Did The Response To The CPRA Request Explain The Agency's Determination As To Whether It Possesses Disclosable Records, Including Any Estimated Date Of Production?

a. If Yes, proceed to next issue.

b. If No, Agency Must Timely Serve Its Determination-Response.

c. *<u>Reminder</u>: Response Typically Due 10 Days After Request Receipt (Unless It Invokes The 14-Day Extension), But Production Is Due A Reasonable Amount Of Time Thereafter.*

8. **TIMELY DISCLOSURE OR PRODUCTION. Did The Agency Either Disclose The Disclosable Information Or Produce The Records With The Disclosable Information In A Reasonably Timely Manner After Serving Its Response-Determination?**

   a. If Yes, proceed to next issue.

   b. If No, The Agency Must Disclose The Information Or Produce The Records With The Responsive Information. (*Redactions May Be Allowed, See Above.*)

9. **COPIES & PAYMENT. Did The Agency Receive Its Chargeable Copying Costs From The Requester?**

   a. If Yes, proceed to next issue.

   b. If No, The Agency *May* Withhold Disclosure Or Production Until Copying Costs Are Paid By The Requester (Unless Agency Waives Such Costs).

10. **WEB POSTING. For CPRA-Disclosed Records, Does The Public Agency Want To Post The Disclosed Public Records On Its Publicly-Accessible Website?**

    a. If Yes, after repeating all but the disclosure-production steps above, the agency may direct future requesters to the *specific* web page with the disclosed public records information.

    b. If No, the agency will likely need to repeat these foregoing steps in full for some future requester.

If all of the foregoing issues have been properly addressed, then the CPRA response and any associated production should be compliant with the requirements of the CPRA.

1. *CPRA Cheat Sheet: Disclosable v. Exempt Police Records.*

With all of the subtleties specified herein above in mind, and with the caveat that whether a law enforcement record is disclosable under the CPRA is often case-specific, here is a brief recap of the policing records that typically are, or typically are not, disclosable.

a. Typically Disclosable Police Records.

- Information From **Arrest Reports**
- Information From **Calls For Service Reports**
- Information Shared By **Alarm/Security Companies, Including Customer Lists**
- Information & Recordings Regarding **OIS & UOF Causing Death Or GBI**
- **Identities Of OIS-Involved Officers**
- Information & Recordings Regarding **Sustained Findings Of Officer Sexual Assault** On Public Members
- Information & Recordings Regarding **Sustained Findings Of Officer Dishonesty In Law Enforcement**
- Criminal **Witness Names & Addresses** (Except Confidential Informants) — *To CPRA-Specified Requesters Only*
- Criminal **Incident Dates, Times, and Locations** — *To CPRA-Specified Requesters Only*
- Criminal **Incident Diagrams** — *To CPRA-Specified Requesters Only*
- Criminal Incident **Witness Statements** (Except Confidential Informants) — *To CPRA-Specified Requesters Only.*

b. Typically Exempt (Non-Disclosable) Police Records.

- Other Police Investigatory Reports & Recordings — other than specified arrestee & call reports
- Autopsy Reports & Photos
- Administrative, Personnel, and Internal Affairs Investigation Records-Files — other than those specified above
- Officer Personnel File Records & Information — other than those specified above
- Officer Home Addresses & Personal Phone Numbers/Contact Information
- Records Or Reports Prepared For Use In Litigation

- Intra-Agency Drafts, Memorandums, and Communications Reflecting Pre-Decisional Deliberations
- Attorney-Client Communications
- Attorney Work Product — Opinion & Some Non-Opinion
- Officer Training Records & Materials — including training bulletins, training manuals and demonstratives/PowerPoints, training logs, training certificates, and comparable documents
- Medical Records & Information
- Terrorism Response Plans
- Most everything else constituting a police record not specified above as being disclosable.

Please see the foregoing sections for additional details.

2. *Exemplar: CPRA Response Form.*

Requesters: Please see [insert website address] for the [public entity name]'s procedures and requirements for requesting public records under the California Public Records Act (CPRA). This form must be completed by you in order for the [public entity name] to be able to meaningfully assist you with your request.

REQUEST — TO BE COMPLETED BY REQUESTER:

<table>
<tr><td>Requester Name:</td><td>Requester Address:</td><td>Requester Phone #:</td><td>Requester Email Address:</td></tr>
<tr><td>Request Date:</td><td colspan="3">Department(s) Believed To Have Responsive Records (check all that apply):
☐ City Hall/Executive ☐ City Hall/Legislative
☐ Finance Department ☐ Fire Department
☐ Health Department ☐ Police Department
☐ Property Department ☐ Sanitation Department
☐ Water & Power Dept.
☐ Unknown or Other Department: ____________
[add/customize departments to suit your public entity]</td></tr>
<tr><td colspan="4">Public Records Requested (Describe, As Specifically and Narrowly As Possible, What Records Or Types Of Public Records You Are Requesting To Access Or Copy):</td></tr>
<tr><td>In-Person Review OR Copies Requested:
☐ In Person Review
☐ Agency Copies Only</td><td>If You Requested Copies, Do You Agree To Pay The Copying Costs*?
☐ Yes
☐ No</td><td>If You Requested Copies, Do You Need Hardcopies (Instead Of Electronic)?
☐ Yes
☐ No</td><td>Do You Need [Agency] Assistance To Clarify Your Request?
☐ Yes
☐ No</td></tr>
</table>

NOTICE: The [public entity name] is not required to create or produce copies of records unless the requester has paid the copying costs. [Cal. Gov. Code §§ 7922.530(a), 7922.505 (formerly Cal. Gov. Code § 6253(b), (e)); Cal. Gov. Code §§ 54985, 81008.]

RESPONSE-DETERMINATION — TO BE COMPLETED BY THE [PUBLIC ENTITY NAME]:

<table>
<tr><td>Request Receipt Date**:</td><td colspan="2">Clarification Needed To Evaluate Request (Explain):</td></tr>
<tr><td>Agency Persons Involved In The Response Decision (Specific Names):</td><td colspan="2">NOTICE: Agency Needs Extended Time To Respond To Request & Basis***:
☐ Single request requires search through voluminous and separate records.
☐ Requested records may be at a separate facility from where request was received.
☐ Another public agency with a substantial interest in the records must be consulted.
☐ Computerized data or data abstract must be compiled or specially programmed.
☐ Other:______________________________.</td></tr>
<tr><td>If Copies By Agency Requested, Copying Fees Paid By Requester*?

☐ Yes

☐ No

☐ Waived By Agency</td><td>Possession Review — After A Diligent & Reasonable Search Of The Records In The [Public Entity Name]'s Possession, Custody, Or Control, And After Reasonable Attempts To Clarify The Scope Of The Request, The Agency Has Determined That:

☐ The Agency Has No Responsive Records.

☐ The Agency Cannot Identify What Records The Requester Is Seeking.

☐ The Agency Has Responsive Records.</td><td>Estimated Date of Record Disclosure-Production:

☐ ________________(date)

☐ Not Applicable Because Permanent Exemption From Disclosure Applies

Location For Inspection If In-Person Review Requested:

______________________</td></tr>
<tr><td colspan="3">Agency's Determination On Disclosure-Production Of Requested Records (check all that apply):

☐ The Agency Has Determined That All Of The Records Requested Are Disclosable Public Records, Which Will Be Produced To You On The Above-Specified Estimated Date Of Production.

☐ The Agency Has Determined That Some Of The Records Requested Are Disclosable Public Records, Which Have Already Been Made Available On The Public Website At The Following Web Address: ______________________________.

☐ The Agency Has Determined That Some Of The Records Requested Are Disclosable Public Records, Which Will Be Produced To You On The Above-Specified Estimated Date Of Production.</td></tr>
</table>

☐ The Agency Has Determined That Some Of The Records Requested Are Exempt From Disclosure, And Thus Will Not Be Produced (Will Be Withheld) At This Time.

☐ The Agency Has Determined That All Of The Records Requested Are Exempt From Disclosure, And Thus Will Not Be Produced (Will Be Withheld) At This Time.

Basis For The Agency's Decision To Withhold Public Records, If Applicable (check all that apply):

☐ Drafts. The records are exempt pre-decisional communications or drafts. [Cal. Gov. Code § 7927.500 (formerly Cal. Gov. Code § 6254(a)).]

☐ Litigation. The records were created for pending litigation against the agency. [Cal. Gov. Code § 7927.200(a) (formerly Cal. Gov. Code § 6254(b)).]

☐ Medical. The records contain protected medical information. [Cal. Gov. Code § 7927.700 (formerly Cal. Gove. Code § 6254(c).]

☐ Law Enforcement. The records are an exempt type of law enforcement investigatory records or training records, and do not pertain to a critical incident or sustained investigation of officer sexual assault or dishonesty. [Cal. Gov. Code §§ 7923.600-7923.625 (formerly Cal. Gov. Code § 6254(f)).]

☐ Law Enforcement (SB 1421, AB 748). The records are exempt police investigatory records that pertain to a critical incident or sustained investigation of officer sexual assault or dishonesty, but remain exempt from disclosure for one or more of the following reasons [Cal. Gov. Code §§ 7923.600-7923.625 (formerly Cal. Gov. Code § 6254(f)) & Penal Code §§ 832.7-832.8]:

☐ A Criminal Or Administrative Investigation Is Ongoing — and disclosure would endanger the successful completion of the investigation and/or a witness, officer, or other person based on the following particularized facts known to the agency:

____
____
____.

☐ Related Criminal Charges Have Been Filed, But A Verdict/Plea Has Not Been Entered.

☐ The Records Pertain To A Complaint That Was Deemed Unfounded Or Frivolous.

☐ The Privacy Of Individuals Identified In The Records Cannot Be Otherwise Protected By Redaction.

☐ Officer Personnel File. The records are *Pitchess*-privileged officer personnel file records unrelated to a critical incident or sustained investigation of officer sexual assault or dishonesty for which the officer was a subject. [Cal. Gov. Code § 7927.705 (formerly Cal. Gov. Code § 6254(k)); Penal Code §§ 832.7-832.8; Evid. Code §§ 1043 & 1045.]

☐ Attorney-Client/Attorney Work Product. The records are privileged attorney-client communications or attorney work product. [Cal. Gov. Code § 7927.705 (formerly Cal. Gov. Code § 6254(k)); Evid. Code §§ 952-954; Code Civ. Proc. § 2018.010, *et seq.*]

☐ Other Statutory Privilege. The records may not be disclosed due to a mandate in federal or California law. [Cal. Gov. Code §§ 7927.700, 7927.705 (formerly Cal. Gov. Code § 6254(c), (k)).]

☐ Public Interest In Non-Disclosure. The public interest in non-disclosure clearly outweighs the public interest in disclosure for the following reasons [Cal. Gov. Code § 7922.000 (formerly Cal. Gov. Code § 6255(a))]: ______________________

____

☐ Other Bases For Withholding: ______________________________________

____

***NOTICE: Unless the [public entity] invokes its right to an extension of time, responses to requests are due 10 days from the request receipt date. Disclosure or production of non-exempt public records is due within a reasonable time after the response date. [Cal. Gov. Code § 7922.535 (formerly Cal. Gov § 6253(c); Motorola Comm'n & Elec., Inc. v. Department of Gen. Serv. (1997) 55 Cal.App.4th 1340.]*

****NOTICE OF EXTENSION: By invoking its right to extend the time for making its response-determination due to unusual circumstances, the [public entity name's] response is now due 24 days from the request receipt date. [Cal. Gov. Code § 7922.535 (formerly Cal. Gov § 6253(c).]*

J. C.P.R.A. LITIGATION: An Overview of the Challenge Procedures, Writ Lawsuits, and Related CPRA Appeal Processes and Standards.

The CPRA permits a requester to challenge a public agency's disclosure determination by means of an expedited judicial process seeking production of the requested public records withheld.[349] However, notably, unlike the Brown Act, there is no criminal penalty for failure to comply with the CPRA.[350]

1. *Forum: Jurisdictional & Venue Mechanics.*

Under the CPRA, any "person" can file a civil action for writ of mandate, injunction, or declaratory relief so as to enforce that person's right to access to public records.[351] Such action should typically be filed in a superior court in the county where the records at issue, or some part thereof, are situated or maintained.[352]

Significantly, this applies even where the requester is a public entity: specifically, where one public entity seeks to compel disclosure of public records from another public entity, the disclosure-seeking agency has standing as a "person" to bring a CPRA action.[353]

a. Reverse CPRA Action.

Along similar lines, a person who believes their rights would be violated by disclosure of public records may bring a CPRA action to enjoin disclosure-production of such records: in what is commonly referenced as a **reverse CPRA action.**[354]

---

349 *See* Cal. Gov. Code §§ 7923.000, 7923.100-7923.500 (formerly Cal. Gov. Code §§ 6258, 6259).

350 *Compare* Cal. Gov. Code § 7920.00, *et seq.* (formerly Cal. Gov. Code § 6250, *et seq.*) *with* Cal. Gov. Code § 54950, *et seq.*

351 *Id.*; *cf. Long Beach Police Officers Assn., supra*, 59 Cal.4th at p. 66 n. 2 (declaring that whether a CPRA action is the exclusive means of enforcing the CPRA is unresolved); *County of Santa Clara v. Superior Ct.* (2009) 171 Cal.App.4th 119, 130 (holding that the CPRA did *not* prevent a taxpayer's Cal. Code Civ. Proc. § 526a lawsuit for injunction and declaratory relief challenging the legality of a public agency's general policies or practices for responding to CPRA requests).

352 *See* Cal. Gov. Code § 7923.100 (formerly Cal. Gov. Code § 6259(a)).

353 *See Los Angeles Unif. Sch. Dist., supra*, 151 Cal.App.4th at pp. 768-771.

354 *See Marken v. Santa Monica-Malibu Unif. Sch. Dist.* (2012) 202 Cal.App.4th 1250, 1264-1268 (citing *Filarsky v. Superior Ct.* (2002) 28 Cal.4th 419, 431).

In such an action, the original CPRA requester is permitted to join the reverse CPRA action as a real party in interest or as an intervener.[355]

However, significantly, the **custodial public agency is <u>barred</u> from bringing a reverse CPRA action or seeking declaratory relief to determine its CPRA disclosure obligations.**[356] The reasoning underlying this lack of authorization for public entities to seek affirmative protection from CPRA disclosure is that: (a) the purposes of the CPRA could be frustrated by the associated lengthy delays of litigation; (b) such reverse actions would force records requesters to defend civil actions they did not initiate; and (c) such reverse actions would chill or discourage requesters from seeking public records — thereby frustrating the purpose of the CPRA and the fundamental right of persons to have access to public records.[357]

2. *CPRA Action Deadlines.*

The CPRA does not have its own deadlines for bringing an action: this likely means that such actions are subject to the civil statutes of limitations, presumably the statute that governs when there is no other specific statute of limitations; and that related doctrines for laches and tolling likely apply to CPRA actions.[358]

Thus, because California law appears to otherwise be silent on the issue, **the statute of limitations for CPRA actions *appears* to be <u>4</u> years from the date of the agency's service of its response-determination.**[359]

Once a CPRA action is filed and served, generally framed as a petition for writ of mandate, the deadline for the public agency to answer that

---

355 *Id.* at pp. 1269-1270.

356 *See Filarsky, supra*, 28 Cal.4th at pp. 426-429.

357 *Id.* at pp. 423, 428-429.

358 *Compare* Cal. Gov. Code §§ 7923.000, 7923.100-7923.500 (formerly Cal. Gov. Code §§ 6258-6259) *with* Cal. Code Civ. Proc. § 343 (setting 4-year statute of limitations when no other specific statute of limitations applies).

359 *See* Cal. Code Civ. Proc. § 343; *Yarber v. County of Santa Clara Prob. Dept.* (N.D. Cal 2009) 2009 U.S. Dist. LEXIS 109871, * 9 (because no other statute of limitations applies to actions brought under the CPRA, the four-year statute of limitations of Cal. Code Civ. Proc. § 343 applies to CPRA enforcement actions); *see generally Barlow v. City of Inglewood* (1948) 32 Cal.2d 688, 693 (the 4-year statute of limitations applies to mandamus proceedings).

complaint-petition likewise appears to be governed by the civil statutes: namely, **the respondent generally has <u>30</u> days from service of the CPRA complaint-petition to file its answer-opposition.**[360]

Once a CPRA action is at issue, the court shall set "the times for responsive pleadings and for hearings" with "the object of securing a decision…at the earliest possible time."[361]

On a practical level, the customary sequence of events for many courts is: (1) the CPRA petition for writ of mandate is filed, initiating the CPRA action; (2) once served, the respondent custodial public entity timely files an answer to the petition; (3) the court then sets a hearing or bench trial date and a related briefing schedule — with a brief from petitioner, a respondent's brief, and a petitioner's reply; and (4) the court then holds the hearing or bench trial and issues its ruling thereafter.

3. *CPRA Discovery.*

Although such mechanisms seem to be rarely used, in a CPRA action, **the litigants *are* entitled to conduct civil discovery**: such as written interrogatories, requests for production, and depositions.[362] This is because a CPRA action is considered to be a "special proceeding of a civil nature" that subjects such action to the Civil Discovery Act.[363]

On a related but contrasting note, the fact that a civil case is pending does not prevent a civil litigant from seeking records through the CPRA, rather

---

360 *See* Cal. Code Civ. Proc. § 1089.5 ("Where a petition for writ of mandate is filed in the trial court pursuant to Section 1088.5, and where a record of the proceedings to be reviewed has been filed with the petition or where no record of a proceeding is required, the respondent shall answer or otherwise respond within 30 days after service of the petition. However, where a record of the proceeding to be reviewed has been requested pursuant to Section 11523 of the Government Code, or otherwise, and has not been filed with the petition, the party upon whom the petition has been served, including any real party in interest, shall answer or otherwise respond within 30 days following receipt of a copy of the record."); Cal. R. Ct. 8.487(a)(1) (opposition to petition for writ of mandate is due 10 days after petition served); *see generally* Cal. Code Civ. Proc. § 430.30, 430.41(a)(2) (setting responsive pleading deadline at 30 days from service); Cal. R. Ct. 8.491 (extending responsive pleading time where review of petition for writ of mandate was sought).

361 Cal. Gov. Code § 7923.000 (formerly Cal. Gov. Code § 6258).

362 *City of Los Angeles, supra*, 9 Cal.App.5th at pp. 284-290.

363 *Id.*

than by civil discovery: and the fact that the custodial public agency is also a party to that civil action does *not automatically* cause the CPRA request to be objectionable on undue burden grounds.[364]

4. *Burden Of Proof In A CPRA Action: Custodial Public Agency.*

Public Entity Has The Burden Of Proof. Generally, the public entity opposing disclosure bears the burden of proving that it was justified in its withholding (or failure to disclose) the requested public records: thus, where the agency denies disclosure-production on grounds of a vague request, despite adequate agency assistance to clarify the request; or on grounds of an applicable exemption (including but not limited to the public interest exemption); or on grounds of a procedural defect by the requester, or comparable grounds, the public entity bears the burden of proof justifying its decision under the facts and law applicable to the case.[365] This is partly because exemptions are construed narrowly.[366]

This is true despite the fact that "a person who seeks public records must present a reasonably focused and specific request, so that the public agency will have an opportunity to promptly identify and locate such records and to determine whether any exemption to disclosure applies";[367] or the fact that "[g]overnment agencies are…entitled to a presumption that they have reasonably and in good faith complied with the obligation to disclose responsive information."[368]

5. *Court Proceedings: In Camera Review & Decisional Orders.*

***In Camera* Review Of Disputed Records Is Mandatory**. After the briefing is completed, where the public records are of the kind that a court is

---

364 *Bertoli v. City of Sebastopol* (2015) 233 Cal.App.4th 353, 370-372.

365 *Los Angeles Unif. Sch. Dist., supra*, 151 Cal.App.4th at p. 767; *accord Michaelis, Montanari & Johnson, supra*, 38 Cal.4th at p. 1071; *California State Univ. Fresno, supra*, 90 Cal.App.4th at p. 831 (holding that the burden of proof falls on the "proponent of nondisclosure, who must demonstrate a 'clear overbalance' on the side of confidentiality").

366 *Pasadena Police Officers Assn. v. Superior Ct.* (2015) 240 Cal.App.4th 268, 284; *American Civ. Liberties Union of N. Cal. v. Superior Ct.* (2011) 202 Cal.App.4th 55, 67; *Dixon, supra* 170 Cal.App.4th at p. 1276.

367 *See Fredericks, supra*, 233 Cal.App.4th at p. 227.

368 *See American Civ. Liberties Union of N. Cal., supra*, 202 Cal.App.4th at p. 65.

permitted to review (i.e., the records do *not* contain attorney-client privileged matter), the CPRA *requires* the court to review the withheld requested records *in camera* — outside the presence and hearing of the requester — in order to determine if the disputed records were justifiably withheld from CPRA disclosure-production under the applicable law and facts of the case.[369]

Obviously, the court cannot compel the custodial public agency to submit for *in camera* review records that are protected by the attorney-client privilege.[370]

The Court's Order. In reaching its determination, in general, the court balances the public right of access to information with the government's need for records to remain confidential (the public interest in non-disclosure), based on the exemption claimed.[371]

If the court determines that the agency **lacked legal justification for withholding** the public records, the court will order the agency to disclose-produce the public records — or show cause as to why the agency "should not do so."[372]

On the other hand, if the court determines that the agency was **justified in withholding** the public records, the court must return any records submitted for *in camera* review without disclosing their contents, and the court must deny the petition-action seeking disclosure by an order supporting the failure to disclose.[373]

Moreover, the court can issue a mixed decision: ordering *some* of the requested public records to be disclosed, while also ordering that the agency was justified in withholding other public records sought by the same requester.[374]

---

369 Cal. Gov. Code § 7923.100 (formerly Cal. Gov. Code § 6259(a)); *see also* Cal. Evid. Code § 915.

370 *Costco Wholesale Corp., supra,* 47 Cal.4th at pp. 737-739; *see also* Cal. Evid. Code § 915.

371 *County of Los Angeles (Anderson-Barker) v. Superior Ct.* (2015) 242 Cal.App.4th 475, 482.

372 Cal. Gov. Code § 7923.100 (formerly Cal. Gov. Code § 6259(a)).

373 Cal. Gov. Code § 7923.110 (formerly Cal. Gov. Code § 6259(b)).

374 *See id.; see also, e.g., Fredericks, supra,* 233 Cal.App.4th at p. 234.

6. *Appeal Process: Appellate Review Of CPRA Trial Court Decisions.*

An appeal from a trial court's CPRA decision is made by an extraordinary writ, wherein the appellate court "'conduct[s] an independent review of the trial court's ruling; [but] factual findings made by the trial court will be upheld if based on substantial evidence.'"[375] Such review is thus limited to whether the agency decision was arbitrary, capricious, or entirely lacking in evidentiary support.[376]

This is because a trial court's CPRA order is not construed as a final judgment subject to traditional, and often lengthy, appellate review: but rather as subject to the expedited process of extraordinary writ review.[377]

As a result, on review of an extraordinary writ to the Court of Appeal seeking to reverse a trial court's CPRA decision (*e.g.*, review of an order or ruling on a petition for writ of mandate to the Superior Court), the appellate court is permitted to decline to review the writ case without a hearing and/or without issuance of a detailed written opinion.[378]

However, simply because the CPRA appellate process is expedited under a constitutionally-approved system, so as to avoid the time delays associated with the normal appellate process from defeating the public interest purposes of the CPRA, appellate review must still occur in good faith: an appellate court lacks

375 *Becerra v. Superior Ct.* (2020) 44 Cal.App.5th 897, 913 (citing *Times Mirror Co., supra*, 53 Cal.3d at p. 1336).

376 *See Helena F. v. W. Contra Costa Unified Sch. Dist.* (1996) 49 Cal.App.4th 1793, 1799; *see also Powers v. City of Richmond* (1995) 10 Cal.4th 85, 111-114; *American Civ. Liberties Union Found'n v. Superior Ct.* (2017) 3 Cal.5th 1032, 1038, 1043 ("**In balancing the interests for and against [CPRA] disclosure, we review the public interest factors de novo but accept the trial court's factual findings as long as substantial evidence supports them.**" (emphasis added).)

377 *See* Cal. Gov. Code § 7923.500 (formerly Cal. Gov. Code § 6259(c)); *Powers, supra*, 10 Cal.4th at pp. 111-114 (holding that, under the amended Cal. Gov. Code § 6259, trial court decisions on CPRA requests are appealable only by the extraordinary writ process of Cal. Code Civ. Proc. § 1067; not as final judgments subject to appeal under Cal. Code Civ. Proc. § 904.1); *but see Mincal Consumer Law Group v. Carlsbad Police Dept.* (2013) 214 Cal.App.4th 259, 265 (appellate court has discretion to review an appeal from a non-appealable order as a petition for writ relief, but only where extraordinary circumstances, such as substantial compliance with procedures coupled with significant injustice otherwise, warrant such extraordinary review).

378 *See* Cal. Gov. Code § 7923.500 (formerly Cal. Gov. Code § 6259(c)); *Powers, supra*, 10 Cal.4th at pp. 112-115.

the authority to deny a *meritorious* writ petition that was timely presented and is procedurally sufficient — including for ancillary reasons, such as because the appellate petition presents no important issue of law, or because the appellate court views the appeal as unworthy of its attention.[379]

a. Deadlines For CPRA Appeal.

Where seeking appellate review of a trial court's CPRA decisional order by way of extraordinary writ, the appellant party must file its petition for appellate review within 20 days of being served with notice of the trial court's order: and the appellant's time to file its petition for extraordinary writ is extended by 5 additional days (*25* days to file the appellate petition) where the trial court served its notice of order by mail.[380]

However, on a showing of good cause by the movant, the *trial* court can extend the appellant's petition-filing deadline by *up to* 20 additional days.[381] Notably, the trial court's authority to extend the time for appellate petition filing is discretionary, and the trial court is empowered to grant an extension of less than 20 days.[382]

Trial Court's Notice of Decision-Order Served:	***Deadline To File Petition Seeking Appellate Review By Extraordinary Writ:***
Order Personally Served On Party	**20 Days** From Service Date
Order Mail-Served On Party	**25 Days** From Service Date
Order Personally Served, Court Grants Extension On Petition Filing Deadline	**Up To 40 Days** From Service Date
Order Mail-Served On Party, Court Grants Extension On Petition Filing Deadline	**Up To 45 Days** From Service Date

379 *Id.*

380 *See* Cal. Gov. Code § 7923.500 (formerly Cal. Gov. Code § 6259(c)).

381 *See* Cal. Gov. Code § 7923.500 (formerly Cal. Gov. Code § 6259(c)).

382 *See id.; State Dept. of Pub. Health v. Superior Ct.* (2013) 219 Cal.App.4th 966, 972 n. 5 (holding that where the CPRA order was mail-served on September 17, 2012, according to the court's postmark, and on October 10, 2012, the public agency requested an extension of the petition filing deadline, 23 days after the order notice date, and where the trial court then granted a 20-day extension, the public agency's filing of its petition for extraordinary writ on October 26, 2012 [39 days after the order-service date] was timely).

Logistically, if the appellate court accepts the writ without a summary denial, the appeal would then proceed on a faster timeframe than a traditional appeal: with the appellate court having the option of issuing a writ (peremptory or alternative), with the losing party having the option of seeking rehearing typically within 15 days of the decision.[383]

b. Stays Of The Disclosure Order: Trial Court Stays v. Appellate Court Stays.

Under the CPRA, once the disclosure order is issued, failure to comply subjects the public agency to contempt sanctions from the issuing trial court.[384] Particularly if the order would require disclosure before the appellate petition filing would be due, the public agency seeking to prevent disclosure while pursuing its appeal must move the trial court for a stay of its disclosure order pending resolution of the appeal.[385]

The standard for the trial court's grant of such a stay is that the public agency must show to the trial court that: (1) the public agency would "sustain irreparable damage" absent the stay, and (2) that its appellate petition has "probable success on the merits."[386]

However, from a practical perspective, as the trial court may seem unlikely to stay its own decision, in the alternative, when the public agency appeals, it also can and should seek an immediate stay of the trial court's decision *from the appellate court.*[387]

c. Standard Of Review: CPRA Appeals.

Disclosure Decision Reviewed On Substantial Evidence Standard. As noted above, on review, the appellate court will conduct an independent review of the superior court's disclosure decision, and the appellate court will

---

383 *See* Cal. R. Ct. 8.268, 8.485-8.490.

384 *See* Cal. Gov. Code § 7923.500 (formerly Cal. Gov. Code § 6259(c)).

385 *See id.*

386 *See* Cal. Gov. Code § 7923.500 (formerly Cal. Gov. Code § 6259(c)); *Times Mirror Co.*, *supra*, 53 Cal.3d at p. 1335.

387 *See, e.g.*, *Agricultural Lab. Rel. Bd. v. Superior Ct.* (2016) 4 Cal.App.5th 675, 687; *St Croix v. Superior Ct.* (2014) 228 Cal.App.4th 434, 440; *see also* Cal. Code Civ. Proc. §§ 1072, 1094.5(g)

affirm and uphold the trial court's disclosure decision where such is supported by **substantial evidence.**[388]

<u>Other CPRA Decisions, Including Fees, Reviewed For Abuse Of Discretion</u>. By contrast, a trial court's decision on **attorneys' fees** or sanctions, or CPRA-related orders *other than* the disclosure decision, is/are subject to a traditional appeal, rather than an appeal by extraordinary writ: which is generally based on an **abuse of discretion** standard.[389]

7. *Attorneys' Fees.*

As part of its enforcement mechanism, the CPRA includes two options for recovery of attorneys' fees: (1) if the **requester** "prevail[s]" in the CPRA litigation, the court "shall" award the requester his or her court costs and reasonable attorneys' fees; but (2) the court "shall" *only* award the respondent **custodial public agency** its court costs and reasonable attorneys' fees "[i]f the court finds that the requester's case is clearly frivolous."[390]

a. Requester Attorneys' Fees.

Notably, as to the **requester**, if he or she prevails in the CPRA action, the award of costs and fees is mandatory.[391]

A requester "prevails" in the CPRA action where he or she "succeeds on any significant issue in the [CPRA] litigation and achieves some of the benefit sought in the lawsuit."[392] Along these lines, "[a] plaintiff is considered the

---

388 *See Times Mirror Co., supra*, 53 Cal.3d at pp. 1332, 1336; *accord American Civ. Liberties Union Found'n, supra*, 3 Cal.5th at p. 1043 ("In balancing the interests for and against [CPRA] disclosure, we review the public interest factors de novo but accept the trial court's factual findings as long as substantial evidence supports them."); *Becerra v. Superior Ct.* (2020) 44 Cal.App.5th 897, 913.

389 *See Los Angeles Times, supra*, 88 Cal.App.4th at pp. 1387-1389; *Butt v. City of Richmond* (1996) 44 Cal.App.4th 925, 929; *Crews v. Willows Unif. Sch. Dist.* (2013) 217 Cal.App.4th 1368, 1379; *see also* Cal. Code Civ. Proc. § 904.1.

390 *See* Cal. Gov. Code § 7923.115 (formerly Cal. Gov. Code § 6259(d)-(e)); *see also Pacific Merchant Shipping Ass'n v. Board of Pilot Commissioners* (2015) 242 Cal.App.4th 1043, 1053 (reviewing and summarizing the CPRA fee-shifting provisions).

391 *See* Cal. Gov. Code § 7923.115(a) (formerly Cal. Gov. Code § 6259(d)); *Garcia v. Governing Bd. of Bellflower Unif. Sch. Dist.* (2013) 220 Cal.App.4th 1058, 1065.

392 *Garcia, supra*, 220 Cal.App.4th at p. 1065 (also holding that the terms "prevailing party" and "successful party" are synonymous under California law); *accord Belth v. Garamendi*

prevailing party if his lawsuit motivated defendants to provide the primary relief sought or activated them to modify their behavior."[393] This is because "'a plaintiff need not achieve a favorable final judgment in order to be a successful party [under the CPRA]. A defendant's voluntary action induced by the plaintiff's lawsuit will still support an attorneys' fee award: on the rationale that the lawsuit spurred defendant to act or was a catalyst speeding defendant's response.'"[394]

Thus, for example, where the public agency never denied the CPRA request, where it produced all of the responsive documents it had before the CPRA action was filed, reached out to a private entity for additional potentially responsive public records, and then produced those additional documents one day after the CPRA complaint was served on the public agency, the reviewing court affirmed that because the responsive documents were produced regardless of the CPRA litigation, the requester-petitioner was *not* the prevailing party; and thus the requester was *not* entitled to recovery of costs and fees.[395]

In other words, where a public agency acts diligently to disclose-produce responsive records, courts are less likely to find that records were produced because of the threat of a CPRA action.[396]

Interestingly, even where a party was *not* the plaintiff-petitioner in the CPRA-related action, he or she may be entitled to recover costs and attorneys' fees under the CPRA where he was the CPRA requester. For example, where a public agency moves for a protective order against a CPRA requester by filing a separate civil action for court relief, and the opposing party requester cites the CPRA as grounds to defeat the protective order motion as to the public records at issue, the fact that the opposing party was not the "plaintiff" in the

---

(1991) 232 Cal.App.3d 896, 901 ("'In order to justify a fee award, there must be a causal connection between the lawsuit and the relief obtained.'")

393 *See Belth, supra*, 232 Cal.App.3d at p. 901-902 (holding that where agency initially denied the CPRA request, then only produced the requested records well after the lawsuit was filed, the petitioner was a prevailing party entitled to recover costs and fees).

394 *Id.*

395 *See Rogers v. Superior Ct.* (1993) 19 Cal.App.4th 469, 482-483.

396 *Compare, e.g, Motorola, supra*, 55 Cal.App.4th at pp. 1350-1351 (diligent entity, petitioner not deemed prevailing party) *with Community Youth Athletic Ctr., supra*, 220 Cal.App.4th at pp. 1430, 1446-1447 (non-diligent entity, petitioner obtained declaratory relief that CPRA was violated, petitioner deemed prevailing party).

civil action does not prevent the requester from recovering his or her costs and attorneys' fees: the rationale underlying this rule is that allowing the recovery to depend on who reached the courthouse first would undermine the purposes of the CPRA.[397]

By contrast, although a requesting party is allowed to participate in a reverse-CPRA action brought by someone seeking to block disclosure of public records by a public entity, where the requester is involved in a reverse-CPRA action, "a requesting party who participates in a reverse-CPRA lawsuit would not be entitled to the recovery of attorneys fees," as would otherwise be the case if the requester was bringing a successful CPRA action for disclosure; this is because, in a reverse-CPRA action, where the agency is *supporting* (not opposing) disclosure and the reverse-CPRA litigant is the one opposing disclosure, "no fees will be incurred if the party [requester] relies on the agency to oppose the effort to bar access to the records."[398]

In other words, a requester is *not* entitled to recovery of attorneys' fees in a reverse-CPRA action because, in that action, the requester and the agency are both on the side of disclosure (otherwise there would be no dispute between the reverse-CPRA litigant and the agency) and, thus, the requester should not be incurring any attorneys' fees in a reverse-CPRA action.[399]

b. Public Agency Attorneys' Fees.

In contrast to the rules for awards of fees and costs to the requester, a **public agency** is entitled to recover its court costs and reasonable attorneys' fees <u>*only* where the requester's case is clearly frivolous</u>: this means that the public agency must show that the requester's case is "utterly devoid of merit or taken for [an] improper motive" — a high bar for most agencies to cross.[400]

For example, where a requester brought a CPRA action: (1) after the public agency had produced all disclosable records; (2) where the public

---

397 *See Fontana Police Dept. v. Villegas-Banuelos* (1999) 74 Cal.App.4th 1249, 1253.

398 *Marken, supra*, 202 Cal.App.4th at p. 1268.

399 *See id.*

400 *Crews v. Willows Unif. Sch. Dist.* (2013) 217 Cal.App.4th 1368, 1381-1384 (petitioner's CPRA action was not frivolous where he did not receive the requested documents until after he brought the action).

agency had gone to extraordinary lengths to accommodate the requests; and (3) where the requester brought the CPRA action before the agency's time to serve a response-determination had even expired, the reviewing court held that the requester's CPRA action was clearly frivolous, and it affirmed an award of court costs and reasonable attorneys' fees to the public agency.[401]

c. Miscellaneous Attorneys' Fees Rules Under The CPRA.

Under the CPRA, **when attorneys' fees are awarded, they must be paid by the public agency, *not* by the public employees or officials who decided to withhold disclosure** of the requested public records.[402]

Finally, even though attorneys' fee awards are meant to be "'fully compensatory'" for all the attorney hours reasonably spent on the CPRA litigation, in deciding the award, **courts have broad discretion in determining whether the amount of hours spent on the CPRA litigation was reasonable**: and courts may reduce the award to adjust the amount to fit what the court believes to be reasonable.[403]

K. Conclusion re CPRA and *Pitchess.*

Even in the summary form offered herein above, the foregoing complexities of the CPRA significantly affect and intersect with the subtleties of *Pitchess* privilege law in a way that a wise practitioner should not ignore.

Particularly in light of the 2019 and 2022 limited exceptions to the CPRA exemptions for *Pitchess*-privileged matter, understanding how police-related records may or may not be CPRA-disclosable, and the role the *Pitchess* privilege system may play in preventing disclosure of certain police records, is key to understanding how better to engage in police-related advocacy that involves law enforcement records and information.

---

401 *See Butt, supra*, 44 Cal.App.4th at pp. 929-930 (affirming award of $3,991 in fees and costs).

402 Cal. Gov. Code § 7923.115(a) (formerly Cal. Gov. Code § 6259(d)) ("The costs and fees shall be paid by the public agency and shall not become a personal liability of the public official involved.")

403 *Bernardi v. County of Monterey* (2008) 167 Cal.App.4th 1379, 1394; *accord Ketchum v. Moses* (2001) 24 Cal.4th 1112, 1133-1134; *Serrano v. Unruh* (1982) 32 Cal.3d 621, 635.

In short, **unless an *exception* to a policing-related CPRA exemption applies, *most* police-related records and officer personnel file records and information are *not* CPRA-disclosable**: and a party seeking such records or information will generally need to proceed with other discovery tools — such as those available in civil litigation or via the *Pitchess* motion system — to obtain such police-related records and information.

14. FEDERAL DISCOVERY: How Do the *Pitchess* Privileges Affect Discovery in a *Federal* Civil Case? (An Introduction to the Federal Analogs to California's *Pitchess* Privileges.)

While, under California law, police personnel and associated internal affairs records are presumed to be protected from disclosure under the *Pitchess* procedure, the state-law protections do *not* control in federal cases — instead, federal law governs procedure in federal court.[1] Along these lines, federal privileges are determined according to common law as interpreted by the federal courts, provided that such decisional law is not superseded by any federal Constitutional or statutory law.[2] In other words, **the *Pitchess* statutes do not *control* discovery or disclosures in a federal case**.

However, although federal courts are not bound to follow California's statutory *Pitchess* procedures and privileges, the *Pitchess* privileges will often affect the outcome of discovery and disclosure in federal cases due to the privacy rights that are implicated by the *Pitchess* privileges and which lie in peace officers' personnel records.[3]

---

1 *Compare* Cal. Evid. Code §§ 1040, 1043, 1045 *with Kerr v. United States District Court, N.D. Cal.*, 511 F.2d 192, 197 (9th Cir. 1975); *Stevens v. Harper*, 213 F.R.D. 358, 365 n. 5 (E.D. Cal. 2002) (concluding that federal, not state privileges, control in federal court in federal question cases).

2 *See* Fed. R. Evid. 501; *Association for Reduction of Violence v. Hall*, 734 F.2d 63, 66 n. 1 (1st Cir. 1984).

3 *See, e.g., Hallon v. City of Stockton*, 2012 U.S. Dist. LEXIS 14665, *2-3, 12-13 (E.D. Cal. 2012) (concluding that "while [f]ederal law applies to privilege based discovery disputes involving federal claims," the "state privilege law which is consistent with its federal equivalent significantly assists in apply ing [federal] privilege law to discovery disputes" — and evaluating the *Pitchess* privileges in its application of the federal official information, law enforcement, and executive-deliberative process privileges that

To summarize, while the *Pitchess* privileges do not apply to a federal civil case, they arguably strengthen a peace officer's constitutionally-based **privacy right** in his/her personnel file information by codifying the officer's reasonable expectation of privacy. Additionally, there are somewhat weaker federal equivalents to *some* of the *Pitchess* privileges — specifically, the **federal official information privilege**, the **federal deliberative-executive process privilege**, and the **federal law enforcement/investigative privilege** — that may be invoked to obtain the kind of *in camera* review/judicial screening to limit production or disclosure of confidential information contained in a peace officer's personnel file and/or the law enforcement agency's internal investigative files in civil cases.

A. The *Pitchess* Statutes' Effect on the Officer's Federal Right to Privacy.

Specifically, although the scope of discovery in federal litigation is typically broad, it is bounded by the limits of relevance.[4] Thus, though the "requirement of relevancy should be construed liberally and with common sense, rather than in terms of narrow legalisms," it is also true that "[d]iscovery of information that has no conceivable bearing on the case should not...be allowed."[5]

Along these lines, in a federal case, a party moving to compel production of documents withheld by the custodial party has the burden of establishing that the requested material is relevant to the moving party's claims in that action: in other words, the propounding party must prove that the requested material, if not directly admissible, "is reasonably calculated to lead to the discovery of admissible evidence."[6]

---

lie in peace officer personnel files); see generally *Noble v. City of Fresno*, 2017 U.S. Dist. LEXIS 194489, *11-15 (E.D. Cal. 2017); *but see Doe v. Gill*, 2012 U.S. Dist. LEXIS 42159, *8-12 (N.D. Cal. 2012).

4 *See* Fed. R. Civ. P. 26(b)(1).

5 *Miller v. Pancucci*, 141 F.R.D. 292, 296 (C.D. Cal. 1992) (excluding from its production order personnel file records and government tort claims related to issues of firearms or equipment misuse, or to racism/prejudice, because those issues had not been alleged in any of plaintiff's operative claims and thus requests for their production could not be reasonably calculated to lead to the discovery of admissible evidence in that case). NOTE: The similarity between this precept and the *Pitchess* privilege case law should be apparent.

6 *World Triathlon Corp. v. Dawn Syndicated Prod.*, 2007 U.S. Dist. LEXIS 1704, *7 (M.D. Fla. 2007); *see* Fed. R. Civ. P. 26(b)(1) (permitting "discovery regarding any matter, not privileged, which is relevant to the subject matter of the pending litigation"); *Oppenheimer Fund v. Sanders*, 437 U.S. 340, 351-352 (1978) (clarifying that "relevance" for purposes of determining if the materials sought are discoverable equates to whether the materials sought are reasonably calculated to lead to the discovery of admissible evidence); *Joseph v. Las Vegas Metro. Police Dep't*, 2010 U.S. Dist. LEXIS 135111 (D. Nev. 2010).

Under revisions to Rule 26, the party seeking discovery must show not only that the discovery seeks material that is "relevant to any party's claim or defense"; but also that such discovery is "proportional to the needs of the case, considering the importance of the issues at stake in the action, the amount in controversy, the parties' relative access to relevant information, the parties' resources, the importance of the discovery to resolving the issues, and whether the burden or expense of the proposed discovery outweighs its likely benefit."[7]

However, when it comes to police officer personnel files, courts are more reluctant to conclude that non-incident personnel file records are discoverable, particularly in light of the officer privacy interests at issue.[8]

To elaborate, police officers have constitutionally-based "privacy rights [that] are not inconsequential" in their police personnel records.[9] Where privacy interests are implicated, the party or person whose privacy is affected may either object to the discovery request or seek a protective order.[10] Where a party or person has served such an objection or sought such a protective order, the court will resolve the issue by balancing the need for the information sought against the privacy right asserted.[11] Where the privacy right is implicated during this balancing, disclosure should be barred wherever such a bar to disclosure would not prevent a fair resolution of the lawsuit.[12] During this

---

7 *See* Fed. R. Civ. P. 26(b)(1).

8 *See generally Breed v. United States Dist. Ct.*, 542 F.2d 1114, 1116 (9th Cir. 1976) (when confronted with an assertion of the right to privacy in records-information, the court must balance the privacy interests of the privilege-holder against the discovering party's need for the information sought — and the court may conduct an *in camera* review of the information or records at issue to determine the applicability of the privilege).

9 *Soto v. City of Concord*, 162 F.R.D. 603, 613 n. 4, 616 (N.D. Cal. 1995); *see Pagano v. Oroville Hosp.*, 145 F.R.D. 683, 695 (E.D. Cal. 1993); *cf. Breed*, 542 F.2d at 1116; *accord Centeno v. City of Fresno*, 2016 U.S. Dist. LEXIS 180013, *42-45 (E.D. Cal. 2016).

10 *Laxalt v. McClatchy*, 809 F.2d 885, 889 (D.C. Cir. 1987).

11 *Perry v. State Farm Fire & Cas. Co.*, 734 F.2d 1441, 1447 (11th Cir. 1984), *cert. den.* 469 U.S. 1108 (1985) (requests for court orders for release of information from government agencies should be evaluated by balancing the need for disclosure against the potential harm to the subject of the disclosure); *Johnson v. Thompson*, 971 F.2d 1487, 1497 (10th Cir. 1992), *cert. den.* 507 U.S. 910 (1993) (denying discovery of names of participants in a medical study due to privacy interests of the individual participants); *Cook v. Yellow Freight Sys., Inc.*, 132 F.R.D. 548, 550-551 (E.D. Cal 1990) (balancing targeted individual's right of privacy against the public's need for discovery in an employment discrimination case).

12 *See Ragge v. MCA/Universal Studios*, 165 F.R.D. 601, 604-605 (C.D. Cal. 1995); *Soto* 162 F.R.D. at 617.

balancing, the federal court is *permitted* — but *not* required — to "give some weight to privacy rights protected by state statutes," as long the federal court complies with federal law governing the weighing process.[13]

Thus, although the *Pitchess* privileges do <u>not</u> control privilege decisions in federal civil cases based on federal law, because the officers have a *federal* constitutional right to privacy, and because their reasonable expectation of privacy in their personnel records is affected by the *Pitchess* statutory protection, the operation of the *Pitchess* privilege can and often will affect the course of discovery in a federal civil case.[14]

1. *Rule 26 Relevance: Tipping The Privacy Privilege Balance.*

In 2015, the U.S. Supreme Court revised Federal Rule of Civil Procedure 26 to limit the scope of what is discoverable in a civil action by redefining discovery-phase "relevance."[15] Specifically, Rule 26(b)(1) was modified to ensure that "[i]nformation is discoverable...if it is relevant to any party's claim or defense and *is proportional to the needs of the case*."[16]

Although the amended Rule still notes that information "need not be admissible in evidence to be discoverable," in order to determine discovery-phase relevance under Rule 26, litigants and courts are required to "consider[] [1] the importance of the issues at stake in the action, [2] the amount in controversy, [3] the parties' relative access to relevant information, [4] the parties' resources, [5] the importance of the discovery in resolving the issues, and [6] whether the burden or expense of the proposed discovery outweighs its likely benefit."[17]

The core rationale underlying the Rule 26 revision was that courts should use Rule 26(b) to "'control excessive discovery'" by "restor[ing] the

---

13 *See, e.g.*, *Marti v. Padilla*, 2011 U.S. Dist. LEXIS 98259, *19 (E.D. Cal. 2011); *Martinez v. Stockton*, 132 F.R.D. 677, 681-682 (E.D. Cal. 1990) (evaluating the privacy expectations under the *Pitchess* privileges in its application of federal privilege); *but see Welsh v. City & County of San Francisco*, 887 F. Supp. 1293, 1299 (concluding that the *Pitchess* privileges do not create any enforceable privacy interests on behalf of the officers).

14 *See Hallon*, 2012 U.S. Dist. LEXIS 14665 at *2-3, 12-13.

15 *See* Fed. R. Civ. P. 26 cmt (2015).

16 *See id.*; Fed. R. Civ. P. 26(b)(1) (emphasis added).

17 *Id.*

proportionality factors [of Rule 26] to their original place in defining the scope of discovery."[18]

From a practical perspective, this narrower threshold for Rule 26 discovery-phase relevance tends to weigh more heavily in the privacy balancing calculus in a way that somewhat strengthens the federal privacy privilege.[19]

Specifically, for example, in conducting its privacy balancing on a police use of force case, with the revised Rule 26 in mind, a court is more likely to conclude that officer personnel files remain private and non-discoverable: *except* as they pertain to similar pre-incident administrative/personnel investigations regarding force that is "sufficiently similar" to the kind of force that is at issue in the instant case, or as to allegations pertaining to the party officers' honesty or dishonesty.[20]

Thus, to illustrate this point, in applying Rule 26 relevance and the federal privacy to an officer-involved shooting case of a human decedent, prior instances of a shooting involving a canine, or post-incident uses of force would *not* be discoverable; nor would instances of alleged dishonesty from decades past in a personnel file held by a prior, non-party police employer.[21]

---

18 Fed. R. Civ. P. 26 cmt (2015).

19 *See Centeno v. City of Fresno*, 2016 U.S. Dist. LEXIS 180013, *15-29 (E.D. Cal. 2016); *Najera v. County of Riverside*, 2019 U.S. Dist. LEXIS 221115, *7-11 (C.D. Cal. 2019); *Noble v. City of Fresno*, 2018 U.S. Dist. LEXIS 44839, 8-11, 20-24 (E.D. Cal. 2018).

20 *See Centeno*, 2016 U.S. Dist. LEXIS 180013 at pp. *15-29 (in an officer-involved shooting case, holding that *post*-incident administrative investigations were *not* relevant/discoverable; that a dog-shooting complaint was *not* relevant/discoverable; and that a pre-incident manual restraint incident administrative investigation was *not* relevant/discoverable; but that a *pre*-incident shooting of a person *was* discoverable); *Najera*, 2019 U.S. Dist. LEXIS 221115 at pp. *7-11 (holding, in an officer-involved shooting case, that where the only alleged misconduct in defendant officer's personnel files was an occasion of alleged dishonesty 20 years prior to the relevant shooting incident, while the defendant was employed by a prior, non-party police employer, Rule 26 and privacy prevented the officer's personnel files from being relevant/discoverable); *see also Noble*, 2018 U.S. Dist. LEXIS 44839 at pp. 8-11, 20-24.

21 *Id.*

PRACTICE TIP: Where a police agency has produced all incident-related records, including an incident-related administrative investigation, under a protective order, that procedural fact tends to shore up the police agency's defense against non-incident officer personnel file discovery, even in federal civil cases.

Particularly when it relies upon a reasonable expectation of privacy raised by the California *Pitchess* privilege, practitioners are likely to find that the federal privacy privilege, coupled with the more stringent application of Rule 26 relevance, is the closest analog one will find to a *Pitchess*-comparable defense against discovery in a federal civil case.

a. 2019 CPRA-Pitchess Amendments and Federal Privacy Privilege Considerations.

Notably, the 2019 amendments to the California Government Code and California Penal Code — effectively making critical incident recordings and officer personnel file records of critical incidents and sustained officer sexual assaults/policing dishonesty into CPRA-discoverable records — are likely to affect the assertion of federal privacy privileges: by removing or at least undermining the officer's reasonable expectation of privacy in the CPRA-discoverable recordings and personnel file records.[22]

B. The Federal Official Information Privilege.

Additionally, under federal law, there are an array of federal privileges that operate in a manner comparable to the *Pitchess* privilege: namely, the federal official information, executive-deliberative process, and law enforcement/investigative privileges.

To elaborate, federal common law also recognizes a privilege for government personnel files and official records under the official information privilege.[23] Under the official information privilege, upon completion of an *in camera* review, federal courts will preserve from disclosure those documents or information that constitute official government information, such as police personnel files.[24] When a party seeks disclosure of police officer personnel files, and the responding party asserts the official information privilege, the

---

22 *See* Cal. Gov. Code §§ 7923.600-7923.625 (formerly Cal. Gov. Code § 6254(f)); Cal. Penal Code §§ 832.7-832.8 (amend. 2019).

23 *See Sanchez v. City of Santa Ana*, 936 F.2d 1027, 1033 (9th Cir. 1990) ("Government personnel files are considered [to be] official information."); *Destacomento Gonzalez v. City of Garden Grove*, 2006 U.S. Dist. LEXIS 97148, *11 (C.D. Cal. 2006) (concluding, in a 42 U.S.C. § 1983 action involving a police shooting, that "the contents of [police] personnel files are likely inadmissible hearsay, are confidential, and are often subject to the official information privilege").

24 *See Sanchez*, 936 F.2d at 1033.

court must then review the documents or information at issue, *in camera*, to "weigh the potential benefits of disclosure against the potential disadvantages": where the disadvantages outweigh the benefits, the privilege bars disclosure.[25]

Where a police agency or comparable defendant has made a threshold showing, in the form of a sworn affidavit/declaration, supporting non-disclosure of the government records or information at issue, upon *in camera* review of such records, the court should *deny* disclosure of such records where: (1) disclosure will thwart government processes by discouraging citizens from giving information to the government/police; (2) disclosure will chill honest self-evaluation and analysis for the purposes of program and/or service improvement; (3) the information sought is evaluative summary rather than factual data; (4) no intra-departmental disciplinary proceedings are likely to arise from the incident; (5) plaintiff's suit is frivolous; (6) plaintiff can obtain the information from other sources or discovery; and (7) the information sought is not important to plaintiff's case.[26]

Thus, for example, in a § 1983 action, where police internal affairs files and related memos were not pertinent to the encounter with plaintiff that was the subject of the action, the court held that the defendant could withhold the police records sought for discovery.[27] Along the same lines, in a § 1983 action, where disclosure of the entire police personnel files sought was not necessary because the internal affairs investigation of the incident at issue was available under a protective order, the court held that the defendant could withhold the police records.[28]

---

25 *See Sanchez*, 936 F.2d at 1033-1034 (affirming non-disclosure of police personnel records where comparable information could be obtained from other sources); *see also Seminara v. City of Long Beach*, 1995 U.S. App. LEXIS 29729, *16 (9th Cir. 1995) (affirming a protective order barring disclosure of police personnel files in a § 1983 action over use of force in part because plaintiff could obtain comparable information from another source).

26 *See Soto*, 162 F.R.D. at 613, 613 n. 4 (N.D. Cal. 1995) (also including the impact on informants, whether the person seeking disclosure is a party, and whether the investigation is complete as potential factors in determining if the privilege applies); *accord Kelly v. City of San Jose*, 114 F.R.D. 654, 668-671 (N.D. Cal. 1987).

27 *Sanchez v. City of San Jose*, 250 F.R.D. 468, 471-472 (N.D. Cal. 2008).

28 *Seminara v. City of Long Beach*, 1995 U.S. App. LEXIS 29729, * 16 (9th Cir. 1995) (affirming the issuance of a protective order barring disclosure of police personnel files in a § 1983 action over police use of force, in part because plaintiff was able to obtain relevant internal affairs information from another source under a protective order); *but see Noble v. City of Fresno*, 2018 U.S. Dist. LEXIS 44839, 8-11, 20-24 (E.D. Cal. 2018) (finding official information and deliberative process privileges did not bar production under a protective order).

C. The Federal Executive or Deliberative Process Privilege.

Federal courts also recognize a privilege in the **executive or deliberative process** of governmental agencies. To elaborate, in order to ensure the frank discussion of legal or policy matters, government documents or materials are privileged from disclosure where they reflect the advisory opinions, recommendations, or deliberations of officials as part of a process in which governmental decisions and policies are formulated.[29] Thus, documents fall under the federal executive-deliberative process privilege where such records were prepared to assist an agency decision maker in arriving at his or her decision, including recommendations, draft documents, proposals, suggestions, as well as other subjective documents which reflect the personal opinion of the writer rather than the policy of the agency.[30]

While purely factual information is not generally protected by this privilege, where factual information is inextricably interwoven with the process by which a policy is made, or where the manner of selecting or presenting the facts would reveal the mechanics of a deliberative process, then the privilege will extend to the interwoven facts as well.[31]

Where a party has properly asserted the federal executive-deliberative process privilege, **the court will *not* resort to *in camera* review of the documents or information at issue unless the party seeking disclosure has met its threshold burden by showing a specific need for such records** — a showing which must be based on more than mere speculation.[32]

Only if the party seeking disclosure satisfies this threshold burden, may the court then review the documents or materials at issue *in camera* in order

---

29 *See Kerr v. United States Dist. Ct., N.D. Cal.*, 426 U.S. 394, 405-406 (1976); *National Lab. Rel. Bd. v. Sears, Roebuck & Co.*, 421 U.S. 132, 150 (1975); *Maricopa Audubon Soc'y v. United States Forest Serv.*, 108 F.3d 1089, 1092 (9th Cir. 1997).

30 *Maricopa*, 108 F.3d at 1093 (holding that documents must be pre-decisional in nature and form a part of the agency's deliberative process to fall under the deliberative process privilege); *accord Federal Trade Comm'n v. Warner Commc'n, Inc.*, 742 F.2d 1156, 1161 (9th Cir. 1984).

31 *See Pacific Fisheries, Inc. v. United States*, 539 F.3d 1143, 1147-1148 (9th Cir. 2008) (holding that "[f]actual portions of documents covered by the deliberative process privilege must be segregated and disclosed unless they are 'so interwoven with the deliberative material that [they are] not [segregable]'" in which case they may be withheld from disclosure); *accord Gomez v. Nashua*, 126 F.R.D. 432, 434-435 (D. N.H. 1989) (prohibiting the deposition of a prosecutor, or production of his notes, regarding the underpinnings of his decision over prosecution of an incident at issue in the civil claim).

32 *See Maricopa*, 108 F.3d at 1093-1095; *Gomez*, 126 F.R.D. at 434.

to balance the interests of the party seeking disclosure against the interests of the party seeking to prevent disclosure.[33] In conducting its *in camera* review, the court should consider that the interest of the party asserting the privilege is strongest where the information in question falls squarely within the definition of the privilege and its disclosure would "undermine the public interest in [the] free, candid, and uninhibited exchange of information or jeopardize the physical security of an individual or governmental institution."[34]

Thus, for example, where documents were prepared rendering advice to a government agency on whether to file a complaint to commence litigation, the court held that the documents were protected from disclosure by the deliberative process privilege.[35] Similarly, where documents were prepared to advise an administrator as to how to deal with specific allegations of unethical and illegal conduct — including recommendations and suggestions from an inferior to a superior reflecting the writer's personal opinion on a proposed course of action — and where the administrator relied on those documents in deciding what to do with the employee at issue, the court held that the documents at issue were protected from disclosure by the deliberative process privilege.[36] Along these same lines, where the police records at issue involved an internal evaluation and discussion about hogtying restraint procedures, the court affirmed that the documents were protected from disclosure by the deliberative process privilege.[37]

D. <u>The Federal Law Enforcement or Investigative Privilege.</u>

The "federal law enforcement privilege is a qualified privilege designed to prevent disclosure of information that would be contrary to the public interest in the effective functioning of law enforcement."[38] The function of the law enforcement privilege is thus to "preserve the integrity of law enforcement techniques

---

33 *See Maricopa*, 108 F.3d at 1093-1095; *Warner Commc'n, Inc.*, 742 F.2d at 1161; *Gomez*, 126 F.R.D. at 434.

34 *Kerr*, 426 U.S. at 405; *Maricopa*, 108 F.3d at 1093-1095; *Gomez*, 126 F.R.D. at 435.

35 *National Lab. Rel. Bd.*, 421 U.S. at 150; *cf. id.* at 158-159 (distinguishing such protected documents from advice memos that were effectively adjudications).

36 *Maricopa*, 108 F.3d at 1094-1095.

37 *Price v. County of San Diego*, 165 F.R.D. 614, 620 (S.D. Cal. 1996); *see also Gomez* 126 F.R.D. at 435 (prohibiting the deposition of a prosecutor, and production of his related notes on his decision regarding a prosecution over an incident at issue in the claim).

38 *Tuite v. Henry*, 181 F.R.D. 175, 176-177 (D. D.C. 1998), *aff'd*, 203 F.3d 53 (D.C. Ci[r.] 1999); *see generally Kelly*, 114 F.R.D. 653.

and confidential sources, protect[] witnesses and law enforcement personnel, safeguard[] the privacy of individuals under investigation, and prevent[] interference with investigations."[39] The rationale behind the privilege is that by "protecting relationships and values outside the courtroom, privileges demonstrate that even though the search for truth is of critical importance in the litigation process, it is not necessarily paramount to all other interests of society."[40]

Accordingly, the law enforcement privilege "bars disclosure of facts" and "investigatory files" where such disclosure might harm law enforcement efforts or investigations.[41] The privilege is effectively asserted where a responsible government official makes a formal claim of privilege after "personal consideration of the information sought," particularly specifying the information for which the protection is sought, and explaining why the information falls within the scope of the privilege.[42]

Once the qualified law enforcement privilege is asserted, the court balances "the government's interests in ensuring the secrecy of the documents in question against the need of the adverse party to obtain discovery."[43] In weighing the competing interests, the court may consider many factors including but not limited to: (1) "the extent to which disclosure will thwart governmental processes by discouraging citizens from giving the information"; (2) "the degree to which governmental self-evaluation and consequent program improvement will be chilled by disclosure"; (3) "whether the investigation has been completed"; (4) "the impact upon persons who have given information of having their identities disclosed"; (5) "the importance of the information sought to the plaintiff's case"; (6) "whether the information sought is factual data or evaluative summary"; (7) "whether any interdepartmental disciplinary proceedings have arisen or may arise from the investigation"; (8) whether the propounding party is an actual

---

39 *Tuite*, 181 F.R.D. at 176-177; *accord In re U.S. Dept. of Homeland Sec.*, 459 F.3d 565, 569-570, 569 n.1 (5th Cir. 2006) (ordering an *in camera* review of the documents at issue to determine the extent of the law enforcement privilege); *Hamstreet v. Duncan*, 2007 U.S. Dist. LEXIS 89702 (D. Or. 2007).

40 *Tuite*, 181 F.R.D. at 185.

41 *See Hamstreet*, 2007 U.S. Dist. LEXIS 89702 at *4; *see also Tuite*, 181 F.R.D. at 176-177; *cf. In re Dept. of Investigation*, 856 F.2d 481, 484 (2d Cir. 1988).

42 *See Hamstreet*, 2007 U.S. Dist. LEXIS 89702 at *7, 10-11 (observing that it is possible for police internal investigation files to fall within the scope of the law enforcement privilege in a civil rights action and ordering government affidavits to support the asserted privilege claims prior to *in camera* review).

43 *Tuite*, 181 F.R.D. at 177; *accord Frankenhauser v. Rizzo*, 59 F.R.D. 339, 344 (E.D. Pa. 1973).

or potential criminal defendant in a criminal proceeding reasonably likely to result from the incident at issue in the investigation; (9) whether the information sought may be obtained by other means of discovery; and (10) whether plaintiff's suit is brought in good faith and is not frivolous.[44]

In sum, although California's *Pitchess* privileges do *not* protect peace officer personnel files from discovery or disclosure in federal actions, **they can affect the operation of some federal privileges** and/or they are substantially duplicated by comparable federal police/governmental privileges.

---

44 *Tuite*, 181 F.R.D. at 177 (denying plaintiff's motion to compel production of government recordings of attorney-client conversations and a related report thereon); *accord Frankenhauser*, 59 F.R.D. at 344 (prohibiting disclosure of evaluative summary, but not factual information, from investigatory files even where the investigation had been concluded for 2 years without any criminal charges or disciplinary proceedings pending).

PRACTICE NOTE: California law has a comparable investigative privilege that is not actually part of the *Pitchess* privilege regime, but which may impact civil litigation involving peace officers. Specifically, pursuant to Cal. Gov. Code sections 7923.600-7923.625 (formerly Cal. Gov Code section 6254(f)), records of ongoing investigations are exempt from otherwise applicable discovery-disclosure requirements. *See also* Cal. Evid Code sections 1040 (official information privilege), 1043, 1045. Thus, "[e]xcept as provided in Sections 7924.510, 7924.700, and 7929.610 [regarding environmental and testing disclosures], this division does not require disclosure of..."

> **Records of complaints to, or investigations conducted by, or records of intelligence information or security procedures of, the office of the Attorney General and the Department of Justice, the Office of Emergency Services and any state or local police agency, or any investigatory or security files compiled by any other state or local police agency, or any investigatory or security files compiled by any other state or local agency for correctional, law enforcement, or licensing purposes....**
>
> [However], a state and local law enforcement agency shall disclose the names and addresses of persons involved in, or witnesses other than confidential informants to, the incident, the description of any property involved, the date, time, and location of the incident, all diagrams, statements of the parties involved in the incident, the statements of all witnesses, other than confidential informants, to the victims of an incident, or an authorized representative thereof, an insurance carrier against which a claim has been or might be made, and any person suffering bodily injury or property damage or loss, as the result of the incident caused by arson, burglary, fire, explosion, larceny, robbery, carjacking, vandalism, vehicle theft, or a crime as defined by subdivision (b) of Section 13951, unless the disclosure would endanger either of the following: (1) The safety of a witness or other person involved in the investigation. (2) **The successful completion of the investigation or a related investigation**....However, **this article does not require the disclosure of that portion of those investigative files that reflects the analysis or conclusions of the investigating officer**.

Cal. Gov. Code § 7923.600(a), 7923.605 (formerly Cal. Gov. Code § 6254(f)) (emphasis added); *but see* Cal. Gov. Code § 7923.625 (formerly Cal. Gov. Code § 6254(f)(1)(A)(4)-(B)) (making critical incident recordings CPRA-discoverable).

15. FEDERAL TRIAL: What Are the Limits to Using *Pitchess* Privileged Matter in a Federal Civil *Trial*?

Absent the operation of a binding protective order or exclusionary order in the federal action regarding specific peace officer personnel records or information that would otherwise be protected by the *Pitchess* privilege, California's *Pitchess* privileges have **no effect** on the admissibility of evidence in a federal trial.[1]

Although, in practice, federal courts are often reluctant to apply the federal equivalents to the *Pitchess* privileges to prevent or limit the discovery of peace officer personnel file information (due to the default federal disfavor of privileges), the availability of federal equivalents to the *Pitchess* privileges often warrants their invocation in at least a minimal attempt to preserve the confidentiality of records and information that is more strongly protected under California law as enforced by California state courts.

1 *See, e.g.*, Fed. R. Evid. 501.

16. CONCLUSION.

The *Pitchess* privileges serve the laudable goal of protecting the privacy and security interests of those dedicated men and women who join our police forces in order to keep our homes, our businesses, our families, and our communities safe — while also preserving their employing public entities' interests in efficient administration of their police departments/officers and preservation of their unique interests in confidentiality of certain information.

As explained in the preceding chapters, peace officer and custodial officer personnel records, and related personnel file information as defined by California law, are generally privileged from discovery or disclosure in California state cases under the *Pitchess* statutory procedures; and may be privileged from discovery in federal cases under analogous federal privileges such as the constitutional right to privacy. Normally, under California's *Pitchess* procedure, which applies in both state criminal and civil court cases, any information that meets the statutory definition of peace officer "personnel file" information is protected from discovery or disclosure to persons/parties outside the scope of the privilege — regardless of where such information is stored; even if it's stored in the officer's memory.

Under the *Pitchess* procedure then, where a party seeks to obtain/discover or publish/disclose *confidential* officer personnel file records/information, that party must make a motion for a <u>court order</u> showing good cause for the records/information to be discovered/produced to the moving party, or published/disclosed to some other party: such as to a jury at trial.

The *Pitchess* procedure has several detailed technical requirements — including specificity, good cause, materiality/manifest necessity, and reasonable belief mandatory thresholds, and other procedural mandates — all of which must be met before the moving party can obtain *in camera* review by the court of the personnel file records/information sought: and only after the court conducts such *in camera* review may any personnel file records/information be produced/discovered to the moving party and/or published/disclosed to a non-party, such as the trial jury. Furthermore, even *after* the court issues a *Pitchess* production/discovery and/or publication/disclosure order, the *Pitchess* procedure imposes several restrictions on what can be discovered/disclosed and on what must remain protected by court order.

However, the *Pitchess* procedure also contains several exceptions, including: (1) the exception for criminal prosecutors' investigations; (2) the exception for release of a complaint to the complainant; (3) the exception for discretionary release of anonymous data by a government agency; (4) the exception for discretionary release of rebuttal facts by a government agency when an officer lies to the media about a disciplinary investigation; (5) the exception for critical incident recordings and records of complaints/investigations involving OIS, UOF resulting in death or serious bodily injury, and sustained findings of officer sexual assault on non-employees and officer policing dishonesty; and (6) the emerging exception from *Pitchess* discovery procedures — but *not* from *Pitchess* disclosure procedures — that applies to the public entity with possession-custody of the peace officer's personnel file information.

Notably, the *Pitchess* procedural protections operate only in *state* court civil and criminal cases: they do *not* apply in federal court cases. However, there are several analogous federal privileges which can be used to protect an officer's and/or entity's interests in federal civil litigation, including privacy, official information, deliberative process, and law enforcement investigation privileges.

In light of the unique complexities of the *Pitchess* privileges and procedures, and in order to avoid the undue expenditure of time and resources that can otherwise accompany misguided or even futile attempts to obtain production during discovery of peace officer personnel files, or to introduce such matter into evidence at the time of trial, civil litigators should familiarize themselves with the unique and detailed protections and procedures that are implicated under California and federal law in relation to such officer personnel file materials and information.

Hopefully, this primer has helped the reader to do just that.

About the Author.

Tony M. Sain is a partner in the Los Angeles office of Lewis Brisbois, a Vice Chair of the General Liability Practice and Co-Chair of its Civil Rights & Police Litigation Defense Task Force, and a member of the National Trial and Appellate Practices. He focuses his practice on high exposure, high-stakes, high-profile matters in a wide variety of catastrophic injury and wrongful death cases across a number of practice areas, including personal injury, tort litigation, as well as police civil rights and public entity defense. Throughout his career, Mr. Sain has served as lead trial attorney in multiple high-profile jury and administrative trials, consistently securing defense verdicts, complete dismissals of claims, and other favorable outcomes on behalf of his clients, as well as racking up an impressive number of wins as an appellate court advocate.

Outside of his practice at Lewis Brisbois, Mr. Sain serves on the panel for prosecuting criminal cases for the Los Angeles County District Attorney's office on a pro bono basis. Mr. Sain was also an adjunct professor for trial advocacy at Los Angeles' esteemed Loyola Law School. He has also trained multiple public entities on the legal implications of changes to key statutes affecting policing, and he has served as a lead lecturer for the California Peace Officers Association's (CPOA) seminar series.

Moreover, Mr. Sain is the author of *"Pitchess Privileges and the CPRA: Polic Officer Personnel and Investigative Records Privileges and their Intersection wit the California Public Records Act,"* a leading resource manual on the intricacie of California's complex officer privacy laws and their intersection with th California Public Records Act.

Mr. Sain is also a Member of the American Board of Trial Advocates (ABOTA): a prestigious and elite association of widely admired jury trial attorneys. Named a Rising Star by Super Lawyers from 2013-2017, he is currently recognized by that publication and by the Los Angeles Business Journal as a top-rated civil rights attorney in Los Angeles. Before practicing law, Mr. Sain served as a senior executive in a variety of corporate and non-profit organizations, where he specialized in high-stakes organizational overhauls and community outreach.

Mr. Sain is a graduate of Princeton University's elite School of Public and International Affairs, where he learned executive-level governance. He is also a graduate of Loyola Law School of Los Angeles's prestigious Hobbs Trial Advocacy Program, and the Williams Civil Rights Litigation Program, and in law school, he also won the Best Advocate in California award in the National Moot Court competition for appellate advocacy.

Made in the USA
Monee, IL
04 November 2026

67375817R00167